Ulaanbaatar beyond Water and Grass

Praise for M. A. Aldrich's *The Search for a Vanishing Beijing: A Guide to China's Capital through the Ages*, available from Hong Kong University Press

'To me (a Chinese) it is Aldrich's open-mindedness—his awareness and acceptance that his values are not universal—that makes his book a delight to read. I take pleasure not only looking at the Old Beijing he so vividly portrays, but, also, in looking at him looking at Old Beijing.'

—Michelle Ng, *Zing Magazine*, Shanghai

'It's not the kind of thing you get from your average tour guide, and certainly not what you get from your average guidebook. For someone who is going to linger here for a few days, and really wants to walk around the hutongs—which really is the most interesting thing to do in Beijing these days—it is a fairly indispensable companion.'

—Evan Osnos, author of *Age of Ambition: Chasing Fortune, Truth, and Faith in the New China*

'Beijing is like the most interesting girlfriend you never had—rich, beautiful, and highly cultured but very, very difficult to understand and requiring a lot of time and thought. Michael Aldrich has produced by far the best crack at interpreting the city to date.'

—Paul French, author of *Midnight in Peking: How the Murder of a Young Englishwoman Haunted the Last Days of Old China*

'M. A. Aldrich's city history was my constant companion on bike rides around town. If a building caught my eye, I could usually find its description in Aldrich, who narrates in the relaxed voice of a patient guide.'

—Michael Meyer, author of *The Last Days of Old Beijing: Life in the Vanishing Backstreets of a City Transformed*

'Like an old friend who knows Beijing inside and out, M. A. Aldrich takes the reader by the arm as they discover the city together. By weaving history, legend and humour, the author portrays, with a sure hand, the rich tapestry of Peking. In doing so, the history of China also unfolds.'

—Valery Garrett, *Asian Review of Books*, Hong Kong

'The stories are what make the book a compelling read, regardless of whether or not you actually make it to the sites he is describing. Some are fact, some are myth, and many span the grey divide between the two.'

—Rebecca Kantor, *Far Eastern Economic Review*

Ulaanbaatar beyond Water and Grass

A Guide to the Capital of Mongolia

M. A. Aldrich

HKU PRESS
香港大學出版社

Hong Kong University Press
The University of Hong Kong
Pokfulam Road
Hong Kong
www.hkupress.hku.hk

ISBN 978-988-8208-67-8 (*Paperback*)

British Library Cataloguing-in-Publication Data
A catalogue record for this book is available from the British Library.

10 9 8 7 6 5 4 3 2 1

Printed and bound by Hang Tai Printing Co. Ltd., Hong Kong, China

This book is for Төмөр Таягт Хүн.

Contents

Preface viii
Acknowledgements xii
Notes on Using This Book xiv

Part I: The City 1
1. The Plan of the City 3
2. Memories 9
3. Faith 40
4. Architecture and Decoration 63

Part II: The Sites 81
5. Eastern Monastic Settlement (Züün Khüree) 83
6. Sükhbaatar Square (a.k.a. Chinggis Khan Square) 99
7. To the South of Sükhbaatar Square 118
8. Between the Monastic Settlements 139
9. Western Monastic Settlement (Baruun Khüree) 160
10. 'Consulate Hill' and Environs 181
11. 'Chinatown' (Maimachin) 204
12. To the South 209
13. Farther Afield 232
14. The Holy Mountain (Bogd Uul) 249

Afterword 253

Glossary 255
Bibliography 268
Index 282

Preface

In the 1920s a Danish scientific expedition travelled to an obscure corner of the Central Asian steppes. Its purpose was to set up an experimental farm to test a new variety of winter wheat and conduct experiments in modern dairy production. The group journeyed overland from North China to the newly independent sovereign state of Mongolia, a country where the Arctic winter conditions made it a perfect testing ground for their experiment.

One of the members of the expedition was Henning Haslund, an anthropologist, musician, and former officer in the Danish army. Haslund was a remarkably capable and outgoing young man whose optimism and cheerfulness impressed everyone who came to know him. Like so many of his countrymen, his open-minded and sympathetic attitude won him many friends among Mongolians who were delighted by his understanding of their customs and his ability to speak the rudiments of their language.

In *Tents in Mongolia* Haslund recalled his days in Mongolia with an infectious enthusiasm. A clear image of the man emerges from the book. He described the joys of boarding a train in Peking to escape to Kalgan, the expedition's first staging post in Inner Mongolia. 'I sank down on a comfortable leather-covered seat, under a whirring punkah, and ordered a Beck's beer, a big bottle.'[1] After weeks spent in the stuffy and insular Western community in Peking, he sensed a great exhilaration in finally being able to slip away from colonial social constraints.

> We now left China, where a 'white' cannot live without half a dozen boys to wait upon him and cannot walk in the street, but must have himself drawn by a sweating coolie. We had done with dancing on roof gardens and with cocktails at clubs. We packed our dinner jackets at the very bottom of our trunks, exchanged the daily, fresh-ironed, spotless linen for shorts and khaki shirts and threw the other rubbish into wagons.[2]

After a crossing of the Gobi Desert enlivened by the Scandinavian camaraderie and conviviality of his colleagues, the expedition caught its first sight of the capital.

> [The city] lay at our feet, traversed by the abundant waters of the [Tuul] river and encircled by [the Holy Mountain's] wooded steeps. The rays of the sun, which for

---

1. Haslund at 21.
2. Ibid. at 27.

> weeks we had been cursing, now threw an enchanting light over thousands of birch and larch trees clothed in autumn foliage. The innumerable gild roofs and minarets of the monastic city, the goal of our desert journey, lay before our enraptured eyes.[3]

Haslund was a witness to a time of extraordinary change in Mongolia. With the assistance of the Red Army, a collection of Mongolian nationalists founded a government that was soon to adopt a strict Marxist-Leninist ideology under the dominating wing of the USSR. A curtain was about to descend on an ancient way of life. Nonetheless, at the time of Henning's arrival, the capital was still an open city for foreign businesses and the tumult that attended Asia's rude introduction to the modern world.

> No town in the world is like [the capital]. Upon us newcomers it made an extremely strange impression. The most conservative eastern life and customs and western innovations like the telegraph, the telephone and the motor-car exist side by side in motely combination. The houses of the Russians clutter around the church with Byzantine cupolas; colossal Buddhist temples rise high over thousands of felt-covered Mongol tents. Mounted Mongols, slippered Chinese, long-bearded Russians and smiling Tibetans swarm between palisaded compounds whose walls are hung with gaily fluttering prayer-flags.[4]

This enthusiastic Dane was one of a small fraternity of inquisitive and restless travellers who recorded their experiences in Mongolia with an open heart and abundant sympathy. In his monumental work *The Modern History of Mongolia*, the British Mongolist Charles Bawden wrote that those who reached the distant city in that era were creative explorers who were articulate enough to write of their inner experiences while being moved by a sense of mourning that the culture of the Mongolians was on the verge of disappearing. Certainly, Haslund had heard people along the Gobi caravan route express a sorrowful expectation that 'the golden days of Outer Mongolia were drawing to close'.[5] Bawden said that such travellers were 'tough romantics, spiritually capable of appreciating the lost horizons and physically capable of making their way there'.[6]

Nearly one hundred years after the Haslund expedition, travellers to Ulaanbaatar often experience the same impressions. A mixture of the commonplace and the exotic creates a dazzling kaleidoscope of images. People wearing Mongolian robes and boots queue in fast-food restaurants for Western brand pizzas, deep-fried poultry parts, and hamburgers. Young professionals savour fine imported French wines while the elderly quaff *kumis*, fermented mare's milk tasting of a cocktail of unsweetened yogurt and club soda with the slightest touch of vodka. The most sophisticated nightlife this side of Europe is on offer in winter temperatures that often drop below those of Nome,

---

3. Ibid. at 66.
4. Ibid. at 68–69.
5. Ibid. at 36.
6. Bawden (1989) at 17.

Alaska. In a city filled with Asia's best English speakers, taxis are neither marked nor metered and frequently create the sensation of hitching a ride in an ashtray on wheels. The unemployed of the suburban tent settlements scavenge rubbish heaps for recyclable water bottles while luxury stores purvey Vertu mobile phones and diamond-encrusted bottles of vodka.

For first-timers, the city never matches their expectations because, for many, Mongolia is only a by-word for remoteness, an isolated place to be mentioned in the same breath as Timbuktu or Patagonia. This stereotype is long-lived and deeply entrenched. In the last century before the Christian era, the Grand Historian of China, Ssu-ma Ch'ien wrote a compendium of all history known to the Chinese world at that time. However, unlike Herodotus, whose misperceptions faded with antiquity, the Grand Historian enshrined a standard Chinese cliché about the inhabitants of the steppes. The nomads of Central Asia, he wrote, 'move about according to the availability of water and pasture, have no walled towns or fixed residences, nor any agricultural activities'.[7] This observation inadvertently insinuates purposelessness on the part of the ancestors of Mongolians and a lack of discrimination, as if *any* water or *any* pasture was suitable.[8] Subsequent generations of Chinese historians picked up on this stereotype and passed it along to the outside world, where it spread far and wide.

If Mongolia is remote, then Ulaanbaatar does not even produce a flicker of recognition in the eyes of most outsiders. Not even the *Financial Times* includes it in its list of global weather forecasts. The capital city usually comes in for cursory treatment by non-Mongolian tourists, who rush out on their adventure tours to verdant mountain valleys, magical lakeside cabins, and the desert's relentless frown, all admittedly the stuff that vacation dreams are made of but nonetheless affirming the jaded assumption that Ulaanbaatar somehow does not really 'matter'.

Indeed, the capital is often dismissed as a 'scar of city' even by some of the purported experts who have devoted many years of their lives to the country. While I do not contest this impression—Ulaanbaatar is not everyone's cup of tea—this one-sided view ignores the dramatic tale of three cities that arose on the banks of the Tuul River, the first under the influence of Buddhism, the second as a consequence of a Communist revolution, and the third as a testing ground for neo-liberal economics with more than a few lashings of Tammany Hall ethics.

Few tangible relics remain of Ulaanbaatar's distant past. This book, therefore, is a subjective journey into the imagination to compose a pointillist dreamscape of long vanished or half-vanished sites. I also set out forgotten dramas and anecdotes, along with my own subjective and quirky digressions, as we make our way through the city. I ask for the reader's indulgence in this poetic licence because I do not attempt to write a 'serious work of scholarship'—too much fun can be crushed in that process. This is an unconventional guidebook written about this unconventional city for today's 'tough

7. Ssu-ma Ch'ien at 129.
8. Lattimore (1962) at 31–32.

romantics', of any origin, who wish to invoke the spirit of this overlooked city on the steppes.

Last, there may be those who take offence that I do not present Ulaanbaatar as a pure Mongolian city without the 'taint of foreign blood' or outside culture. Such negative patriotism is not only ahistorical, but dangerous. I side with the nineteenth-century American satirist Ambrose Bierce who observed that patriotism is not the last refuge of a scoundrel; it is the first.[9]

M. A. Aldrich
Three Harbour Village, Formosa
Festival Day of Ayush
Full Moon, First Month, Year of the Female Red Fire Bird
12 March 2017

9. Bierce at 323.

Acknowledgements

Many friends and colleagues helped me to paint this portrait of Ulaanbaatar, and I owe them all a debt of gratitude: Delgermaa Altantuya, B. Anand and his staff at Zaya Hostel, Jamie Barr, Turtuvshin Bat-Erdene, Byambasuren Batbayar, Batmonkh, Solongoo Bayarsaikhan, Anudari Bold, Chinguun Bolormaa, Stanley Boots, Greg Buhyoff, Batbayar Byambasuren, Nicholas and Anne Cheffings, Mark Connelly, John Cooper, David Craigen, Aart DeJonge, the late Chris Dorman, Mendtuvshin Enktaivan, Tuvshinzaya Gantulga, Urtaa Gereltekh, David and Claire Getzinger, John and Noel Gorton, Laurent Gouiffés, Bolormaa Gulguu, Gary Hamp, Niel Isbrandtsen, Naranchimeg Jukov, Deen Kaplan, Janice Law, Erik Leyssens, Christine Lin, Mark McConnell, Doug McGay, Chris and Leila Melville, Lukas and Teresa Nikol, D. Odkhuu, Erdenedalai Odkhuu, Nominchimeg Odsuren, George Olsen, Scott Palmer, Lisebeth Ruitjer, Jeff Shane, Steven Schwenk, Yue Shen, Chris Smith, Nicholas M. Smith, OBE, Jim Stent, Myagmarsuren Tsoggerel, Baigalmaa Tsookhuu, Anthony Woolley, and David Wyche.

Turuu Bat-Erdene cheerfully and enthusiastically agreed to help me with the research and the site visits for this book. Without his keen support and willingness to help me explore every alley and old broken down building I would not have been able to finish the present work. I also thank him for correcting the spelling of Cyrillic Mongolian words in the text.

Aubrey Yang agreed to take on the work to design the maps in this book. I am grateful to him for his care and diligence in preparing the illustrations and for working through several rounds of revisions. Janice Law and Lukas Nikol kindly provided me with copies of their photographs.

The celebrated Mongolist Jack Weatherford was a source of wise counsel and support during this project. Similarly, former ambassadors Jonathan Addleton and Chris Stuart provided encouragement and exchanged viewpoints with me despite the pressures of their busy schedules. His Excellency Clifford Borg-Marks, former ambassador of the Republic of Malta to Mongolia, visited me many times in Ulaanbaatar where he shared with me his legendary stories about life in Asia 'back in the day'. Greg Buhyoff went through early drafts of chapters and offered me his thoughts. Aart DeJonge shared his insights and valuable experiences in Mongolia and Asia.

I owe an immense debt to the scholarly work of Zsuzsa Majer and Krisztina Teleki, who have undertaken groundbreaking research on Mongolian Buddhism. Their survey on the fate of pre-revolutionary temples is more than a significant addition to the field; it evokes the spirit of a vanished world. Professors Majer and Teleki compiled information on old and newly built temples and recorded interviews with elderly monks who had personal recollections of the sangha before the purges. Their work can be found at the website for the Mongolian Temple Historical Project, www.mongoliantemples.com. I often thought of them fondly as the 'two Budapest bodhisattvas' as I sought to recreate old Urga in my mind, an exercise not too far removed from trying to visualize a mandala.

Long-time UB resident Don Croner deserves the Polar Star for his books and website on Central Asian history and culture. I yield to no one in my admiration for his empirical understanding of Mongolia. Don's writings often focus on the life and culture of the herder and the Mongolian world beyond UB and are highly recommended.

I apologize to anyone whom I have forgotten to include in my acknowledgements. If I have not mentioned you, it is an inadvertent oversight attributable to the creeping effects of advancing years, a failing memory, and fine arkhi. I ask for your indulgence.

Most of all, I am grateful to Mei-Chih Chuang for putting up with a spouse who just had to take us to the coldest capital city on the globe. Of course, the views expressed in this book, and doubtless its many errors, are all my own.

Notes on Using This Book

'There isn't really much culture here, you know.' Or so was the declaratory judgement of a mid-level diplomat at an embassy shortly after my move to Ulaanbaatar in 2009.

Perhaps this misguided view can be understood in light of the paucity of information in English about Mongolia and its capital city. It is an opinion reinforced by contemporary travel books in which an author flaunts his or her own exceptionalism for travelling in an 'outlandish' country like Mongolia. Some of the guidebooks on the market strain at the bit to get past UB and introduce their readers to the scenes of natural beauty, inadvertently slighting the contention that Mongolia has a history and civilization that ought to be appreciated side by side with the more well-known cultures in Asia.

These misperceptions provided me with the grit determination to offer something new, something that might help open people's eyes and see UB differently. To paraphrase the great Carlos Celdran of Manila, you can't change the way UB looks, but you can change the way you look at UB.

I have divided this book into two parts. The first contains detailed chapters about Ulaanbaatar as a more 'serious' offering to provide the reader with a deeper appreciation of this unknown city. Chapter 1 sets out the cosmological plan of the original settlement and explains how the appearance of the city changed over time while remaining true to its core character. This is followed by the chapter 'Memories', which sets out Mongolian history viewed through the prism of the city from ancient days to the twenty-first century. Here I introduce themes and famous people whom we will encounter later on during our perambulations. Chapter 3, entitled 'Faith', paints a mosaic of the spiritual beliefs held by Mongolians and the institutions that supported these beliefs. This will hopefully make the city's surviving temples and shamanistic sites more accessible and help visitors take away more than a perfunctory impression of them. Chapter 4 introduces the reader to an overview of Mongolian architecture and ornamental decoration, another overlooked topic.

Brief discussions on Mongolian music, drama, literature, sports, and cinema are set out elsewhere in the book. I hope that these cursory introductions will whet the appetite of those who might pick up where I leave off and write a better and more thorough treatment of these topics.

The second part of the book sets out tours in the city and its environs and presents more subjective impressions. Chapter 5 starts with a description of a handful of eighteenth-century tent-style temples that have managed to survive. It then takes the reader on a tour of the imagination into the centre of the old monastic city as it looked one hundred years ago.

In Chapter 6 we enter terra firma as we embark upon a visit to mostly tangible sites (and sights) at the city's main square, enlivened (I hope) with my own idiosyncratic commentary. Each subsequent chapter moves farther from the centre of the city to more distant locales.

Throughout the book, I mention to black-and-white photographs of certain sites. A good collection of these is in Bayasgalan Bayanbat's *Ulaanbaatar Then and Now*, which can be found in book stores in UB and is a useful companion to this book.

Getting Around

Ulaanbaatar is not a pedestrian-friendly city. I recommend the reader to procure transportation by motor car for most of the visits to the sites described in these pages. Taxis range from professional radio-dispatched service to filthy wrecks. I recommend cutting a daily rate for visiting these sites if you meet a decent driver. Alternatively, public transportation costs very little, but there are few bus stops that are easily identifiable to a newly arrived traveller without the language. Furthermore, street addresses are seldom used or recognized. Directions are usually given by referring to landmarks, such as 'take the alley way next to the Cuban embassy until you pass a Khanburger joint'.

A winter visit is challenging, not only for sub-zero temperatures but the treacherousness of icy sidewalks, which can lead to nasty spills and broken bones for those from less northern climates. However, there is a much less 'touristed' feeling at that time compared to the summer high season.

Traffic congestion in recent years means that travel within the city can be agonizingly slow. There is a popular quip about a driver offering a ride to a friend walking by. He retorts, 'No, thanks, I am in a hurry.'

Accommodations

The quality of hotels ranges from ersatz five-star splendour to boisterous knocking-shops. As business standards come and go, it is somewhat futile to make recommendations for a place to stay. An international brand is also no guarantee of the quality that you may be accustomed to elsewhere. Personally, I find small guest houses to be more welcoming and personable than the dark, impervious behemoths that have cropped up in both the communist and capitalist years. Zaya Hostel is the best of the small inns.

Language, Romanization, and Names

Frustratingly, there is no standard method of romanizing Mongolian. This book is no more nor less consistent than other works in print. I add certain key words in Mongolian Cyrillic in the hope that this lessens confusion between the languages. I do this also to give primacy to the local language in this missive that seeks to give pride of place to Mongolian culture. At times I also use Sanskrit and Tibetan terms as these may be better known among Westerner readers. Chinese terms are in *pinyin* and sometimes simplified characters; when older forms of romanization are more recognizable to Westerners, I use them instead.

As I explain in Chapter 1, I call the capital city of Mongolia by three different names, depending on the historical context. I also use the traditional name 'Peking' in lieu of the officially-sanctioned *pinyin* spelling 'Beijing'. 'Peking' has a more elegant appearance that conjures up the pageant of that city's past. As a graduate of a Jesuit university, I will stick with tradition, at least in this one instance.

Mongolians do not have surnames, which, in case you were wondering, were probably an invention for tax collection and state surveillance in most parts of the world. In Mongolia the custom is for someone to have a personal name conjoined with a patronymic, which is usually the personal name of the father. Sometimes, the second part of the name is the mother's name (as in the case of Choibalsan) or it may be the name of the person's clan affiliation from long ago, if known.

As an illustration using English names, a person named John with a father named Peter would probably be known as John Peter. His daughter, named Naomi, would be Naomi John. In official documents, the patronymic precedes the personal name. In this case, the suffix *iin* (ийн) is added to the patronymic, similar to Peter*'s* John or John*'s* Naomi.

People use different styles to render a Mongolian name into English, which results in inconsistencies. For example, the woman mentioned above might present her name as J. Naomi or Naomi J. The protocol is to call her Ms. Naomi or just Naomi.

Mongolians also use nicknames and abbreviated personal names. Nicknames like 'Bonehead' or 'Horsehead' sound like Mafioso titles; they are not likely to be shared with you. Abbreviated personal names are similar to the Western custom where John becomes Jack. 'Nominchimeg' may go by 'Nomio', 'Batbayar' becomes 'Bagi', or 'Erdenedalai' is known as 'Dalai'. Some people adopt Westernized names as an accommodation to non-Mongolians, which is helpful when encountering tongue-twisters like Terbishdagva.

Food and Beverages

Mongolian cuisine is predicated on its natural environment, and it cannot be denied that it is a trying place for vegetarians. Historically, dining customs embarked on a circular migration that went from the use of hands (for gnawing on a boiled mutton rib), to chopsticks for noodles (sometimes), to a fork and a knife for Russian cuisine, and then back to using hands (for hamburgers and pizza). While healthier alternatives have become popular, people still say that 'meat is a meal, but a meal with no meat is no meal'.

Meat was traditionally prepared by boiling, the least wasteful method, to conserve fuel, an understandable concern given the winter temperatures that drop to minus 40 degrees. It was also taboo to roast meats because some Buddhist Central Asians, unlike their Muslim neighbours, believed that the gods are offended by the smell of barbecued flesh. (Roasting meat wastes fuel, too.) The primary if not sole seasoning was salt as a necessity on the steppes. Sometimes green onions were added. Mongolian specialties on offer in Ulaanbaatar's restaurants are often a local adaptation of northern Chinese cuisine. Russian cuisine introduced the liberal use of mayonnaise, pickled vegetables, sausages, and preserved cold meats.

Buuz (бууз) are steamed meat dumplings usually made with mutton, similar to Chinese *baozi* (包子). *Khuushuur* (Хуушуур) are lightly fried meat-cakes often filled with mutton and diced onions. For travellers coming from points to the south, khuushuur are similar to Chinese *roubing* (肉饼), but much larger. These two are the standard fare offered in many quick snack places throughout the city and in the countryside. Buuz and khuushuur are typically served with a semi-synthetic soy sauce sold under the trademark Maggie. I find that they taste their best when flavoured with a fiery Sichuan chilli paste, but that is too radically spicy for some of my Mongolian friends. (Take your own jar of this condiment with you if this sounds appealing.) *Tsuivan* (цуйван) is fried noodles made with mutton and carrot and cabbage shavings. *Khorkhog* (хорхог) are sheep ribs cooked in a pressure cooker and then eaten by tearing off a piece with the mouth and cutting it free with a knife—pointy-nosed Westerners are advised to use caution. It is cooked with potatoes and other root vegetables. The ribs are roasted with black porous stones which wind up covered in fat and handed out at the start of the meal. These are not mementoes to be taken home, or an hors d'oeuvre, as famously assumed by some visiting investment bankers, but are meant to improve the circulation of the blood in one's hands. As these are piping hot, you will need to flip the stone from one hand to the other until they cool down.

Mongolian mutton is very tasty as it is grown organically. As noted fifty years ago,

> [Artemisia], and several species of wild garlic and wild onion, and a plant that has a smell something like sage, give Mongolian mutton a flavor that eaters of the prim American lamb chop cannot even imagine.[1]

We should land a knockout punch on the myth of 'Mongolian barbecue'. The 'original' Mongolian barbecue was first sprung on an unsuspecting public in 1955 at the Genghis Khan Restaurant in Taipei, possibly as an excellent way to pawn off ingredients that had started to spoil. This type of restaurant wormed its way to Hong Kong

---

1. Lattimore (1962) at 18.

'Careful eating the *khorkhog*, Comrade!'. Photo by author.

and then to other eateries in the Chinese diaspora before showing up in Ulaanbaatar as purportedly a Japanese cuisine in the 1990s.

Mongolian cuisine is ubiquitous in UB. For this reason, I do not have any recommendations for a Mongolian restaurant as they all tend to be equally fine because of the simplicity in the preparation of the food. In these chapters I point out a handful of other restaurants that have unique or interesting cuisine on offer, either by the standards of UB or elsewhere.

For those curious about the history of Mongolian food, there is no more fascinating resource than *A Soup for the Qan* by Paul Buell and Eugene Anderson, which details the fusion cuisine (and recipes) of the Mongolian court during the Yuan dynasty.

Mongolian vodka is of excellent quality but dangerous potency. Since Mongolian trademark practice is still in its infancy, various conglomerates have registered deceptively similar marks using the likeness of Chinggis Khan (who appears to be glaring out from some labels with a severe hangover). Other national symbols, such as Zanabazar's Tantric Soyombo emblem, have been ripped off as brands for vodka, too. I recall the days when the only spirit on the shelves of most shops was the trusty blue-labelled *arkhi*.

Local beers tend to follow the bland lead of American lagers, though GEM ale, whenever available, is a fine tipple that calls to mind English ales. Imported wines are available in the high-end shops.

The high altitude and dryness of the climate dehydrates visitors. Be sure to drink plenty of bottled water and keep some on hand in your hotel room in the evening in case you wake up parched.

Conduct

To me, fine nightlife means a single malt scotch and a good book by a fireplace so that I can salute the Goddess of the Hearth. That said, expatriate connoisseurs assure me that the nightlife in UB is as sophisticated as night-time haunts in Europe, with electronic music at ear-splitting decibels and light shows designed to induce epileptic fits in life forms higher than a clam.

While I do not wish to overemphasize this point, you need to maintain a certain Western 'streetwise' sense about you. One cannot take personal security as a given (as in many other Asian cities). Things can be a little dicey once the sun sets and the vodka flows. The foreign press has made much of groups of nativists, and they are certainly a nuisance betraying the tradition of their country. Nonetheless, you need to keep your wits about you. One should embrace the Taoist recommendation to be 'yielding like water' and flow away and around potential unpleasantness. For men, nightlife with Mongolian female companionship may bring with it the predictable consequences of alpha males wanting to maintain the purity of the herd.

Mongolia is the other half of Asia, the one without the oppressive crush of a large population or an agricultural and sedentary tradition made burdensome and heavy through political Confucianism. Asia of the steppe (as opposed to Asia of the sown) has been little appreciated outside a small circle of academic scholars and those who have 'gone native'. Nor is it often written about with affection. By giving a priority to Mongolian culture and an appreciation of its people, you will discover an overlooked jewel that, like all good things, pays rich rewards for the investment of time and patience.

Part I

The City

1

The Plan of the City

At its core, the amorphous spirit of Ulaanbaatar has all the versatility and fecklessness of one of the air signs of the Western zodiac. These qualities transformed the appearance of the capital into three vastly different cities over the centuries. In the sixteenth century it donned the robes of a lama and laid the foundations for Mongolian sedentary society. The settlement matured into a sacred city on par with Lhasa or Varanasi by the late nineteenth century. Then, in 1921, it traded its monastic robes and mitre for a black worker's cap and the high-collared tunic of a commissar, looking faithfully to Moscow for direction, if not inspiration. After the fall of communism in 1990 it morphed into a free-market entrepreneur, with a baseball cap worn backwards, tooling around town in an SUV while listening to Mongolian hip-hop as a badge of faux patriotism.

The city's mercurial personality is seen in its many names. Among Westerners long ago, it was called Urga, or Ourga, a mangling of the Mongolian *örgöö* (өргөө), meaning 'esteemed residence' or 'palace' of an important person.[1] In 1924, it took the name Ulan Bator (Улан Батор) or 'Red Hero'. 'Ulan Bator' is an imprecise Latin rendering of its classical Mongolian name as put through Cyrillic Russian. It also looks irritatingly like the name of a minor Star Wars character. In the 1990s an accurate rendering of its name, Ulaanbaatar (Улаанбаатар), from its Cyrillic Mongolian spelling, came on the scene, though this has been ignored by most Anglophone news outlets, which continue to use Ulan Bator.

In these pages I use one of these three names to refer alternatively to the three main historic phases of the city. Urga is the name I use for the city from antiquity to the formal establishment of the Mongolian People's Republic (MPR). Ulan Bator covers the period from 1924 to Mongolia's renunciation of Marxism-Leninism in 1990. The post-communist city is Ulaanbaatar or, in sympathy with the overused letter *a* on my keyboard, UB.[2]

1. The term originally referred to the flap in a tent used to cover its circular smoke hole. Lattimore (1962) at 61.
2. In Mongolian, too, the city has been called by a maddening multitude of names. Aside from Örgöö, it was called Khüree from the early eighteenth century, though this went through several modifications: Ikh Khüree (Great Monastic Settlement), Bogdiin Khüree (Monastic Settlement of the Patriarch), Khutagtiin Khüree (Monastic Settlement of the Incarnate One), and Ariin Khüree (Monastic Settlement of the North). Coming to the twentieth century, its name became Niislel Khüree (Monastic Capital) in 1912. Finally, we land on the name Ulaanbaatar Niislel Khot (Red Hero Capital City) in 1924. See Teleki (2008) at 12.

In the eighteenth century Urga coalesced into two roughly circular settlements like orbs in the upper sky of a Buddhist painting. One of the orbs was a monastic encampment, or *khüree*, which is a mobile collection of felt tents arranged in the shape of an inverted *U* with the residence of a high lama at its centre. A khüree is the nomadic counterpart to cosmological designs often applied to Asian cities. It has the same shape as the mobile hunting camps of the Manchu nobles or the travelling encampments of the Tibetan Sakyapa Buddhist patriarch. While lacking an intricate theory of urban design, unlike Peking, or Baghdad during the Abbasid Caliphate, the shape of a khüree determined the basic contours of monastic settlements.

The other orb was a trading post built by Chinese merchants who sold the manufactured necessities of life otherwise unavailable on the steppes. Their clientele consisted of mostly Mongolian herders and monks. The residents of the trading post attempted, haphazardly, to follow Chinese urban design by enclosing their settlement with a wooden 'city wall' plastered with mud to create a semblance of sturdiness. The second orb did not resemble in the least the grand walled cities of China because of cost—the interests of the merchants were practical rather than ceremonial—but it soon acquired all the accoutrements of a Chinese settlement in non-Han lands, such as opera halls, temples, and restaurants.

Urga took its prestige from being the residence of the Jebzundamba Khutugtu (Жавзандамба хутагт), or the Revered Noble One. This exalted lineage produced the Buddhist patriarchs who were the spiritual leaders of Northern (or Khalkha) Mongolia.

In the early nineteenth century, a third orb joined the other two. The patriarch established a 'university town' to the west of his khüree as a centre for higher Buddhist learning. This turned into a second monastic district. The original one was called the Eastern Monastic Settlement, or Züün Khüree (Зүүн Хүрээ), and the other the Western Monastic Settlement, or Baruun Khüree (Баруун Хүрээ). The tradesmen district, a 'Chinatown' in fact, was called Maimachin (Маймачин), from the Chinese *maimaicheng* (买卖城), meaning 'buy-sell city'.

During the nineteenth century Urga began to lose its nomadic character as it set down tenuous roots. Nonetheless, it still had the appearance of a transitory camp that could be disbanded rapidly. Wooden palisades enclosed felt tents and a few wooden houses, looking like the forts of the Hudson Bay Company in early nineteenth-century Canada. These palisades were conjoined to form unpaved roadways meandering through the settlement. Non-monastic dwellings for lay Mongolians grew to the south of the two religious centres while the Khalkha nobles built wooden courtyard town houses along the northern bank of the Tuul River for their occasional visits to Urga. Despite the appearance of Chinese architectural forms, fixed sites of worship, and other urban touches, it remained a loose hodgepodge of randomly positioned felt tents and wooden buildings well into the twentieth century.

However, that was almost not the end of the story. Some bright bulb in the 1990s coined a new name, Aziin Tsagaan Dagina, or, in a translation ripe for misunderstanding, 'Asia's White Fairy'. This suggestion mercifully slipped back into obscurity after its airing.

Gate for a khasaa in the ger district. Photo by author.

A view familiar to nineteenth-century visitors. Photo by Lukas Nikol.

Life was simple and basic compared to other Asian cities. Most residents of Urga were disinclined to walk any distance and travelled around on horseback. They purchased their water from Chinese labourers hauling barrels from the Tuul River and its tributaries. Dried dung, or *argol* (аргал), was the fuel used for heating and cooking, wood being too valuable for combustion while the extraction of coal risked provoking the ire of underground spirits. Illumination was by way of lamps burning a wick in oil. Rubbish was left festering in the roads outside the palisades until the visit of an

Communist building mural. Photo by Lukas Nikol.

important person or a special religious holiday necessitated a rapid clean-up. Despite monastic protests, a marketplace gradually grew up between the two monastic settlements. By the late nineteenth century, a small tsarist diplomatic mission had become a nucleus for a Russian colony on 'Consulate Hill'.

Coming on to the stage in the third decade of the twentieth century, Ulan Bator was a complete repudiation of Urga and its traditions. Its distinctive shape arose through the gradual adoption of Soviet urban design implemented by teams of Mongolian and Russian architects. Gone was the ramshackle chaos of the lamas and tradesmen. A main square formed the centre around which concentric paved ring roads connected neighbourhoods with newly built apartment complexes. Heated water and electricity were supplied from power stations. Dorian, Ionian, and Aeolian columns, recalling their distant origins on the Aegean Sea, decorated public buildings along with delicate and subtle Mongolian motifs shorn of religious associations. Modern hospitals, schools, cooperative stores, museums, opera halls, cinemas, and macadamized roads replaced the hard scrapple existence of urban life under monastic rule. Thanks to Soviet technical guidance, urban planners placed buildings in locations for the best use of air and light.

The municipal authorities created discrete suburbs called microdistricts as the city expanded beyond the outer ring road; however, construction perennially lagged behind migration to the city. Felt tents were always being added to the suburbs and were never fully replaced by modern housing.

By the mid-1960s, Ulan Bator had completed its metamorphosis into a carefully designed Siberian provincial capital built in accordance with a tastefully restrained

Soviet neoclassicism. It was a city pleasing to the eye if unexciting to those seeking more libertine excitements or bourgeois consumerism.

With the advent of Ulaanbaatar, time went backwards. The appearance of the city reverted to an unplanned settlement with helter-skelter construction that marred the carefully crafted Soviet design. Some justify the lack of planning on the excuse that Mongolians are nomads unfamiliar with such foreign concepts. In truth, there has been little desire to preserve the Soviet patrimony of Ulan Bator and an intense hunger to make a quick buck. The city was also inundated with herders uprooted in the aftermath of neo-liberal economic policies in the 1990s. The sprawling '*ger* districts' or the newly settled outlying suburbs are a throwback to nineteenth-century Urga; its residents depend upon water trucked in and have to make do with minimal,

'Sacrifice zones' for the free market. Photos by Lukas Nikol.

if any, public utilities. The Mongolian capital became a 'sacrifice zone' for a new set of imported economic theories.

As UB entered the twenty-first century, the downtown district tossed up ill-placed skyscrapers that look, for all the world, like they have somehow managed to pull up sticks and wander up from Hong Kong or Singapore, setting themselves down uninvited next to Soviet monuments, felt tents, and the few surviving Buddhist temples. Once important buildings fell victim to the wrecking ball or were robbed of their former dignity in the rush to embrace modernity. The resulting jumble resembles a surrealistic Central Asian city dreamed up by Terry Gilliam as a modern-day Xanadu. Or perhaps it suggests an alternative reality for Lhasa if the Tibetan capital had been able to escape the clutches of the 'Fatherland'.

The chaotic face of Ulaanbaatar hides the stories of its past, locking them away in the stony forgetfulness of neglected or misunderstood buildings—that is, until we release them.

Ger district. Photo by Lukas Nikol.

2

Memories

The Tuul River Valley was fated to be the site of the Mongolian capital for several reasons.[1] Water, a scarce commodity on the arid Mongolian plateau, was available in abundance at the confluence of the Tuul and Selbe rivers. The surrounding mountains provided shelter from fierce windstorms that afflict Central Asia in spring and autumn. Its central location at the heart of Khalkha Mongolia ensured that it would become the main commercial relay station between Siberia and China.[2]

Perhaps the most significant reason was the reverence felt by ancient steppe dwellers for the spiritual forces of nature. The Holy Mountain, or Bogd Uul (Богд Уул), was the home of a powerful protective spirit. Mongolians envisaged this 'patron saint' of the river valley as a majestic bird or *khangarid* (хангарьд), perhaps modelled on the sacred Garuda, the legendary bird-god of India. The khangarid became the symbol of Urga, and today it adorns the municipal flag of Ulaanbaatar.[3] Whenever I see this symbol, I hear faint echoes from the Mahabharata and its narrative about the epic clash between two Indian clans. Rabindranath Tagore's comment on the Indonesian islands applies equally to Ulaanbaatar: 'I see India everywhere, yet I do not recognize it.'

Aside from these natural attributes and spiritual elements, the rise of Urga to a capital city was linked to two historical events—the second conversion of Mongolians to Buddhism and the conquest of China by a tribe from Manchuria.

The people of the steppes had learned of Buddhism long before Chinggis Khan's consolidation of Mongolian tribes in 1206. A formal conversion began in 1253 when

1. The main historical overviews for Mongolia are Baabar and Bawden. Perdue describes the evolution of geopolitics in Central Asia from the fifteenth to eighteenth centuries. Weatherford (2004) is the essential starting point for a study of Chinggis Khan. Grousset and Prawdin are older and engaging historical overviews.
2. By the early nineteenth century, Urga was the most important staging post between Kiakhta, a Siberian border town, and Kalgan, the first major settlement on the south side of the Gobi Desert. Both Kiakhta and Kalgan have lost their historical significance as inland 'port' cities where divergent cultures converged on account of trade. Kiakhta fulfilled a role similar to Hong Kong and Macao on the south flank of the Chinese empire. It was a trading city where new innovations in thought and technology created a mixed Sino-Mongolian-Russian culture, complete with its own patois. Kalgan, meaning 'gate' in old Mongolian, was the functional equivalent of the various 'gate' (*men* 门) ports along the China coast. It too had a broadly cosmopolitan culture that did not survive the installation of Communist rule. Today it is a nondescript Chinese city called Zhangjiakou (张家口 or 'Zhang Family Pass').
3. The *khangarid* was forced into 'temporary retirement' during the Communist era.

Ovoo on snow-clad steppes. Photo by author.

the dominant monastic rulers of Tibet shrewdly submitted to Kublai Khan's empire to forestall an invasion of their Himalayan homeland. As a result of this diplomacy, Kublai Khan was introduced to, and perhaps entranced by, the sorcery and the ritual pageantry of Vajrayana Buddhism. Or so say Chinese accounts. When the Yuan dynasty collapsed in 1368, Buddhism appears to have faded from the landscape. Mongolians sought refuge in the shamanist traditions of their ancestors and drifted away from the dharma.

After producing one of the world's most cosmopolitan empires, Mongolia fell into a dark sleep while its elites bickered, causing needless turmoil across the steppes. Khalkha Mongolia, formerly the region of the empire that was home to the Chinggisid founders, broke up into three provinces, or aimags. These were loosely defined regions whose borders continually shifted because of clan alliances. Each aimag was ruled by a hereditary khan under whom smaller principalities were governed by lesser princes in service to their khan as vassals. The original 'three aimags' of Khalkha Mongolia were the Tsetsen Khan Aimag in the east, the Tüshetu Khan Aimag in the region surrounding Urga, and the Zasagtu Khan Aimag to the west, with each aimag named after the title of its ruling khan. In the early eighteenth century, the Sain Noyon Aimag was carved out from the Tüshetu Khan Aimag. (These four aimags continued to be the main internal boundaries of Khalkha Mongolia into the twentieth century.)

The Second Conversion began in the late sixteenth century when a Tibetan monk, Sonam Gyatso, arrived in the Ordos, the Mongolian region within the bend of the Yellow River in what is now China's Inner Mongolia Autonomous Region. As the leading monk of the 'Yellow Hat' branch of Buddhism, he proposed a mutually beneficial bargain to the Altan Khan, the leader of the Ordos Mongolians. The Tibetan patriarch declared him to be a reincarnation of Khublai Khan as a boost to his prestige. In return, the Altan Khan promised the monk his military support against rival religious factions. During this summit meeting, the literal meaning of the name of Sonam Gyatso was translated as 'Dalai Lama'—Ocean Teacher. This mixed Mongolian-Tibetan phrase came to be used as the title of the senior monk in the Yellow Hat tradition. It was retroactively applied to the incarnations of his two spiritual predecessors, making Sonam Gyatso the Third Dalai Lama.[4]

Other nobles soon followed in the footsteps of their Ordos Mongolian cousins. Specifically, the Abatai Khan of the Tüshetu Khan Aimag converted to Yellow Hat Buddhism at the urging of Sonam Gyatso. He founded the Monastery of the One Hundred Treasures, or Erdene Zuu Khiid (Эрдэнэ Зуу хийд) in 1586 near the old imperial capital Kharakhorum. In support of the new religion, the khans launched purges against indigenous shamanist practitioners and competed to back the Yellow Hat branch in its disputes with other branches of Buddhism. Tibetan philosophy, medicine, art, science, and music, which were all influenced by Indian culture, flowed into the steppes while Mongolian culture drifted back to Tibet in a mutual exchange between the two civilizations.

A descendant of the Abatai Khan, Gombodorj perceived the significance of the rise of the Yellow Hat faith among Mongolians. He arranged for his son to be inducted into the clergy, giving him the clerical Sanskrit name Jnanavajra, or Zanabazar (Занабазар), meaning 'Thunderbolt of Wisdom'. In 1639 the clergy recognized the four-year-old Zanabazar as the reincarnation of Taranatha, a revered Tibetan scholar and founder of the Jonam branch of Tibetan Buddhism. The child was given 108 households as servants—in effect, these serfs were the 'seed assets' that eventually grew into the massive estates owned by his successors. In 1647 Zanabazar's clan took the boy to Peking as the Jebzundamba Khutugtu to pay homage to the recently installed Manchu emperor of China. (Being adept when it came to covering all his bases, Gombodorj also anointed another son as his successor-khan of Tüshetu Khan Aimag, placing both state and pulpit in the hands of his family.)

From the Second Conversion until the 1930s, Yellow Hat Buddhism was the predominant Buddhist sect in Mongolia and shaped the social context for Urga's pre-eminence in the late eighteenth century.

* * *

The other key players for the eventual rise of Urga were the Manchus, a semi-nomadic people from the forested regions to the north-east of China proper. The political ascendancy of the Manchus began as the Ming dynasty entered terminal decline in the early seventeenth century. In 1644 they successfully laid siege to Peking and installed the Qing dynasty, which eventually brought all China under its rule.

4. Many historians state that the Altan Khan bestowed this title on Sonam Gyatso. The current Dalai Lama rejects this interpretation. See Laird at 143.

Symbol for *Svayambhu*. Photo by author.

Manchus shared many traits with Mongolians. They were a martial people who celebrated horsemanship and archery, and they had practised shamanism as their native belief before encountering Buddhism. On the other hand, they had adopted agriculture as their primary economy as well as Chinese administrative principles and political philosophy, thus beginning the slow but inexorable process of Sinicization that led to the near extinction of the Manchus as a separate people.

In their ascent to power, the Manchus initially allied with the Mongolian khans whose territories bordered on Manchu lands. As cultural cousins, the khans of eastern Inner Mongolia viewed the Manchus as senior partners in an imperial alliance for riches to be extracted forcefully from China. They accepted Manchu suzerainty over their domains in exchange for recognition of their royal privileges and the right to call on the Manchu throne for defence in times of trouble.

As in most political alliances, the motivation for this accommodation was, of course, power and wealth, not altruism. Contemporary Mongolians sometimes condemn the treacherous scheming of the Manchus—the Mongolian word for Manchu has a secondary meaning of 'smarminess' or 'duplicity'—but certainly they were no less treacherous than Mongolian elites competing for power against other Mongolian elites.

At first, Khalkha Mongolia remained beyond Manchu suzerainty because of its isolation, thanks to the Gobi Desert being a buffer. This isolation collapsed when Galdan Boshogtu Khan, the leader of a Zungarian tribe of Western Mongolians, sought to conquer Greater Mongolia in its entirety. Claiming to be the defender of the dignity of the Yellow Hat patriarch, Galdan used an alleged slight by Zanabazar to a representative of the Dalai Lama as the pretext for launching a war despite grave warnings to keep the peace from the Manchu court. In 1688 Galdan launched a full-scale invasion of Khalkha Mongolia, razed the Monastery of the One Hundred Treasures, and sent the Khalkha nobles along with Zanabazar and his monks fleeing to the open arms of the Manchus.

Seizing the opportunity, the Kangxi Emperor of the Qing Empire met the Khalkha elites at the Inner Mongolian city of Doloon Nor where they pledged fealty to the Manchus in exchange for military support against Galdan. Under the terms of the alliance, the highest ruling prince of each aimag retained the title of khan, though each khan came under the direct authority of the Qing emperor, whose approval was needed for any hereditary succession. The boundaries of the aimags were also fixed, and within each aimag the khan oversaw the lesser princes of each principality, or *khoshun*, again subject to affirmation by the throne. (These khoshuns are more commonly called 'banners' in Western historical writing.) The Patriarch, Zanabazar, was also recognized as the highest ecclesiastical authority in Khalkha Mongolia, but his powers were likewise subject to the ultimate authority of the emperor. The estates of the patriarchs grew in size over time so that they operated as a fifth aimag. By 1691 Khalkha Mongolia was formally incorporated as an autonomously governed territory within the Qing Empire and remained as a protectorate until 1911.[5]

While the Khalkha elites pursued obvious personal objectives for declaring their allegiance to the Manchus, they did not embark upon this oath lightly or view it as a dishonourable undertaking. The nobles were taken into the Manchu empire as higher-ranking allies rather than vanquished foes, like the Chinese.[6] Likewise, the Kangxi Emperor demonstrated his commitment to the Khalkha Mongolians by personally leading a joint army of Manchu, Mongolian, and Chinese troops against Galdan, defeating him at the Battle of Zuunmud near the Tuul River Valley. Galdan fled from the battle and eventually took his own life (or was poisoned) in 1697.[7]

Despite their battlefield losses, Galdan's descendants continued to raise merry hell on the borders of Khalkha Mongolia and in Tibet, where their supposed military support for the dalai lamas became a transparent excuse for them to invade Tibet and loot the country three ways from Sunday. Zungharian resistance against the Manchus continued until 1759 when the Qianlong Emperor, having decided enough was enough, invaded the Zungharian domains and committed one of the first acts of genocide in the modern era, butchering or enslaving the Zungharian people and laying waste to thousands of square acres.

* * *

5. Cheney at 24–32.
6. See Elverskog on Mongolian-Manchu relations.
7. In an act of unspeakable vindictiveness, the Kangxi Emperor had the desiccated remains of Galdan brought to Peking, paraded in front of the Forbidden City, sliced up, ground into dust, and then scattered throughout the streets of the capital. At that time, Chinese believed that the treatment of the remains of a deceased directly impacts upon the deceased's condition in the afterlife. In other words, the Kangxi Emperor sought to grind Galdan into the dust and rubbish of Peking's streets for all eternity, an unsubtle message to one and all of the consequences of challenging the emperor.

Zanabazar was fortunate to fall on the winning side of the conflict between the Zungharians and the Manchus. His pledge of loyalty to the Kangxi Emperor ensured generous imperial support for his monasteries. In time, the emperor and the lama became friends.

I doubt that Zanabazar was ever drawn with any personal enthusiasm to the deadly geopolitics of Central Asia. He seems to me to have been more an 'intellectual's intellectual'. A giant of a man, he was an accomplished polymath, the Leonardo da Vinci of Mongolia. He cast exquisite bronze statues of the Buddhist pantheon using Newari and Tibetan techniques. He researched the therapeutic properties of the waters of Mongolia's hot springs, revised monastic architecture, composed poetry, wrote religious treatises, invented a new Mongolian clerical alphabet, and adapted Buddhist rituals to Mongolian culture.[8]

He was also susceptible to affairs of the heart—a shortcoming that reinforces his appeal today—and fell in love with a woman who served as model for his famous bronze sculptures of the Buddhist saint Tara. Today, his portrait gazes out from the 100-togrog note, so for the observant visitor there is a daily reminder of his talents.

However, the imperial successor to the Kangxi Emperor distrusted Zanabazar, considering him to have been too close to his recently deceased father. The Yongzheng Emperor was a surly and cunning young man who may have helped the elderly lama 'change his vestments' during a trip to Peking for the Kangxi Emperor's funeral in 1722. Two years later, the Second Patriarch was found incarnated in Khalkha Mongolia in the person of the great-grandson of Zanabazar's brother and duly enthroned.

Zanabazar is the first of eight incarnated lamas, or *khutugtus* (хутагт), sometimes called 'Living Buddhas' (from the Chinese *huofo* 活佛), that were officially recognized by the Qing court as the Yellow Hat ecclesiastical leaders of Khalkha Mongolia. They were the third most senior lamas in Khalkha Mongolia's Buddhist hierarchy after the Dalai Lama and the Panchen Lama. Each of these eight patriarchs was an object of intense adoration by ordinary herders because of their purported supernatural powers and their infinite wisdom transcending mundane understanding. They were also as rich as Croesus because the nobility, the clergy, and the ordinary laity showered them with lavish donations. These gifts became the basis of the treasuries of the patriarchs, which remained outside the jurisdiction of the aimags of the nobles.

* * *

In the early eighteenth century, there were few notable sedentary settlements in the Tuul River Valley because Mongolia was still a nomadic society. The Monastery of the One Hundred Treasures was rebuilt but the patriarchs held court in mobile felt tent encampments that moved twenty-eight times between 1639 and 1855. These encampments were called *örgöö* or, starting from the reign of the Second Patriarch, khüree.

8. Croner (2006) traces the career of Zanabazar and identifies important sites in contemporary Mongolia from episodes in his life.

In fact, until the middle of the nineteenth century, the encampment called Urga by foreigners did not have a fixed site. It was to be found wherever the Patriarch 'hung his hat', or, more accurately, pitched his tent. This is because the locus of ecclesial authority depended upon the person of the nomadic patriarch.

In 1721 the Scottish physician John Bell arrived at the Patriarch's court as a member of a Russian diplomatic delegation en route to Peking.

> What they call the Urga is the court, or the place where the prince and the high priest reside; who are always encamped at no great distance from one another. They have several thousand tents about them, which are removed from time to time. The Urga is much frequented by merchants, from China and Russia, and other places; where all trade is carried on by barter, without money of any kind. The Chinese hither bring ingots of gold, damasks, and other silk and cotton stuff, tea, and some porcelain; which are generally of an inferior quality, and proper for such a market. The Russian commodities are chiefly furs of all sorts. Rhubarb is the principal article which is exchanged for these goods, great quantities whereof are produced in this country, without any culture. The Mongols gather and dry it in autumn; and bring it to this market, where it is bought up, at an easy rate, both by the Russian and Chinese merchants.[9]

By the 1730s Mongolian commerce became wrapped up with a new and fateful commodity. After Russians became tea addicts, caravans regularly crossed the Gobi Desert to purchase tea grown in the central Chinese provinces.[10] In order to be closer to their customers, Chinese merchants from Peking, Tianjin, and Shanxi province set up trading posts in the Tuul River Valley under licences from the Qing authorities.

The Manchus did not look favourably on the growing tea trade because they preferred Khalkha Mongolia as a militarized defence zone against foreign encroachment. Since they were also keen not to incorporate Mongolia into China proper, the Qing authorities only reluctantly permitted Chinese merchants to trade there on temporary terms that required them to return to China periodically. Nor could the Chinese bring their families with them. Non-trade businesses, such as moneylending, were forbidden. However, not being fully conversant with new innovations like trade or a money culture, Mongolian elites cavalierly borrowed large sums in silver from Chinese merchants in 'grey market' transactions for the purchase of imported luxuries. They passed the burden of loan repayment on to their serfs.

9. Bell at 92. Elsewhere in his memoirs, Bell, ever the Scotsman in his distaste for waste, condemns the Mongolian practice of boring a hole through the thickest part of the rhubarb, which led to the stalk decaying. During a trek to the Bogd Uul, you will see amazing amounts of rhubarb growing wild. It is a pity no one ever thought to introduce rhubarb wine to Mongolia, which is the old chestnut of English country vintners and other eccentrics. As long observed by the home-brewing crowd, it is impossible to make a bad bottle of rhubarb wine.

10. It is interesting to compare this with the rise of tea as the indispensable beverage in western Europe and the Americas on account of the seaborne China trade. European tea-drinking habits contributed to the rise of sugar plantations in the Caribbean and the slave trade. The story of the tea trade between Russia and China is told in Avery and Bamana.

Around the same time, the Tuul River Valley and its surrounding regions saw the construction of more and more monasteries. While these institutions often started off as mobile encampments, they soon followed the example of the Monastery of the One Hundred Treasures by setting down roots at fixed locations. The Manchu throne provided financial support as an inducement for the clergy to set up permanent monasteries, which made things easier for tax collection, military planning, and government surveillance.

It was in this era that Urga's 'Chinatown' began to emerge as a collection of warehouses and a few merchant shops on the north bank of the Tuul River.

* * *

The warmth between Khalkha nobles and Manchus dimmed to a distant memory by the middle of the eighteenth century as Mongolians grew frustrated with Manchu demands to support the never-ending imperial wars with the Zungharians. Another problem was the inevitable inclination of the Qing emperor to micromanage Khalkha affairs with the heavy bureaucratic hand that is as famously Chinese as chopsticks (or whinging about 'hurting the feelings of the Chinese people').

In 1755 the ill-fated Chinggünjav rebellion broke out just as the Qianlong Emperor was formulating aggressive military plans against Zungharia, Tibet, and the Muslim lands of today's Xinjiang.[11] Led initially by a cousin of the Second Patriarch, the rebellion convinced the Qianlong Emperor to break the potentially seditious relationship between the Mongolian elites and their Buddhist clergy. The Qing court declared that after the death of the Second Patriarch, all subsequent incarnations had to be found in Tibet and born of Tibetan parents.

The Qianlong Emperor could make this demand to change clerical procedure because he was more than just a secular ruler in the eyes of the clergy. The dalai lamas had declared the Qing emperors to be reincarnations of Manjusri, the bodhisattva of wisdom. This brought about an extension of secular power into the spiritual domain, a circumstance that provokes unrest in Tibet to this very day. The nominees for the position of patriarch had to be approved by the emperor's court in Peking, then by the dalai and panchen lamas, and finally the name of the candidate had to be drawn from a golden urn in a Peking temple containing balls of dough, each with a slip of a paper and a name inside, a little like the Mark Six lottery.[12]

The Manchu court also decided that Khalkha nobles needed more on-site supervision and appointed a civilian Mongolian high commissioner, or *amban*, directly responsible to the throne for affairs in the Tuul River Valley. Thinking things over,

11. Incidentally, a monumental statue of the leader of the rebellion, Chinggünjav, glares down an avenue named for him in western UB. After Mongolian nobles abandoned him, he was run down by the Manchus while trying to escape to Russia. He suffered a ghastly execution in Peking.
12. This temple still exists as a place of worship/tourism in Peking. It is colloquially known as the 'Lama Temple' and formally as the Palace of Peace and Harmony, or Yonghegong (雍和宫). For descriptions of the temple in the early twentieth century, see Arlington and Lewisohn and Lessing (1942).

the Qianlong Emperor decided to station an additional amban there in 1761, one of Manchu descent, as a precaution against the risk of Mongolian collusion. The country was slowly being drawn more tightly into the Qing Empire.

* * *

Some writers say that Urga was formally established in 1778 because the khüree of the Fourth Patriarch finally settled down in the Tuul River Valley that year. This confuses Urga as a sedentary settlement with Urga as the residence of the patriarch. In fact, the historical record shows that while the encampment for the patriarchs stayed within the Tuul River Valley from that year, the 'residence' was still moved at the whim of the patriarch and the clergy whenever there was an inauspicious sign (but always subject to the approval of the Manchu throne). In 1778 Urga began to report to the Qing court directly, but this was more an administrative matter rather than the foundation of a future capital city.

More tension arose between Manchus and Mongolians as the eighteenth century wore on. The Third Patriarch did not make it past his sixteenth birthday in 1773, which may be taken as a sign that the Mongolian elites were not overly thrilled to have monastic authority put into the hands of a non-Mongolian.

His successor was a khutugtu remembered as the 'Terrible Fourth', who almost made it to his fortieth birthday in 1813, a remarkable feat of longevity for such a politically important and thus controversial lama. The Terrible Fourth founded the first Khalkha *datsan*, or monastic college, for the study of Buddhist philosophy to lift Urga's scholastic standards to match those in Tibet.

The Terrible Fourth earned his nickname because he was alarmed at the failings of the monastic community. He famously enforced discipline by punching, beating, and kicking lamas for laziness and breaches of monastic discipline. In 1797 the Terrible Fourth issued an encyclical letter condemning excessive trade and moneylending as well as brawling, rowdyism, singing, archery, chess-playing, and smoking as impermissible violations of discipline. He also feuded constantly with Chinese merchants whose businesses encroached upon the scholastic atmosphere of his colleges. Perhaps he foresaw the karmic consequences of the decline of Buddhist morality for Mongolia.[13]

* * *

Along with the rest of the Qing Empire, Mongolia went into a decline in the nineteenth century. At the imperial level, the Qing court treated the patriarchs, and their extended families, as less deserving of the imperial dole. Each new patriarch came from successively declining social strata in Tibet, which suggests that the Peking authorities selected candidates whose families had fewer expectations of material privilege.[14]

13. A poem by the Terrible Fourth, a desperate and touching plea for people to return to the purity of Buddhism, is available in English translation in Sarközi at 89–93.

14. The First to Fourth Patriarchs were born in the aristocratic classes in Mongolia and Tibet. The Fifth came from a wealthy commoner family. The Sixth Patriarch was born into a family of humble muleteers and the

While Peking treated the patriarchs with less care, Mongolian nobles were still invited to attend lavish diplomatic missions to keep them and their reserves of soldiers on side. Indeed, some Mongolian nobles still closely identified with the Qing and fought on its behalf.[15] For many, China was still the source for the better things in life despite corruption, mismanagement, and Han chauvinism.

Manchu authority disintegrated more rapidly in the latter half of the nineteenth century. More and more Chinese tradesmen and artisans moved to Mongolia to set up businesses without licences from Peking, thereby evading regulatory controls and taxes (a time-honoured Chinese pastime). Another enduring source of friction between Chinese and Mongolians took root because Chinese merchants dumped shoddy goods rejected in Chinese markets and sold them at outrageous prices on usurious credit terms or loaned money at interest rates starting at 30 per cent. Mongolian elites were easy targets for these nineteenth-century payday lenders because they were hopelessly addicted to imported luxury goods (not unlike the addiction to Apple iPhones and luxury rags in Ulaanbaatar today). Many Mongolian elites had no comprehension of the implications of chronic debt. The treasuries of the monasteries soon enthusiastically jumped on the lending business bandwagon, charging interest at rates ranging from 100 to 200 per cent per annum.

The failure in the rule of law was accompanied by an increasingly lax morality among some of the monks, who disregarded their monastic vows and lived dissolute lives. High-ranking lamas lorded it over lesser monks, who often lived in poverty as virtual slaves, often receiving no more than starvation rations. In a city that consisted primarily of a male population, prostitution flourished—as did venereal disease, which rose to pandemic proportions.

Those who fought back against social decay wrote biting satirical commentaries on corruption and ostentatiousness. Injannashi, a prince from south-east Mongolia, ridiculed spoiled aristocrats, pampered clergy, and thick-headed herders in his novel *The Blue Chronicle*. The 'mad monk' Danzanravjaa penned poetry decrying the erosion of values in society.

> And oh, the old get older without collecting merit—what a shame!
> And oh, the young get dressed up without straightening their minds—what a shame!
> And oh, the wise don't join their Dharma minds—what a shame!
> And oh, the princes are showy when they serve—what a shame!
> And oh, the monks study by day in the monastery and wander the streets at night—
> what a shame!
> And oh, the students pray openly and stuff themselves in secret—what a shame![16]

Seventh Patriarch came from a lay family. This decline was reversed with the selection of the Eighth Patriarch, who was born into a high-ranking family in Lhasa.

15. For instance, Prince Senggerinchen (called 'Sam Collinson' by British troops in a begrudging sign of affection) was the most capable general fighting against the Anglo-French invasion force during the 1860 Opium War.

16. Wickham-Smith at 166. For more on Danzanravjaa, see Kohn.

'Khuulich' (or 'Storyteller') Sandag composed *üge* poems, voicing plaintive cries from inanimate objects about their mistreatment, mirroring the common people's victimization by the powerful. Using conversational language, Sandag described the fears of a piece of porcelain in his short poem 'What the China Cup Said':

> Don't let the children see me!
> Place me in the wardrobe,
> If I make a sound, then I'm dead![17]

Nevertheless, all classes of Mongolians rallied around the patriarchs whose stock continued to rise despite their foreign birth and unmonkish behaviour. The treasuries of the patriarchs reached their wealthiest levels, benefiting from donations from the faithful and supplemented by the work of tens of thousands of serfs, or *shabi*.

* * *

In 1855 the official residence of the patriarch shifted its location for the last time and settled down in the middle of what is today Ulaanbaatar. The power and prestige of the patriarchs also ensured that Urga became the political, ecclesiastical and cultural centre of the country. The presence of Qing ambans and administrators directly corresponding with Peking, plus a thriving Chinese merchant community, reinforced the inevitability of the city's destiny as a capital.

This accidental city on the steppes was a chaotic sprawl at this time, with little order other than the general outline of a khüree. Thomas Knox described the appearance of the city in the 1860s: 'Urga is not laid out in streets like most of the Chinese towns, its by-ways and high-ways are narrow and crooked, and form a network very puzzling to a stranger', an impression which still greets today's visitor navigating the back alleys of UB.[18]

Knox was one of the first Western authors to introduce Urga into English language travel literature. A survey of this genre shows that while Knox was a decent man, many of these writers pandered to their audience's sense of racial superiority and the prevailing taste for macabre and shocking stories about 'uncivilized' races. The nastiness of these stiff white people makes for some distastefully unpleasant reading today, but they did leave important historical records of the impression that Urga had on its visitors.[19]

17. Wickham-Smith at 167–68.
18. Knox at 168.
19. One scholar has commented on the theme of persistent nastiness in Western travel writings from the nineteenth century through the 1990s in contrast to thirteenth-century European and Persian travellers' accounts that are less biased and attempt to explain the cultural reasons for different customs. It is hard to disagree with this proposition as the writings of William of Rubruk, Carpini, Marco Polo, and John of Montecorvino are far more sympathetic and far less offensive than the works of modern authors such as Harry Francke, Beatrix Gull, Silvio Micheli, Nicholas Przelanksky, Tim Severin, or Robert Storey. See Endicott at liii. The crux of the difference is that thirteenth-century writers were not being coached on how to appeal to mass-market tastes by publishers motivated by their self-assured knowledge of 'what the public wants to read'. Instead, they sought to illuminate the unknown.

Mongolian funerary customs in Urga routinely came in for condemnation by visiting authors. The remains of the deceased were left exposed to the elements and eaten by wild dogs or birds of prey. (The rapid consumption of the remains by animals was an auspicious sign indicating that the soul had left the body and was on its way to a better incarnation.) Packs of wild dogs infested Urga, a menace often remarked upon by Western authors. Urban myths abounded about a lama or Cossack being attacked at night by wild dogs leaping and dragging the unfortunate rider from his saddle to the ground, with only a bloodied boot or torn piece of uniform to be found in the morning. A few Western authors took a ghoulish delight in describing how wild dogs carried body parts from the charnel grounds into central Urga. One of these proud representatives of Western civilization went so far as to quarrel with locals when she tried to abscond with a skull as a souvenir.[20]

Other mundane matters drew more nasty one-sided criticism too. Without a sanitation system, human refuse was left in the streets wherever dropped for packs of scavenging wild dogs. Personal physical hygiene was unknown and clothes were seldom washed. Travellers with Puritan morals could not resist writing in shock at the prevailing 'immorality'. Libertine enticements were on offer in the Chinese settlements where the availability of wine, women, and song (and easy credit) accounted for the fortunes of the Chinese. Bored by their studies and the monotony of daily chanting in an all-male community, younger monks seldom could resist the temptations of Chinatown, whose merchants were no Puritans when it came to sensual distractions. While explicit commentary was 'just not done' in the Victorian and Edwardian eras, few Westerners refrained from pious condemnations of the sexual mores of Mongolians.

Most writers did not attempt to discern the internal logic of Mongolian customs. Burial in the ground was felt to be polluting as well as an affront to the spirits of nature. Wood was too expensive and rare to burn for cremations. Water was both a scarce commodity and the home of water spirits who would take offence at the misuse of their abode for something so climatically unwise as bathing. Laundry was a reckless proposition because the thunder spirits were offended by people spreading out clothes to dry on the steppes; the offenders risked being hit with a thunderbolt. Mongolians saw human waste in concentrated areas, such as in a WC or an outhouse, as a disgusting gathering of matter that otherwise could be quickly disposed of by wild dogs. As herders who were exposed to the unvarnished facts of life from a young age, Mongolians never embraced the cult of virginity of Chinese society or Victorian Europe. In Buddhist thought, sexual acts were not sinful per se but violations of monastic discipline and distractions from the quest for enlightenment. While Mongolians might be critical of lapses by high lamas, they distinguished between the person of an incarnation as a corrupted vessel and the divine spirit contained therein.

20. See Gull at 214–15. The Buddhist prohibition against taking life, in any form, was the theological basis for the inhibition against killing stray dogs. Travel writers bemoaned the elusiveness of a good night's sleep on account of the howling of dog packs. This complaint is eerily reminiscent of the stories told by the first Western travellers in Lhasa just after the region was reopened to tourism in the 1980s.

A handful of foreign authors had the openness of mind to see that Mongolians are delightful. Lamas offered friendship and goodwill to non-Mongolian travellers who approached their temples with respect and courtesy. The Russian anthropologist Aleksei Pozdneyev, who spoke Mongolian and studied Buddhist rituals and theology, contested the popular portrayal of 'evil' lamas as a one-sided and cruel verdict.[21] John Sheepshanks, the bishop of Norwich, passing through Urga on his way to Europe, penned an agreeable portrait of the lamas whom he met. The Finnish scholar Gustaf John Ramstedt was a close friend of highly placed nobles and lamas whom he helped at various times, including looking after a Mongolian diplomatic delegation in Saint Petersburg in 1911. Reflecting the easy-going nature of Americans in Asia in the nineteenth century, Knox also recorded his favourable impressions:

> The Mongols are a strong, hardy, and generally good-natured race, possessing the spirit of perseverance quite as much as the Chinese. They have the free manners of all nomad people, and are noted for an unvarying hospitality to visitors. Every stranger is welcome and has the best the host can give; the more he swallows of what is offered to him, the better will be pleased the household.[22]

Old Knox seemed to have had some problems choking down unseasoned boiled mutton for dinner, but at least this did not colour his recollections of the people he met.

* * *

Rapid global change had a profound impact on Mongolia at the beginning of the twentieth century, and the gamesmanship of the Tournament of Shadows was felt in Urga. Britain and Russia had their zones of interest in Tibet and Mongolia while Japan nibbled away at Korea. The Qing court was struggling to retain power over its collapsing empire while Chinese revolutionaries built up momentum and nurtured irredentist attachments to non-Han regions, such as Mongolia, Xinjiang, and Tibet. Concurrently with these machinations, the Mongolian elite began to contemplate a complete break with their political past.

By this time, Urga had acquired a different appearance from the temporary encampment a century earlier. More permanent structures built in brick and stone were erected along its meandering alleyways. The faithful flocked to its religious festivals 'from hundreds and even thousands of miles around'.[23] The population had risen from 1,500 in 1820 to 20,000 in 1910.[24] Chinese shops increased a hundredfold from 1875 to 1890 and even more followed in the years leading up to the declaration of Mongolian sovereignty. A Russian community of around five hundred clustered

21. See Pozdneyev (1978) at 243–44.
22. Knox at 167.
23. Binsteed at 869–70.
24. Urga's population statistics are a notoriously tricky historical topic because of nomadism.

near the consulate along with a small collection of expatriates from Sweden, Norway, Denmark, Germany, the United States, and Canada.

The Eighth Patriarch continued to be the only person around whom Mongolians could rally. Despite his foreign birth, he embraced Mongolian nationalism and deeply resented any infringement of his authority. He pointedly and consistently refused to go to Peking to pay tribute to the Qing emperor. While both Mongolian and non-Mongolian accounts say that he led a dissolute life that led to syphilitic blindness and alcoholism, he nevertheless continued to enjoy the undimmed adoration of Mongolian ordinary people, nobles, and clergy.

The Qing dynasty's dysfunctional government suddenly unravelled in October 1911 when discontented Chinese soldiers seized the central Chinese city of Wuhan. As province after province declared independence from the Manchus, the Eighth Patriarch announced on 29 December 1911 the establishment of an independent theocracy that was to rule Mongolia during an 'autonomous period' until 1920. To symbolize his new status, the Eighth Patriarch took the title Bogd Khan, which had been reserved exclusively for use by the Qing emperor before then. Without the Manchus on the throne, the Mongolian elites decided that they were not beholden to its successor, the Republic of China. The 1691 alliance had come to an end along with the Qing dynasty. Mongolia inaugurated a Buddhist theocracy independent of China, but not free from the dangers of geopolitical intrigue.

Nonetheless, people in Urga rejoiced upon the declaration of the theocracy:

> It seemed that establishing their government was comforting for the people. During the reign of the Manchu Emperor, the local nobility and the officials had the head of household—poor and rich alike—on Tsagaan Sar, as the sun rose, burn incenses and juniper on a high place while kowtowing to the south. Now all men and women prayed in the direction of Urga before the emblem of the Jebzundamba Khutugtu—the Grand Lama of Urga, offering the choicest milk or tea.[25]

* * *

The autonomous period was an era of intellectual and cultural ferment in Urga. A rising intelligentsia introduced new scientific ideas that triggered clerical opposition. While Mongolians attempted to decipher a world of newly-discovered hegemons with unexpected importance for their country, technological innovations flooded in, such as automobiles and airplanes, photography and printing presses, weaponry and electric power.

Tsyeben Jamstrano, a Buryat Mongolian destined to die in Stalin's gulags, published a monthly journal called *Shine Toli* (the New Mirror), which had an explosive impact on received wisdom and public opinion. His journal introduced revolutionary concepts, like the heliocentricism of the solar system, the spherical shape of the earth, and a translation of the French historical novel *La Bannière bleue* about the

25. Sambuu at 53.

Chinggisid Empire. The literate public had the chance to read excerpts of modern literature by foreign authors such as Tolstoy, London, Verne, and Stevenson. Jamstrano translated an article by Ramstedt on the common origins of Mongolians and other Central Asian people, a view that departed radically from the popularly believed myth of descent from legendary Buddhist kings in India. The first edition of the New Mirror sold out immediately, but later the clergy forced Jamstrano to close the journal. Other newspapers appeared, published by Mongolian language printing presses set up with tsarist Russian support. Buryats staffed secondary schools offering a modern curriculum for the first time.[26]

Some problems proved intractable. Jamsrangiin Sambuu, a herdsman who later became president of Mongolia, noted that the declaration of independence had not brought a new sense of social responsibility among the elites:

> In the capital at that time, there were many lamas and princes, officials, clerks and couriers wearing the hats with peacock feathers as their symbols of rank. There were ecclesiastical and secular minsters wearing their multi-coloured jackets who met here and there, looking like black crows as they swaggered and spoke in little groups with the deputy ministers, the Da Lama who was the administrator of Urga, and the chiefs of the five Ministries who sat in their green and yellow sedan chairs.[27]

Thrift continued to be an unknown virtue:

> At this time, in the capital, the majority of both the secular and clerical feudal lords wandered about the shops, and the owners of these shops offered them great feasts while, at the same time, cheating them into authorizing the repayment of vast amounts of debt. With a nod of the head, they were able to get both the principal and interest on those debts allocated to [their districts], which stripped the people of their assets. The lower officials and especially the scribes and relay attendants were continually anxious about the amount of the debt that would come from them.[28]

* * *

The autonomous period was also racked by conflict with China. Mongolian soldiers and Chinese warlord armies fought on the steppes, committing senseless atrocities as the old order collapsed. In order to instil fear among the Chinese, General Sandagdorjiin Magsarjav revived a dark custom from antiquity. He offered the hearts taken from dead Chinese soldiers to the state standard and insisted upon his men tasting blood from the enemy's corpses. Massacres took place with a sickening regularity on both sides. Travellers wrote about sun-bleached skeletons littering the steppes on the approach to Urga.[29]

---

26. King at 60–63.
27. Sambuu at 55.
28. Ibid. at 57–58.
29. See Onon (1976) at 114 for a translation of a hagiographic essay composed by Choibalsan about Magsarjav and these bizarre battlefield rituals.

Despite its declaration of sovereignty, Mongolia's international status was murky and remained so until its admission to the United Nations a half century later. In this void of diplomatic clarity, China and Russia continued manoeuvres over the fate of the theocratic state, agreeing in 1915 that Mongolia was an autonomous region under Chinese suzerainty. The Peking warlord government stationed a Chinese 'high commissioner' in Urga with instructions to reclaim Mongolia at the first opportunity. The cabinet of the warlord government in Peking considered a secret plot for the assimilation of Mongolians through intermarriage with Chinese, a failed plan whose memory stoked exaggerated fears among Mongolians in the twentieth-first century.[30]

The nobility grew discontented with the theocracy as the decade drew to a close because their estates were taxed to support increasing central government expenditures. They had lost personal and state subsidies from the Manchus as well as titles and other sundry insignia of prestige that came with fealty to the Qing government. By late in the decade certain factions of nobles held secret negotiations with the Chinese high commissioner to abrogate autonomy.

In 1919 the Peking government of warlord Duan Qirui decided to bring matters to a head and dispatched the ambitious and thoroughly obnoxious General Xu Shucheng to force a formal revocation of Mongolian sovereignty. Known by the nickname 'Little Xu', he demanded that the Patriarch and his nobles rescind autonomy in a humiliating ceremony held on 1 January 1920. Little Xu also insisted on reinstating previously cancelled debt obligations to Chinese moneylenders and stationed troops in Urga, who imprisoned Mongolian notables whom Xu considered to be too nationalistic.

Both Chinese warlords and revolutionaries applauded Little Xu as a hero for retrieving Mongolia for China. Even the proponent of republicanism, President Sun Yat-sen, sent a laudatory telegram congratulating him on his reclamation of wayward Mongolia for the fatherland.[31] These insults to Mongolian dignity deepened antipathy towards its southern neighbour.

* * *

By the summer of 1920 Little Xu had placed the Patriarch under house arrest. Desperate to obtain help from any corner against the Chinese warlord government—be it the Bolsheviks, the White Russians, the Americans, or the Japanese—the Patriarch turned to all of them as potential saviours. He also gave his fateful consent to a handful of men to travel secretly to Irkutsk and ask for support from the Soviets.

These envoys were the nucleus of the Mongolian People's Party (MPP), a group that had come into existence on 25 June 1920 through the merger of two Urga factions.

---

30. Howard-Gibbon at 21. See Billé for a discussion of twenty-first-century Mongolia paranoia about China and Friters on Mongolia's unclear status under international law.
31. In November 2014 I attended the inaugural meeting of the Hong Kong Mongolian Chamber of Commerce at the China Club in Hong Kong. The ceremony was held in a room decorated with a large oil painting of the Empress Dowager, Sun Yat-sen, and Mao Zedong, all of whom regarded Mongolia as Chinese territory. I do not believe that any of the Mongolian officials in attendance were aware of the historical irony or the unintended insult.

One faction was the East Khüree Group, partially drawn from the monastic community. The other, the Consulate Group, was formed by Mongolians exposed to modern ideas while working at the tsarist legation or other Russian institutions in Urga.

Two members of the MPP had a huge impact on Mongolian historical memory. Damdiny Sükhbaatar, the youngest member, was an energetic revolutionary whose political awakening came about from having to perform harsh corvée labour for the nobility. While he was not the initiator of the party, Mongolian propagandists posthumously reengineered his life story to cast him as the Lenin of their revolution. He passed away in 1923 under mysterious circumstances that were convenient for his eventual canonization. The other, Khorloogin Choibalsan, was a former monk who had attended technical schools in Irkutsk. A deputy official in the MPP at first, he was destined to become the dictator of Mongolia and a willing executioner for Joseph Stalin in the 1930s.

As the MPP representatives sought Soviet assistance, Urga fell into a storm of white terror. A psychotic Russian noble of Baltic German descent, Baron Roman von Ungern-Sternberg, led a force of White Russian Cossacks to Mongolia. The 'Mad Baron' believed in a twisted form of Buddhism that rationalized senseless bloodshed as a justifiable way to speed people on to a better incarnation. He saw himself as a reincarnation of Chinggis Khan and sought to create a Holy Buddhist Kingdom in Central Asia as the first step for the eventual defeat of the Bolsheviks. In February 1921 he 'liberated' Urga from Little Xu's warlord army and promptly plunged the city into a reign of terror, randomly killing soldiers and civilians for real or imagined offences such as dereliction of duty or socialist sympathies. He reinstated the Patriarch as head of a puppet theocratic government, but he proved to be too bloodthirsty even for the likes of General Magsarjav, who regretted allying himself with a psychopath.

The Bolsheviks decided to destroy the threat posed by Ungern-Sternberg in the south of the Siberian border once and for all and agreed to send troops to help the MPP seize control of Urga. By 6 July 1921 an auxiliary of Mongolian soldiers under Sükhbaatar supported by the Red Army captured Urga, forced Ungern-Sternberg to flee, and ran him to ground in the desert. Afterwards, he was shot by a firing squad in Irkutsk.[32]

The success of the Mongolian revolutionaries came at a convenient time in the evolution of Communist ideology. While Marx had envisaged industrial societies as ripe for revolution, he felt that Asia had not reached a level of economic development that could support the transition to a communist state because it had not yet entered into a capitalist phase of production. After the defeat (and execution) of leftist revolutionaries in Europe, Vladimir Lenin was forced to revise Marxist theory. During a session of the Third Comintern in June 1921, Lenin redirected Communist agents to other parts of the world, declaring that 'backward' societies like China and India could

32. See Alioshin, Ossendowski, and Palmer for more on Ungern.

'by-pass capitalism' and achieve communism directly. This doctrinal innovation gave a theoretical basis for the application of Marxist-Leninist principles to Mongolia.[33]

Sükhbaatar's partisans fought for two objectives that were destined to clash. They saw themselves on a mission to transform the nation into a full member of the socialist fraternity. They also sought to support Buddhism, taking inspiration from Tibetan legends about an apocalyptic battle between good and evil before the ultimate triumph of a universal kingdom called Shambhala. The partisans were indistinguishably 'red' in their devotion to the Bolsheviks and to red-faced Buddhist protectors, like Jamsran. Their religious fervour comes through in one of their marching songs:

> The war of North Shambhala,
> We march to the holy war of Shambhala,
> We will die in the war
> To be reborn as warriors of Lord Shambhala.[34]

On 11 July 1921 the Mongolian revolutionaries declared the Patriarch to be the equivalent of a constitutional monarch (without a constitution) and vested political authority in the MPP. This sleight of hand did not extinguish the reverence held by ordinary Mongolians for the Patriarch or the Buddhist clergy, however. Within the new government, an internecine struggle for power began among the revolutionaries. Some of the losers in these struggles were dispatched to the execution grounds while others were to pass on from unexplained illnesses like Sükhbaatar in 1923. Blind and feeble, the Bogd Khan followed him in May 1924.

The Patriarch's passing allowed the soon-to-be-renamed Mongolian People's Revolutionary Party (MPRP) to abolish the lineage and implement a new structure of government.[35] The Russian legal expert P. V. Vseviatskii drafted a new constitution in Russian, which was translated into Mongolian and adopted by Parliament without revision (or discussion). The theocracy was eliminated and the country renamed the Mongolian People's Republic (MPR). The constitution also granted the state the power to deny civil rights to class enemies and created a state monopoly over natural resources and trade. The implementation of these powers was delayed until a radical leftist political swing five years later.

The 1924 constitution also changed the name of Urga to Ulan Bator, a reference to an unspecified 'red hero' often thought to be Sükhbaatar.[36] The revolutionary name could also be seen as a subtle allusion to Jamsran, a red-faced wrathful demigod and the protective deity of Mongolia.

---

33. See Appignanesi and Zarate and Hopkirk.
34. Becker at 125.
35. To be precise, the MPP adopted the new name MPRP in 1925. In 2011 it revived its older name to distance itself from its Communist roots. Quick as a wink, an MPP faction broke off from the party, adopted the rejected name MPRP and set about campaigning with the intention of confusing the electorate. Intellectual property is a nascent field in Mongolia.
36. The word *Baatar* shares the same root as the Hindi/Urdu word *Bahadur* for a brave warrior, demonstrating the interlocking nature of cultures and languages.

The MPR and the MPRP were reluctant to discard all the trappings of the past at this juncture. The government even passed a resolution declaring the Soviet Union to be the Shambhala promised by the Buddhist deity Maitreya and that the next Bogd Khan would be incarnated there. Some in the MPRP even wishfully contemplated a synthesis of communism and Buddhism.

However, younger revolutionaries decried the clergy as parasites. The monastic community reacted by equating Lenin with Langdarma, a reviled king who tried to root out Tibetan Buddhism in the ninth century.[37] The radicals and the clergy entered into an uneasy five-year truce while the MPRP struggled to get its house in order.

* * *

Despite the political and social tumult, travel writers visited Mongolia in unprecedented numbers from 1912 to 1928, thanks to newly constructed rail lines in Siberia and North China. These travellers preserved a fascinating image of Urga in the middle of a drastic metamorphosis:

> By 1928, the Mongolians ceased to wonder at cars and aeroplanes and saw nothing extraordinary in the modern omnibuses circulating in a city filled with fantastically dressed lamas, a mixed population attired in bright silks of all colours and camel caravans that differed in nothing from the caravans of ten centuries ago, or in fast aeroplanes flying at prodigious speeds over monasteries crammed with weird instruments for driving out devils from the bodies of the 'possessed.' Pious pilgrims who crawl to the monasteries on their bellies return home of an evening and turn on the electric light. In one wing of the public hospital in Urga, which is equipped with all the latest medical appliances, the lama doctors still continue to treat the sick with magic and herbs.[38]
>
> These years were a period of rapid development in Mongolia. The transformation of Urga proceeded at a truly staggering rate. Almost daily, new colours and sounds were introduced into the life of this kaleidoscopically colourful and lively city. Cinemas were opened one after another and the Parliament building, between sittings, was also used as a theatre, for which purpose it had been partly designed when it was built. The theatrical programme consisted mainly of Mongolian historical plays, particularly of the period of Djenghis Khan, and the Parliament-theatre was always thronged to the doors with grateful audiences. In addition to cinemas and a theatre, there were also dance-halls where Mongolians took to dancing with the same careless abandon as post-war Europe.[39]

The cost of living in Ulan Bator was no bargain. Daily necessities were far more expensive than in China. Personal tastes were also well on the way to being Westernized. Ma Ho-t'ien, a Chinese Nationalist intelligence agent and later a member of the

---

37. Becker at 125.
38. Gelata at 191.
39. Ibid. at 190.

Green Gang faction in Shanghai, recorded his astonishment at how expensive Ulan Bator was:

> Everything is several times more expensive than in the big cities of China with the highest cost of living... Prodigality flourishes in Urga. Almost every man and woman has a fox-skin or sable-skin hat costing anywhere from ten to well over a hundred dollars. The prices of their leather boots range from ten to several tens of dollars . . . Most teachers have adopted Western fashion in clothes and many of the schoolgirls boast scarfs and high-heeled leather slippers.[40]

By the mid-1920s, the hallmark of contemporary UB nightlife—nightclubs, dancing, and women in high-heeled shoes—had already made landfall.

Ma was also struck by the comparative freedom from conservative social conventions, especially between the sexes. He described the easy-going manner of a group of secondary school students that stood in contrast to rigid Confucian societies:

> As we were eating dinner around the inside of the camel men's tent this evening, three girl students seventeen or eighteen years of age dropped in on us. We asked them to sit, and they sat; we invited them to eat, and they ate. They chatted and laughed with great informality . . . Then several other boys and girls of the same age as these first girls trooped in and wanted to examine everything that caught their eye. The girls displayed no inhibitions as they amused themselves by leaning against the boys or putting their hands on the boys' shoulders . . . This, one might say, was freedom unconfined. They maintained that all Mongols of both sexes above fourteen years of age had lovers, but I cannot vouch for the truth of that.[41]

Despite the state's communist orientation, Western and Chinese businesses did not disappear from Urga but actually expanded between 1923 and 1928. At first, the Soviet Union scarcely had control over its own economy let alone being able to support Mongolia's. As a consequence, foreign businesses seized upon trading opportunities in Ulan Bator despite the country's unsettled political direction. For instance, a large British firm that specialized in the world market of frozen meats went into Mongolia on a large scale. American firms exported furs and sheep intestines (for which there was a great demand in processed meats and sausages).[42] There was even an English language newspaper, the Urga Dawn, a little broad sheet that came out 'not less than six times in the month' with mostly insubstantial news on social events and probably lots of advertising.[43]

Nevertheless, the new government gradually tightened restrictions on foreign businesses. Low-level customs agents detained foreigners for months on end with no clear explanation why while high-level MPRP politicos filled their days with plots

40. Ma at 77–78.
41. Whatever you say, Mr. Ma. Ibid. at 45.
42. Lattimore (1962) at 112.
43. Haslund at 74.

against factional rivals. Arriving travellers were brusquely searched; those lucky enough to wrangle an exit visa received the same treatment on the way out.

There were ample opportunities for humorous cross-cultural clashes. In one instance, our friend Haslund used his wits to have the last laugh over some roughneck customs agents. While on his way back to his experimental farm, a revolutionary vanguard of customs agents caught up with him and scrutinized his baggage. Haslund fooled them into believing that a box of Christmas crackers, ornaments, and tinsel actually contained potent utensils for the dark arts of magic and exorcism. He played the scene perfectly. He brought out each piece with exaggerated fear and reverence to stoke the apprehension of the guards. Then, trembling, he lifted up a Christmas cracker and pulled it. As the toy flew apart with a bang, Haslund quickly put on the rubber Charlie Chaplin mask that shot out from the cracker and danced a menacing jig, looking like a 'wrathful' protective deity of some foreign Buddha. The guards went to pieces and fled in panic.[44]

For Mongolians, the doors to the world beyond the USSR had not completely closed (yet). Seeking the keys for modernity, the MPR sent forty students for studies in Germany, which was the second most popular destination after the Soviet Union. This evoked an admiration for all things German.[45] Predictably, doctrinaire revolutionaries struck back and advocated the Soviet Union as Mongolia's one and only friend. By the 1930s the hardliners had won the upper hand and called back all students from 'bourgeois' countries.[46]

* * *

By 1929 Joseph Stalin was in charge in Moscow, Leon Trotsky was under house arrest, and Soviet control of the economy had entered into ascendancy. Sensing the changes in Moscow, the MPRP adopted aggressive leftist policies urged by its revolutionary youth league. With a firmer grip on their own economic affairs, the Soviets helped to set up the Mongolian Cooperative Centre as the state monopoly on foreign and domestic trade, forcing out Chinese and Western merchants. As part of leftist policies, young revolutionaries insisted upon a livestock collectivization program that was incomprehensible to herders and their centuries-old collective wisdom. High lamas were also subject to persecution while traditional Mongolian customs and festivals were banned as remnants of the feudal order.

---

44. Haslund at 178–80.
45. You can still find echoes of this fondness for all things German today. I recall walking along Sambuu Street early one morning, back at a time when I wore a full beard and could pass, on visual inspection, for a scholar of Kant and Kierkegaard from Bayern (rather than my actual identity that day, which was a hung-over American). I came across a group of elderly Mongolians meeting up for their daily calisthenics. Everyone took me to be a German and exploded in warm welcomes, backslapping, and early morning heartiness. (I fear that I confused matters further by saying 'Ich spreche keine Deutsche', which was manifestly untrue.) It was clear that my new-found friends had the times of their lives as students in the German Democratic Republic, even with its Stasi surveillance, watery lager, and gristle-filled sausages.
46. Wolff.

It was not a bad time to be a cadre, though. The state confiscated the assets of the estates of lamas and nobles while reaping the benefits of its trade monopoly. Communist cadres delighted in the prerequisites available to them, such as automobiles for 'state business' and shopping privileges at the co-ops.

The MPRP was not ready for the ensuing blowback, perhaps because they were too focused on the benefits of party membership. Or maybe they were too self-confident from having figured out how to 'by-pass capitalism'. The collectivization program failed since many herders simply disappeared across the border into Inner Mongolia.

When the young cadres sought to impose harsh policies on the monasteries, they learned at first hand that the monks were anything but pacifists when it came to defending their faith. The increasing viciousness of the government led to violent retaliation by monks in western Mongolia and a return to the sickening massacres of the autonomous period. With the country convulsed in a civil war, the MPR pleaded for help from the Soviet army, which sent in tanks and airplanes to blast the monks into submission. Shocked by the failure of collectivization and the inability of the MPR to knock out the monasteries, Stalin instructed the Mongolian communists to halt the leftist attacks as he moved more units of the Red Army into Mongolia.

The 'Engineer of Human Souls' had more important worries than the incompetent leadership of the MPRP at that time. In 1933 Japan had set up a puppet state in Manchuria as a springboard for further encroachment into North China and Inner Mongolia. The Japanese sought to present themselves to Mongolians as co-religionists who would bring about a Buddhist renaissance. In pursuit of this goal, the Japanese military in Manchuria recruited Inner Mongolian princes with money and empty promises of independence while Japanese intelligence agents masqueraded as lamas in monasteries on Mongolia's border.

The Japanese threat was both real and convenient for Stalin. It had been less than two decades since the Japanese army had occupied large swathes of the Russian Far East along the Trans-Siberian Railway. Japanese encroachment reignited the spectre of losing Siberia, a threat that also conveniently provided the excuse for a purge of suspected 'Japanese agents' among Mongolians, regardless of the plausibility of the allegations. The elimination of an older class of bureaucrats brought in a new generation of administrators untainted by the past or professional experience.

Stalin selected Choibalsan to lead a 'Great Purge' from 1937 to 1940 for the final destruction of the monastic community and the intelligentsia of the old society. Twenty-one thousand executions took place, temples and monasteries razed, sutras burned, and bronzes melted down for ammunition. After nearly 400 years as the bedrock of Mongolian culture, Buddhism was torn out root and branch. It subsisted in a handful of lamas who barely survived the cataclysm.

In Ulan Bator the purge produced an atmosphere of fear for older class enemies. A younger generation beat a frenzied retreat to the distractions of cabarets and nightlife. The show trials put on by Choibalsan mirrored the ones in Moscow, but the white terror did not seep as thoroughly through Mongolian society as in the Soviet Union.

As a reward for services rendered to Stalin, Choibalsan rose to the top of the MPRP as the paramount dictator of Mongolia.[47]

Throughout the 1930s Ulan Bator was an obscure and isolated outpost that only made occasional advances in terms of material uplift. New construction distantly followed architectural trends in the Soviet Union but Mongolia had entered a stage of isolation accentuated by the world depression and the country's absorption into Stalin's political orbit. After the purge, there was a flurry of new construction as the MPR recycled wealth extracted from the monasteries.

Japan made a miscalculation that had a profound impact on Mongolia and the course of the Second World War in the spring of 1939. Its military command had concluded that Mongolia was ripe for an invasion because of popular discontent attributable to the Great Purge. An invasion was launched from Manchukuo into the Khalkha River border region. Stalin responded by sending General George Zhukov, who, with his deputy, General Jamyangiin Lkhagavasuren, led the combined Soviet and Mongolian land and air forces that handed the Japanese a thorough drubbing.[48] Hostilities ended by August 1939.

After Hitler's invasion of the Soviet Union, Mongolia was a supportive ally of the USSR, supplying raw materials and collecting donations for the war effort. While distance insulated the country from the Nazi invasion in Western Russia, Mongolia formally joined the Allies in the Pacific conflict for one week in August 1945. Mongolian and Soviet soldiers fought the Imperial Japanese Army in Manchuria and Inner Mongolia, briefly entering North China and supporting the Chinese Communists in the civil war with the Nationalists.

* * *

Despite wartime upheavals, Ulan Bator's economy embarked on an upward trajectory after the defeat of the Axis powers. As noted by Owen Lattimore, 'The war economy was a boom economy, and Mongolia made great progress'.[49] This led to the MPR's golden age during the early 1950s. Choibalsan had buried any prospect of domestic unrest by breaking the power of the Buddhist church and the nobility. The threat from Imperial Japan was shattered, and the rise of a Chinese Communist government sheltered the southern border since Peking waived its irredentist aspirations for Mongolia (for a while). The country settled comfortably into the Soviet bloc and benefited from the post-war reconstruction boom in the socialist states.

Yumjaagin Tsedenbal, Choibalsan's apparatchik apprentice and a slavish Slavophile, inherited political power upon Choibalsan's death in 1952 and maintained an iron grip over the country until 1984. Mongolian scholars and artists were given some slack to explore Mongolian folk culture (so long as Buddhism came in for the

47. For detailed background on the Great Purge, see Jerryson (2017) and Kaplonski (2014).
48. A monumental statue of Lkhagavasuren keeps guard, prudently enough, on Peking Street (but he is facing the wrong way for these troubled times—his back is turned to the Chinese embassy).
49. Lattimore (1962) at 136.

obligatory rhetorical kicks) but this occurred in the aftermath of the Cyrillic alphabet replacing the traditional Mongolian script, thereby cutting off Mongolians from their literary heritage.

When Mongolia was under Soviet tutelage, the Soviet Union generally lived up to its reputation as an elder brother, at least for a while. It supported new institutions such as high schools and universities, a modern infrastructure (for the times), Western medicine and healthcare, cinema and opera, and a diverse industrial base. Mongolians were able to benefit from scholarships to study science and technology in Eastern bloc countries and acquired a sophisticated taste for European ways.

Ulan Bator completed its transformation into a well-planned and picturesque neoclassical city thanks to Soviet subsidies and technical expertise. A joint Soviet-Mongolian group of architects was set up in 1953 with the task of creating a twenty-year plan for the design and reconstruction of the capital. The designers called for a combination of inner and outer ring roads, with large avenues connecting all parts of the city and a basic north–south axis running from the Zaisan recreational area through Government House to the north.

The pace of change was rapid. By the mid-1950s, the 'New Ulan Bator' was unrecognizable to those who knew its roughly cut wooden palisades and unpaved roads in the days of the Bogd Khan. Aside from fellow travellers from the Communist bloc and Japanese prisoners of war, no outsider visited Ulan Bator for more than a few days from the late 1920s until the mid-1950s when Mongolia tenuously opened its door to visitors from the West.

In 1956 the British Communist and winner of the Lenin Peace Prize, Ivor Montagu, recorded his impressions of a newly risen city built upon the ruins of the lamaseries.

Aerial view of city centre's layout from the north. Photo by Doug McGay.

> Space is no problem. There is no crowding. Avenues and squares are large. White is the town, its architecture following the imposing mood of Soviet building of the past decade, white quiet classic lines, columns and porticos, but no ornaments.[50]

The great American Mongolist, Owen Lattimore, visiting in 1962, recorded this impression:

> Rapid growth has made Ulan Bator a uniquely beautiful city. Stretched along the northern side of the Tula River, it will eventually be a city about twenty miles long and four or five miles wide, in a wide plain almost enclosed by mountains with bare southern slopes and forested northern slopes, giving the landscape a variegation of colour and shadow. Because the population has grown too fast for the builders to keep up, there are still many wooden-fenced rectangles in which people live in the old round white Mongol tents, which make a striking contrast with the modern buildings. Because the city is in an earthquake zone, few modern buildings are more than four stories in height. For some reason, Ulan Bator escaped the plague of atrocious 'wedding cake' architecture which was inflicted on Moscow and also on Warsaw in the Stalin era. The prevailing architecture is square and simple. Many buildings are a dazzling white, but others are pastel coloured, which under the right sunlight which prevails for most the year gives the city, in spite of its northern latitude, a Mediterranean mellowness. The sharpest contrast between old and new is in the fact that while many people are still living in tents, heat and hot water are piped underground to the modern buildings from a central heat, power and lighting plant.[51]

Not every visitor found the 'New Ulan Bator' to be appealing, though. The bitterly sardonic British journalist, René MacColl, dismissed the city with his classic wit and colonial arrogance: 'So in Ulan Bator, the mixture on view was as unconvincing as a cocktail put together by someone's maiden aunt.'[52]

Major socialist holidays gave the authorities an opportunity to showcase proudly the capital of the second communist country, a city that seemed to combine the future and, inadvertently, the past in the eyes of one Western visitor. The first British diplomat stationed in Mongolia, Reginald Hibbert, recorded the appearance of Ulan Bator during a political festival:

> All the town was decorated, that is to say that all the main buildings had red flags and strings of electric lights all over them and elephant sized pictures of the leading Mongolian and Soviet bosses and Marx and Lenin. In the background were regiments of women with red and blue flags, who waved them in unison according to the directions given by a man on the roof of the government building who signalled with his red and blue flags. The town looked very gay—as gay perhaps as Piccadilly Circus 100 years ago.[53]

50. Montagu at 50.
51. Lattimore (1962) at 173–74.
52. MacColl at 21.
53. Hibbert at 85.

Nevertheless, while the MPR could have boasted that its people 'never had it so good' in those days, Soviet contributions also caused Mongolia to become too dependent upon its 'elder brother' to solve its problems. This laid the foundation for a passivity that turned toxic once the Soviet Union could no longer come up with innovations and problem-solving plans needed for the country's progress.

* * *

The year 1966 stands out as a turning point for socialist Mongolia. On the one hand, the MPR authorities basked in the glow of hosting an official visit by Leonid Brezhnev that was meant to be a reward for its alliance with Moscow against Peking during the Sino-Soviet split. (Mao's boorish attitudes and irredentist hopes easily persuaded Tsedenbal and the politburo to stay the course with the Soviets.) On the other hand, a terrible flood in the summer of 1966 revealed the ineptitude of a government unable to attend to the urgent needs of its people at a time of a crisis. This foreshadowed the eventual demise of the system.

Progress continued to stall out in the 1970s because of Tsedenbal's mediocrity and his refusal to consider any innovation that did not originate in the Soviet Union. With the onset of the Brezhnev stagnation, the urban design of Ulan Bator fell into the same 'brutalist' torpor that afflicted urban construction elsewhere on the globe.[54] 'Commies love concrete,' or so wrote P. J. O'Rourke in the 1980s.[55] Sites in Ulan Bator like the Third Apartment Building District and Secondary School No. 40 in the Communal Apartment Building District are examples of brutalist architecture meant as gifts from Brezhnev and his Soviet engineers (who cut corners on quality and workmanship in order to win bids for the construction projects).

By the late 1980s the socialist world was ready to turn against the venal lies and craven dishonesty that had come to the fore in place of the ideal society promised by Marx and Engels. A British diplomat, John Colvin, insightfully commented on the creeping malaise:

> Communism in Mongolia was nevertheless an unnatural concept, originally not much more than an excuse for ridding the country of Chinese private traders. The excuse had now become ossified into doctrine and its coincidence with Soviet objectives a source of feather-bedding for the Mongol. Although, for instance, the M.P.R.'s increased per capital income was presented as the result of Communist method, it was more precisely the result of Russian subsidy . . . Certainly, the commitment of the leadership to narrow Marxism/Leninism and to Soviet power still evoked no obvious enthusiasm among the people, especially the younger generation.[56]

54. Nothing captures the turgidity and pointlessness of the Brezhnev era better than *History of the Mongolian People's Republic*, a joint effort of the USSR Academy of Sciences and the MPR Academy of Sciences. Its relentless lack of creativity and doctrinal heaviness are excellent indicators of the coming implosion of the Soviet system.
55. O'Rourke at 74.
56. Colvin at 189.

The Soviet Union cashiered Tsedenbal in 1984, recalling him to Moscow to live out his remaining years. Jambyn Batmonkh was appointed as the prime minister for the last act in the MPR's reign.

* * *

As often happens with revolutions and other 'black swan' events, there was no foreshadowing of the changes that burst on the scene in 1989. Jasper Becker, a journalist for the *South China Morning Post*, attested to Ulan Bator's nondescript and downtrodden appearance in May of that year:

> Ulan Bator was a curiously muffled and sedated city. The broad avenues, undisturbed by any motor traffic, unsettled me. They were unnervingly quiet. It seemed not so much repressed—there was no visible evidence of controls—as sunk in funeral torpor. The absence of certain things gradually became noticeable—the lack of spontaneity, of people talking together in animation, of any kind of emotion except a grudging patience . . . A huge poster towered over the city centre with a blood-red picture of Lenin. Underneath he proclaimed: 'The Party is our soul.'[57]

But not for long—a huge social upheaval was in the wings. By December students, returning home after seeing perestroika in the Soviet Union and elsewhere, launched protests demanding democracy, personal liberty, and a new government. Faced with nationwide demonstrations and a hunger strike in the main square, Prime Minister Batmonkh laudably decided not to follow the bloody example of Deng Xiaoping at Tiananmen Square and relinquished the MPRP's monopoly on political power. In 1992 Parliament enacted a new constitution that introduced a participatory political system and guaranteed personal freedoms for speech, religion, and expression. There soon followed the withdrawal of Soviet troops and advisers, who had lost the halo of 'elder brotherhood' during the years of stagnation.

The Western media scarcely paid attention to this bloodless transition to a participatory democracy when more advertising could be sold by reporting on videogenic events like the Persian Gulf War. The withdrawal of Soviet subsidies pushed the Mongolian economy over the precipice. In the search for new sources of funding, the government turned to the IMF and agreed to implement its 'shock therapies' in exchange for donor-funding.

This Faustian bargain brought about a hard landing for those who had to jump, hurriedly and without preparation, on to a new entrepreneurial merry-go-round spinning at a dizzy speed. Society turned into a Darwinian gamble overnight, without safety nets for those who were most vulnerable in the transition—the urban working class and herders.

By 1995 Ulaanbaatar had begun to revert to the hard-scrabble life that existed before 1921. Shortages in the markets were the norm. Fledgling entrepreneurs in UB set up kiosks or *mukhlag* (мухлаг) at bus stops and thoroughfares to sell single

57. Becker at 39.

cigarettes, chocolate, chewing gum, and *undaa* (ундаа), a dubious-looking yellow fizzy drink sold in sturdy glass bottles. The kiosks soon carried signs with the acronym *tuz* (түц), which stood for 'fast-service-spot'.

With fast-service in mind, nightlife in Ulaanbaatar exploded, rivalling the excesses of Bangkok's Patpong as the removal of the restraints on personal conduct produced a boom in hedonism. Discos featured Bolivian bands playing Andean music while, during intermissions, audiences were entertained by black-light lesbian sex dance performances, with the 'artistes' wearing only blond wigs, red lipstick, black boots, and sunglasses.

'Hungarians are known to say, "What is worse than Communism? The things that come after it."'[58] This maxim was equally true for UB. Under the cover of IMF-sponsored privatization programmes, Mongolian officials sold off state assets to their cronies for a pittance. The creed of 'less government is better' produced an incapacitated government without the experience to respond to social problems from the collapse of state power and the introduction of neo-liberal policies.

With the honourable exception of a privatization project overseen by a dedicated American diplomat, the Great Barbecue helped to introduce the idolatry of Western materialism and a toxic free-market faith that scarred the face of the city. An unrestrained construction boom in Ulaanbaatar tossed overboard all sense of perspective, light, and air that had been carefully crafted in the 1950s. The city succumbed to a surge in billboard advertisements, cheap imported right-hand drive Japanese automobiles, and the occasional Lonely Planeteer, among other disgraces. Traffic clogged the city's streets and parking marred the appearance of apartment courtyards. Unkempt petite bourgeoisie extensions were slapped on in the front of buildings and rented out as beauty salons, notaries, convenience stores, and mobile phone service centres in the scramble to make a togrog. Healthcare, once a hallmark of the previous regime, was cut back, partially at the insistence of ADB policy wonks who claimed the doctor-to-population ratio was too high.[59] Factories fell into disrepair and the above-ground piping system for heated water began to fall apart. The arrival of Louis Vuitton and Zegna outlets were hailed as signs of Mongolia's entry into the 'real world' of false gods.

While these years witnessed a transformation in the form of government, it failed as a social revolution in the classic sense. The elites continue to be from the same Soviet-trained privileged classes who would have governed the country without any change to the system. The transformation did not bring about a transfer of power, or equal opportunity for all. The pursuit of profit produced a generation of Soviet-inspired oligarchs whose wealth put them at the very top of Mongolia's one per cent while the common people or *ard* (ард) lived more precarious and uncertain lives. People from 'important families' still expect continued deference from lowly citizens who come from 'normal families'.

58. Lankov at xv.

59. Rossabi at 168–69.

* * *

The record of the free-market plutocracy is not entirely dark. The personal liberties granted under the 1992 Constitution allowed a young generation to explore the world, study overseas, and nurture the innate Mongolian talent for cosmopolitanism. This led to the blooming of a marvellous generation of Mongolian professionals with a sophisticated world view that is remarkable, uplifting, and vastly stimulating. Those who seized the opportunity to cultivate intellectual curiosity are a remarkable class with whom dinner conversation often turns to a wonderful array of topics ranging from the African essays of Ryszard Kapuscinski, the architecture of Esfahan, or Josef Stiglitz's economic theories with an ease that ought to bring shame to the supposed well-educated of the transatlantic world.

However, other Mongolians saw the fortunes to be made from the new system and eagerly joined in, singing the lyrics of free enterprise while committing violence against the ard through corruption (which is the time-honoured way in Mongolia). When an older relative asked one of my colleagues why she worked such long hours every day, her response epitomized the stance of the progressives of her generation against the swindlers: 'I have to work hard because I don't steal.' The promise of 1990 is an unfinished revolution that will have to be completed by a new generation of Mongolia's cosmopolitan professionals and thinkers over the objections of Soviet-trained crony capitalists and their spoiled neo—liberal princelings and princesses.

* * *

In the twenty-first century Mongolia came to the world's attention because of its natural resources. Most of the foreign newcomers had little interest in the history or culture of Ulaanbaatar, seeking splendid isolation in gated communities. However, a

Young Mongolian professional-in-training. Photo by Lukas Nikol.

few discerning travellers, like Steve Bodio, celebrated the kaleidoscope of disparate cultures and savoured the liberating chaos of Ulaanbaatar:

> The streets were a festival of culture collisions. A red-robed Buddhist priest with an ear flapped cap and boots with turned up toes cut between two Mercedes sedans at a traffic stop. An ad proclaimed 'St Valentins Day' in English and Cyrillic characters. Sleek Japanese-made cars, looking like police cars anywhere, proclaimed 'POLICE' in English only, on their sides. A bearded man rode along the sidewalk on a pony, past a drunk pissing into an iron-hard snow bank decorated with used condoms. People here were obviously hardy . . . Everybody seemed to be smiling; women grinned right into your face.[60]

For Bodio, the hidden history of this ever-changing city came together in a sudden satori-like flash:

> Out in the freezing night, my mind flipped over. It came to me in my alcoholic buzz that this was more than the home of an ancient culture; it was a road map to the next century, an enjoyable but disconcerting nightmare, like a cyberpunk novel. Out in the freezing, black-fogged streets the tenth century passed through a mosaic of 1950s Russia and the Twenty-First. Soviet cars, Chinese Jeeps, and black-windowed BMWs and Mercedes roared past ponies on their way to eighties Eurodiscos with mirrored balls and restaurants glowing with silken tents. Ulaanbaatar was Stalinist sculpture, Japanese sedans, e-mail, and expatriates. The air stank of dung, exhaust, coal smoke, and piss, embedded in a fog so cold it froze your lungs. It was medieval; it was science fiction. And—I had to admit—I loved it.[61]

Certainly, it is not Paris in the springtime. Gritty, quirky, frustrating, unconventional, compelling, all these words do justice to this ever-changing phantom on the banks of the Tuul River. For those mindful of its elusive, mercurial soul against the backdrop of this historical pageant, it is impossible not to love it.

---

60. Bodio at 76.
61. Ibid. at 82.

Graffiti in downtown Ulaanbaatar. Photo by author.

3

Faith

Only the delusional could live on the steppes and believe in Nietzsche's Übermensch. In ancient times, a herder faced an implacable and unforgiving environment where the struggle for survival made it impossible to exalt the self over the supernatural or the collective wisdom of one's neighbours. Life unfolded on a stage of distances so vast that one could never forget one's own insignificance before the cosmos. Each season brought a new threat to survival—the 'starving times' of spring, the floods of summer, the illnesses of fall, and the harshness of winter.

Sedentary societies assume that nomadic life is a primitive stage of development that ought to be supplanted by agriculture. The great American Mongolist Owen Lattimore rejected this view on the basis of his own experience with Mongolian herders and caravans. He felt that agricultural societies are a more simplistic and unsophisticated world of planting seeds and watering fields, a task not requiring the extensive skills of the nomad who lives in a more complex environment. The herder needs multiple abilities to care for livestock since each animal has widely different needs. The harsh extremes of weather demanded an adaptability and range of skills that stand in contrast to the 'produce and consume' cycle of farming in temperate climates.

Nor could women be relegated to the back rooms of homes as 'inside people', to use East Asian jargon. Nomad women took on a wide array of responsibilities—milking the livestock, making felt, caring for children, churning butter, separating curds from raw milk and making cheese, sewing clothes, and a thousand other household tasks—that created a sense of selfhood that was not conducive to passivity. There was a division of labour based on gender but it was also carefully integrated, with men and women jointly working hard to maintain the delicate equilibrium for survival. Louise Waugh captures the pressures of nomadic life in the far west of Mongolia in her brilliant book *Hearing Birds Fly*.

Such daily struggles reminded the herder that life was lived on a knife's edge where extinction could result from a simple mistake, like losing one's way back home in a snowstorm after searching for lost livestock. A human being was a puny thing in the face of nature, which could be a kindly preserver or a wrathful destroyer. The herder was well aware of personal limitations and the need for assistance from powerful invisible forces. Sky and earth, fire and water, grass and mountains were living spirits rather than inanimate objects for plunder. A separate cathedral or temple was not required to instil a sense of the sacred as the sacred was already manifested everywhere and in everything. This awareness yielded a non-scriptural faith passed on in an oral tradition until the twelfth century.

The herder believed in a supreme deity called the Eternal Sky, or Möngke Tenger (Мөнх Тэнгэр), conceived of as an unembodied male force who reigned over the universe but who did not rule it personally. The Eternal Sky was supported by two sons and ninety-nine other *tenger*s or deities. These lesser deities were the spirits with dominion over the sun and the moon, the four directions, the five winds, doorways (a key location requiring supernatural protection), rain and clouds, grasses, wealth, fertility, and livestock. The precise identity of these deities varied throughout Mongolia because there was no way to enumerate all the invisible forces of nature that inspire awe, reverence, and fear—there was no 'definitive list' of deities. How could the infinite be limited to a list?

The herder also believed in the complementary force Mother Earth, or Etügen Ükh (Этүгэн Эх) who nurtured the terrestrial world as the female counterpart to the Eternal Sky. Another significant female deity was the goddess of the hearth, who was the spirit protecting the home and family lineage.

Other spirits asserted their powers locally. The khangarid made its home in the Holy Mountain while the spirit of a powerful shaman, the Dark Old Man, lived in Songgino Mountain to the west of UB, where he is buried. Every plot of land, stream, mountain, and crossroad had its own lord or 'owner' or *gazriin ezen* (Газрын эзэн).

The spirits of the herder's ancestors did not leave the earthly realm for a separate paradise but continued to be present on earth to bless, guide, and reprimand their descendants. This reverence for the ancestors encompassed not only one's direct family but the founders of clans as well as Chinggis Khan as the progenitor of the Mongolian people. Ancestor reverence took the form of daily milk libations (or its counterpart with distilled spirits) tossed into the air by the matron of the family and ceremonial events like marriage rituals and summer solstice ceremonies when the ancestral spirits were propitiated.

A herder kept two *ongon*s (онгон), following a custom first observed by European travellers in the thirteenth century. The ongons were doll-like figurines made of felt, wood, or metal and were believed to be the material foundations for the souls of the ancestors. The herder placed an ongon of the family patriarch in a special place facing the entranceway of the felt tent and two others on each side of the doorway. The family 'fed' the ongon by smearing its mouth with butter or dairy products before communal meals. An ongon of a relative was installed in the family's felt tent three years after his or her death, a time frame which marked the disintegration of the body and the permanent liberation of the ancestor's soul into the spiritual world. After the Second Conversion, the herder's family had to keep this custom in secret because Buddhist missionaries attacked any competition for alms for their newly arrived bronzes of Buddhas and bodhisattvas. (Ongons were revived in recent years in the form of ceramic statues of a jolly husband and wife placed on family altars).

The herder also revered native deities, such as the White Old Man, or Tsagaan Öbgön (Цагаан Өвгөн), who was an ancient spiritual guardian with the power to bless the herds and preserve their fertility. He was envisaged as a bald man with a long spindly white beard and heavy eyebrows, walking with a staff capped by a dragon's head. Some saw in him a simultaneous emanation of kindly saints from other traditions, such as the Taoist Old Man of the South Pole, or Nanji Laoren (南极老人), the God of Longevity (Shou 寿) of the Three Stars (San Xing 三星), the 'Laughing Buddha' (Budai 布袋), and even Saint Nicholas of the Russian Orthodox Church.[1] In contrast to the White Old Man, Jamsran was an angry red-faced warrior, thought to be a violent and ill-tempered patron deity of Mongolia whose immense strength crushed all opponents and inflicted upon them a flesh-tearing and bone-cracking death. The Great Bear constellation was revered as the Seven Old Men or the spirits of fate, circling overhead in a pattern that traced out a swastika or *khas* (хас), one devoid of the hateful connotations of the Nazis. The Polar Star was the Golden Nail, or *altan gadas* (алтан гадас) that held in place the skies overhead and anchored the universe.[2]

If someone in the herder's family had a mind for the metaphysical, she or he would have known that the universe was divided into three separate worlds, one layered on the top of the other, and connected by the Tree of Life, a concept possibly inspired by the image of smoke rising from a hearth and escaping through the smoke hole in a tent. The Tree of Life was the intermediary between earth and sky and reinforced the deeply held conviction that trees are sacred beings that serve to bridge the material and spiritual worlds.

The bedrock of Mongolian spirituality was the herder's belief in the mystical connection between nature and the self, between the quick and the dead. The Mongolian poet Nyamsuren captures this cyclical sentiment:

> I tread upon the grasses now;
> But later they will grow upon me.[3]

* * *

The herder appreciated that ill fortune could signify a falling from the favour of the spirits. Since the world consisted of a myriad of spirits at every turn, any misplaced act such as building a house, moving a rock, burying the dead, washing one's hands in a stream, or going in the wrong direction in a felt tent, could provoke the spirit's anger and cause bad luck, sickness, or death.

The herder might seek the advice of a specialist as an intermediary to find out precisely the cause of the troubles. These specialists were shamans, or *udgan* (удган)

1. Pozdneyev (1978) at 135.
2. For an overview of Mongolian native deities, see Heissig (1980) at Chapter 5.
3. Wickham-Smith at 174.

for the female practitioners and *bö* (бөө) for the male ones.[4] While some may wince or protest, a 'shaman' might be described as the more elegant and politically correct name for what passes as a 'witch doctor' or a 'sorcerer' in Western popular consciousness. The shaman remedied the spiritual causes of misfortune and suffering, or, in a darker context, the troubles maliciously brought down by enemies.

The latent talents of a novice shaman were detected when young. The path to becoming a shaman involved a symbolic destruction of the self through a bout of intense illness, such as rabies or a psychotic episode. The shaman-to-be 'deconstructed' her or his personality with a violent visualization of cutting away of flesh and bone, followed by a flight to the invisible realm of the spirits where contact was made with its celestial inhabitants. This process of a breakdown of one's identity, to be followed by a symbolic rebirth as a shaman, was guided by a practising shaman who introduced the acolyte into a lineage. Once initiated into these mysteries, shamans entered into ecstatic states through fasting, drumming, and dancing in order to revisit the spirits on behalf of a petitioner. The shaman determined whether ancestral spirits were dissatisfied and thus causing the distress or whether the petitioner had offended a nature spirit by some act or omission. Or if an enemy had another shaman cast a curse on the petitioner.

Aside from investigating spiritual disorders, the herder might also retain a shaman for divination or a magic spell. A shaman could divine the prospects of success for an endeavour or invoke powers to bring about good weather. The methods of divination were ancient practices that we can track to the early years of the first millennium BCE. Scapulimancy was a popular method where a shaman placed a well-scraped sheep shoulder bone in a fire; the resulting cracks were the answer to the inquiry. Beads could be thrown and then 'read' based on how they landed. In times of drought, the herder asked the shaman to perform a ritual to bring about rain. Or, when pestilence stalked the grasslands, the shaman would be called on to disperse the plague by raising posts crowned with livestock skulls. In distant times, shamans advised the ruling classes on how to conduct human and animal sacrifices to bring about good fortune and appease wrathful spirits.

The rituals of divination can be separated into voluntary and involuntary interpretations of events, the former being in response to a request from a layman and the latter being a shaman's interpretation of omens, such as the behaviour of a flock of birds or a dream. Another example of the 'involuntary interpretation' of an omen was the interpretation of the behaviour of a horse ridden by a shaman-doctor on the way to see a patient. The behaviour of the horse would forecast the malady of the patient.[5]

As 'fixers' of specific supernatural problems, shamans were outside the mainstream of society. They were not, and still are not, the correct intermediaries for rituals to

4. Some writers see a connection between the term *bö* and the pre-Buddhist faith in Tibet called *Bon-pa*. They suggest that there was a uniformity of belief and practices connecting the ancient belief systems from Siberia to the Himalayas. See Ermakov.

5. Bawden (1994) at 55–56.

worship natural spirits. They were sought to dispel bad fortune and to 'correct misunderstandings' with the spiritual world, as well as other types of dispute resolution, rather than to perform the ceremonies to revere natural forces. Their powers also evoked fear, especially when practised for the harmful purpose of 'black shamanism'.

Shaman during an intermission. Photo by Janice Law.

Shamans passed their customs and rituals in a non-written lineage to acolytes. By the sixteenth century they had formed their own professional association, called the Council of Shamans, to discuss common challenges such as competition from the arrival of Buddhist missionaries and the maintenance of professional skills, standards, and fees. The profession was purged by the incoming Buddhists and their princely supporters, who demanded people burn their ongons and reject shamans as healers and divine intermediaries. The Buddhist purges pushed the shamans to the outer edges of Mongolian society while the monks absorbed other traditional Mongolian beliefs to the extent that they were not antagonistic to the dharma and the authority of the monasteries.[6]

Some Buddhists acted horrendously during the purges and violated their monastic vows of non-violence. Those who were found worshipping an ongon or initiating an acolyte were robbed of their livestock, depriving them of wealth and status. Shamans were 'fumigated' by having dog excrement smeared on them. Recidivists were punished more brutally. The memory of this persecution still causes the outrage felt by some shamans regarding the treatment meted out to their spiritual predecessors.[7]

* * *

While Buddhism was practised in isolated monasteries in Mongolia during the first millennium, it did not sweep the country fully until the seventeenth century. The religion introduced a new set of beliefs that became intertwined with Mongolian spiritual traditions and customs.

Except for diehard purists, disentangling 'pure Buddhist' and 'pure Mongolian' beliefs does not seem to be too profitable or too feasible a pastime. Buddhism arrived already 'premixed' with indigenous Tibetan accretions, many of which were analogous to Mongolian beliefs. There is a tendency for some historians to present the conversion to Buddhism as a one-way transmission of 'higher' Tibetan culture that displaced

6. For a general overview of shamanism in Mongolia, see Atwood, Bawden (1994), Ermakov, Purve and Purvee.
7. Bawden (1994) at 205.

more 'primitive' Mongolian ways. This view is gradually disappearing as more research reveals that Mongolians and Tibetans exchanged beliefs and customs. Buddhism in Mongolia was constructed on the foundation of Mongolian spirituality and was never a wholesale import that displaced existing beliefs.[8]

For the herder, many of the principles of Buddhism were opaque, however. The lamas did not proselytize the tenets of their beliefs, and the herder knew of Buddhist ceremonies as a spectacle whose significance was esoteric in the extreme. The lamas did not give sermons to the herder to make sure that he or she understood the faith, and the ceremonies at the monasteries were never envisaged as participatory events for the laity. The herder might have been more interested in a lama making rain or curing an illness, casting a horoscope or perhaps reciting a good story from the canon of Buddhist adventure epics.[9]

The herder's son might have been inducted into the monastic community. These institutions were solely for men, and nuns appear not to have been a part of the Mongolian Buddhist tradition in an active way until modern times. Mongolian practice followed closely the forms of ordination and instruction in Tibet.

At a basic level, the herder's son might have become an *ubashi* (үбаши), a term that refers to Buddhist laymen who had made a vow to follow the five general Buddhist precepts against the taking of life, theft, unchaste behaviour, intoxicants, and lying. He might have studied some Buddhism at a monastery, but otherwise led a secular life, living with his family, working as a herder or wagoner and even taking a wife. Until the age of seven or eight, an ubashi could be ordained as a *bandi* (банди) and take up residence in a monastery. A bandi pledged to obey the instructions of a personal teacher, or *bagsh* (багш).[10] At age 15, the bandi who had learned some of the sutras could take the vow of ten precepts to become a novice lama or a *getsül* (гэцэл).[11] Upon completing his studies to the satisfaction of his bagsh, a getsül could then become a fully ordained monk, or *gelen* (гэлэн), by taking 253 vows during an ornate ceremony before the entire monastic community.

After entering the monkhood, the future for the herder's son depended upon his talents or, if his family were well off, their connections with the monastic power structure. The monasteries needed a large army of monks for their routine functioning. As a recruited youth, he might work as a manual labourer, a cook, a tea-brewer, a bodyguard, or a sweeper. If he had a facility at managing money, he might work in the monastery's bursars or as a procurement agent for supplies. He might also enjoy the opportunity to acquire the skills to become a craftsman of religious paraphernalia or to

8. Wickham-Smith at 178.
9. Pozdneyev (1978) at 389; see also Lattimore (1941), Lattimore (1962).
10. The title *bandi* took on a tertiary and sordid meaning of catamite given the prevalence of pederasty among the lamas. Bawden (1997) at 43. *Bagsh* seems to be Persian or Sanskrit in origin and was the basis for the modern Chinese word for the holder of a doctorate, *boshi* (博士).
11. In addition to a reiteration of the vows against unchaste behaviour, lying, theft, killing, and taking intoxicants, the candidate also swore off songs and dances, music and shows, perfumes and jewellery, luxurious 'chairs', eating outside of the monastery's daily schedule for meals, and owning silver. Pozdneyev (1978) at 203.

carve woodblocks to print Buddhist sutras and treatises. If he had the capacity (and the good fortune) to learn how to read and write, he might find himself launched down the path of learning the intricacies of Buddhist thought, acquiring the credentials to be a physician or astrologer, or perhaps rising within the administrative hierarchy of the monastery or becoming a venerated philosopher.

At the head of the Khalkha Mongolian sangha was, of course, the Jebzundamba Khutugtu or, as I call this ecclesiastical office in these pages, the patriarch. As a group, Urga's monasteries were supervised by a Da Lama, or Great Lama. In turn, each monastery was under the general supervision of an abbot, or *khamba* (хамба), who in turn was supported by a vicar, or *tsorji* (цорж), the lama in charge of day to day affairs. A *shireetü* (ширээт) presided over divine ceremonies. These three were considered to be the highest authorities in a monastery. The *gesgüi* (гэсгүй) was the overseer of the lamas and the disciplinary master who meted out punishment to misbehaving monks. This is an ancient office in Buddhism, and some of its holders included historical luminaries such as Ananda, a disciple of the historical Buddha, Nagarjuna, and the First Dalai Lama. Another important personage was the choir master/precentor, or *umzad* (умзад), selected for having a deep bass voice to lead chanting. Other ranks included assistant monks to provide tea to the participants, the caretakers of the altars, and musicians.

One class of monks had a special role because of their studies of the magical formulas to exorcise evil spirits, to perform prayers and rites to control rain, and to determine the place of rebirth for deceased laity and monks. They took over some of the functions of the shamans.[12]

The high lamas were the ones who learned the complex philosophical principles underlying Buddhism. For the ordinary monks, it could be an insurmountable task to become conversant with these concepts since the language of the liturgy was Tibetan.

> It is to be remembered that the prayers are not said in the vernacular, which none but the very few learned understand. Moreover, the most sacred Dharanis, which were originally delivered in Sancrit, are thought to be of such efficacy that each syllable, each letter, has a magic virtue. They may not therefore be translated into another tongue, but when written in the sacred books, while the ancient language is preserved, each Sancrit letter is rendered by its equivalent letter in the Tibetan language. Thus they are no more intelligible to the Mongol than a Greek sentence if written in old German characters letter for letter would be to the ordinary Englishman.[13]

This explains why the monasteries in Urga did not emphasize translations of sutras into Mongolian, partially because it was a question of spiritual if not magical efficacy. But it was also a question of prestige. Lattimore recalled that one of his guides for his caravan journeys, a Khalkha ubashi named Arash, simply felt that anything sacred written in Mongolian, as opposed to Tibetan, was vulgar and ignorant. This was

12. Pozdneyev (1978) at 229–30.
13. Sheepshanks at 88–89.

Buddhist monk making the rounds. Photo by Janice Law.

not a denial of pride in being a Khalkha but a reflection of Arash's reverence for the orthodox practices of his faith.[14] This was also the perspective of the Eight Patriarch, who ordered a reprinting of the Tibetan language canon in 1908–1911, ignoring a Mongolian translation published at the order of the Qianlong Emperor in 1740.[15]

Broadly speaking, gelen monks had two options open to them depending upon their interests and proclivities. Contemplative, *dayanchi* (даянч), lamas were those who withdrew from society, usually on a temporary basis, to engage in extensive meditation for a complete liberation of mind from matter. Such lamas were highly esteemed by the laity as saints. *Tsanid* (цанид) lamas, on the other hand, embarked upon the acquisition of knowledge from Buddhist treatises in theology, philosophy, logic, rhetoric, poetry, ethics, medicine, astrology, or alchemy in accordance with their intellectual aptitude.[16]

As accomplished scholars, the tsanid lamas of Mongolia were experts at explaining the intricacies of the history of Buddhism and expanding upon the symbolism of the staggering assortment of deities. Sadly, these polymaths are unknown to the English-speaking world.

Many young boys did not choose to enter the monastic life but were 'given' by their families to the monasteries. The tedium of life could be unbearable, and it was even worse for the reincarnate monks whose lives were darkened by alienation and loneliness because of their exalted status. Some travellers sarcastically observed that monastic life seemed to be a combination of a boy's school and a juvenile detention

14. Lattimore (1941) at 90–91.
15. As a contrast to the Eight Patriarch, the Third Mergen Lama of Inner Mongolia promoted the use of Mongolian as a liturgical language. See Atwood at 40 and generally Humphrey and Ujeed.
16. Pozdneyev (1978) at 265 et seq. and 278 et seq.

centre. Nevertheless, sympathetic foreign visitors felt a genuine religious sense beyond the missionaries' condemnation of supposed superstition.[17]

* * *

It would have been a tsanid lama who could have led us through a discussion of the complex history of his faith and its journey from India to north of the Gobi Desert. The rise of Buddhism had a profound influence on Mongolian culture and the origins of UB and therefore has a material bearing on our understanding of the city.

Buddhism arose as a reformist faith on the south side of the Himalayas in the fifth century BCE long before the amalgamation of the steppe tribes into the Mongolian nation.[18] While historical records are lacking, its principles appeared to be considerably different from the original beliefs of the herders on the steppes. Two of Buddhism's core beliefs—karma and samsara—were deeply engrained in Indian thought but did not seem to have parallels among the views of Mongolians and East Asians until after the introduction to Buddhism.

The Buddha (or the Awakened One) was a noble named Siddhartha Gautama of the Shakya tribe. At birth, the soothsayers predicted a great future for him as a king or a religious figure. His father tried to lead him away from religion and raised him in closed-off luxury, but he slipped outside the palatial walls one day and came across, in rapid succession, a corpse, an elderly person, a terminally sick patient, and an ascetic mystic. Never having seen such things before, these shattering discoveries galvanized him to search for a spiritual explanation of suffering. After a period of extreme ascetic fasting, Gautama rejected the path of material deprivation and went off to mediate beneath a Bodhi tree. Forty days later he awakened to the nature of the self and the conditions that cause human suffering.

His first sermon took place at the deer park in Sarnath with an elaboration of the four noble truths—an explication of the causes of birth and rebirth and the method to achieve liberation from mortal existence and suffering. The four noble truths hold that life is suffering; suffering is caused by desire; to end suffering, one must end desire; the ending of desire may be accomplished through the 'eight-fold path' governing right action, thought, and disposition. The sermon in the deer park is celebrated as the Turning of the Wheel. It is often memorialized in sculpture of two deer adoring an eight-spoke wheel.

For the rest of his life, the Buddha took on a ministry and preached his method of spiritual salvation to nobles and commoners, friends and family. The Buddhist canon says that he performed miracles, subdued evil demons, and taught an ever-expanding

17. See, for example, Lattimore (1941) at 198.
18. Ch'en, Conze and Rapole provide excellent introductions to Buddhism. Bell, Powers, Tucci and Waddell (1972) are good starting places to explore Vajrayana Buddhism. Wallace's superb collection of essays is one of the few books devoted to Mongolian Buddhism. Humphrey and Ujeed describe the traditions of Vajrayana as practised in a monastery in Inner Mongolia. The Namgyal Monastery's opus is a useful introduction to Kalachakra imagery. Getty is still a helpful book about northern Buddhist deities. McArthur can be helpful for newcomers to understand Buddhist artwork.

body of disciples. At the age of 80 he was prepared to pass away, confident that he would not be reincarnated but would enter a state of bliss beyond feeling called *parinirvana*. His disciples pleaded with him to delay his extinction. Granting their request, he remained for another five years, passing away after having accidentally eaten a plate of rancid pork.[19]

The Buddha's teachings were eventually recorded in a canon that reveres the 'three jewels', namely the Buddha (or the progenitor), the dharma (or the teachings of the progenitor), and the sangha (or the monastic community of followers of the progenitor). The original eighteen disciples of the Buddha came to be known as the *arhats*, a term later applied generally to monks. The Sanskrit term for teacher, guru, referred to highly learned monks and was translated into Tibetan as lama and later into Mongolian as *lam* (лам).[20]

The Buddha believed that there may be ways to salvation other than his. Accordingly, he ruled out a doctrinaire approach or preaching punishment for non-believers. This anti-dogmatic view opened the door for Buddhism to absorb local beliefs so long as they were consistent with Buddhism's basic assumptions.

According to tradition, the Buddha's followers held a council in Vaisali about one hundred years after his death. Contemporaneous records do not exist, though apparently disagreements divided his followers. At the risk of gross oversimplification, one group maintained the necessity of holding to the precise practices and ideas advocated by the historical Buddha. This group saw the Buddha as a distinctly human being whose path to enlightenment requires discipline, many reincarnations, and removal from the material world. This group later evolved into Theravada (or the Way of the Elders), which is the prevailing form of Buddhism in South East Asia today.

The other group believed that this approach was too limited, too intellectual, and simply too dry for the average person. How could the historical Buddha have solved the riddle of human existence only to become extinct after fifty years? How do you reach out to people who do not have the intellectual capacity to grasp this dry message? What emotional comfort is there in advocating repeated incarnations while living an austere life as a monk?

This other school is the Mahayana, or the Great Vehicle, a metaphor for a way to enlightenment suited to many people. It dismissed proto-Theravada Buddhism as too focused on individual salvation and held that salvation was available for all feeling beings, even within one lifetime. They further contested the historical narrative that the Buddha only existed for a short ministry on earth and then 'bugged out'. Instead, they argued that the Buddha had always been imbued with supernatural power and existed in countless forms beyond time and space. In Mahayana, the Shakyamuni Buddha (a name for the historical Buddha taken from his tribe) gradually morphed into a deity as one of many other 'emanations' or manifestations of a supreme Buddha.

19. Some traditions say it was poisonous mushrooms.
20. Technically, only monks with a high level of education ought to be called lamas, though the term is generally used in English to refer to all monks following the Mongolian or Tibetan form of Buddhism.

Under Mahayana Buddhism, enlightenment yields wisdom and compassion simultaneously. The followers of this school fashioned an innovation—the bodhisattva, a compassionate enlightened being who chooses to delay entry into parinirvana and remains engaged with worldly matters until the liberation of all sentient beings. It is claimed that Shakyamuni Buddha presented these views in the Second Turning of the Wheel—a preaching called the Prajnaparamita Sutra delivered at Vulture's Peak in India to a select number of disciples. Anti-Mahayanists derided this as an invention where the Mahayanists falsely 'put words into the mouth' of the historical Buddha to justify their theological creations.

Mahayana faith also emphasizes the important concept of 'nothingness', or *sunyata* in Sanskrit. Nothingness refers to the belief that no component of the universe has an existence independent of any other component. We perceive the components only in their relation to others. One's own awakening is achieved by fully grasping 'nothingness' through the rejection of dualism, which obscures and blights our lives.[21]

Mahayana Buddhism is sometimes referred to as the Northern School because it was transmitted from northern India and Central Asia to China, Korea, Japan, and Vietnam starting around the first century BCE. In this process, it evolved into new sub-branches, such as Zen, Pure Land, and Mind Only, which became the main sects in East Asia.

* * *

Starting from the fifth century, Mahayana Buddhists in India entered into a prolonged philosophical exchange with Hindu devotees of Shiva. From this exchange arose a new branch of Mahayana Buddhism called the Vajrayana.[22] A vajra is a thunderbolt-shaped weapon made of a hard substance capable of piercing all other materials. It is also likened to a diamond, implying that its teachings can penetrate obstacles with the rapidity of a thunderbolt and the toughness of a diamond. According to this tradition, the Buddha initiated a legendary king into this tradition during the Third Turning of the Wheel, which was a sermon delivered at Dhanyakata in India. This teaching was said to have been held in secret for many centuries to avoid the misapplication of its principles. It is also the form of Buddhism that rose to prominence in Tibet and Mongolia.

Vajrayana Buddhism teaches that there is a mystical interconnection among the physical world, the phenomenal world, and the mind of living beings that can be experienced through the cultivation of wisdom and the practice of ritual. With guided practice and proper training, the Vajrayana Buddhist can channel the forces of the universe into the microcosm of his or her own being. The similarity between humans

21. In a different context, I. F. Stone neatly summarized this notion in his book on the trial of Socrates. 'All knowledge may be reduced to comparison and contrast; if only one thing existed in an otherwise void universe, we could not describe or "know" it.' Stone at 6.
22. Vajrayana Buddhism is sometimes called Tantric Buddhism from the Sanskrit word 'tantra' referring to the treatise which expounds its beliefs.

and the universe is propounded in a phrase found in Vajrayana works: 'As it is outside, so it is within the body.' This belief in 'energy flows' within and beyond the body is a complex religious and medical theory only slightly understood in the West.

Vajrayana theorists often speak of 'common' and 'uncommon' levels on which all phenomena occur. All events occur on exoteric levels that comport with a 'common' person's view of reality. Concurrently, these events also occur on an esoteric level that defies or confounds common perceptions. This is reminiscent of the dilemma of the same objective reality perceived through classical and quantum physics. Phrased another way (and again, at the risk of gross oversimplification), the Vajrayana common and uncommon levels of reality can be analogized to the dilemma in quantum physics that elemental particles of matter appear to exist in two places at the same time, something not contemplated by classical physics. This quandary points to the arguable possibility of two realities existing for the same phenomenon.

An acolyte of Vajrayana Buddhism, like the herder's son, had to be guided by a learned lama in these complex esoteric beliefs and rituals lest the powers contained in them cause psychic injury. There are 'secret teachings' or rituals and beliefs that should be disclosed to an acolyte gradually and under strict supervision to make sure that he or she has acquired the requisite wisdom for their safe use.

Vajrayana Buddhism landed on the fertile soil of Tibet where it took root and merged with the existing beliefs of the Tibetan people.[23] It was first supported by the famous King Songtsen Gampo in the seventh century because, purportedly, his two main wives, a Nepalese and a Chinese, were devotees of the dharma. After a period of resistance and rejection, Buddhism was able to get a foothold in Tibet, partially thanks to the efforts of Padmasambhava, a flamboyant Indian guru and the foremost practitioner of Tantric rituals. Padmasambhava advocated a religious regime through which a practitioner acquired the power to transcend pleasure or greed to achieve a superior state of awareness.[24] We will often come across depictions of Padmasambhava during our wanderings among UB's Buddhist temples.

Legends about Padmasambhava are a collection of mysterious and contradictory allegories that supposedly represent higher principles rather than an actual historical record in a Western sense. As a youth, Padmasambhava broke free of living a coddled existence, somewhat like young Gautama, but did so by openly killing several court officials as punishment for the atrocities that they had committed against the dharma in their prior lives. This incident forced Padmasambhava to go on the run as an outlaw. While travelling through India, he cultivated a form of meditation in cemeteries and cremation grounds where demons and ghouls taught him to overcome attachment to mundane perceptions. In the process, he honed his Tantric skills for magic as well as his power to debate theology, acquiring the talents for a persuasive and charismatic advocacy of Buddhism. He defied convention by conduct that led his enemies to accuse him

23. Laird provides a highly readable account of the history of Tibetan Buddhism drawn from his interviews with the Fourteenth Dalai Lama. See also van Shaik.

24. In Mongolian, Padmasambhava is known as *Lowon Badamjunai* (Ловон Бадамжунай).

of fornication, drunkenness, and deception. His followers explained this behaviour as esoteric parables pointing to more complex, hidden truths that are meant to shatter conventional thought.

The king of Tibet asked Padmasambhava to pacify outraged local spirits that had prevented the construction of a monastery in the city Samye and to convert them into 'protectors of the faith'—*dharmapala* in Sanskrit or *choijin* (чойжин) in Mongolian—which he did through his supernatural powers. Thus began the tradition of the frightening protective deities that we associate with Tibetan artwork.

By the eleventh century Tibetan Buddhist thought was flourishing, producing a golden age of new theological schools over the next three centuries. Once again, at the risk of gross oversimplification, Atisha, one of the last great Indian Buddhist gurus, came to Tibet to reform monastic practices and founded the Kadampa, a highly disciplined branch of Vajrayana Buddhism. The Kadampa evolved into the Sakyapa order and much later into the Gelukpa. At the same time as Atisha, an Indian guru introduced meditational practices that eventually produced the Kagyüpa sect. Padmasambhava's teachings also continued to enjoy ongoing popularity among nonconformists seeking unconventional practices outside monastic institutions. Their branch came to be called the Nyingma, or the Ancient Teachings.

In the fourteenth century a monk named Tsongkhapa (the 'Man of the Onion Valley') founded the Gelukpa sect, which emphasizes monastic discipline and celibacy, along with other innovations in theory and practice.[25] The Gelukpa began a gradual rise to prominence, competing against other sects and seeking political and military support from rulers in the Himalayas and beyond. These branches of Tibetan Buddhism came into conflict because of ecclesiastical politics. The substance of the dispute was not religious but political—the control of wealth and power.[26] The Gelukpa branch came to be colloquially called the 'Yellow Hat sect' because of the headwear worn by Tsongkhapa. The term 'Red Hat' came to be loosely applied collectively to the non-Gelukpa branches.[27]

* * *

This medieval golden age saw three significant innovations in the practice of the Vajrayana. The first innovation related to monastic leadership. The leaders of a monastic lineage in Tibet were often drawn from an influential clan. For instance, in the Sakyapa branch, the Khön family has produced the hereditary leaders of that lineage for the past forty-one generations. Other lineages looked askance at this because of the risk of factional struggles within a family for the appointment of the next monastic leader.

---

25. In Mongolian, Tsongkhapa is known as *Bogd Zonkhov* (Богд Зонхов). The Gelukpa branch is Gelügba (Гэлүгба)
26. Lattimore (1941) at 307–8.
27. In Mongolian the Yellow Hat Sect is called Shariin Shashin (Шарын Шашин). The Red Hat Sect is Ulaan Shasin (Улааны Шашин).

Both the Kagyüpa and the Gelukpa avoided this risk through the institution of a *tulku* or a *khutugtu* (хутугту). A khutugtu is popularly perceived as the incarnation of a learned lama. In fact, Buddhism rejects the concept of an eternal soul or ego. A khutugtu's ego is not reborn but rather is a type of energy of the mind that carries on from one life to the next. Those with advanced spiritual awareness, such as a high lama or a bodhisattva, are able to direct this energy at death. The 'next' incarnation is not a continuation of the life of the previous khutugtu or that khutugtu's personality but is a continuation of positive qualities, wisdom, and blessings from that person. These energies are not necessarily directed to one incarnation; they may be divided and manifested in several persons or simply in one person. The term *emanation* is perhaps more accurate than reincarnation.

Before death a khutugtu provides clues about his next emanation. Other evidence is found by colleagues of the deceased lama based on interpreting the reflections of the surface of a certain lake in Tibet or through consultations with oracles. Using these clues, a lama is dispatched to interview possible candidates born shortly after the khutugtu's passing. They examine indicative markings on the child and see if he recognizes former colleagues or possessions, such as a tea bowl or a rosary. The child is then raised by the clergy and trained to perform the functions of the khutugtu.

The second innovation was a compilation of the Buddha's sayings into the Kanjur (meaning 'translated sayings'), a canon of 108 volumes of Tibetan translations made under the supervision of the Sakyapa lama Bu-ton Rinche Drup. Bu-ton also supervised the compilation of the Tanjur, or 'translated treatises' of 225 volumes of commentaries. The Kanjur and Tanjur are the orthodox canon of Vajrayana Buddhism. The possession of these works was a mark of distinction for a Vajrayana monastery.

The third innovation was the Kalachakra or *düinkhor* (дүйнхор), the 'Wheel of Time', which reached its fullest expression in the Gelukpa branch. The Kalachakra is a religious treatise that sets out meditative techniques and metaphysical theories that aim to accelerate a practitioner's path to enlightenment. The practitioner of Kalachakra envisages becoming a deity of the Buddhist pantheon, summoning its spiritual power while also controlling and funnelling bodily energy to create a state of awakened bliss. The teaching is divided into exoteric and esoteric segments. The exoteric segment is propagated openly and addresses the universe, astrology, geography and prophecies regarding the future of the world, such as Shambhala. The esoteric segment is reserved only for those who had been initiated into the Kalachakra through ceremonies conducted by a learned lama.[28]

The initiations are conducted on different levels. The lower levels entail the Dalai Lama or another high-ranking lama conducting an initiation at a gathering, even on a mass scale, where the faithful pledge to follow Buddhist principles. Before initiation into the Kalachakra, an adherent invokes a personal protective deity, *yidam* in Tibetan or *yadam* (яадам) in Mongolian, from among the Buddhas, bodhisattvas

28. See J. Newman, Powers.

and dharmapalas and seeks to visualize the self as that protective deity. In this way, the initiate 'destroys' the self and becomes a 'deity' in a symbolic way that is reminiscent of the shaman's self-destruction and rebirth. A practitioner might select a treatise or system of belief and visualize it as the protective deity for meditation and faith. Such treatises include the Kalachakra, visualized as a blue coloured deity in the embrace of his consort, or the Prajnaparamita Sutra, imagined as a kindly female goddess.

For higher levels of initiation, a lama might be guided to engage in *yabyum*, a sexual meditation where the lama retains his bodily fluids and achieves a heightened state of awareness during sexual embrace. Other practices might include conducting this ritual in a charnel ground or consuming loathsome matter in order to overcome dualistic thought. This system of faith and meditation is a way to tap mystical energy inherent in each individual for rapid enlightenment; it carries with it grave physical and psychic risks if misused or wrongly applied to black magic.

Some commentators emphasize the spooky or erotic side of these practices instead of the mainstream message of Vajrayana teachings. While 'method' or ritual is celebrated in this tradition, wisdom is of equal importance and hence methods that lead to spiritual degradation are contrary to the faith. Many lamas have stressed, over and over again, that the practices are meant to be meditative techniques not to be applied literally and certainly are not for the pursuit of prurient pleasure or power. In the Gelukpa tradition, Tsongkhapa refrained from relying upon such practices, creating a precedent in favour of celibacy in that branch. At the same time, Vajrayana Buddhism does not shy away from sexual imagery but regards sexual energies as a reflection of the cosmic order.

There are echoes in the Kalachakra about the danger of using supernatural powers for improper purposes, not unlike the use of shamanist skills to cause harm. Certain monks cultivated this aura purposely as a way of manipulating the gullible. In the early twentieth century, Dambijantsan, the 'False Lama' from the Volga River delta, raised a guerrilla army to fight gamin troops and the central government in Urga, trading off his reputed powers in the dark arts that he reinforced with unimaginable blood lust.

* * *

When the herder visited Mongolian monasteries, he would have seen artwork depicting a wide spiritual pantheon populated with a hierarchy of Buddhas, bodhisattvas, and other deities that can be confusing, complicated and, at times, contradictory. A general understanding of some of these personages helps make a visit to UB's temples more meaningful.

To start off, the historical Buddha is supplemented by legendary Buddhas in the Mongolian tradition. It is often said that the 'Buddhas who have been, are, and will be, are more numerous than the grains of sand on the banks of the Ganges'.[29] Mahayanists

29. Getty at 10, citing the Aparmita-Dharani.

say that there were countless Buddhas before the Shakyamuni Buddha, though little is known about them.

At the apex of the Vajrayana Buddhist hierarchy is the eternal Adi-Buddha or Angkhan Burkhan (Ангхан Бурхан). This is a godlike entity that transcends time, space and perception, existing independently of itself and others. It is unknown and unknowable. The Adi-Buddha has a similar role as the Eternal Sky in native Mongolian belief. Sometimes it is described as the primordial Buddha that brought forth other Buddha forms.

The Adi-Buddha issued an emanation that is an exoteric, perceivable form of itself known as the 'Thunderbolt Bearer' or Vajradhara and in Mongolian as Ochirdara (Очирдара). Vajradhara is generally worshipped as a supreme deity and the 'patron Buddha' of Mongolia.[30] Subordinate to Vajradhara are the Five Tathagata Buddhas (or the Five Victors, in the sense that each of these Buddhas represents a victory over passion and ignorance by having entered parinirvana). In Sanskrit these five are Vairocana (the Illuminator), Akshobya (the Imperturbable), Ratna Sambhava (the Jewel Born), Amitabha (the Infinite Light), and Amoghassiddhi (the Unfailing Success). The Five Tathagatas have always been Buddhas during their existence and collectively constitute the whole of the universe whose constituent parts are emanations from each of them. For instance, the five elements, the five senses, the five cardinal points (with the centre being the fifth), the five basic colours, the five flavours, and the five sounds all correspond to one of these Five Tathagatas. In artwork and philosophical texts Vajradhara is sometimes conjoined with the Five Tathagatas as the 'senior' Buddha.

Two Tathagata Buddhas stand out in Mongolia. The Amitabha Buddha is highly popular because his association with infinite light signifies that he is the Buddha of longevity and healing. In UB's Buddhist temples, his statue is frequently donated by devotees as offerings for the well-being of friends and family. The Amoghassiddhi Buddha is also symbolic for Mongolia because this Tathagata's directional realm is the north.

Vajrayana practitioners added other Buddhas to the pantheon. Manla or Otochi (Оточ) is the blue 'Healing Buddha' who restores the health of his devotees when properly worshipped. He is somewhat unorthodox because of his role as the restorer of health, a dualistic endeavour, but nonetheless he enjoys popularity as the patron saint of Buddhist medical colleges.

Another highly popular Mongolian deity straddles identities as both a Buddha and a bodhisattva. This is Maitreya or Maidar (Майдар), the 'Future Buddha', a bodhisattva living in the heavenly realm Tushita. This bodhisattva will lead sentient beings in a battle against the enemies of the dharma. At the final victory of good over evil, the bodhisattva Maitreya will become a Buddha and inaugurate the kingdom called Shambhala.

30. It is sometimes said that since Vajradhara was absorbed in divine quietude, he delegated the realm of sentient beings to another emanation of the Adi-Buddha—Vajrapani or Ochirvaan (Очирваань).

The Maitreya legend was sometimes turned into the belief in the triumph of Buddhists, and especially Mongolian Buddhists, over their enemies. Some Mongolian Buddhists saw the Bolshevik revolution as the beginning of this ultimate conflict, and, true to form, tsarist, Soviet and Japanese military and espionage agents attempted to manipulate this expectation. In Moscow several Bolsheviks sought to exploit the Shambhala legend as a way to expand Soviet influence from Mongolia into Tibet. Baron Ungern-Sternberg also believed in this 'end-of-times' battle and sought to rally Mongolians to his side as he unleashed a vengeful bloody war as the prelude for Shambhala.[31]

Each Tathagata has a corresponding bodhisattva. When the bodhisattvas are depicted in a form to symbolize Tantric teachings, they are usually accompanied by a corresponding Shakti or feminine force. The most commonly encountered bodhisattvas in UB are Avalokitesvara, Manjusri, Vajrapani, and the two female deities Green Tara and White Tara.

Avalokitesvara is the famous bodhisattva of compassion that has enjoyed extensive popularity in Asia.[32] This bodhisattva is depicted in a multitude of appearances in Buddhist art, ranging from a multi-headed and multi-armed male deity to a goddess of compassion in forms strikingly similar to the Virgin Mary in Roman Catholicism. Manjusri, the bodhisattva of wisdom, wields a sword to cut through the knot of ignorance and troubles. Vajrapani is the protector of water serpents or nagas and therefore the god of rain. He was the object of prayers whenever there was a drought; he also had the power to assist herders in locating lost livestock. In the seventeenth century Vajrapani was absorbed into the cult of Chinggis Khan, who was seen as his earthly emanation.

The Taras are peaceful maternal goddesses. They are sometimes seen as a female form of the Tathagata Amoghassiddhi and the bodhisattva Maitreya. There is also a legend that they projected emanations into to the Nepalese and Chinese wives of the Tibetan king who first introduced the dharma to the Himalayas.

On the same spiritual level as the bodhisattvas are the ten dharmapala or the protectors of the dharma—fierce deities or *dogshid* (догшид) with horrifying countenances who pledged to wage war without mercy against the enemies of the dharma. They are often depicted trampling enemies and wearing necklaces of skulls and other body parts or in sexual embrace with an equally horrifying consort. Their appearance is meant to demonstrate their supernatural power and their revulsion against sin and ignorance.[33] Legends about the dharmapalas became popular stories recounted by travelling monks for herders before campfires.

Yama or Erlig Khan (Эрлэг Хаан) is the king of hell. He sits in judgement of the deceased while undergoing the same torments as other sentient beings. Yama was

31. See Alioshin, Ossendowski, Palmer, Znamenski.
32. In Mongolian, Avalokitesvara is known as Migjid Janraisig (Мэгжид Жанрайсиг).
33. Kalsang sets out an overview of protective deities; Nebesky-Wojkowitz is the definitive scholarly work on protective deities and oracles.

once a monk who had completed an esoteric cave meditation lasting for nearly fifty years. When he was on the verge of enlightenment, two thieves went into his cave with a bull that they had stolen and cut off its head. When they noticed the lama, they moved to kill him, too. Yama pleaded with them to spare his life, explaining that since he was on the verge of enlightenment, his death at that very moment would rob him of the benefit of years of sacrifice. The thieves killed him anyway and cut off his head. Enraged by this cruelty, Yama re-entered his body, put on the bull's head as a replacement, and ripped the thieves to pieces. He then went on a binge of murders in a fit of anger and frustration, nearly depopulating Tibet.

Yamantaka or Jigjid (Жигжид) is the sworn enemy of Yama and an emanation of Manjusri. Yamantaka is as powerful as Yama, as indicated by the fact that he too has the head of a bull. In response to the pleas of Tibetans, Yamantaka took up the challenge to defeat Yama and cast him to hell. These two dharmapalas convey the lesson that rage creates death and death must be overcome by wisdom.

Sridevi or Baldan Lkham (Балдан Лхам) is the chief protectress of the Gelukpa branch and the most fearsome and loyal of the protective deities. According to legend, she supposedly vowed to convert her husband, a Sri Lankan king, to the dharma or, failing her vow, she pledged to exterminate the royal lineage. When her husband rejected Buddhism, she kept her vow and in a rage, murdered their son and left Sri Lanka, travelling first to Tibet, then China and Mongolia. Baldan Lkham is supposed to have made her home in East Siberia.[34]

We briefly met Jamsran (Жамсран) in Chapter 2. He is a red-faced warrior god also known as Begtse before the Second Conversion. According to legend, he tried to prevent the Third Dalai Lama from coming to Mongolia, but he failed because the Tibetan holy man out-gunned him with superior magical skills. In his submission to the Dalai Lama, Jamsran vowed to defend Buddhism in addition to continuing on as a protector of Mongolia. Before his conversion, he had a taste for supplicatory offerings of blood, hearts, and kidneys, a preference that was mostly suppressed by the lamas.[35] While highly revered, he occupies a lesser position in the Buddhist hierarchy as a deity who was late in pledging allegiance to the Buddhas and bodhisattvas.

Mahalaka or Gombo (Гомбо) is a protector usually depicted with a black face and multiple arms holding a trident. In the late sixteenth century, the Altan Khan proclaimed him to be the patron saint of Mongolia after meeting the Third Dalai Lama. The Qing emperors honoured his spirit with a temple next to the Forbidden City for the printing of the Mongolian Kanjur. Since black is the colour that incorporates all other colours, Mahalaka's coloration suggests the power to overcome and merge all things as a symbol of non-dualism.

34. Getty at 149–50.

35. It is also said that Jamsran was already a part of the Tibetan Buddhist pantheon in the early sixteenth century and therefore another spiritual import. Wallace, 'What Do Protective Deities, Mongolian Heroes, and Fast Steeds Have in Common?' at 205.

Hayagriva or Damdin (дамдин), the horse-headed wrathful protector, was unsurprisingly a favourite of horse traders and herders in Mongolia. The image of the Mongolian wind-horse was inspired partially by Hayagriva and incorporated into the Mongolian state logo. It is depicted on prayer flags, carrying a wish-fulfilling stone, or *norbu*.[36]

There are many lesser deities. The Maharajas of the Four Directions or Makharaz (Махараз) assisted the Shakyamuni Buddha during his earthly existence and defend the four gates of Mount Meru, the Buddhist centre of the universe. *Dagina* (дагина) or *khajid* (хажид) are female spirits, taking wrathful or mild forms as the consorts of the deities. Nagas are water-spirits, thought to be beings that are part snake and part human. These were the spirits who felt aggrieved by the pollution of lakes and rivers or otherwise by the misuse of the waters that made up their domain. Citipati, or *dürteddagwa* (дүртэддагва)—the 'Skeleton Lords'—are two protectors in the form of dancing skeletons. They were originally male and female meditators whose deep concentration made them oblivious when thieves attacked them and cut off their heads.

Finally, the White Old Man joined the Buddhist pantheon on account of a legend that he was an assistant to the historical Buddha and therefore an ally of the dharma from the very outset. His critical role as a protector of the herds and a guarantor of their fertility also made it impossible for the lamas to ignore him, though he remained at a lower level of sacredness than others in the pantheon.

* * *

Going back to the herder, he (or she) was likely to have little comprehension of Vajrayana's complex theories. Rather, the herder went to the monasteries for the same reasons as the ancestors went to an udgan or bö—they were looking for a solution to a specific problem, such as stopping a drought or locating stolen property or lost livestock. Divination, such as scapulimancy or throwing dice or coins and interpreting the results of the throw, became tools of the trade of monks, purloined from the shamans.

The monasteries also insisted that the herder had to pay the clergy as a fee-collecting intermediary in order to invoke blessings or assistance from nearly all the deities, with the exceptions of Hayagriva and the two Taras. This 'toll-free' direct contact contributed greatly to the popularity of these three deities.

The custom of *khadag* (хадаг) also permitted direct communion with the spirit world. The original practice appears to have started in the early twelfth century in Tibet and Mongolia where people tied coloured strips of cloth or *dartsug* (дарцаг) on trees and other spiritually significant places. In the nineteenth century, the Mongolian

36. The state logo was originally designed by none other than Stalin. During a meeting with Choibalsan in 1940, Stalin advised that the logo should emphasize the country's role as a livestock producer. He insisted that the logo show the 'five animals' of Mongolian herds along with a man on horseback. See Baabar at 376. The motif of the five animals parallels the corresponding ancient Chinese custom of the 'five grains' which provide the essential sustenance of sedentary life. In 1961 the emblem was revised slightly, and it was revamped to appear unquestionably like a wind horse in 1992. See Gulik for more about Hayagriva.

practice absorbed a social custom that started in Lhasa—one would send a piece of white silk as a calling card ahead of a visit to an honoured person. This evolved into giving a long, narrow bolt of coarse blue or white silk as a symbol of a long life or a sign of devotion and respect. Blue khadags were favoured in Mongolia and soon came to be placed in sites where the 'lords of the land' lived, such as in trees, bridges, and ovoos.[37]

* * *

Vajrayana Buddhism survived the first fifteen years of the revolutionary government of the MPR but was brutally crushed by the Great Purge, leaving hardly a trace on the Mongolian cultural landscape. Lower ranking lamas were defrocked and returned to secular life while the cadres seized building materials from the monasteries and recycled them into new construction whenever possible. Beyond the scrutiny of the state, herders preserved their own religious practices on the remote steppes.

A gradual relaxation came about in the years after Stalin and Choibalsan. By 1960 Gandantegchenlin Monastery was allowed to reinstate Kalachakra initiations. Ten years after that the MPR permitted the establishment of a Buddhist university. The current Dalai Lama visited Ulan Bator in 1979 in a sign of further relaxation of state policy.

With the 1990 demonstrations, the MPR abandoned its official hostility and allowed the resumption of shamanism, Buddhism, Christianity, and Islam. Shamanism expanded in renewed popularity without the centralized structure of an institution, leading some Mongolians to dismiss urban shamans as doubtful practitioners who earned their qualifications through the equivalent of a mail-order correspondence course. Some Mongolians say that a real shaman will never claim to be one.

Mongolian Buddhism experienced a renaissance starting in the years after the implosion of the MPR. At the request of the abbot of Gandantegchenlin Monastery, the Fourteenth Dalai Lama made a public announcement in September 1991 that the Ninth Patriarch of Mongolian Buddhism was alive and well in India. It had been widely believed that the Urga lineage of the Jebzundamba Khutugtu died out with the passing of the Eighth Patriarch in 1924.

The Ninth Patriarch, Jambal Namdo Choiji, was born in Lhasa in 1930 and recognized by the Tibetan regent, Reting Rinpoche, as the incarnation of the Bogd Khan in 1935. His identity remained a secret, though this meant that after his induction into the clergy, he was treated as simply another novice youth without the special comforts usually provided to important *tulku*s. At one point, he left the clergy, started a family, and earned his living as a farmer. In 1959 he fled to India from fear of being discovered and used as a propaganda tool by the Chinese Communists.

The Ninth Patriarch visited Mongolia briefly in 1999 despite criticism from politicians concerned about the possible political role that he could assert. In November 2011 he returned to Ulaanbaatar and took up residency at Gandan Monastery. He

37. Atwood at 298.

passed away in March of the following year. As approved by the Dalai Lama, his body was mummified and preserved in a secret room in a building on the grounds of the monastery.

During a visit to Ulaanbaatar in November 2016 the Fourteenth Dalai Lama announced that the Tenth Patriarch had been reincarnated in Mongolia but did not provide any specifics about the child's identity or the procedure by which he was identified. The Mongolian newspapers, which are overtly manipulated by their owners to report news in keeping with their business interests, did not uniformly endorse this development. Some outlets claimed that the child was found in one of Mongolia's wealthiest families, suggesting that financial considerations entered into the process of identification. Certainly, not all elements of the Mongolian government welcome the revival of a potentially rival source of sovereign authority. The announcement of a Tenth Patriarch also triggered outrage in Peking over this demonstration of the Dalai Lama's clerical authority. Until the child's enthronement upon taking his vows as a bandi, the abbot of Gandan monastery will continue to be the ecclesiastical leader of all of Buddhist Mongolia.

* * *

Contemporary Buddhism appears to be on two tracks in Mongolia. In the main monasteries, the lamas have resurrected many of the old rituals, chanting prayers in Tibetan and resuming their former role as intermediaries between the laity and the spirit world. A supplicant may request the monastery for 'reading of a sutra' or *jasaa* (жасаа) by a monk for good fortune or the health of someone in the family. Some monasteries post a fixed 'price list' of their recommendations for prayers directed to obtain certain results. A *gürem* (гүрэм) can also be 'booked' to pray to the Buddhist deities for a good rebirth of a recently deceased relative. The laity may also participate in religious rituals, in a limited way, by sponsoring a ceremony at a monastery, such as offering food for the lamas or donating butter lamps for the altars.

The laity seek these billable spiritual services to improve prospects for health, wealth, or romance in the unquiet age of competitive free market profiteers and 'sink-or-swim' economic policies, though one has to wonder whether these services pander to superstition rather than offering spiritual insight and solace. Certainly, stories abound about lamas driving about town in BMWs. The use of Tibetan as the liturgical language also prevents inclusive participation by the laity (and many of the monks, in truth).

There may be a disconnect between older ritualistic forms and modern innovations in Vajrayana Buddhism. Since the flight of most leading lamas from their homeland, Tibetan Buddhism has been 'modernized' in the lands of their exile. Specifically, the Fourteenth Dalai Lama advocates meditation and a thorough understanding of Mahayana principles rather than the mechanical performance of rituals. These days, modernized lamas give sermons to the Mongolian faithful, who are puzzled and perhaps bored by this innovation when what some of them want is a spiritual quick fix so that all their dreams come true.[38]

* * *

In the aftermath of the liberalization of the 1990s, people in UB revived folk divination rituals as a way to grapple with the uncertainties of a society adrift. Both Buddhists and shamans offered soothsaying as a way to make some order in the chaos, as recorded by the Italian journalist Tizano Terzani in his book about fortune telling in Asia.

During his visit to UB, Terzani met a lama specialist in scapulimancy for a forecast. Following a ritual from before recorded history, the lama took the shoulder blade of a freshly slaughtered sheep, scraped it clean and purified it over burning juniper incense. He then placed the bone in a fire and examined the resulting cracks to see the answers to Terzani's questions. But even this ancient form of soothsaying had lost much of its sophistication—cracks running up the bone meant yes while those going down meant no.[39] Before the Great Purge, treatises elaborated at great length about the nuanced meaning of each crack and chip.[40]

On the same trip, Terzani met an udagan who predicted his future through a shamanist combination of numerology and images gleaned in the reflections of mirrors. She asked him to choose three numbers under ten. She next conducted a calculation on a Buddhist rosary to produce Terzani's 'magic number' and sought an image in the mirror that she wore on her chest that reflected another image from a mirror behind Terzani. She refined her divination by examining the shape of Terzani's eyes and skull before giving him some fairly innocuous predictions.[41]

* * *

While the uncertainties of modern life draw people to divination, magical rituals, and Buddhist ceremonies, these quick fixes are far removed from the contemplative foundations of Mongolian spirituality as perceived by the herder.[42] The Mongolist and musician Simon Wickham-Smith has insightfully observed that:

> Buddhism is an imported tradition, never completely comfortable in a land inhabited by people more attuned to the spirits of the wind and the hills and the grasses, and to the ever present heaven, than to the world of Buddhist contemplation and philosophy.[43]

38. See Even.
39. Terzani at 290 et seq.
40. See Bawden (1994), 'On the Practice of Scapulimancy among the Mongols'.
41. Terzani at 296 et seq.
42. See Buyagdelger for a discussion of the relationship between shamanism and social anxieties in modern Mongolia.
43. Wickham-Smith at 161.

Contemplative reverence for the spirits of nature has been the time-honoured way in which Mongolians have met the challenges of the life on the steppes, and it remains their spiritual foundation beneath the concrete sidewalks and asphalt highways of UB.

Oil lamps at a shrine. Photo by author.

4

Architecture and Decoration

A circle is one of the simplest and most ancient symbols of the divine. It can be found on the walls of Neolithic cave dwellings and on the tools forged during the early Bronze Age. Pre-Slavic peoples worshipped nature in circular forest clearings. For the ancient Egyptians, a circled dot represented the sun god Ra while the same character meant the sun in ancient Chinese oracle writing. Japanese calligraphic masters draw a circle as the totality of heaven and earth and all being while the *keter*, the uppermost *sephirot* or topknot of the Tree of Life of the Kabbalah is a circle.[1]

The circle imitates the sun and the moon in their progression across the skies and symbolizes complementary forces in Buddhist *thangkas*.[2] In the system of numbers, a circle came to mean a complete balancing of positives and negatives. It can be seen as a subtle allusion to the Mahayana principle of nothingness as the essence of the all. The 'sun direction', *naran züg* (наран зүг), or clockwise circumambulation describes the correct way to approach sacred places among most Central Asians, with the revered site always on the right-hand side.

On the grasslands the circular canopy of the sky is a constant reminder of one's place within a perfectly formed universe. It must have been because of the impulse to revere the Eternal Sky that herders built their homes in round-shaped felt tents, which proved to be perfectly suited for nomadic life on the steppes. When Russians first came across these structures during their imperial expansion into Central Asia, they called them *yurta*s. Mongolians prefer to use their own word, *ger* (гэр).

The shape of a ger has remained unchanged since William of Rubruck's mid-thirteenth-century description in the record of his diplomatic mission to Kharakhorum. It is assembled around a wooden *toono* (тооно), a circular outlet or smoke hole in the roof of the ger. The toono tracks the circular progression of the sun as the sunlight falls through it upon different parts of the interior throughout the day. The main walls of a ger are set up with a circular wooden lattice frame with poles

1. This chapter relies upon work by Anderson, Beer, Eberhard, Guo, Liang, Luvsandorj, Pozdneyev (1978), Teleki, N. Tsultem, Williams.
2. *Thangkas* are religious paintings on cloth that originated in Tibet. They were designed to be easily transported by nomads and served to be a visual representation of a Buddhist theological 'sermon' for unlettered commoners. They are highly stylistic and certainly an unforgettably powerful form of religious artwork. See Jackson and Jackson for an introduction.

Early Türkic rune. Photo by author.

attaching the top of the frame to the toono. The lattice frames are covered in felt, which provides superb insulation in the brutal winter and can be rolled up for ventilation in the summer. The entire structure can be assembled in an hour and transported easily as needed to tend to the herds.

The features of a ger are both functional and symbolic. There are two poles or *uni* (унь) anchoring the toono to the ground. The two uni bring to mind the duality of the universe and its division into complementary forces of light and dark, birth and death, male and female, growth and decay. The east or 'left' side of the ger is for the exclusive use of women while the west or 'right' side is for men and their guests. Between the uni is the hearth, which is the home of the sacred fire god and the protector of the residents of the ger. (It is poor form to cross between the two uni since it is disrespectful to step over the spirit of the hearth.) The doorway of a ger always faces the south, a custom found throughout Asia. According to Chinese cosmological theories (among others), a residence ought to have a south-facing entranceway because a host, ruler, leader, or deity should sit on a throne, chair, cushion, or altar on the north side of a building when receiving visitors, subjects, servants, or supplicants. Others point to the practical consideration that a southern exposure uses the sun's warmth effectively and avoids fierce crosswinds.

Ger at the Monastery of the Great Tara. Photo by author.

A ger must have been the first Buddhist temple in Mongolia, and later its design inspired stationary temples built with wood planking instead of felt. More permanent circular structures were constructed on square foundations. In contrast to a circle, a square symbolizes the earth and implies stability. These mixed design temples required the erection of four main columns, or *bagana* (багана), connected to the toono. These were sometimes interpreted as symbols of the four elements or the four directions. The placing of circular superstructures over square foundations hearkened to the circle and square motifs in mandalas, an Indo-Tibetan artistic design brought to Mongolia with Vajrayana Buddhism.

Mongolians later constructed temples in pyramidal shapes with semi-domed roofs and square cupolas, or *gokhon* (гохон), placed over the toono. This elegant innovation is also found in Manchu architecture. By the late nineteenth century a Russian Mongol specialist noticed that few Buddhist temples were housed in felt gers but were mostly set up in permanent structures of stone or wood.[3]

The rectangular tent, or *maikhan* (майхан), is another portable shelter. A maikhan is set up between two poles and a cross-beam with the flaps of the tent held in place with pegs pounded into the ground. These are temporary and informal shelters for celebrations such as summer sporting events, or other ad hoc uses. The maikhan evolved into the more permanent *asar* (асар), a rectangular-shaped pavilion or gatehouse attached to fixed structures as an antechamber or vestibule.

In the nineteenth century two new architectural styles appeared in the Urga monastic community. These were Tibetan and Chinese forms combined with Mongolian motifs.

3. Pozdneyev (1978) at 55.

Stationary ger-style temple in the Dashchoilin Monastery. Photo by author.

A Tibetan temple is built with stone in a square shape, with narrow windows, a flat roof, and inward sloping walls painted white with brown or black trim along the top. The outside walls are devoid of decorations. Multi-tiered roofs, an innovation from India, appeared on Tibetan temples at the end of the first millennium CE. In North Asia, Mongolian/Manchu square cupolas were added to these solid fortress-like structures. The Temple of Avalokitesvara at Gandan Monastery and the Puntsoglin Monastery are classic examples of Tibetan monastic architecture.

Chinese architectural theory favoured single-storey temples with the buildings symmetrically placed along a north–south axis. This arrangement was aligned to the general principles of orderliness required by an impersonal yet ethical universe. This custom of *feng shui* (literally wind and water 风水) resulted in the positioning of a building so that it takes advantage of latent positive energy and avoids darker, harmful forces.

The main entrance of a Chinese-style temple faces to the south, too, often with a protective spirit screen at the southernmost point. The spirit screen or *yampai* (ямпай) prevents malicious spirits from drifting into temple grounds. Since these harmful spirits draw their power from the darker and slower *yin* (阴) forces of nature, they lack *yang* (阳) agility and quickness, which renders them incapable of navigating sharp turns around a spirit screen to sneak past the main gate of a temple.

A central walkway usually leads from the spirit screen to a main gate and entranceway of a Chinese-style temple. Outside the main gate are typically two flag towers on which celebratory or ritual flags or lanterns were raised.

In the main antechamber of some temples, there may be statues of the Maharajas of the Four Directions or Dörwön Makharaz (Дөрвөн Махараз). These guardian-kings rule over the four continents that make up the Buddhist universe and protect the dharma from its enemies. Yulkhorsung is the white guardian-king of the eastern continent; he is depicted strumming a lute that fires off thunderbolts to subdue enemies. Phakyepo, the blue guardian-king of the south, is usually depicted drawing his sword for combat. Chenmizang is the red guardian-king of the west. He holds a stupa, which can be turned into a supernatural weapon, and a *naga*, a serpent like creature with formidable powers. Manthose is the yellow king of the north, holding a mongoose, likewise an animal that can transform itself into a warrior, and a banner of victory that, when opened, shoots thousands of flaming arrows at an enemy. The four deities are envisioned as the guardians to Mount Meru, which is the centre of the universe in Vajrayana Buddhism.

Beyond the antechamber, there are sometimes drum and bell towers in the first main courtyard of a Chinese temple. These are for marking the time for ceremonial rituals and the opening and closing of the temple's gates. If an emperor had ordered the construction of the temple, the courtyards might have imperial marble stelae enclosed in pavilions. A stela is a rectangular marble slab often decorated at the top with the image of a dragon. On these were carved important announcements, such as decrees from the Qing court or records of meritorious service or historic events. These were often carved in the four major literary languages of the city: Manchu, Mongolian, Tibetan, and Chinese.

Continuing along the central walkway, rectangular courtyards are set out sequentially along the axis. On the walkways are often placed large metal incense burners, or *boipar* (бойпор), with engravings in Tibetan, Mongolian, and sometimes Chinese for the burning of pounded juniper, or *arsh* (арц). At the north end of each courtyard is the main temple, or *gol süm* (гол сум), of that section where devotional rituals or services took place. The one-storey halls placed on the east and west sides of the courtyard served ancillary purposes, such as storage, housing, or libraries. Passageways on each side of the main hall lead to additional courtyards.

Chinese-style temples were built with weight-bearing pillars to support heavy tiled roofs; walls were not load-bearing but rather were barriers against the weather and safeguards for privacy and security. Roofs were gabled with eaves sweeping upward, a form that deflected harmful spirits away from people below. A complex system of brackets called *dougong* (斗拱) or *khaalt* (хаалт) distributed the pressure on the building's supporting pillars evenly. Lintels and brackets were richly decorated with Buddhist geometric designs and paintings of flowers, legendary literary characters, mythical beasts, and historic sights.

Other Chinese motifs include green tiled gabled roofs and *wenshou* (吻兽) or zoomorphic images placed on the upturned eaves. On Urga's temple roofs these are a bird, a fish, and a lion. The round end tiles on the beams of a roof often depict the face of a lion in imitation of the lion motifs placed on the beams of Lhasa's seventh-century Jokhang Temple by Nepalese craftsman. Other motifs commonly painted on the wooden palisades of a temple are the 'earrings of the prince' (an allusion to the

Dougong roof brackets at the Monastery of the Great Tara. Photo by author.

Buddha's noble birth, now a common design on wedding rings) and the endless knot of Indra. These appear more commonly on the palisades in the ger districts nowadays.

The Vajradhara and Buddha Temples at Gandan Monastery are said to be classic examples of Chinese temples, though the courtyard does not cohere to the symmetry usually required by Chinese custom for the arrangement of a temple complex. The Museum of the Bogd Khan, however, is a late Qing project that faithfully replicates a traditional Chinese temple layout and deploys square cupolas, a novelty for most Chinese temples. The Russian-influenced White Palace next door might have started the precedent in UB for randomly placing buildings side by side despite conflicting architectural styles.

At its simplest, a Vajrayana temple in Mongolia has two buildings: an assembly hall and a pavilion or temple for its protective deity or *sakhius* (сахиус). In the planning stages, monastic astrologers and geomancers determined by divination the appropriate protective deity for a temple's patron saint. This took into consideration how the temple fit with the landscape and its nearby earth spirits. Uncharacteristically for a Chinese government, the Qing authorities did not heavily regulate the construction of temples in Mongolia; the lamas only had to make sure that a new monastery did not infringe upon any arable land under cultivation.[4] For larger monasteries, a *tsogchin dugan* (цогчин дуган), a 'cathedral-like hall' was the site for the monks to meet for services.

Inside the main halls there may be a glass cupboard with sculptures or bas relief and an altar along the northern wall holding statues of Buddhas and bodhisattvas.

4. Pozdneyev (1978) at 48.

During services the lamas sit in rows on the east and west sides of the hall facing each other on rows of low seats or *javdan* (жавдан).

For those nationalists searching for a 'purely Mongolian' temple, all Buddhist temples have frustratingly non-Mongolian decorations brought from India by way of Nepal and Tibet. These decorations function as a visual esoteric language to convey Buddhist principles or historical events from the life of the Shakyamuni Buddha.

Over the main gate of Buddhist temples are two gilded deer, sitting in adoration around an eight-spoke wheel, another reminder of the circle as a symbol of the universe and perfection. The wheel represents the dharma while the deer alludes to the Buddha's sermon in the deer park at Sarnath. On the sides of the beam for the roof of the temple are two sea dragons or *zhiwen* (蜘吻), sometimes called more generally *chimeglel luu* (чимэглэл луу) in Mongolian. These are aquatic dragons that perform the practical function of anchoring the main beam while providing the mythical form to protect the temple from fire since they are watery creatures native to the sea.[5] Upturned eaves on the roofs are capped by *makaras*, another type of sea dragon and a stylistic variation of the *zhiwen*.

Door knockers on temple gates often take the form of a zoomorphic creature—the *kirtimukha*, meaning the 'face of glory' in Sanskrit. Its Mongolian name is *zeebad* (зээбад). The zeebad comes from a Hindu legend about a quarrel between Lord Shiva and the deity Rahu. In a move of audacious chutzpah, Rahu attempted to put the moves on the wife of Shiva, the god who is famously known by the title World Destroyer, no less. Shiva conjured the zeebad, a ferocious beast of uncontrolled fury, and sent it after Rahu. Just as the zeebad had beaten the tar out of Rahu, the libidinous mutt pleaded

Roof decorations on the temples at Gandan Monastery. Photo by author.

5. Villier at 101.

with Shiva for his life. Feeling that he had sufficiently demonstrated his masculine authority, Shiva called off the zeebad. (What *is* it with the male of the species?) In outrage at being denied its final fruits of victory, the ravenous zeebad turned on itself and, starting with his tail, devoured itself until all that remained was its jawless head. Shiva was duly impressed with the zealous sense of duty of the zeebad, not to mention his overwhelming ferocity, and rewarded the creature by putting it at the head of his security detail. The zeebad was to remain for all eternity outside the threshold of Shiva's palace. Since the zeebad was missing its jaw, I imagine that it was not able to express its opinion about this so-called reward. This decorative motif spread throughout Asia, with people often unaware of its South Asian origins.

On the flanks of the main gate of the temples are stone lions, or *arslan* (арслан), a decoration found all throughout East Asia even though lions are not indigenous to the region. Lions are a symbol of the Buddhist empire of King Asokha and, as an artistic decoration, hitched a ride with the dharma's transmission from India to East Asia. Stone lions are placed before imperial, royal, or religious sites, with the male lion, always set to the right of an entrance, playing with a ball symbolizing the world and the female lion and its cub to the left. People beseech the favour of the lions by rubbing butter over their months just as ancient Mongolians smeared butter on the mouths of their ongons. (*Arslan* is one of those marvellous words that show the linguistic web that binds together distant cultures; the Mongolian word is the same as the Turkish.)

The walkways leading to the main gate of a temple are usually flanked by wooden or bronze prayer wheels, which are devices that originated in eleventh-century Tibet. At that time, lamas required the faithful to recite prayers posted on wooden panels at the entrance of a temple before entry. However, as the prayers grew longer, they needed to be printed on both sides of the panels. These panels were placed on a swivel to assist the supplicants in their recitation. With illiteracy being the norm in the Himalayas, many Tibetans simply turned the panels while reciting prayers from memory. This led to this practice of turning canisters filled with Tibetan sutras where each spin is equivalent to the recitation of its contents.[6]

A gilded *ganjir* (ганжир) or 'treasury' is a vessel shaped like a vase or a lotus. These are located on the centre of the roof of a temple and are filled with sutras and other religious documents. On the four corners of the roof underneath the cupola are the *jaltsan* (жалцан) or victory banners symbolizing Buddhism's triumph over ignorance and superstition. Like the ganjir, these cylinders are filled with sutras.

A common motif painted on the doors and walls of the monasteries is the Eight Treasures of Vajrayana Buddhism. These treasures are the wheel (a symbol of the Buddha's teaching as well as samsara), the conch shell (the voice of the Shakyamuni Buddha and the awakening from ignorance), the flag (symbolic of the victory of Buddhism over falsehood), the umbrella (an allusion to the Buddha's royal birth),

6. Pozdneyev (1978) at 57–58.

the jar (a funerary urn for lamas and a reminder of the impermanence of the material world), the two fish (freedom from the restraints of this earthly world), the lotus (symbolizing perfection arising from the mundane, just as a lotus rises from the muddy bottom of a pond to bloom on the water's surface), and the mystic knot (reflecting Indra's knot, or the interconnection of all phenomena and emptiness). Indra's knot or *ulzii utas khee* (өлзий утас хээ) has become a symbol of good fortune found on the wooden palisades of ger homesteads. Another frequent motif is the double-vajra or *natsagdorj* (нацагдорж) which are two interlocking sceptres with five-spoke crowns, a symbol of a doubling of the powerful effect of the thunderbolt of enlightenment.

Arrayed horizontally along the trim just below tiered roofs or square cupolas, there is often a row of multiple circular silvery shapes. These are called beads, *erikh* (эрх), or mirrors, *toli* (толь). The beads refer to the ornate jewellery draped over statues of Buddhas and bodhisattvas as well as the rosaries used by the lamas. The mirror is the symbol of pure consciousness, a perception of reality unclouded by ignorance or desire.

Temple interiors are often decorated in red, an auspicious symbol that represents Jamsran, the patron saint of Mongolia, and the positive (yang) forces of the universe. Multiple uni or bagana are decorated with four-fingered dragons rising from sea and climbing past clouds.

On the altars there may be dough offerings or *sor* (сор). The shape of a sor is roughly triangular, though there are many different forms depending upon the purpose. These days, they are often made of plastic as 'permanent' offerings on a temple's altar.

The sor goes back to a legend about the Shakyamuni Buddha and an ogress with 500 ogre-children. To feed her numerous offspring, the ogress kidnapped children from the villages near the Buddha's monastery. The Buddha elected to use his powers of persuasion to correct her behaviour. He captured one of her children and hid him under a begging bowl. When the distraught ogress searched for her lost child and failed to find him, she pleaded with the Buddha for his help. The Buddha reasoned with the ogress, asking her to imagine the suffering of others, particularly the people in the villages with only one child and to compare that with her own grief from losing only one of many children. The ogress was struck with remorse and pledged to stop feeding others' children to her own. The Buddha then rewarded her by revealing her missing son under the begging bowl. From that day on, the Buddha's disciples made daily dough offerings to the ogress as a reward so that she would always have the means to feed her children.

The sor ceremony evolved to serve multiple purposes. A sor offering was a way to petition the temple's deities to remove hindrances and obstacles. Later, it was recast as a method of exorcising the accumulated sin of a community by burning the sor once it had been offered to the deities as a way to absorb harmful karma. In Urga this ritual took place on the twenty-ninth day of the last lunar month.

Mongolian temples are graced by stupas or *suburgan* (суварга), which are reliquaries for the cremated or mummified remains of high lamas—a practice that reportedly dates back to the time of the historical Buddha's burial. They are meant generally to symbolize the actual person of the Shakyamuni Buddha. Other theories say that a stupa represents the five elements of the universe (as determined by the Indo-Tibetan tradition): earth, water, fire, air, and ether.

There are general monastic principles that govern the construction of a stupa, though there is much leeway for local variation. In Mongolia the stupas are an adaptation of Tibetan forms. The plinth (or base) is called the Lion Throne after the chair that the Buddha used during rituals and lectures. It is square in shape, representing the earth and the four cardinal directions. The dome is likened to a drop of water while the spire symbolizes the fire of enlightenment. The upper spire with its stylistic parasol represents air while the crescent moon, the sun, and flame at the very top symbolize space and enlightenment. The hierarchy of the stupa reflects the process of enlightenment and the divisions between ordinary sentient beings, bodhisattvas, and Buddhas. The rituals for constructing a stupa are elaborate and require the builders to meditate in preparation and engage in reverential acts in the course of construction.

At Gandan Monastery many stupas are constructed in the form called the fully ornamented enlightenment stupa. Two long faux-silk pendants hang from each side

Devotee praying before a stupa. Photo by Janice Law.

of the granite spire. The pendants are painted yellow to simulate golden jewellery and precious jewel tassels. On the dome is a plaque with a mantra, the symbolic number ten, or images of the Buddhas or bodhisattvas. The main stupa is often surrounded by eight smaller ones symbolizing events from the Buddha's life: his birth, his victory over Mara while meditating under the Bodhi tree, his first lecture in the deer park, his performance of miracles to overpower demons and heretics, his descent to the lower realms to teach the dharma to his mother's reincarnation, his reconciliation of factions among his followers, the extension of his life at age 80, and his passing away.

* * *

Into Urga's mosaic of Mongolian gers and Vajrayana temples, Western architectural forms arrived from Russia during the mid-nineteenth century. These new entrants were constructed as utilitarian and functional outposts for diplomats, merchants, and settlers of small holdings.

The first two-storey Western building was the Russian consulate, whose barricaded rectangular design was a distinct contrast to the surrounding gers, Buddhist temples, and Chinese courtyards. When the Russians added an Orthodox chapel to the consulate in 1872, it presented the first non-Buddhist religious decorative motif with its modest spire, adding a new message to Urga's Buddhist sermons in stone, wood, and brick. Around the same time, Russian homesteaders moved to the Tuul River Valley and built their rectangular log cabins or *izbas*. As they prospered, the homesteaders replaced the log cabins with peasant-style wooden buildings with steep gables to prevent snow building up on the roofs.

Innovative Russian architectural forms gradually appeared in Urga as the twentieth century replaced the nineteenth. In Western Russia architects were experimenting with extrapolations of wooden peasant houses, featuring innovations that were usually beyond the budgets of Urga's frugal Russian peasants, such as sharply pitched roofs with prominent gables, ornate Siberian window frames, and intricate wooden gingerbread fretwork along roof edges. These eventually showed up as decorations on the homes and shops of Urga's nouveau riche. They can be seen today at the Ulaanbaatar History Museum and the Europa Restaurant, near the former Russian diplomatic enclave.

In the aftermath of the Russian Revolution of 1905, Russian intellectuals sought new artistic directions to revitalize their country and embrace 'futurism' for a utopian world where form would not be beholden to the past. Russian futurists joined the October Revolution in the quest for the new society envisaged by Lenin and his 'scientific socialism'. This quest spawned different theories of Soviet architecture that came to influence the appearance of Ulan Bator greatly, though there was often a considerable time lag, sometimes decades, between the development of a stylistic innovation and its introduction to Mongolia.

The constructivist school of design arose early on in the Soviet Union, advocating that 'real construction' had to be based on expediency, utility, and economy.

Siberian-style log cabin 'sawed in half'. Photo by author.

Russian peasant-style house. Photo by Lukas Nikol.

Ulaanbaatar City Museum, former house of Buryat Russian merchant. Photo by author.

Constructivist forms emphasized sturdy designs without elaborate decorations. Perhaps the most famous example in the Soviet Union was the Shabolovka Radio Tower, designed by Vladimir Shukov, and completed in 1922. The Radio Tower fit constructivist theory perfectly—it performed the essential utilitarian function of providing the first direct radio communications across the entire Soviet Union while it was 'decorated' only by a scientifically minimalist appearance with a steel beam lattice design. Architects hailed it as a groundbreaking and progressive advance from the architectural style of the Eiffel Tower. (The Moscow Radio Tower foreshadowed Ulaanbaatar's own television tower, which was constructed in 1967.)

Not all constructivists agreed on this direction, though. The rationalist faction of constructivism argued that the power of the abstract form creates an aesthetic encouraging scientific thought among the working classes. Abstract geometric designs and new angles and curves were seen as heralds of a new futuristic age where the functional and the fantastic would merge. (In UB a neglected site of uncertain age near Peace Bridge uses a rationalist design.)

Other Russian architects focused on the Soviet Union as a multi-ethnic state. Moisei Ginzburg advocated adapting regional secular designs from the non-Russian Soviet republics. He felt that while religious motifs should be abandoned as cultural 'dead ends', secular architecture from ethnic minorities should be improved and promoted in Central Asia and elsewhere.[7]

Against this backdrop of architectural innovations, Russian contractors invented an urban design theory in light of the pressing need to improve transportation and rectify unsanitary and crowded conditions in the industrial slums of Soviet cities.

7. Anderson at 120.

MongolKino building, an example of constructionist architecture. Photo by author.

Rationalist architecture south of Peace Bridge. Photo by author.

With an eventual impact upon the appearance of Ulan Bator, the contractors reshaped the urban design of Moscow by implementing a radial-concentric street network in the form of its famous ring roads. New Soviet residential districts were constructed with an emphasis upon proportion and light, resulting in staggered rows of three-storey buildings, such as the apartment complex on Traktornaia Street in Leningrad. The design of apartment complexes along Western Peace Avenue and 'Beatles Square' took inspiration from the Traktornaia Street project while Moscow was the inspiration for the layout of the 'New Ulan Bator' of the 1950s.

* * *

As already noted, these Soviet architectural trends were barely felt in faraway Mongolia when they first came into fashion in West Russia. The MPR authorities retained German architects in the 1920s to design the now-vanished neoclassical building for the State Printing Press. A Hungarian in Ulan Bator independently came to the same view advocated by Ginzburg and designed the 'Green Domed Theatre' incorporating the domed roof of a ger. A few important buildings were erected in accordance with constructivist principles, but these are now obscure or forgotten, such as the former Lenin Club, the present KinoMongol building, and the Internal Security Agency's

Neoclassical residential building. Photo by Lukas Nikol.

Exhibition Hall, 'national in form but socialist in content'. Photo by Lukas Nikol.

headquarters. In the main, the monasteries and khasaas still dominated the appearance of Ulan Bator before the Great Purge.

Constructivism lost momentum in the Soviet Union during the 1930s because of practical and ideological obstacles. Constructivist buildings required large quantities of steel frame and reinforced concrete, both of which were strains on nascent Soviet industry. Moreover, the 'boss' himself, Comrade Stalin, said that he preferred neoclassicism as a way to emphasize the grandeur of the Soviet revolution and its assimilation of previous architectural heritages. (It also used far less steel because it relied primarily on masonry.) The architects saw which way the wind was blowing and fell into line—'they looked for precedents in the urban ensembles of the Italian Renaissance, the French city of the ancien régime, contemporary planning in Fascist Italy and even the architectural fantasies of the American draughtsman Hugh Ferris.'[8] Constructivism was dismissed because it erred in thinking that Soviet architectural theory was merely 'to produce machines'.[9]

It took a decade for Soviet neoclassicism to arrive in Ulan Bator. The Ard Cinema (now a Mormon chapel) and the Mongolia State University were two early examples from 1935 and 1940. However, Ulan Bator's 'golden age' of neoclassical design had to wait until after the war with Nazi Germany. With Soviet assistance, the MPR authorities constructed the highly vaunted political and cultural buildings around the newly paved Sükhbaatar Square. Just as the Greek-derived Cyrillic alphabet was making its easternmost landfall in Mongolia, Greek architectural symmetry and proportion arrived as the ornaments for Ulan Bator's new urban look. The State Opera Hall, the National Library, and the Children's Cinema drew heavily from Greek temple designs while incorporating subtle Mongolian decorative motifs.

Residential housing followed the Soviet neoclassical form pioneered by Arkadii Mordvinov for the residential projects at the base of Gorky Street (now Tverskaia Street) in Moscow. The apartments along east Jigjidjav Street deploy similar shallow balconies and a rhythmic repetition of windows, cornices and pilasters, but on a smaller scale.

* * *

Khrushchev called a halt to neoclassicism in 1955 saying that it was a wasteful, bourgeois perversion. Pointing to the 'over-the-top' Wedding Cake palaces in Moscow, he argued, 'We are not against beauty but against excesses,' and inaugurated 'modernism'.[10] The former Café Bear Cub, the Urgoo Cinema on Ard Ayush Avenue, and the former Ard Cinema on Baga Toiru Street recall modernism, which advocated a more conventional use of geometric shapes than rationalism as well as landscaped spaces with lawns in front of buildings to provide urban 'breathing space'. Around the same time,

8. Ibid. at 158. Incidentally, Ferris was the creator of the perspective drawings of gothic art-deco buildings that inspired the dark brooding look of Batman's Gotham City.
9. Ibid. at 148.
10. Ibid. at 216.

Soviet-trained urban designers endorsed the creation of urban satellite settlements or 'microdistricts', which soon sprang up in Ulan Bator beyond the ring roads.

Ginzburg's recommendation of using local vernacular motifs also reappeared in Ulan Bator, leading to a spate of buildings that applied Mongolian designs to modern uses. These can be seen in the National Drama Theatre and the ger-inspired Exhibition Hall. To use the lingo of the era, such buildings were 'national in form but socialist in content' (whatever that means).

In the 1970s Brezhnev declared that the Soviet bloc had achieved 'developed socialism', an ideological gimmick that meant substituting stasis for progress. Following his lead, Ulan Bator's architecture was notable for identical residential and office complexes—the apartment complexes to the west of Gandan Monastery come to mind as an example—where uniformity was occasionally interrupted by innovative monumental 'individual construction' projects, such as the Lenin Museum or the Wedding Palace. The era of the Brezhnev stagnation projected totalitarianism and authoritarianism in non-monumental building design.

* * *

In the aftermath of Communism, functional blue glass high-rise designs are the order of the day, and they are implemented without regard to urban planning or local setting. On the drawing board these monumental buildings might elicit the excitement of the wealthy owner of the real estate project, a 10-year-old boy or President Trump (same intellectual and emotional capacity actually), but they have left the face of the city scarred and its streets chaotic. The concrete jungle of today's Ulaanbaatar has returned its residents to a version of the unplanned urban design of old Urga put through a filter of science fiction. The city has completed the circuit from the perfection of the circle to the sturdiness of the rectangle and now to the desperation of the jagged edge.

'Developed socialist' residential complex from the 1970s. Photo by Lukas Nikol.

Lenin Museum, an example of 'individual construction' from the 1970s. Photo by author.

Part II

The Sites

5

Eastern Monastic Settlement (Züün Khüree)

The Eastern Monastic Settlement or Züün Khüree (Зүүн Хүрээ) was the religious centre of Urga and the site of the official residence of the patriarch.[1] For non-Mongolians trekking across stony deserts and undulating grasslands, the first sighting of Urga's fantastical buildings must have seemed as otherworldly as the lunar scenery in Georges Méliès's *A Trip to the Moon*. Monks dressed in scarlet robes chanting mysterious prayers and lay residents wearing exotic costumes topped by elaborate headwear would have looked like apparitions from a universe far from the familiar and predictable Euro-American world.

Only three main buildings of the Eastern Monastic Settlement survive to the present day. They are all Mongolian ger-style temples that were requisitioned as storehouses for Buddhist artwork looted from other monasteries during the Great Purge. In 1941 the temples were appropriated by the Ulan Bator circus, a form of entertainment newly imported from the USSR, for use as a training ground for performers and a stable for animals.

After fifty years of this less-than-exalted use the Mongolian government reallocated two of the three main buildings in 1990 to the revived Dashchoilin Monastery of the Eastern Monastic Settlement, or Züün Khüree Dashchoilin Khiid (Зүүн Хүрээ Дашчойлон Хийд) along with two much smaller gers that survived the 1930s. (These other two are now the monastery's library and a monastic tailoring/embroidery workshop.) The Dashchoilin Monastery is located on Akademch Sodnom Street in Eighth Khoroo of the Sükhbaatar District, which is located to the east of what was once the centre of the Eastern Monastic Settlement.

A noble from Tüshetu Khan Aimag founded the 'Prince's Aimag', or Wangain Aimag (Вангайн Аймаг), in 1740, and the current ger-temple was built for it in 1790. The temple continued to be an active site of worship until the Great Purge. In its day, it was notable for having a set of the twelve volumes of the Prajnaparamita Sutra written in vermilion ink (which was returned to the temple's care in the early 1990s).[2]

The Wangain Aimag is now the tsogchin dugan for the Dashchoilin Monastery's monks, who meet every morning to chant prayers from 9:00 a.m. to 1:00 p.m. Its

1. See Teleki (2008).
2. Teleki at 113–16.

interior has been redecorated—the ceiling is painted a light blue and the beams and pillars are red and gold. In the morning hours, effulgent sunlight streams through the toono, illuminating the victory banners and thangkas over the monks as they pray. On the main altar are bronzes of the Shakyamuni Buddha, the bodhisattva Maitreya, and Tara, as well as a set of plaster sculptures of arhats. At one side, there are thousands of small statues of Zanabazar in five different hand gestures, or *mudras*, in the glass-covered cupboards.

Next to Wangain Aimag is the Enkhem Tonni Aimag (Энхэм Тонни Аймаг). This structure was also built in 1790 and reconsecrated as the temple for the monastery's protective deities, Baldan Lkham and Jamsran, at the time of its revival in 1990. In the antechamber are the Maharajas of the Four Directions. The interior of the temple proper is decorated in red, the symbolic colour of the wrathful protective deities of the monastery. On the west side of the temple's interior, monks read jasaa for supplicants, who sit on the nearby benches and pass among themselves an urn containing burning juniper incense, fanning the smoke over their heads while waiting their turn for consultations. The bronzes of the two protective deities are placed above the seats for the main disciplinary master and his assistant on each side of the interior entranceway. Hanging from the ceiling are large thangkas of Yamantaka (Jigjid) and Vajrapani (Vachibani) in the centre, Sitamahakala (Gongor) and Mahalaka (Gombo) on the left, and Sridevi (Baldan Lkham) and Yama (Choijoo) on the right. The main altar has a bronze of Tsongkhapa and his two disciples. Set out elsewhere on the altar are bronzes of the Tathagata Buddhas and the dharmapala. The Enkhem Tonni Aimag was founded as an institution in 1737 with the approval of the Second Patriarch, who sought to unify the protective deities for all Mongolian lineages initiated by his great-grand uncle, Zanabazar.[3]

In 1999 the Dashchoilin monastic authorities added the concrete Gandanchoinkhorin Aimag (Ганданчойнхорын Аймаг). Its main image is a copper Shakyamuni Buddha gilded with gold. On its walls is a mural of the Vajrayana Buddhist pantheon, namely the eight main disciples of the Buddha, the sixteen arhats, the ten dharmapala, the protectors from the four continents, the White Old Man, a Mongolian prince holding a tiger by a chain, and eight stupas with eight auspicious symbols, among many others. A set of huge rosary beads decorate the altar. The Gandanchoinkhorin Temple is used primarily for providing jasaa readings or casting horoscopes for the laity.

Outside the grounds of the monastery to the west, the Ikh Daginiin Aimag (Их Дагины Аймаг), built in 1903, is still used as one of the administrative offices of the circus. It was commissioned in honour of Dongogdulam, one of the wives of the Bogd Khan and a purported *dagina*, or female goddess. Despite being the wife of the Patriarch and a female goddess to boot, Dongogdulam's fortunes were limited—she died within a decade of the consecration of the temple. Her replacement-spouse was

3. Ibid. at 109–11.

Wangain Aimag, now the Main Assembly Hall of the Dashchoilin Monastery. Photo by author.

a woman who quickly grasped that an improper marriage to a highly placed incarnate lama could do wonders for disposable income. The new wife had been the consort of a famed wrestler who, upon learning that his missus was eagerly sought for the Bogd Khan's bed, gallantly gave her up with a shrug.

Today's Dashchoilin Monastery does not capture the grandeur of Urga in the era of the patriarchs, but we can reconstruct in our imagination how the Eastern Monastic Settlement looked, thanks to a map of Urga painted by the artist Jügder in 1913 for the Bogd Khan.[4]

The Central Square was a vast unpaved oblong expanse with its narrow ends on the north and south perimeters. It was enclosed on the east and west by rough-hewn wooden fences with prayer wheels 'as plentiful as fire plugs' that were kept in nearly perpetual motion by passing lamas and pilgrims.[5] The south gateway of the Central Square was a red imperial arch with green tiled eaves built on the orders of Peking in 1883 to welcome the Eighth Patriarch to Urga. Two stone lions flanked the imperial arch (and later in the mid-twentieth century, they were posted for duty in front of the Museum of Natural History, where they still stand guard, like demoted zeebads).

From the imperial arch, the Holy Walkway, or Zalrak Zam (Залрах Зам), ran along the main north–south axis of the Central Square. Porters carried the Eighth Patriarch in his sedan chair along the Zalrak Zam whenever he travelled between the Eastern Monastic Settlement and his other palaces.

On the north side of the square was the Yellow Palace, or Shar Ordon (Шар ордон), the official residence of the patriarchs. The palace took its name from the

4. Full-scale copies of the map may be viewed at the Temple of the Oracle Lama and the Bogd Khan Museum.
5. Meignan at 322.

Stone lion, formerly in front of the Holy Walkway. Photo by author.

yellow wooden palisade that enclosed it. The Manchu court had granted the Eighth Patriarch the privilege to use the imperial colour yellow as a sign of its favour.[6]

The Central Square and the Zalrak Zam were positioned in accordance with the geomantic principle of placing the main entrance of a royal palace at the north end of a 'divine walkway'. For a nineteenth-century traveller, the Holy Walkway would have appeared like a Central Asian version of Tiananmen Square or the courtyard outside the main royal palace for the Nguyen kings in Vietnam. When approaching the Yellow Palace along the Holy Walkway, travellers would inevitably have had the impression that with each step they were drawing closer and closer to a celestially chosen ruler.

The Central Square was used for religious events that also served social functions. It was the site of the twice-yearly ceremony for the Tsam—a Buddhist masked dance ritual performed by lamas to exorcise harmful karma from the settlement. In the summer, it hosted the traditional quasi-religious Mongolian sporting contests that later morphed into the secular Naadam festival.

Outside the main entrance of the Yellow Palace, pilgrims waited to receive the blessings of the Patriarch. The monks ran a red string from the interior of the Yellow Palace to the Central Square where the end of the string would be handed to a pilgrim,

6. Pozdneyev (1978) at 362.

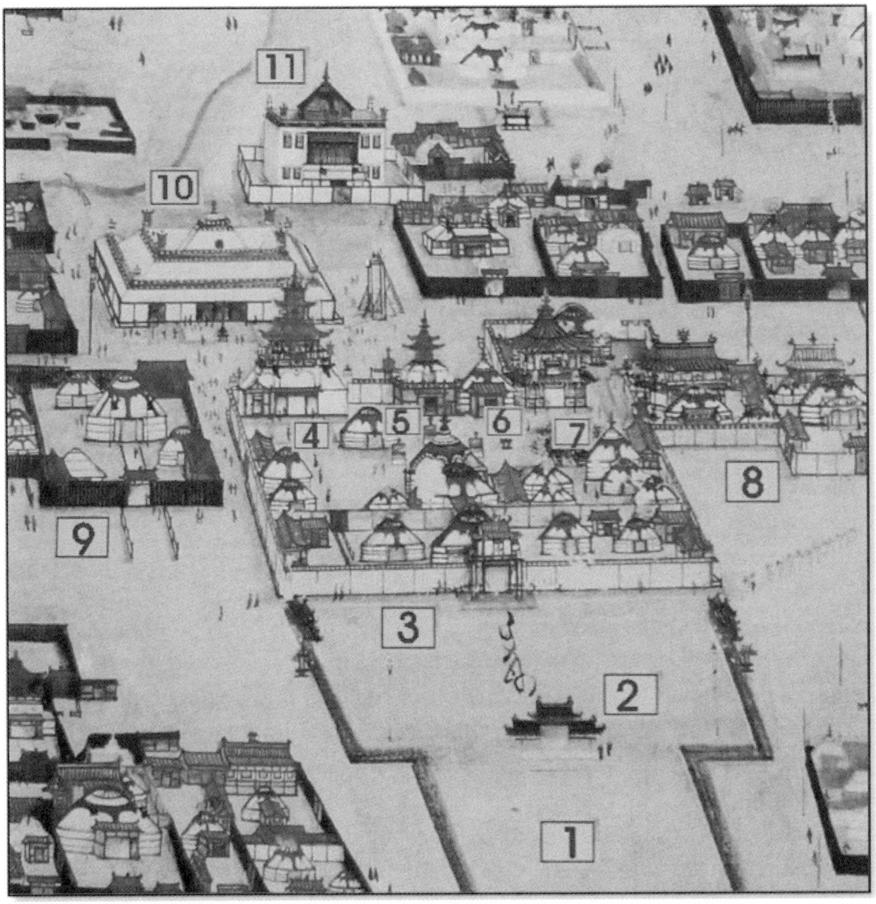

Central Square, Eastern Monastic Settlement. Graphic designed by Aubrey Ding-Shan Yang, original map by Jügder, 1913, Bogd Khan Museum.

Key

1. Holy Walkway
2. Triumphal Arch
3. Yellow Palace
4. Dechingalav Temple
5. Temple of the Bodhisattva Tara
6. Temples of the Three Bodhisattvas
7. Octagonal temple
8. Temple of Vajradhara
9. Western Palace
10. 'Massive White' Assembly Hall
11. Temple of Maitreya

who was instructed to give a tug. The Patriarch, or more likely an unseen proxy holding the other end of the string, would tug back to signal a blessing being sent through the cord by the highest Buddhist authority in Khalkha Mongolia.

As observed by a British travel writer,

> [The] devotions [of the pilgrims] form an important item in their daily routines; though perhaps, to an unbeliever in the Mongol Buddhist faith, these devotions may seem to take a form which is somewhat astonishing. Still, it cannot be denied that they are carried out with great sincerity . . . The 'prayer boards' are also placed for public use in various parts of the city, and on which are continually to be seen prostrate figures lying on their faces, and thus literally humbling themselves to the very dust.[7]

Behind the main gate of the Yellow Palace were fifteen temples. On each side of the walkway within the Yellow Palace there were two palatial gers for the Patriarch. These were not his main place of abode since he owned many other palaces in Urga and elsewhere. Generally, he preferred to be elsewhere away from the site of his clerical duties.

To the north-west of the Patriarch's gers was the Dechingalav Temple, the site for the initiation into the Kalachakra and a notable structure in the city. The temple traced its origins to the Second Patriarch, who in 1729 formed a lamas' 'working group' to introduce the Kalachakra into Khalkha Mongolia. (Those familiar with the Mongolian administrative process might recognize, with a shudder, this long-entrenched administrative vehicle for delaying decisions and avoiding responsibility. The concept of a 'working group' might have been somewhat more suited for religious matters given the gravitas accorded to the faith, but the sceptic in me doubts it.) The temple sites for the Kalachakra initiation remained mobile until 1806 when the Fourth Patriarch ordered the construction of this ornate temple after his own initiation by the Dalai Lama during a pilgrimage to Lhasa. The building burned down in 1892 and was then rebuilt with the same facade and interior. It had a Mongolian mezzanine surmounted by a square cupola and a gilded roof decorated with small bells that were the source of uninterrupted melodic tinkling—a delightful Buddhist sound heard in Asia from Siberia through Tibet into Burma and beyond. Every year on the first day of the last lunar month, the lamas held the Kalachakra initiation ceremonies. The Dechingalav Temple was also the personal temple for the patriarchs. Consequently, it was the temporary resting place for their remains while the astrologers sought an auspicious day for their immurement in a stupa.

The Temple to the Bodhisattva Tara stood directly to the north of the Patriarch's gers. Next to it was the Temple of the Three Bodhisattvas in honour of Avalokitesvara, Manjusri, and Vajradhara, built at the order of the Fourth Patriarch in 1793. Near the gers was an octagonal shaped wooden temple, originally built as a palace for the Third Patriarch, dedicated to the Vajra. To the east of this was the Vajradhara Temple which

7. Price at 282–84.

had a bronze of its deity cast a century earlier by Zanabazar. (This bronze is now on the main altar of the Vajradhara Temple in Gandan Monastery.)

The 'Massive White', or Bat Tsagaan (Бат Цагаан), was the main tsogchin dugan of the Eastern Monastic Settlement. In the late nineteenth century, the Russian Mongolist Pozdneyev compared it favourably to the grand cathedrals of Europe.[8] It was a large square-shaped Tibetan building with its exterior walls splashed with whitewash and its roof crowned with a square cupola.[9] One hundred eight pillars supported its roof, an auspicious number referring to the number of volumes in the Kanjur. (The entire Kanjur was recited here during an annual three-day festival.) The tsogchin dugan accommodated 2,500 lamas for routine rituals. For vow-taking ceremonies and other special events, additional felt tents could be laid on and attached to the hall to accommodate up to 10,000 lamas. The interior of the Massive White was not ornately decorated; there were only rows of low benches placed perpendicular to the main altar and a 'lion throne' in front for the Patriarch. On the main altar, there was a large bronze of Shakyamuni Buddha, or Ikhiin Zuu (Ихийн Зуу), cast by Zanabazar. (This bronze is also now in Gandan Monastery.)

Zanabazar inaugurated the Massive White as an institution for lama convocations in 1654. Like other monastic institutions in Khalkha Mongolia, it was not set in one fixed place but could be dismantled to accompany the patriarchs in their wanderings until the nineteenth century when it was settled for what was expected to be a long duration. It maintained the original appearance designed by Zanabazar.

Outside the Yellow Palace to the west was the Western Palace, or Baruun Örgöö (Баруун Өргөө), a ger-temple for the veneration of the Abatai Khan, the great-grandfather of Zanabazar, the builder of the Monastery of the One Hundred Treasures, and one of the main supporters of Buddhism at the outset of the Second Conversion. It served as a site for worshipping Jamsran and other pre-Buddhist Mongolian deities absorbed into the Buddhist pantheon. Inside were logs that were roughly hewn into shapes of fierce heroes of olden days.

> Faces painted red, barred teeth, enormous bulging eyes, high raised brows . . . were everywhere in evidence here. The logs were clothed in khyak (mail) and duulga (helmets) made of steel and ornamented with gold. The Mongols held these heroes in special veneration, and each person upon entering the yurt deemed it his duty to press his forehead to their shoulders in the hope of thus receiving a small portion, at least, of their heroic strength.[10]

This temple was where, in 1920, Sükhbaatar, Choibalsan, and other proto-revolutionaries put their foreheads to the shoulders of the red wrathful deities, swore an oath

8. Pozdneyev I (1997) at 54.
9. Following the Tibetan custom, monks threw a coat of whitewash on the exterior of multistorey stone building rather than apply it with a brush.
10. Pozdneyev I (1997) at 60.

to defend Mongolia and Buddhism from gamin invaders, and then left to seek the help of the Bolsheviks.

Old photographs reveal the stunning exterior of the Temple of Maitreya, or Maidariin Süm (Майдарийн Сүм), another of Urga's famous sites of worship, which stood to the north-west of the Yellow Palace. The temple was part of the plans of abbot Agvaankhaidav for the propagation of Maitreya in Urga. The abbot was a devotee of Maitreya because the bodhisattva had visited him during a childhood dream.

The temple was first constructed in the Chinese style but burned down repeatedly. The Mongolians lamas sought the guidance of the Panchen Lama, who interpreted these disasters as a sign of Maitreya's displeasure at the absence of Tibetan motifs in the temple's design. In 1860 the temple was rebuilt in a square shape with white wooden walls and a domed roof with an interlocking green and brown design. Within the temple, there was a magnificent masterpiece of Mongolian art, a 16-metre bronze statue of the Maitreya bodhisattva seated on a lion throne. It had been cast in Doloon Nor in 1834 at the request of the Fifth Patriarch. Along the north wall behind the Maitreya bronze were bronzes of the five Tathagata Buddhas. Ten thousand Ayush Buddha bronzes, cast in 1799, were placed along the eastern and western walls. It was said the interior was identical to the celebrated Tibetan 'cathedral' in Lhasa, the seventh-century Jokhang Temple, the most holy site for the dharma in Tibet.[11]

Beyond the Yellow Palace the settlement consisted of meandering alleyways formed by 3- or 4-metre wooden palisades that enclosed lots, or khasaas. The entrances to the khasaas were weather-beaten red wooden gates with a beam or two as lintels bearing plaques with the symbol OM or the Svayambhu. Inside the khasaa there were at least two gers, one for use as a dormitory for the monks and the other as their kitchen. Occasionally, well-off lamas built wooden summer homes in their courtyards. The overall impression must have not been that different from the ger districts in Ulaanbaatar today.

The custom of enclosing each residence with a wooden palisade was a borrowing from the Chinese, who favoured walls around their houses for privacy and security. On the steppes Mongolians did not erect fences, given that there was no need to denote personal space, but urban settlements were a comparatively late innovation to which this Chinese custom was applied.

The Eastern Monastic Settlement was not designed for pedestrians but for people on horseback, just as Ulaanbaatar today is not the most pedestrian friendly city in the world. In the dry weather, the streets became a whirl of dust storms. In the summer rains they were impassably flooded mud ruts that then turned into slippery ice-covered paths in the dead of winter.

While nineteenth-century visitors commented on how the streets appeared to be empty of people, the Eastern Monastic Settlement was in fact a beehive of activity behind the wooden palisades. Several gers housed woodblock printing presses that

11. Pozdneyev I (1997) at 61–62; Teleki at 76–78; Tsultsemin at 143–47.

Urga as orientalist exotica. Source: *Mongolia: The Tangut Country and the Solitudes of Northern Tibet*, Nikolai Mikhailovich Przhevalski, London, 1876.

prepared Buddhist sutras, philosophical treatises as well as literary and historical works in Mongolian and Tibetan. Other ger-temples were the sites of 'eternal assemblies', where convocations of lamas were in continual session to chant prayers and seek the intervention of the gods.

In 1900 there were thirty aimags in the Eastern Monastic Settlement. Linguistically, the term *aimag* (аймаг) was applied to many broadly similar concepts. In its most elementary meaning, it refers to a territorial subdivision. As noted in Chapter 2, it was also the name used for the four main subdivisions of Khalkha Mongolia. In Urga, the ecclesiastical authorities subdivided a monastery into aimags when it had grown too large for unitary administration. To avoid regionalist friction, lamas from the same locality in Khalkha Mongolia were assigned to the same aimag. Other aimags came into being to handle specific tasks, such as the preparation of food or the printing of books. (In the twentieth century the term came to mean political and administrative subdivisions of Khalkha Mongolia, hence its modern meaning province.) In Urga each aimag was assigned a separate khasaa that contained a ger-shaped temple along with other gers for use as sleeping quarters or kitchens. Each aimag was assigned a sequential letter of the Tibetan alphabet to indicate the chronological order of its establishment. (These days, the Bayangol Hotel is a pale shadow of this custom since it never got up the velocity to go beyond Buildings A and B.)

In addition to the aimags, the khasaas near the Yellow Palace also contained *datsans*, or monastic colleges for the study of the higher philosophical arts of Vajrayana Buddhism. The datsans were sheltered in Mongolian temples capped with square cupolas and upturned eaves or, sometimes, in a large ger. Each datsan was dedicated to one of the main fields of study. The courses were taught by highly qualified lamas with higher degrees obtained in Mongolia or Tibet.

Training in philosophical debate was an important element of the curriculum. Debates were conducted in the Tibetan style of aggressive argumentation. One lama would circle his opponent, present a proposition and then lift his right hand behind his head, bring it forcefully down with a boom on his left hand, and accusingly point at his opponent. The opponent had to refute or expand upon his interrogator's proposition.

Questions on Buddhist metaphysics went something like this:

> What is the difference between a man sitting on a tree and a man standing on the ground?

Or this:

> Does the mountain called Bukung Buru mentioned in the book of the Buddha rest *in* the ocean or *on* the ocean?[12]

This was no ivory tower gathering at high tea to consider carefully another's view and proffer gentle rejoinders. The debates were aggressive, entertaining, and often raucous, with the audience hooting at a poor showing by a quailing contestant or aggressively cheering champion debaters. In the hands of a skilled examiner, the cross-examination could lead to the humiliation of those ill-prepared for the contest or to a sophisticated journey into Buddhist logical argumentation.

Pious pilgrims, both laymen and clergy, would engage in a circumambulation of the Eastern Monastic Settlement along its outer pathways. As an act of devotion, a pilgrim would lie down on the ground with arms extended above the head and mark the length with a stone. The devotee then stood up, took two or three steps to the stone, and repeated the process. This continued for a course of prayer around the entire perimeter of the settlement. The hands, knees, and elbows of the devotees were wrapped in leather to lessen wear and tear. A learned lama composed a treatise describing the correct manner of performing this ritual given its importance as an act of devotion. Nonetheless, this was an extreme form of worship (that can occasionally be seen in Lhasa these days along the Barkhor and the remaining segments of the Lingkhor). Some devotees performed this act of piety for the entire distance of the pilgrimage

12. Perry-Ayscough at 102.

from their home to Urga. As one observer remarked in 1914, 'These pilgrims will continue this slow and awkward process for perhaps 100 miles before reaching Urga; and when it is remembered that at the best of times the Mongol dislikes walking and is accustomed to ride from the earliest infancy,' it was a testimonial to the faith of the common herders.[13]

A pilgrimage was not an exercise in pure piety, however. Like the journey taken by the band of travellers in *The Canterbury Tales*, it was also a diversion, a chance to visit the main commercial hub of the region, meet other Mongolians, and exchange gossip and news about the goings-on among the nobles and lamas. It was an opportunity to pick up some of the basic necessities for life on the grasslands and attend religious pageants, sporting contests, and Peking operas in the Chinese quarter. People thought little of undertaking a tiresome and extended journey of hundreds and hundreds of kilometres to partake of the merriment and excitement to be found in Urga.

For the less pious, travel to the Urga did not have to be made by crawling but on horse-drawn contraptions in the age before the automobile. The most notorious was the Peking cart, which was an enclosed two-wheeled wagon with no springs pulled by horses, camels, or oxen. The wooden wheels of a Peking cart slowly lost their circular shape through travelling over rough roads. They were gradually bumped into octagons, then hexagons, and then near squares, with increasing torment for its occupant. The famous (and thoroughly obnoxious) Russian explorer Przhevalskii commented on this mode of transportation during his visit to Urga in the 1870s.

> The traveller usually disposes himself in a Chinese cart, which presents the appearance of a great square wooden box, set on two wheels and closed in all sides. In the forepart of this machine, there are openings at the sides, closed with small doors. These holes serve the traveller as a means of ingress and egress to his vehicle, in which he must preserve a recumbent position head foremost in order that his legs may not be on a higher level than his head. The shaking in this kind of car baffles description. The smallest stone or lump of earth over which the wheels may chance to roll produces a violent jolting of the whole vehicle and consequently of its unfortunate occupant. It may be easily imagined how his sufferings may be aggravated when travelling with post horses at a trot.[14]

A more comfortable way to make the journey to Urga was on horseback or by Bactrian camel, which created the impression of gently rolling travel on an overstuffed sofa. The latter became the preferred transport of nineteenth-century Russian traders who had come to appreciate the nuances of life and travel in Mongolia.

The daily monastic regime in Züün Khüree started with early morning chanting followed by tea breaks and then other ceremonies. At 11:00 a.m. the Yellow Palace closed its gates for the day. The laity could enter other parts of the Eastern Monastic Settlement, but women had to leave by 6:00 p.m. In the afternoon, pilgrims and monks

13. Ibid. at 145–46.

14. Przhevalskii at 4–5. Some have compared the Peking cart to Air China.

headed to the marketplaces to pass their leisure time, loaf, or get up to mischief, often with a tribal bent. As more Chinese merchants moved to Urga, there were more altercations between Mongolians and Chinese. Throughout the nineteenth century, the patriarchs issued proclamations forbidding monks from brawling but to no avail. With time, Chinese migrants learned the wisdom of refraining from going out alone or at night and to seek entertainment in 'safe' establishments for Chinese. As the American traveller Thomas Knox noted laconically, 'The Mongols have no great friendship for the Chinese inhabitants.'[15]

In the course of the lunar calendar year, Urga saw many festivals but perhaps the two most festive in the Eastern Monastic Settlement were the annual circumambulation of the Maitreya bronze and the annual Tsam dance rituals.

On the first day of the fifth lunar month the monastic community brought out one of the Maitreya bronzes from its main temple for a constitutional around the Eastern Monastic Settlement. The ceremony attracted thousands of pilgrims from the Buddhist communities in Mongolia, Buryatia, China, Tibet, and even Kalmykia at the mouth of the Volga River.

All of Urga was busy in preparation for days in advance; lamas and laymen went forth and made what we would call 'municipal repairs' that had been ignored over the preceding year. Young monks were dragooned into gathering up all the rubbish from the pathways and shifting them to Züün Khüree's outer ring road while tradesmen moved their market stalls to other parts of town.[16]

The long train of participants in the ceremony was made up of three processions of monks moving forward side by side. The lamas and others pushed carts laden with Buddhist relics while beating large drums and gongs and blowing horns and oboes. The centrepiece of the procession was a bronze Maitreya placed upon an elaborately decorated carriage 'pulled' by a green wooden horse symbolizing Amoghassiddhi. The Maitreya bronze was sheltered from the sun by multicoloured umbrellas and banners. In contemporaneous black-and-white photographs, the main cart creates the impression of a top-heavy load, precariously close to tipping over. The *Five Treatises of the Maitreya* were also brought out and placed in the carriage for the ceremony. Mid- and low-ranking lamas carried other ritual objects on each side of the main cart while behind it came the bright yellow sedan chair with the Patriarch and then the other ecclesiastical dignitaries, abbots of temples, disciplinary masters, chanting masters, and teachers of higher Buddhist studies, all dressed in their finest robes.[17]

The circumambulation went in a clockwise direction, going first to the western gate of the settlement and continuing along its perimeter until the Maitreya bronze was brought back with pomp along the Holy Walkway from the south. At each of the four gates, the procession took breaks while the lamas refreshed themselves on snacks provided by the monasteries.

15. Knox at 168.
16. Price at 297.
17. Ibid. at 299.

This was a spectacle to see and to be seen at. Thousands of nobles, pilgrims, tradesmen, prostitutes, and herders gathered on the sidelines in their finest fashions. An English visitor wrote in 1892:

> I don't think I ever saw a more gorgeous display of costumes and jewellery. Some of the women were dressed in the richest of silks and were literally one mass of silver decorations from head to foot . . . most of the elite were on horseback.[18]

Another English visitor noted the appearance of the crowds on this special day.

> At the time of my visit, the city was full of rough, simple shepherds and their wives who had come on pilgrimage to bring their presents and to take part in the adoration of their incarnate God. They appeared to me, from my acquaintance with them during the whole time I was in Mongolia, to be rough, simple, honest and ignorant people.[19]

The festivities did not always go smoothly. Fist fights between the monks and Chinese onlookers and other altercations broke up the sanctity of the event. As the nineteenth century wore on, more Chinese shops cropped up on the pathway for the ceremony, thus bringing formal and successive complaints lodged by the lamas with the authorities in Peking. In true Chinese bureaucratic manner, the Peking authorities usually ignored a problem when there was no compulsion from 'on high' to resolve it.[20]

The Tsam ceremony was held on the third day of the ninth lunar month. These days, an abbreviated version is performed at various boilerplate Mongolian culture-day festivities and other forums in UB.

Sometimes described as meditation as a performance art, the Tsam celebrates the triumph of Buddhism over evil. The traditional Urga Tsam was first performed in 1811 based on a seventeenth-century script by the Fifth Dalai Lama. Two months before the ceremony, the participating lamas went into extensive preparations such as *yidam*- or deity-focused meditations and rehearsals. During their meditations, the lamas visualized a mandala as the motif for the dance; each lama focused on becoming the deity that he was to represent within the mandala and manifesting the attributes of the deity during the dance.

The lamas wore colourful costumes and masks depicting bodhisattvas and dharmapalas. The ceremony was performed before a gigantic thangka unrolled in the Central Square to the sound of horns, drums, and cymbals. The ceremony began as two lamas wearing skull-masks of the Citipati circled the Central Square and chanted prayers. Other Citipati carried a triangular box containing a human figure moulded in dough or *balin* (балин) and placed it in the centre of the square. The dough figure represented all the sins and corruption accrued in Urga since the previous year's ceremony.

18. Ibid. at 297.

19. Sheepshank at 90.

20. See Pozdneyev I (1997) at 48–49; Tsultemin at 147–49.

Tsam ceremony in Ulaanbaatar. Photo by Janice Law.

The Citipati were followed by the assistants of the Lord of Death, Yama, dressed as deer. This might have been an allusion to the Shakyamuni Buddha's sermon in the Sarnath deer park about overcoming death and decay through the Four Noble Truths. Next, a 'Tibetan lama' came out to engage in some slapstick to make sure the less spiritually minded stayed on for the show. (In Tibet this slapstick character was a Chinese monk, a parody that perhaps could not have happened in more strictly controlled Mongolia with its detachments of Chinese soldiers and merchants spoiling for a fight.)

After the comic interlude, the main figure of the ceremony appeared. This was Yama or Hayagriva, followed by ten fierce deities, who came out and joined the main figure, slowly leaping from foot to foot and brandishing swords, skull cups, and axes. The Red Protector, Jamsran, typically was part of this slow dancing ensemble given his status as a patron saint of Mongolia. The near end of the ceremony was foreshadowed by the White Old Man, the indigenous Mongolian spirit, who came out and was followed by the thirty-two 'black hat' lamas. In closing the ceremony, a lama wearing a stag mask ceremoniously tore apart the dough figure as a symbol of the dharma's conquest of evil and the dispersal of sin.[21]

Both the Maitreya procession and the Tsam dance ritual have been revived at the Dashchoilin Monastery. It is worthwhile to plan your visit to Ulaanbaatar to coincide with these events.[22]

Perhaps the single most important ceremony in the history of the Eastern Monastic Settlement was the inauguration of the sovereign theocratic government in 1911 and the elevation of the Eighth Patriarch to the status of the emperor, or Bogd Khan.

21. Other Tsam dances are based on themes such as the Choijin Lama or King Geser.

22. A collection of pre-revolutionary photographs of a Tsam ceremony at the Monastery of the One Hundred Treasures is in Baasansuren.

On 29 December 1911 the ceremony began at the Hour of the Horse, 11:40 a.m., as the Patriarch and his consort (and erstwhile dagina), Dongogdulam, rode to the Eastern Monastic Settlement in a yellow four-wheeled horse-drawn carriage, preceded by high-ranking lamas and flanked by soldiers wearing traditional costume. The carriage was driven eastward into the Central Square at a dignified pace followed by the nobility on foot. The entire square was filled with lamas, lesser nobles, and commoners trying to catch a glimpse of the ceremonies but kept to a respectful distance by whip-wielding lama bodyguards.

The Holy Couple first went to the Eastern Ger Palace and then walked along a path of wooden planks draped with yellow silk to the Temple of the Three Bodhisattvas and then to the Western Palace for the enthronement ceremony before an altar to the Abatai Khan. Lamas prostrated themselves three times as representatives of the sangha while the aimag princes declared the Eighth Patriarch as the emperor of Mongolia under the regnal title Exalted by All, or Olnoo Ergegdson (Олноо Өргөгдсөн), with 1912 as the first year of the regnal cycle. At this point the five ministries of the government were brought into formal existence and the emperor and empress withdrew to the Eastern Palace to receive the symbols of imperial rule: a thunderbolt crown, a jade seal of office, a golden plaque and the 'nine whites' consisting of a white camel and eight white horses loaded with silks and furs. Mongolians recorded that a rainbow appeared overhead precisely (and conveniently) at the moment when the Bogd Khan was enthroned.

After a brief banquet the Bogd Khan and his wife, now the Mother of the Country, returned by carriage to the Green Palace with military and monastic escorts and thousands of commoners kneeling in the streets.[23]

This moment of triumph for Mongolia was to be rescinded on this same stage before the decade was out. In 1919 the Peking warlord government launched a plot to seize Mongolia forcibly and incorporate it into the Republic of China. Through the machinations of certain Mongolian nobles and the support of newly arrived Chinese troops, Xu Shucheng forced the Bogd Khan to revoke Mongolian autonomy by sending a petition requesting direct rule by the Peking government. After Peking accepted this petition Xu insisted that lamas and nobles, including the Bogd Khan, undergo a three-day fast as a purification ritual before the formal retrocession to Chinese sovereignty—an absolute insult resented by all Mongolians (except those standing to benefit from it) because the office of the Bogd Khan was perceived as beyond reproach and his person beyond impurity.

On 1 January 1920 the ceremony was held in front of the Yellow Palace. The Bogd Khan and other Mongolian dignitaries had to arrive on foot (while Little Xu arrived in his car) with Chinese soldiers lining both sides of the Holy Walkway to the platform for the ceremony. The Bogd Khan was then required to face towards the north, in the traditional manner of barbarian envoys before the Son of Heaven, and kowtow nine

23. See Batsaikhan at 94–101, quoting several sources.

times to a portrait of the Chinese acting president Duan Qirui and the five-coloured striped flag of the Republic of China. Xu, of course, was standing next to the portrait to bask in radiated glory.[24]

Within two years the Red Army and Mongolian revolutionaries reclaimed the country's sovereignty without the panache of ceremony. Within five years the MPR abolished the lineage of the Jebzundamba Khutugtus. The Eastern Monastic Settlement was soon to be erased from the face of Ulan Bator except for the three main temples at the Dashchoilin Monastery.

At this point, we should let these images of Züün Khüree fade from our imagination like the ghostly impressions of passers-by in an old daguerreotype. It is high time to visit more tangible sites.

24. Baabar at 193.

6

Sükhbaatar Square (a.k.a. Chinggis Khan Square)

The centre of Ulaanbaatar has recently suffered from a split personality disorder. I am referring to the massive square plaza in front of Government House, a public place that was originally designed for socialist demonstrations. The square had started life as a humble and undistinguished stretch of dirt and rocks when the MPP named it after Sükhbaatar in 1925. It retained this name until 2012 when, keen to put some distance between contemporary Mongolia and its communist origins, President Elbegdorj renamed it Chinggis Khan Square. As he was a member of the long-standing party in opposition to the MPP, a few observers detected a none-too-subtle motive for the square's new identity.

The new name was part of the ongoing revival of the cult of Chinggis Khan, which had flourished for centuries before the MPR snuffed it out as a relic of nationalist superstition. During Soviet times Mongolians were obliged to downplay the contributions of the progenitor of the Mongolian people, not the least because his descendants conquered the nascent state of Rus and kept it under their heel for two centuries.

Government House and a photographer's start-up in the free market. Photo by Lukas Nikol.

When the 800th anniversary of Chinggis Khan's birth rolled around in 1963 Prime Minister Tsedenbal cancelled the celebrations to put his Soviet patrons at ease.

Since 1990, the official policy of disapproval has been reversed, and Chinggis Khan is back in the spotlight. He is held forth as a totem of national pride, a focus for spiritual supplication, and a brand of really good vodka. In the revived Mongolian spiritual pantheon, he is deeply revered as the progenitor of the nation (true) and a kindly and forgiving philosopher-king (not so true). This reverence can be seen in little porcelain images of Chinggis Khan occupying places of honour in family shrines and in the portraits adorning the walls of luxury apartments. The state continuously promotes this reverence, perhaps because there are so few other national heroes around whom most Mongolians can rally.

The relentless praise of the Great Khan wears thin over time, though. By pointing to Chinggis Khan as a role model for the solution of a wide array of problems afflicting the country, Mongolian politicians begin to sound as implausible as Jean-Claude Juncker exhorting the Euro-zone to new glories (or economic recovery) by emulating Charlemagne.

As a new coat of paint, the renaming of the square did not work out so well, either, because most people called the plaza by its old name, Sükhbaatar Square. With its landslide victory in the 2016 general election, the MPP reinstated the old name, leaving us with a tale of two squares reflecting the tribal nature of Mongolian politics.

The square's role as a centrepiece for the city slowly started to emerge in the 1920s when the MPR commissioned one of its first major construction projects to the north of what was then a barren lot named after a dead superhero. Joseph Gelata, a former POW from Hungary, was retained to design and construct a social and cultural centre for the revolutionary capital. Funding was provided by the Ministry of Finance and the Chamber of Commerce for foreign businesses (who were soon to be turfed out from the country, notwithstanding the donation). People called it the 'Green Domed Theatre'.

Gelata is one of the first of the twentieth-century architects to apply the shape of a ger to a modern construction project. He might also have been the first instance of a long tradition of non-Mongolian consultants being hired, and occasionally paid, by the Mongolian government. He had come to Mongolia in 1920 as an escapee from the Russian civil war and remained in the country until the beginnings of the 'leftist deviation' in 1928. While in Mongolia, he settled down, took a Russian wife, and generally made himself useful at odd jobs whenever the revolutionary government was in need of someone with a dab hand at Western technical skills. In his memoirs, *The New Mongolia*, he paints an inexact but generally positive picture of Ulan Bator, though he could never remember the correct names of temples or explain cogently the reasons for local rituals. This imprecision turns his book into a somewhat foggy collection of impressions. Perhaps he let his curiosity about the customs of the land be too easily satisfied with glib explanations by his acquaintances, who might not have been well-suited to the role of anthropological informants.

The Green Domed Theatre, formally known as the People's Club, stood on the current site of Government House. It was a low square building topped by a dome-shaped roof over an auditorium. After its opening, the Green Domed Theatre was the main forum for the performance of modern Mongolian dramas and operas.

We cannot mention the long-vanished Green Domed Theatre without a digression to give a nod to Dasdorjiin Natsagdorj, the founder of modern Mongolian literature and drama, whose plays were premiered there.

Natsagdorj was of noble birth, a career impediment in the socialist era, and a free intellectual spirit, which had an even more dreadful impact on his career prospects, somewhat like being a Taoist mystic in a corporate boardroom. As a child, Natsagdorj became enchanted with the pageantry of Peking operas that were staged in the small theatres of the city. Later he went to Berlin where he translated modern European literature into Mongolian and adapted Freudian psychoanalysis theory for character development in his short story writing.[1] When he returned to Mongolia, the so-called Writers' Circle of young authors and poets shunned him because of his 'bad' class background.[2] Nevertheless, classic fiction and poetry flowed from his pen. In a posthumous reversal of fortune, his poem, 'My Homeland', is now regarded as a masterpiece of Mongolian literature for its imagery, phrasing, and rhythm, invoking the spirit of the poetry written by ancient itinerant bards in praise of heroes and battles. It did not do him too much good in his lifetime. The literary elites still ostracized him.

His first play, *Prince Sando*, used motifs borrowed from modern drama. The play is based on the historical Sando, the last Manchu amban in Urga, and a thoroughly Sinicized Manchu, who hailed from the central Chinese city of Hangzhou. On the basis of the historical record, Prince Sando seems to have been an ambitious and possibly tediously energetic administrator (and an enthusiastic amateur archaeologist, incidentally). As a loyal Manchu noble, he sought to reverse the decline of the Qing court in Mongolia but in attempting to do this, he came across as not quite the diplomat in Mongolian eyes. In the play, Natsagdorj depicts the amban as a brutal and two-faced manipulator of Mongolian class divisions. The performance ends with an animated stage scene where the 'impersonalized masses' rise up and arrest Sando, a climax slightly at odds with historical facts but a novel innovation for the staging of a play in Mongolia at the time.

Later, Natsagdorj tried his hand at satire. The play *Not I* had the soon-to-be stock character of a greedy and licentious Chinese merchant who is outfoxed at every turn by the common people. The merchant is subjected to abuse as the Mongolian characters find ways to pull out his beard, trick him into putting on women's clothing, and finally get him to hide in a sack when revolutionaries arrive on stage. The play takes

1. Wickham-Smith at 170.
2. The Writers' Circle (*khuvsgalyn aran zokhiochdyn bulgem*) was founded in 1929 under the direction of the MPRP's Central Committee to create a modern and revolutionary form of Mongolian literature. Natsagdorj became a formal member of the group later on. Or so said the USSR and the MPR Academies of Sciences in *History of Mongolian People's Republic* at 475.

its title from the closing punchline; when the revolutionaries come looking for the merchant, they demand to know who is in the sack. He shouts out, 'Not I!' At the time the audience must have found it to be a wildly funny Marxist foray into vaudevillian slapstick.

Turning from comedy to pathos, Natsagdorj wrote *Tears of the Reverend Lama*, a short story about a rural monk who comes to the capital and falls for a scheming Chinese prostitute plying her wares in the Khüree Market. The woman tricks the poor rube out of all his savings and possessions. In the end, the heartbroken lama reflects upon his fate as he is locked out of their home while his paramour ecstatically embraces another lover. The short story was later turned into an opera.

Natsagdorj is perhaps most celebrated for writing the libretto for Mongolia's first modern and most famous Western-style opera, *Three Sorrowful Hills*. The opera premiered posthumously at the Green Domed Theatre in 1942 with a musical score composed by Bilegiin Damdinsüren. It tells the story of the struggles of a herder named Yundun, his beloved girlfriend, Nasalmaa, and their attempts to overcome the wicked Prince Baldan. After the introduction of the characters, the plot moves to the Prince kidnapping Nasalmaa and trying to force her to marry him. Secretly, at the same time the Prince conspires with an evil-hearted harpy, Khorolmaa, to pass false stories about Nasalmaa's unfaithfulness to Yundun so that Khorolmaa can catch him on the rebound. With the assistance of friends drawn from the ranks of the ard, Yundun defeats Prince Baldan in battle and the lovers are married as the curtain falls.

The original ending of the story, however, had both Yundun and Nasalmaa tragically dying in battle. Like the financiers of Hollywood blockbusters, the MPRP authoritarians insisted that Mongolia's first opera should be capped with a happy ending.

Leaving aside his literary accomplishments, Natsagdorj made a permanent contribution to the Mongolian fashion scene by wearing a fedora hat with a traditional Mongolian *del*, a look that still cuts an impressive image in the twenty-first century.

In his personal life, Natsagdorj was a mess. Burning out the patience of his first wife, he married again and was, in his own way, a devoted spouse to his second wife. When the government arrested him in 1932 for the crime of celebrating Tsagaan Sar, he composed desperate love poems for her on small scraps of paper in his jail cell. While his restless spirit marked him as someone destined to perish in the idiotic brutality of the Great Purge, fate intervened. In 1937 he cheated Choibalsan and his henchmen of the chance to exterminate him. On a June evening, he died a penniless, inebriated death on an Ulan Bator street, like fellow artists Edgar Allan Poe and Stephen Foster. I often wonder about the incomplete poem that he was undoubtedly composing in his head as the shadows closed in.[3]

Moving from its contribution to the arts, the Green Domed Theatre was used for sinister purposes as well. The MPRP held its conferences there to slug out disputes over rightist and leftist deviations, collectivization programmes, anticlerical policies,

3. See Atwood at 400; see also Gerasimovich, and Hangin.

and internecine factional struggles. The Green Domed Theatre hosted the carefully staged and utterly mindless show trials of lamas and other class enemies during the Great Purge. Grainy black-and-white photos from the 1930s show Mongolians mingling outside the building as the proceedings were blared out by loudspeakers across the square. (If you have a masochistic desire to relive the interrogations of the hapless class enemies, then the reader is recommended to visit the local tax bureaus and lodge an appeal against a confiscatory tax decision. Or better yet, sit in the waiting area of a certain embassy and listen to a consular officer interrogate Mongolian visa applicants.) The theatre burned down in the 1940s, undoubtedly the revenge of maligned spirits who suffered unfairly here.

To the south of the Green Domed Theatre, Sükhbaatar Square was the main site for mass political demonstrations in the 1930s. Old photographs reveal people carefully lined up in processions around a wooden podium, decorated with large portraits of the Soviet leadership. This image invokes S. Buyannemekh's satirical poem 'The Seventy-Year-Old Woman and the Seven-Year-Old Boy Scout' which takes place against the backdrop of such a mass demonstration. In it, a young pioneer meets a confused old woman at the May Day celebrations. She mistakes the red scarf worn by the boy for a khadag, the caricatures of imperialists on posters for Buddhist protective deities, and the demonstration for a religious procession. As a Soviet academic observed, 'That which would not at all surprise the children of pre-revolutionary Mongolia would be alien and incomprehensible to today's children.'[4] And so must the pioneer feel the same confusion now in his old age at the onslaught of hip-hop and the tinsel of luxury goods.

After the Second World War, Sükhbaatar Square was paved, with no lesser dignitaries than 'Little Joe' Choibalsan and his sidekick, Tsedenbal, showing up to do a spot of physical labour by twirling a shovel for the camera. Nonetheless, Ulan Bator was still just barely reclaimed wilderness. At night, people needed to take care in walking across the square since wolves came down from the mountains looking for prey. From the vantage point of the Ulaanbaatar Hotel, a British diplomat noted that the immanence of nature was a vibrant element and not a distant memory in the capital city: 'As I sit and write, overlooking Peace Street, the main street of the town, I can see the beginning of the steppe about a mile away, with wooded hills white with frost rising beyond.'[5] Even in the 1990s cows and horses could still be seen rambling across the square, cropping the grass growing between the flagstones.

At the beginning of 1990, Sükhbaatar Square became the epicentre of Mongolia's democracy movement. Having been exposed to perestroika in the USSR and the collapse of communist regimes in East Europe, young Mongolians launched demonstrations with the support of workers, intellectuals, and lamas against the ham-fisted policies of the government. Hunger strikes and daily demonstrations shattered the mid-winter torpor of the capital. It was within the halls of the grey building on the

4. Gerasimovich at 63.
5. Hibbert at 20–21.

Political festival in front of the Green Domed Theatre during the 1930s. Photo by author.

square that Prime Minister Batmonkh made the decision to follow the lead of East European governments and voluntarily ordered the politburo to resign en masse.

Over the past century, the square has been the national stage upon which major events have unfolded: Choibalsan's funeral and burial, Tsedenbal's enthronement, May Day and Naadam celebrations, Brezhnev's 1966 visit, the temporary shelter set up for refugees of the Great Flood in the same year, the welcome ceremony for the Mongolian cosmonaut Jügderdemidiin Gürragchaa, the democratic revolution, the burning of Robert Friedland effigies, Christmas trees, and even an opening party in a temporary structure shaped like an Louis Vuitton suitcase for its flagship store next door in Central Tower. (And they say nothing ever happens in UB.)

The centrepiece of the square was, and is still, the equestrian statue of Sükhbaatar, placed at an auspicious spot. When the general rode into Urga to liberate it from the clutches of the capitalists and imperialists, he momentarily stopped to proclaim the altruistic objectives of the Red Army and its Mongolian partisans. As he spoke, his horse seized the opportunity for a prolonged bout of urination. (I have been trying to find a way to describe the event neutrally, but cultural normativism can only take you so far before things start sounding silly.) Some foresighted onlooker, whom history records as rejoicing in the name 'Bonehead' Gavaa, buried a marker there as a reminder of this auspicious spot, which is why the authorities positioned the statue here in 1947. (Before you accuse me of a cruel *South Park*–inspired joke by fabricating a story

Family day on the square. Photo by Janice Law.

about horse whizz, auspicious signs, and some guy called Bonehead, I refer you to the Wikipedia entry for Sükhbaatar Square or the locally printed *Ulaanbaatar City Guide*. As said many times before, 'You couldn't make this up if you tried.')

The traditional Mongolian script on the pedestal sets out a quote from Sükhbaatar:

> If we are able to unite our strength, then for us nothing will be impossible and we shall attain the heights of happiness for all.[6]

Astute students of Mongolian history will recognize this quote as part of a long and exasperating tradition of encouraging Mongolians to work together rather than against each other.

On the south side of the statue, you can barely make out a bas relief depicting Chinese gamin soldiers being given a bum's rush from the capital by Sükhbaatar and his boys on horseback. A recent renovation of the statue has obscured the image, perhaps intentionally. Nowadays, with a dependency on Chinese markets and investment, the authorities may have concluded that it is better to obfuscate this patriotic image. Throughout the history of the MPR, official publications sought to stir resentment at evildoers from the south without explicitly using the term *Chinese*. 'Manchu colonialism' was much decried.[7] Later such adventuring was attributed to the Kuomintang rather than to China per se once the Chinese Communists came to power. You need to speak in code if you want to keep a lid on the common loathing of China.

6. Montagu at 50.
7. See Sanjdorj.

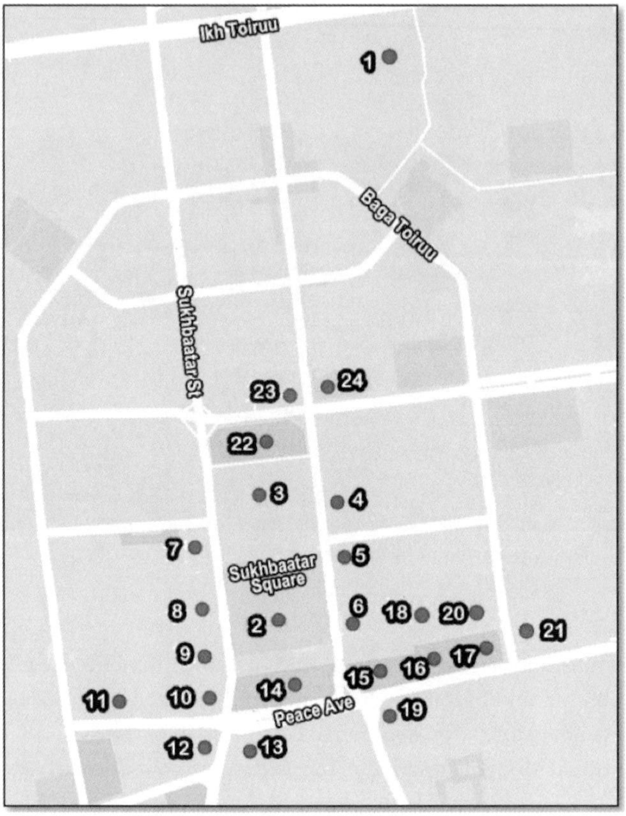

Central Ulaanbaatar. Map by Aubrey Ding-Shan Yang.

Key

1. Dashchoilin Monastery
2. Sükhbaatar Square
3. Government House
4. Site of former State Printing Press building
5. Central Cultural Palace
6. National Academic Theatre of Opera and Ballet
7. Site of former Trade Union Building
8. Site of former Altai Hotel
9. Mongolian Stock Exchange
10. Office of Telecommunications and Postal Services
11. General Post Office
12. Zorig statue
13. Site of former Lenin Club
14. Garden Park and World Peace Bell
15. Marco Polo statue
16. Mongolian herder statue
17. Ulaanbaatar Monument
18. Independence Palace
19. Ministry of Foreign Affairs
20. Ulaanbaatar Hotel
21. National Pedagogical University
22. Great State Seal Monument
23. Site of former Public Retail Store No. 8
24. National University of Mongolia

Equestrian statue of Sükhbaatar marks the spot. Photo by Janice Law.

Government House rose on the north side of the square with Soviet financial support and the additional boost of Japanese POW labour. Following the design of the Eastern Monastic Settlement, perhaps inadvertently, the situs of political power was placed on the north perimeter of the successor to the Yellow Palace's Central Square.

As a result of one week of warfare in August 1945, Soviet-Mongolian forces captured 15,000 Japanese soldiers, who were sent to Mongolia as prison labour for construction, logging, stone-cutting, and mining projects. Some were sent to build the rail line between Ulan Bator and the Soviet Union. Those Japanese who survived starvation and harsh treatment were repatriated in 1947, though five remained in the country facing charges of war crimes until finally freed in 1955. One prisoner recalled:

> I was sentenced to twenty years in June 1946 and put into prison . . . In this prison there were Japanese 'spies,' Chinese, Buryats, White Russians, Tibetans in addition to the Mongols—a total of approximately 800. They ranged from youths of about fifteen or sixteen to the very old. Without any clothes except for one flea-infested shirt, we worked around the clock from 7 am to 1:30 am In spite of the long hours of work, we were given very little to eat because of the food shortage. About 1950 or 1951, everyone came to recognize the good the Japanese had accomplished in Ulan Bator and this reflected on our lives in prison.[8]

Technical expertise and a good work ethic for free? What's not to love about involuntary labour? It is even better than unpaid internships.

The stern building earned an appropriate nickname, the 'Grey Palace', and housed a rubber-stamp legislature endorsing all decisions from the politburo. After Choibalsan's death in 1953 a mausoleum patently modelled on Lenin's Tomb in Red Square was

8. Rupen at 262.

constructed for the marshal's remains and the reinterred body of Sükhbaatar. The authorities sought to embalm Little Joe but found that they were too late—he was already rotten.

In the 2000s the government decided to give a facelift to this dreary building. Messrs Sükhbaatar and Choibalsan were dug up and popped into a smallish mausoleum in the Altan-Ölgii National Cemetery. The Lenin tomb replica was taken down, and a new modern pastiche was added to honour the ancient khans, complete with a seated statue of Chinggis Khan in imitation of the posture of Honest Abe in Washington, DC. Two other seated khans, Ogedei and Khublai, along with two standing generals, Muqali and Bo'orchu, are on his left and right flanks.

To the east of Government House, there is a barricaded construction site on the ruins of the former State Printing Press. The original building had been designed by the German architect Kavel Maher in the 1920s. It was a fine white two-storey building with large windows and graceful rooftop facades. The press took over the task of publishing reading material from Russian-run printing shops and the woodblock printers at the monasteries and turned publication into a state monopoly. By the early 1930s there was a profusion of publications following the progress made years earlier by Jamstrano with *Shine Toli*. There were even several issues of something called the *Lama News*, presenting a Marxist interpretation of theological topics in Mongolian and Tibetan before things turned nasty.

According to the word on the street, the sale of the State Printing Press site was the cause of former president Nambaryn Enkhbayar's conviction for corruption in 2012. Financing stalled for whatever building was planned to take the place of the State Printing Press, and it remained fenced in by a large blue aluminium border several metres tall, something like a modern equivalent of the wooden palisades that enclosed the khasaas in Urga. As a sign of the times, a foreign-invested mining company leased advertising space on the fence and erected a billboard in a propagandistic attempt to argue its position, and instil guilt, regarding the state's taxation laws on resource extraction. Right in the face of Government House, the billboard used the symbol of a Tsagaan Sar cake being disproportionately sliced up to make its point about the division of royalties and profits between the state and the company. Imagine the reaction of senators in Washington, DC, or Canberra to such a stunt pulled outside Capitol Hill or Parliament.

The Central Cultural Palace Building is the curious white-and-gold trimmed structure directly to the south of the construction site. Built in 1987 as a gift from the Soviet people, it is the home for the Mongolian National Gallery of Modern Art and the Mongolian Theatre Museum, both founded in the same year.

My fondest memory of the Central Cultural Palace Building is completely unrelated to what goes on inside: a stencilled graffiti portrait of Prince Damdinsuren on one of the outside columns. The prince was a spirited general who fought battles against warlord invaders in the southern part of the country during the autonomous period. In photographs, Damdinsuren comes across as a pretty tough customer (even though he had a penchant for wearing pointy hats). In 1920 the Peking gamin army in Urga tortured him to death (or in current neocon parlance, 'applied enhanced interrogation techniques with maximum prejudice'). As he was succumbing to his wounds, he asked that his comrades-in-arms in the prison prop him up against his cell wall so that in death his corpse would not be found bowing to his Chinese tormentors.

The stencilled graffiti was, I believe, a silent approbation to a government divorced from the realities of the ard as well as to the elites and their nativist wastrel offspring tooling around town in SUVs and listening to Kanye West.

Proceeding farther to the south, the orange neoclassical National Academic Theatre of Opera and Ballet of Mongolia is the nicest structure on the square. It is decorated with baroque ornaments that include Grecian dramatic masks, Doric columns, and a couple of crumbling concrete lions created by sculptors S. Choimbol, Davaatseren, and N. Jambaalt. Within the portico overhead are white plaster statues of four Mongolian musicians holding Mongolian instruments, each melding local motifs with classical forms. The theatre was designed by the Soviet architect Gerhard Kozel and completed in 1949.

During the 1950s Mongolian musicians were trained at the Bolshoi and elsewhere in the Soviet bloc in order to be able to bring Western opera to the steppes. Today, the theatre boasts a Mongolian and European repertoire, such as *Three Fateful Hills*, *The Magic Flute*, *Chinggis Khan*, and *Swan Lake*. While a night at the opera starts at the unusually early hour of 5:00 p.m., the quality of the opera is very satisfying. Not surprisingly, the performances are staged in a dark, moody ambiance consistent with older Russian traditions.

The Central Tower, completed in 2006, is the newest and most prestigious commercial eyesore in downtown Ulaanbaatar. Its ground level is renowned for leasing space to Eurotrash luxury stores selling worthless toys to the well-to-do, but this scope of business operations is not necessarily an adequate recipe for the quiet life. Not too long ago, the city was alive with rumours that a hyper-masculine Mongolian celebrity had an uncontrolled freak-out when the credit card facility at one store did not recognize his credit, thus launching the old bruiser into a tirade that led to him trashing the store. No wonder this purveyor of fine rubbish wanted to open a store in UB if it meant keeping *this* type of clientele out of its shops elsewhere in the region.

From here if you cast your eyes westward on the square, you will see a multistorey black behemoth structure built for the Ulaanbaatar municipal government. It goes by the apt nickname 'the Death Star'.[9]

On the north-west corner of the square is another neoclassical structure, the former Trade Union Council Building, now allocated to the Ulaanbaatar Bank and the municipal authorities. On its roof is the political slogan 'May Mongolia Prosper!' The next building to the south is the former Altai Hotel, completed in 1948. This was the first modern hotel to accommodate visitors from Communist bloc nations and the

9. I am grateful to Doug McGay for telling me about this.

occasional visitor from less confrontational countries like Denmark and Italy, as well as fellow travellers, like the British communist Ivor Montagu. It lost its status as Ulan Bator's primary hotel when the Ulaanbaatar Hotel opened its doors in 1961 around the corner.

The next main building to the south is the Mongolian Stock Exchange. This building was completed in 1948 as the Bat-Ochiryn Eldev children's cinema (named after a Mongolian politico of the 1930s) and later became simply the Children's Cinema. Its current deployment demonstrates the government's unintended talent for recycling old institutions for comparable purposes.

Mongolians have the same soft spot in their hearts for children as do the Russians. The Children's Cinema is a site of pleasant childhood memories for many Mongolians born in the 1970s. One friend recalls the enthusiasm in his circle when the cinema screened the North Korean epic *Hong Gil-Dong*, a transparently Marxist Robin Hood adventure set in the seventeenth century. It was also the closest a child could get to a James Bond flick in those days. The film became a status symbol, with one spoiled brat boasting about having seen the film forty-seven times in the same obsessive manner as today's Star Wars addicts.

The current use of the Children's Cinema as the Mongolian Stock Exchange makes me reflect upon the efforts of consultants to help Mongolia. I recall once seeing a partner from a major white-shoe law firm with the stock appearance of a lawyer typecast by Hollywood: chiselled Nordic features, blonde hair, unsmiling blue eyes, and a 'power tie'. He was being interviewed in the dining room of the Ulaanbaatar Hotel by foreign journalists. His brief was to bring the Mongolian Stock Exchange into line with global standards. I remember him saying, 'So we have seen a promising start, but obviously there remains a lot of work to be done.' Yes, he was certainly right about that, *since this interview happened over twenty years ago* and progress still remains illusionary in what is the world's smallest stock exchange. Later I was told that his pro bono measures amounted to photocopying the Delaware Company Act and posting it by FedEx to the Ministry of Finance. Contemporary legal advice from Wall Street firms still seems to involve printing standard form documents off the server and otherwise packaging documents with an indifference to whether the client understands the terms and conditions. Or maybe this level of advice is adequate—Mongolian governmental clients sometimes do not care about the legal consequences of their transactions so long as hidden agendas are served.

The Office of Telecommunications and Postal Services, constructed in the late 1940s, stands at the south-west corner of the plaza. It was recently defaced by an advertisement for a sugary carbonated beverage of zero nutritional value. Better to stick to kumis or *suutei tsai* or *arkhi* or just plain water so long as it has not been poisoned by the leather tanners along the Tuul River.

While we are on the topic of advertisements, billboards have defaced the appearance of the square, not to mention the entire city. Some former socialist states understand that national dignity is sometimes more valuable than the opportunity to make a cheap buck. Will some Mongolian statesman stand up for a removal of these visual blights from the square?

Attached to the Office of Telecommunications and Postal Services along Peace Avenue is, unsurprisingly, the General Post Office, another 1950s neoclassical concoction with stately Russian windows and high ceilings. It is one of the main sites in Ulaanbaatar for surrealistic professional advice on whether certain products imported by post for personal use are dutiable.

Across the street from the Telecoms Office is a statue of Sanjaasurengiin Zorig, the soft-spoken, modest, and highly principled architect of Mongolia's political revolution in 1990. His career arc began in the 1980s when, dissatisfied with the ossification of the MPR's government, he called for reforms modelled on Japan. In 1990 he was a leader of the student democracy demonstrations and afterwards became a major figure in the opposition Democratic Party as well as one of the drafters of the 1992 constitution. After being elected to Parliament, he went through the indignity of being a target of despicable insinuations because of his mixed Russian-Mongolian parentage. In 1996 his party joined the Democratic Coalition which had swept to power in the general election. Zorig distinguished himself from the run-of-the-mill politician by adhering to the highest ethical standards, a distinction that was to cost him gravely. In 1998 he was under consideration to be the prime minister–elect when unknown assassins broke into his apartment and murdered him.

Crossing Chinggis Avenue at the south-west corner of the square, we come to the former Lenin Club, built in 1929. The club went through several renovations over the decades but was nonetheless the main place for entertainment and social functions in Ulan Bator for many decades. Among its other uses, it was the first of many night clubs where young Mongolians discovered jazz music and ballroom dancing in the 1930s. During the Great Purge, these distractions rose to frenetic levels as an escape from the pressure of the show trials. Myself, I love the image of young Mongolians dancing to the 'King Porter Stomp' or being serenaded by one of the handful of Soviet jazz bands. The notion of Soviet jazz at that time ought not to be too much of a surprise—even Shostakovich wrote his jazz suites during Moscow's own show trials.[10]

These days, the former Lenin Club has hit hard times. After a brief stint under new management as the Saint Petersburg Club, the building now stoops to renting commercial space to convenience stores selling faulty goods (like matches that do not spark), stationery stores trading in overpriced A4 paper, and a garish billboard that all but covers the club's facade on the plaza.

Next to the Lenin Club stands the Blue Sky Tower and Hotel, an eyesore made in imitation of Dubai's overdone hotel with its dhow sail design. (The relevance of this motif to a landlocked country remains unclear.) More importantly, there is an unexplained mystery about why it took so long for the building to receive its occupancy permits from the governmental authorities. For months, unproven rumours abounded

10. See Starr for an extensive discussion of the vicissitudes of Soviet jazz from the earliest days to 1980.

about structural flaws, which somehow disappeared, perhaps pursuant to the magical formula to be found in the flash of a brown envelope.

Across Peace Avenue, 'Garden Park', which looks neither like a garden nor a park, was originally a larger attempt at greenery on the edge of the Gobi Desert. Old photographs indicate that it used to occupy more surface area, but today new construction encroaches as relentlessly on the park as did the Chinese merchants on the pathway for the Maitreya procession. Accentuating the free-market values of the age, the government has turned the south end of the square into an open-air car park, with plans to build a multilevel one on the same spot. Nonetheless, Garden Park does have a few things that are worth a remark or two.

Directly to the south of Government House is a pavilion constructed for the World Peace Bell, a gift to Mongolia from the United Nations Association of Japan some fifty or sixty years ago. It was cast from coins collected from children around the world. On World Peace Day (21 September), representatives of Mongolia's religions take a break from competing in the market place of beliefs to come here and ring the bell for peace. If the ceremony could be more efficacious and, say, induce heart attacks in neocon foreign-policy geniuses in the world's capitals, I would be out there every day ringing away like mad. Alas, alas.

Further to the east, you will come to a bronze statue of Marco Polo, with a feathered cap and pigeon roosting on his shoulder, across from the Ministry of Foreign Affairs. Since we have no true portraits of the famed Venetian, one wonders about the inspiration for these avian touches. But more importantly, it is far from certain whether the Venetian ever made it this far north in the course of his wanderings in Kublai's empire. A better choice for 'whitey on the square' would have been the long-forgotten French silversmith, Guillaume Boucher, who actually lived and worked in Mongolia.[11]

Guillaume was a Parisian artisan who was employed to cast silver liturgical artwork for the Francophile court in Hungary. His timing for this commission left something to be desired. Shortly after he arrived in the dual capital of Buda-Pest, Ogedei Khan seized the city and forced its craftsmen to Central Asia to be put to work for the family business. In his thirteenth-century account of travelling, on foot, from the Black Sea region to Mongolia, the famous Flemish Catholic ambassador William of Rubruck found Guillaume busily at work in his silversmith studio in Kharakhorum. Guillaume designed and built the renowned silver tree fountain which dispensed, as a classic example of medieval Mongolian multiculturalism, mead, rice wine, grape wine, and kumis.[12] The fountain used hydraulic pressure to force the beverages into pipes within the tree trunk and on up to be dispensed by spouts at the top of the tree. On top of the structure stood a silver angel blowing a trumpet, which must have looked inspiring even without being hammered by mixing kumis and grape wine. A fanciful

11. For a delightful little book recounting the story of Boucher, see Olschki. For more on the Catholic missions to Mongolia, see Dawson, Rubruck, and Spuler.
12. Rubruck at 208.

eighteenth-century Dutch impression of the Silver Tree of Kharakhorum graces the 5,000-togrog note as a reminder of this foreign craftsman (and his involuntary labour) who unquestionably lived and worked in Mongolia.

Continuing a little further to the east, there is a bronze statue of what appears to be a cowboy astride a bucking bronco by Frederic Remington, the nineteenth-century artist who was famous for his paintings and sculptures of scenes from the American Wild West. Like Norman Rockwell's paintings on the covers of *The Saturday Evening Post*, Remington's style and subject matter traded on sentimental images of an America that was, like its native population, already in the process of being exterminated. Photographs from the early 1950s reveal that it was already in situ in Ulan Bator in 1955, a time of rising tension with the United States and all things American.

Closer inspection reveals that the bronze is actually of a Mongolian herder taming a wild horse. While the bronze's style appears to be borrowed from Remington, it creates a false impression of a similarity between the cultures of the American cowboy and the Mongolian herder. Mongolian herders have a far more caring and gentle relationship with livestock because of their reverence for nature. Animals were not just a source of wages but supplied food, housing, clothing, fuel, and transport—in essence, the sustenance of life on the steppes. 'The best symbol of the difference between the American West and Mongolia is the cowboy eating canned, corned beef. This, to a Mongol, would be just fantastic.'[13]

Moving on to the east, you will come across a statue of a dragon-faced tortoise with a stela on his back. This type of statue has been used in China since the third century CE and then later throughout Central Asia, Japan, and Korea. Stone tortoises mark a historical event or commemorate a literary or other achievement by a worthy individual. While this marker does not purport to derive from distant antiquity—it was erected by the municipal authorities in 1994—it is said to be the location of a *balbal* statue that had been set up at the centre of the settlement in 1778.

The historical record on this is murky. Balbals are Türkic statues found throughout Central Asia all the way to the Caspian, the Ukraine, and East Prussia. As of the middle of the first millennium CE (and possibly much earlier), such memorials were placed over the graves of local chieftains, but their purpose is uncertain in the absence of written records. They might represent the chieftain over whose tomb they stand or a spirit that had been drafted to serve as the guardian of the tomb. In the latter case, this might have been a reworking of the ancient practice of walling in soldiers or ministers in the chieftain's tomb to join him in the afterlife.

As far as I have been able to determine, the site acquired the name of the Hollow of the Stone Man in ancient times. Perhaps a balbal had stood on this site for centuries. However, it is even less clear why this site should be regarded as the founding place for the city in 1778. As already explained, the 'city' of Urga was wherever the ruling patriarch was to be found. These residences did not 'settle down' until 1855.

13. Lattimore (1941) at 186–87.

More disturbingly, there was an ancient tradition of immuring a person to be the protector spirit of a city elsewhere in Asia. Was some poor 'volunteer' selected for this detail back in antiquity? Or in 1778? And if so, why? It is a strange choice if this date alludes to the decision of the Qing colonial government to let Urga report directly to the court. This ought not to be a foundation date since this was an act by the Manchus, not Mongolians.

Near here, Ulaanbaatar experienced its first riot since the years of pitched battles between lamas and Chinese traders. It broke out after the general election in July 2008. It had been widely rumoured that the MPRP had rigged the vote, sparking protests which turned violent. The masses burned out the MPRP headquarters, a building humbly named the Independence Palace, and looted nearby museums. Four people were shot and another died from poisonous gases emitted by the fire. In the aftermath, the MPRP elected to form a coalition government with the opposition DPP as a way to bury the hatchet (and a few unfortunately placed demonstrators).

Later, the MPRP cum MPP built a new, taller, and bigger modern headquarters in its place with generous subsidies from the government and donations by its membership. The rebuilt 'palace' opened its doors in November 2011. Its luxurious decoration and construction materials compel some to wonder about the construction cost for the 'palace' compared to the state budget for healthcare facilities, air pollution prevention, and utilities for newly settled herders in the ger district. But the shiny elegance of the building distinctly shows that thanks to its old pedigree, the MPP does understand how to get things done. Certain things, that is.

The Ulaanbaatar Hotel, completed in 1961, appears on the north side of Peace Avenue to the east of the Independence Palace. This site was where the Manchu and Mongolian ambans set up their residences in the late eighteenth century. The Ulaanbaatar Hotel itself comes in for quite a roasting in most travelogues about Mongolia. While Owen Lattimore politely commented on its 'Danish' interior design, nearly all other writers were unable to resist taking a kick at this testimonial to Prime Minister Tsedenbal's addiction to all things Soviet. Perhaps the most insightful comment came from Reginald Hibbert, the first British diplomat resident in Mongolia that the hotel staff seemed to play at running a hotel rather than really running one.[14] (His views were not a toss-away comment of some smug interloper; the British embassy was initially located on the second floor of the hotel.) The little wings on the sixth floor at the western and eastern ends of the building were presented as a creative advance in architectural form at the time but fail to elicit the slightest notice today. The boredom associated with a posting in Ulan Bator used to lead the diplomatic inmates of the hotel to wager on which of the elevators on each side of the main stair case would arrive first when summoned. Certainly, its restaurants never passed the test of demanding Western foodies in the pre-capitalist era. Indeed, in 1993 a carrot was the closest you could come to a green leafy vegetable in the dining hall. Westerners compared the nightlife in the hotel's pub to the barroom scene from Star Wars.

14. Hibbert at 156.

Nowadays, the owners of the privatized Ulaanbaatar Hotel assert that it is a five-star institution. Since there are no global criteria to regulate this certification, *any* hotel can assert that it provides five-star accommodations. Well, if President Obama can win the Nobel Peace Prize and then fling predatory drones at Muslim weddings in Waziristan, it must be all right for the Ulaanbaatar Hotel to give itself five stars.

Formerly, a statue of Lenin with a rapidly advancing gait stood in front of the hotel. He has now been replaced by a sedentary statue of the writer Natsagdorj, which had been set up in the Children's Park in 1968. The park surrounding the statue has been a notorious after-hours pick-up point for libidinous old men and young women looking to earn some extra cash.

Across the street, the Ministry of Foreign Affairs, with its olive walls and steeple-like obelisk, was designed by N. M. Tschepetilnikov, the architect who also designed the State University of Mongolia and Choibalsan's former residence on what is now Seoul Street. Due to the encroachment of high-rise buildings, it has lost its former majesty as the diplomatic centre of what once was one of the two independent sovereign states of Central Asia (the other being Afghanistan).

Across the street from the Garden Park and the Ulaanbaatar Hotel is the National Pedagogical University. It too was a part of government office buildings built in the early 1950s (though its third floor was a later addition). On its roof there are signs that proclaim in Cyrillic and in ancient script: 'Let the Mongolian Spirit Flourish Forever' along with our khangarid winking at us from the Ulaanbaatar municipal emblem.

Retracing our steps to the north side of Government House, our tour takes us to a park that is notable for its statue of the Great State Seal of Mongolia, a monument erected in 2007. It is scarcely noticed by visitors to the building.

In Asia a seal was a token of the authority and the right to rule, similar to a crown or a sceptre. It also served the practical function of indicating the irrevocable acceptance or authentication by the state of the terms of any document to which it was affixed. In other words, it was the 'official' signature of a state or a government. When Sükhbaatar and his revolutionaries first presented a letter without the Bogd Khan's seal to the Irkutsk Bolsheviks, the commissars advised the embryonic MPP that it needed to get its own seal tout de suite for official correspondence. The personal use of seals is still carried on in Mongolia and elsewhere in the form of the 'stamps' used on binding contracts and other documents to confirm the commitment of its owner.

Chinese emperors held the seals of their predecessors and the preceding dynasties as a symbolic demonstration of their right to rule. This same significance was attached to the state seals of other Asian powers. Popular culture referred to this custom in the first Mongolian feature-length film, *Tsogt Taij* in the scene where the dying Ligdan Khan expresses his concern for the whereabouts of the state seal.[15]

The Great State Seal monument is a large-scale replica of the seal used by the prime minister. The elevation and departure of a prime minister to or from office is

15. The film *Tsogt Taij* can be viewed with English subtitles at https://www.youtube.com/watch?v=pmZTeLPL17U.

accompanied by a formal ceremony that features its handover from or to the speaker of the Parliament. Along the base of the monument base are Hunnu-Syanbi runic symbols representing the ancient alphabet and names of the various tribes that roamed the steppes before and after the Christian era. On the top of the monument is a lion, a symbol of power and sanctity as we have already discussed. On each side of the square pedestal is a replica of the impression of state seals used through Mongolian history. On the south side of the monument, in a place of honour and facing Government House, is a replica of the great seal used during the Yuan Empire. On the west is a copy of the Bogd Khan's seal. The northern side shows the seal approved by the Great Hural in 1924 for use by the MPR government. On the east is a replica of the impression made by the state seal under the 1992 Constitution.

Across the street from the park and along the first ring road are surviving examples of neoclassical residential projects from the 1950s. Sadly, these housing estates enclose communal courtyards that are crowded with opportunistic additions, and their exterior is marred by uncoordinated extensions for shopfronts. At least some of these extensions provide an opportunity for convivial nourishment. On the south-east corner of the housing estate is Le French Bistrot, a fine dining venue, which is located in a building that once housed a shop with the punchy name Public Retail Store No. 8. A few doors down is Le Triskell, specialising in fine Breton crepes and hard cider.

In the area bounded by the first ring road you come across a neighbourhood that better preserves the image of the city from a time of more careful urban design. In and around the buildings for the German and Cuban embassies are tree-lined streets with modest-sized buildings designed to create a notion of community. These days, the area is a site for restaurants, bars, and antique shops and makes for a pleasing stroll.

Off to the north-east of the park are the neoclassical buildings of the National University of Mongolia. Completed in in 1947, this institution of higher learning was originally named Choibalsan State University. A statue of Choibalsan still stands in front of the entranceway to the university, impervious to the change in temperament that has run his buddies Vladimir and Uncle Joe out of town on a rail.

Choibalsan's legacy is surprising to outsiders. Instead of being reviled for mass murder and torture, some people argue that he should be given the benefit of the doubt (as if there are two sides to the question of an atrocity). Others excuse him by challenging critics to explain 'what else could he have done in such challenging times', moving the conversation away from what he did do and whether he deserves to have a statue in his memory. For his fans, he is regarded as a national hero who kept Stalin's expansion at bay. Others claim that he was an emanation of Jamsran.

Inside the main courtyard of the university, away from the street, there is a semi-circular auditorium. This was the site of an unusually civil debate in the middle of the Cold War. In 1961 United States Supreme Court Justice William O. Douglas visited Mongolia in a bit of personal diplomacy to encourage official communication between Ulan Bator and Washington.

Justice Douglas was a gruff, cantankerous Woody Guthrie–style leftist who stood firmly on the side of civil rights, individual privacy, and the environment during the flowering of the Roosevelt Republic. As a youth, he worked with the International Workers of the World and supported political programmes to give the working class an even chance in sharing the blessings of this world. His arch-conservative opponents gave him the disparaging nickname 'Wild Bill' because of his down-to-earth cowboy manners, his love of nature, and his general lack of bourgeois refinement. (I do not know if he met Jamsrangiyn Sambuu, but the two of them might have gotten on like a house on fire, shooting back glasses of arkhi and exchanging stories about living off the country and herding livestock.)

Bill acquitted himself superbly in Ulan Bator during his lecture at the university. Photographs show him at the lectern in the auditorium with murals of Soviet luminaries on the walls looming over him. His commitment to individual liberty was at the core of his jurisprudence and his ideal of Western liberalism:

> Progress could not be determined merely by the amount of food production, factories, hospitals and doctors – important as they were. Progress, I said, could be judged only by taking into account spiritual values. 'I would judge a society by a poet's standard,' I said. 'Is the mind free? Is it allowed to explore all horizons? Or does some official say, 'This you shall not believe, that you shall not publish'? No torrent of denunciation descended on me, as it has on similar occasions in Russia.[16]

In an article in *National Geographic Magazine* the globetrotting justice elaborated on the breath of fresh air and open-mindedness that he encountered from his Mongolian hosts:

> No group placed a Marxist roadblock across our conversation, as is done in Russia, though we often stirred the coals of controversy. My statement, made again and again, that Karl Marx could not possibly have written *Das Kapital* if he had lived in the United States in the mid-twentieth century, was met with interest, not antagonism. The capitalism about which Marx wrote, I told them, was as long buried as their ancient capital, Karakorum.[17]

I wonder if Bill might be tempted to revise this view these days.

For this jurist who had worked his way on a cattle-freight train from his native Washington state to study law at Columbia University, it was in his character to extend the hand of friendship and goodwill to Mongolia. His trip gave the small handful of American Mongolists cause to hope for a new era in the relationship between Central Asia and the United States. Alas, other earth-shaking crises in the Cold War's Manichaean clash submerged any constructive thinking among the denizens of Foggy Bottom, who would not listen to him. Diplomatic ties only came about seven years after Douglas' death while other more important foreign events, like meeting the national security threat posed by Grenada, preoccupied the thinking of the Masters of the Beltway.

---

16. Douglas at 345.
17. Ibid.

7

To the South of Sükhbaatar Square

To the south-west of Sükhbaatar Square, there is a single-storey brown building on the west side of Chinggis Avenue, currently serving as the district headquarters of the Democratic Party. It was built in the constructivist style in the early 1930s for the Ministry of Animal Husbandry and Crops, and later, in the 1950s, it housed the Montsame News Agency, the MPR's equivalent of Tass or Xinhua.

There are photographs of the building taken in the 1930s showing a huge fleet of automobiles parked in front for use by state officials, perhaps a karmic foreshadowing of the traffic now choking Chinggis Avenue. Since traffic jams ceaselessly impinge on our exploration of the city from here, this is a good spot for a brief digression about the Mongolian love affair with the combustion engine.

These contraptions first appeared in Urga during the Peking-to-Paris automobile race of 1907, an event for the idle rich at the outset of the motor age and one that continues today for idle rich adventure tourists.[1] In 1915 the Bogd Khan imported the first car, a Ford Model T from Tianjin along with the kerosene needed to power it. From this humble start, within a decade Mongolians embraced the automobile with the same gusto that they once reserved for fine horseflesh. According to Lattimore, Mongolians quickly developed discerning tastes; the most popular make was the older Ford Model A instead of the more stylish later models with low ground clearance. The older model was designed for America's unpaved roads, making them ideally suited to Mongolia's dirt tracks. The ongoing importance of ground clearance on rough roads is the obvious reason why today Ulaanbaatar is awash with SUVs.

By the late 1920s automobiles had become such a hallmark of prestige and privilege for cadres that they attracted satirical commentary. In 'A Story of Cars', S. Buyannemekh used the literary device of giving voice to inanimate objects in order to comment on the prevailing abuse of prerogative. In the story, two state automobiles lament the treatment meted out by their owners-officials. One complains, 'I went with the boss to the public baths, then to the meat bazaar, and to the Russian and Mongolian shops; we bought bread, sugar, and cigarettes . . . and now I am taking the boss home.' The other emits this *cri de cœur*:

---

1. Le Munyon at 661. For the Peking-to-Paris race, see Barzini.

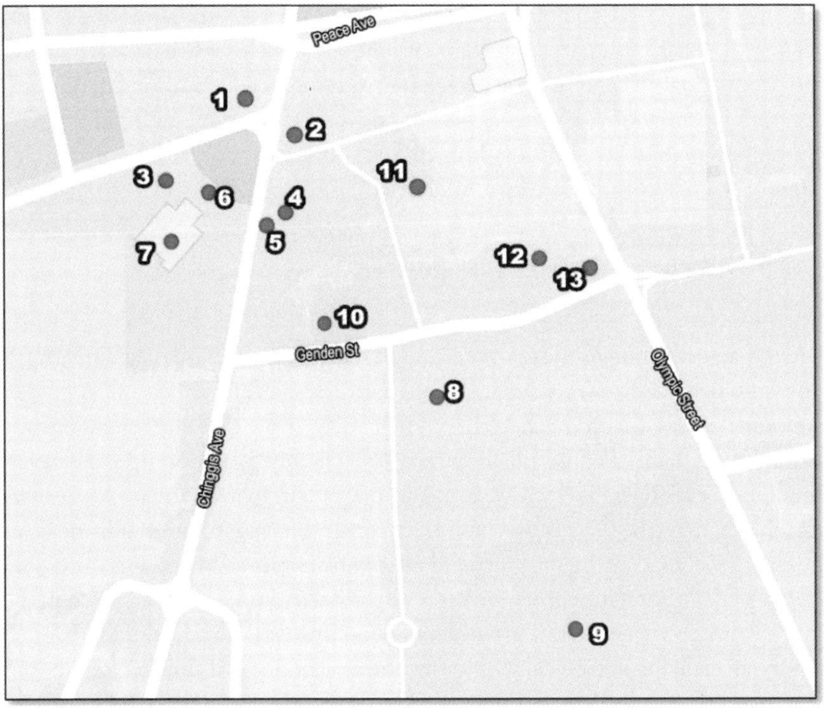

South of Sükhbaatar Square. Map by Aubrey Ding-Shan Yang.

Key

1. Site of former Ministry of Animal Husbandry
2. Site of former Bambaruush Kafe
3. Grand Khan Irish Pub / Suit Fight Club
4. Central Library
5. Rinchen statue
6. Tsedenbal statue
7. State Drama Theatre
8. Children's Centre
9. Children's Park
10. Exhibition Hall
11. Temple of Choijin Lama
12. Wedding Palace
13. Memorial Museum for Victims of Political Repression

> Oh, our boss calls me a state car but he is wholly unaware of what mercy is. Day and night he arranges to transport his household, he crams in up to ten people not caring whether or not there is room. On sand, over rocks, he flies at top speed. I am exhausted. I have no more strength, all my nuts and bolts are loose, my wheels are broken and there is no one to pity me![2]

In the 1930s Mongolia imported Ford Model A automobiles manufactured by the joint venture between Ford Motors and the Soviet car manufacturer GAZ in Moscow. As the Soviet auto industry developed, Volga sedans, Lada compacts, and

2. Gerasimovich at 46.

the ubiquitous grey UAZ-452 off-road vans arrived to share Ulan Bator's streets with herders on horseback. After 1990, western automobile franchises began to sell luxury cars while individual entrepreneurs arranged for the importation of second hand automobiles from Japan. Soon UB's streets were impossibly congested.

Current driving habits owe something to past equestrian practices as noted in this observation by a nineteenth-century traveller:

> An abundance of space naturally has an influence on how the Mongols relate to those around them; for example, when walking or riding horses, Mongols are never concerned with avoiding collisions with others.[3]

Directly across Chinggis Avenue is a round building that was once the Bambaruush Kafe (or Cafe Bear-Cub), a restaurant famous for its sweets and ice cream. A golden statue of a little bear sat up on the roof of the cafe to show that the restaurant was meant for 'young cubs'. People still respond with dreamy-eyed nostalgia on recalling childhood occasions, like birthdays and primary school graduations, when their parents took them to the Cafe Bear-Cub for ice cream sundaes, followed by a movie at the Children's Cinema or a merry-go-round ride at the Children's Park. It is a pity that this symbol of childhood innocence and its sentimental memories was sacrificed in the wake of privatization. In a later incarnation, the building was the home of the Havana Moon pub, specializing in tropical mojitos for the very untropical climate. It is now an outlet for overpriced cashmere products.

Set back across the street is the Grand Khan Irish Pub (or 'Irish' as it is universally called by Mongolians), a dining institution for the local elite and expatriates and perhaps the most successful of all the ersatz Irish pubs in Ulaanbaatar. At the time of the short-lived investment boom of 2012, the 'Irish' experienced a veritable invasion of grey-suited foreigners scheming to cut 'megabuck' deals in the resource sector while keeping an anxious eye on their luxury watches so they wouldn't miss the next flight home. It is said that one night two rival gangs of roving investment bankers had an exchange of words that degenerated into an all-out brawl. I wonder if they ate the wounded.

Sitting outside on the porch of the Irish on a summer evening, you might witness motorcycle aficionados parading past on their bikes and making an infernal racket. This nuisance too has a long pedigree as seen in this account from the 1920s:

> One of the strongest men in Mongolia was the war minister, Danzan . . . We often saw him in his Mongolian riding dress driving through the streets of Urga in a rattling 'Harley-Davidson', which set camels and ponies off at a gallop.[4]

Across Chinggis Avenue is the yellow neoclassical State Central Library, an underfunded repository for priceless historical documents and cultural artefacts. It always reminds me of a conference held there long ago to honour Owen Lattimore, an unconventional if not heroic scholar of Central Asia.

3. Price at 243.
4. Haslund at 74.

The 'Irish' featuring Guinness stout and investment bankers in cage fights. Photo by Janice Law.

Lattimore learned to speak Mandarin like a native while growing up in the Chinese coastal city Tianjin. As a young man, he worked as a purchasing agent for a foreign export trade company, and, among other duties, Lattimore travelled throughout North China collecting raw wool for shipment to the coast. Unlike other Westerners of his era, Lattimore took delight travelling in person with trade caravans to remote oasis towns and obscure villages in Inner Mongolia where he soon picked up Mongolian. Without the tedium of a higher degree, Lattimore embarked upon a career as a scholar who penned influential accounts of Central Asian life, history, and culture.

During the Second World War, Lattimore encouraged the Roosevelt administration to rally in support of Mongolian sovereignty. In 1944 he accompanied United States Vice President Henry Wallace on a goodwill mission to Siberia, China, and Mongolia where he met Choibalsan and interpreted for the vice president. Lattimore convinced Wallace about the progress that Mongolia had made since 1921 and urged him to recommend the United States government to reject any proposal for the restoration of Chinese sovereignty.[5]

In 1950 Lattimore was a professor at Johns Hopkins University when Senator Joseph McCarthy accused him of being a high-ranking Soviet spy who had disclosed state secrets to Moscow. (The only significant state secret known to Lattimore might have been that the State Department had no clue about dealing with Asia, but never mind.) Summoned to testify before Congress, Lattimore fought back tenaciously. At the outset of the Senate hearings, he condemned McCarthy to his face and vigorously defended his professional record against this abuse of congressional authority. While expressing his feisty contempt for McCarthy and other red-baiters, he called out their

5. Baabar at 402, quoting Clubb at 348.

deceit unflinchingly as the true threat to national security. It took Lattimore five years to prevail over an accusation of perjury but, in the end, with the assistance of attorney Thurman Arnold, he was acquitted of all charges. It was also an unrecoverable loss of five prime years stolen from his professional life.

There were few people in Lattimore's corner for this battle. While Johns Hopkins University stood by Lattimore, it did so with little relish and more in the interest of asserting its administrative independence than protecting freedom of inquiry. Lattimore could only count on feeble support from most fellow scholars while the Communist bloc resoundingly condemned his non-Marxist interpretation of Asian culture and accused him of being an American spy. Once the worst of the witch-hunt was over, the administration of Johns Hopkins University treated him with indifference. He left the United States to pursue a more rewarding and remunerative career setting up the East Asian studies programme at Leeds University, which continues to turn out superb Asia specialists.[6]

At the time of its accession to the United Nations, Lattimore was invited to visit Mongolia despite discouragement from Johns Hopkins. His new friends and fellow scholars in Ulan Bator showed him the utmost respect, finding him to be a perceptive and respectful intellectual who acquired his insights through empirical experience on the caravan trail with common herders rather than through the narrow prism of diplomacy, espionage, or academia. (There can be a thin line separating those three.) His books are brilliant in their analysis of Central Asian life and history while his legacy stands for a combination of intellectual perceptiveness, integrity, and empathy.

In 1969 the MPR's Academy of Sciences paid Lattimore the sublime honour by inducting him as its first non-Mongolian member. At the induction ceremony in one of the conference rooms in the State Central Library, Lattimore gave a speech in fluent Mongolian and tied it off with an alliterative Mongolian song-poem that he composed himself. His hosts were awed by the performance of this undemonstrative owlish man. I imagine him walking out the Library and down its stairs with a sprightly step afterwards, cherishing this affirmation of his knowledge and character.

In front of the Central State Library is a statue of Byambyn Rinchen, a board member of the Academy of Sciences at the time of Lattimore's induction and a celebrated scholar of Mongolian folklore. Ironically, a statue of Stalin had once occupied the plinth where Rinchen now stands.

By the end of the communist era, the Stalin statue had sunk to the level of being a well-known rendezvous point for exchanging foreign currency on the black market. British journalist James Pringle recorded that the black-market rate yielded twenty-five togrogs to one US dollar as opposed to three togrogs at the official rate in 1989. 'You make the connection beneath Stalin's statue, and the money exchange is effected outside a nearby lamasery.'[7]

6. For the saga of Lattimore's trials and tribulations, see Lewis.

7. Pringle at 33.

The student demonstrators pulled down the Stalin statue during the 1990 revolution. For a while, a large talismanic stone replaced the 'Engineer of Souls' in a bow to traditional shamanism.[8] Soon, Rinchen climbed up on the plinth, and the statue of Stalin was moved to one of UB's strip clubs, a fate that might have pleased the old lecher. It is now said that he is in a box behind the library, which goes to show the inelasticity of karmic retribution.

Rinchen is a revered figure today though he endured campaigns of political repression from time to time during his career. He was born on the northern Mongolian border and grew up in Kiakhta when it was a major commercial and cultural crossroad like Dejima or Kalimpong. Rinchen came of age as the new and the old mixed freely, allowing him to acquire a cosmopolitan viewpoint while being well-versed in Mongolian traditions. He learned Russian and Manchu and later studied at the Oriental Institute in Leningrad from 1923 to 1927. Afterwards, he returned to Ulan Bator to join the Writers' Circle, penning anticlerical poetry (with unflinchingly partisan titles such as 'For the Yellow Parasites'). At one point during the Great Purge, he was slated for execution but he was spared that fate because of a bureaucratic oversight. In the 1940s he began his rise as a scholar at the Academy of Sciences, the State University, and the State Printing Press. In 1947 he translated the *Communist Manifesto* into Mongolian (which raises the question whether anyone before that date actually knew what all this Marxism stuff was about. Perhaps the politicos just learned enough to mouth the vocabulary as some undoubtedly do now when towing the Washington Consensus line). In 1956 Rinchen published a historical novel, *The Rays of Dawn*, which told the story of a Mongolian family experiencing the tumult of the early twentieth century.

Rinchen deeply mourned the demise of the traditional Mongolian script and the adoption of Cyrillic as the official alphabet. He foresaw that this would cut off Mongolians from centuries of folklore, legend, and wisdom. This, he knew, would yield a loss of identity that could never be remedied by any amount of socialist literature, such as the 1948 Stalin Prize–winning blockbuster *Steel and Slag*.[9] He went so far with his irrepressibly impish instinct for satire to write a poem about the failure of the Phags-pa script in the thirteenth-century Yuan dynasty, implicitly ridiculing the conversion to Cyrillic in his day. His masterful command of Mongolian lore and wisdom allowed him to skewer the geniuses in charge, often without their knowing it. Rinchen also took immeasurable delight in bursting the balloon of pompous Soviet Mongolian specialists, who paraded about town like Russian Colonel Blimps and inevitably fell victim to his practical jokes and subtle put-downs. Scholars beyond the Iron Curtain with a genuine interest in Mongolia found him to be an open-hearted and delightful gentleman who cherished the opportunity to bring Mongolian studies into the global mainstream of learning. His correspondence with the Indian scholar Lokesh Chandra

8. Juergensmeyer at 120.
9. If you can find a copy of *Steel and Slag*, you can kill time stone dead by reading this drama on the heroic efforts of the manager of Soviet steel foundry to meet higher production quotas from the state.

is filled with wonderful allusions to Indian legends that were still being retold around the hearths of herders' gers. In his letters, he jotted down aphorisms written in all the different Mongolian scripts that had been in use since the thirteenth century.[10]

Because of his unwillingness to follow the lead of the MPRP uncritically, the party condemned him as a bourgeois nationalist in 1959 and again in 1960 with several politburo members even threatening to have the old sage dragged away and shot for his counter-revolutionary views. Towards the end of his life, official harassment took the form of repeated demotions. This persecution hastened his death from cancer in 1977. (I always nod to his statue in homage when passing by the Library.)

In contrast to Rinchen, a statue of Prime Minister Tsedenbal stands across the street in front of the State Drama Theatre. Tsedenbal was an introspective loner who began his political ascent as a member of Choibalsan's inner circle. He was well-suited to the tastes of Moscow's power elite and, as a consequence of his deferential attitude to Moscow, in 1952 he inherited the position of prime minister, which he held until 1984. During his time in power he skilfully derailed any de-Stalinization programme encouraged by Khrushchev and deployed his favourite fine arts henchman 'Horsehead' Lhamsuren to crush intellectual or cultural innovations such as abstract art, folklore, survey-based sociology, or a reappraisal of Buddhist art and literature. He advocated unthinking reliance on Soviet models for development—the country just narrowly missed having Russian promulgated as its primary language of education—and helped to transplant the ennui of the Brezhnev stagnation to Mongolia. Thankfully, his three-volume work on political theory was never translated into English. In his last ten years of power, he suffered memory loss and dizziness, becoming increasingly erratic in his behaviour. His domineering Russian wife, Anastasia Ivanovna Filatova, wielded power in her own right because she enjoyed a close friendship with Leonid Brezhnev. In an unpardonable violation of old Soviet virtues, she refused to let her offspring play with 'Mongolian children' for fear of infectious diseases and shut them away in the gated communities for the elites.[11]

Tsedenbal is placed right across from Rinchen's statue, an irony that would not have been lost on the old master. Some bright light has given Tsedenbal a chair (no less) while Rinchen has to stand amid the diesel fumes on Chinggis Avenue. It goes to show that even in the afterlife doddering apparatchiks and party hacks still get better rations than maverick intellectuals.

Behind Tsedenbal we find the State Drama Theatre where local troupes perform both Mongolian and foreign plays. The theatre was constructed in 1960 on the basis of a design by B. Chimed, the architect of the Ulaanbaatar Hotel, and A. Khishigt. The Municipal Revolutionary Youth League provided support for the project—you can just barely make out the Mongolian Youth League logo over the portico—after it turned a leaf towards pacific endeavours. (The league started out as a radical wing of the MPRP responsible for the leftist excesses in the 1930s.) The building has a square

10. See Chandra.

11. Atwood at 548–49.

cupola derived from Buddhist temples, a touch that is reminiscent of Ginzburg's theory for the combination of national character and modern forms. This impression is reinforced by the neoclassical Doric columns cleverly decorated with Mongolian ornamental touches, such as horse heads and the three jewels.

The State Drama Theatre hosts Mongolian and foreign plays as well as folk music performances. Mongolian drama remains mostly unknown outside the country. Its origins are rooted in seventeenth-century Buddhism when lamaseries staged religious-themed pantomime morality plays for the spiritual cultivation of monks. Gradually, the characters were given voice as performances spread from the monastic centres to ger encampments.

A drama from Tibet, *The Journey into Hell*, became popular in late eighteenth-century Mongolia. Its main character is Lady Choidshid, who, falling into delirium from a severe fever, dreams that she has died and descends into the kingdom of the underworld where she witnesses the judgement of the dead before Erlig Khan, the bullheaded king of hell. Erlig Khan reviews each person's life and demands that they answer for, defend, or explain their choices. When he comes to Lady Choidshid, the king consults his records and tells her that her time has not yet come. She then awakens and exhorts one and all to follow the dharma.

The Journey into Hell enjoyed enduring popularity with successive generations of Mongolians. The German Mongolist Walther Hessig recalled how Mongolian exchange students in the 1920s could recite sections by heart, just as his German students might have been able to do with *The Threepenny Opera* or, for those from a lesser age, *The Rocky Horror Picture Show*.

Traditional Mongolian drama reached its zenith with a nineteenth-century play attributed to poet, iconoclast, and 'mad monk' Danzanravjaa. Born in 1803 to a poor herding family, Danzanravjaa grew up in a Nyingma monastery where the lamas concluded that he was the fifth incarnation of the Noyin Khutugtu. Since the monastery did not adhere to the doctrines of Gelukpa discipline and its vows of celibacy, Danzanravjaa took to this license with gusto, having two wives and a taste for strongly distilled inspiration. This mad monk travelled throughout the steppes, observing the follies of society in a combination of light-heartedness, irony, and melancholy that underlay his anti-establishment feelings. He despised the pomposity of Manchu officials and their impositions on the ard, and the officials, in turn, hated him as an irritant to the existing order.

As a two-fisted troublemaking drinker, womanizer, and radical poet-priest, the ecclesiastical authorities denied Danzanravjaa entry to Urga on one occasion, hoping to leave him stranded and alone on the south bank of the Tuul River. Not one to walk away from a fight, he retaliated by throwing his own festival of music and poetry there, something that must have been the best counterculture concert before Monterey Pop. He met his end poisoned by a former lover recruited by the Manchu court or one of its local quislings.

In 1831 Danzanravjaa's rewrote *The Life History of the Moon Cuckoo*, a well-known morality play that had been previously performed as a staged narrative. Perhaps following the conventions of Peking opera, Danzanravjaa added dialogue and music with lyrics to be sung by the actors and actresses—Mongolians had no hang-ups against women appearing on stage—moving the story beyond pantomime to drama. He also took on the role of theatrical director. The performers wore Peking opera make-up painted directly on their faces instead of wearing Tsam masks. The opera was a smash sensation in eastern Mongolia.

The title of the opera refers to cuckoos stealing the nests of other birds. The play relates the tale of a Buddhist prince and his karmic destiny. As the opera opens, the father of the prince arranges for Lagayana, the son of an aristocrat, to be raised as the prince's playmate and best friend. Unknown to the characters, a karmic enmity afflicts the two boys because they had been deadly enemies in past lives. The young prince comes of age and marries Princess Altan, a devotee of the dharma who encourages her husband to draw close to Buddhism.

When the two princes are still young, a Hindu Brahmin teaches them to animate a dead body by projecting their consciousness into it. The plot thickens when the prince's devotion to Altan offends one of his concubines. (There is a contradiction in having a beloved spouse and a harem, but never mind; the prerogative of royals has always been the enjoyment of one-sided privileges.) The concubine seduces Lagayana and stokes his jealousy of the prince. Together they plot his destruction.

One day, the young men come across two dead cuckoos in a wooded field. Lagayana persuades the prince that they should leave their bodies and animate the birds in order to better explore the woods. When the prince projects his spirit into one of the birds, he becomes transfixed by the fruit, birdsong, and flowers of the field. True to his devotion to Buddhism, he gives a discourse on the dharma to the other birds. While the prince is distracted, Lagayana flies back and enters the prince's body. Lagayana as the prince throws his true corpse and the corpse of the other cuckoo into the river, leaving the prince stranded in the body of the other cuckoo. Lagayana, in the body of the prince, returns to the palace and claims that his friend 'Lagayana' drowned in the river. Altan finds the character of the 'prince' to have changed—he abandons his Buddhist faith and acts mean-spirited and base.

At this point in the opera, the Buddha himself arrives on stage and takes the form of a cuckoo to keep company with the prince, who falls into desolation. The Buddha explains Lagayana's treachery as well as its karmic basis, softly breaking the news that the prince cannot go back to his old life. The prince flies to his palace to tell the truth to his family and friends, who take revenge on Lagayana and the unfaithful concubine. Karmic destiny cannot be reversed, and the prince cannot revert to human form. He accepts his fate and spends the rest of his life preaching the dharma to his fellow birds.

This proto-modern musical had been all but forgotten after the communist revolution. In the late 1950s the folklorist Damdinsuren happened across an incomplete copy of the libretto in the archives of Gandan Monastery. Intrigued by the dialogue and lyrics, he went on a countrywide search for the missing sections, eventually assembling the entire libretto in the early 1960s.[12] The opera has been set to modern music, with performances staged at the State Drama Theatre from time to time. It is worthwhile to attend a performance if your visit coincides with one.

The State Drama Theatre's troupe also performs Western plays. Ann Hibbert, the wife of the first British diplomat to Mongolia, recalled the memorable reaction of an audience to a performance of the Mongolian version of *King Lear* (or in this case, perhaps *Lear Khan*) in 1966:

> The audience must have been very like the audience Shakespeare was writing for . . . The straight drama of the play came out, expressed of course in contemporary Mongolian, and the audience threw themselves into it like true Elizabeth groundlings. There were sharp intakes of breath at the disgraceful way the daughters behaved to their aged father. There were angry mutterings over Edmund's villainy and cheers when the traitors met their deserts. It was really highly entertaining.[13]

In the tourist season the State Drama Theatre also hosts nightly folk-music performances as does Tumen Enkh, the performing arts auditorium in the Children's Park. While these are touristy pre-packaged offerings, they are nonetheless an excellent way to have an overview of Mongolian folk music at one go.

The pride of place for Mongolian folk instruments certainly goes to the horsehead fiddle, or *morin huur* (морин хуур). This is a bowed two-stringed instrument that produces a deep cello-like sound. The head of the instrument above the tuning pegs is often in the form of a green horse's head, just like the wooden horse that pulled the Maitreya cart during the annual festivals for the bodhisattva.

The origin of the morin huur is told in a suitable legend. Each night, a 'celestial herder' descended to earth on his winged horse for a tryst with a steppe girl, serenading her with music and then quietly leaving her bed to fly back to the heavens at dawn. Since the steppe girl grew unhappy with his disappearances, she secretly cut off the

Oversized morin huur.
Photo by Janice Law.

12. For a fine account of the detective work conducted by Professor Damdinsuren to recover Danzanravjaa's lost masterpiece as well as an overview of premodern Mongolian theatre, see Heissig (1966) at 211–30.
13. Hibbert at 166.

horse's wings one night. The next morning, her lover failed to notice this and tried to fly off, only to crash back to earth, killing the horse. The grieving herder fashioned a morin huur in memory of his beloved horse.

While the shape of the morin huur is a time-honoured custom, Mongolian musicians were not averse to innovations for improving its sound. In the 1960s the Soviet violin maker Denis Vladimirovich Iarovoi and his Mongolian pupils invented a new design for the morin huur to make it more suitable to the acoustics of a concert hall. The bow was straightened and symmetric sound holes added, among other changes.

No instrument captures the essence of the grasslands like the morin huur. Its deep vibrato immediately conjures images of distant horizons, dramatic cloudbursts, and the bible black of the Mongolian night.

This effect also reaches near perfection in the vocal music called the long songs, or *urtyn duu* (уртын дуу). The 'length' of the songs refers to drawn out words and melodic phrases that are sung with trills and glissandos to suggest a horse galloping along the contours of hills and valleys. There is also a genre called short songs, or *bogino duu* (богино дуу), that emphasize lyrical treatment of topics like religion, legendary heroes, horses, mountains, rivers, romance, and satires about libidinous lamas.

Throat-singing, or *khoomii* (хөөмий), has entered the repertoire of world music as a celebrated example of Mongolian culture. This was not always the case. Throat-singing was an art form in the western parts of the country and derided as low-brow musical entertainment by the clergy. After the establishment of the MPR, Mongolian ethnographers, inspired by their Soviet counterparts, began to rediscover, catalogue, and record throat-singing music.

Khoomii singing requires a constriction of the larynx to create a whistling overtone of two or even three voice lines over the main voice. The whistling effect is said to emulate the sounds of the wind and water. It used to be exclusively a male art form because the wind and water were thought to be male forces of nature, although female throat-singers have begun to appear in recent years.

In contrast to these forms of secular music, Tibetan religious music arrived in Mongolia along with monasteries, scholar-missionaries, and the sutras in the sixteenth century. Tibetan chant is based upon distinct notes though the orchestral music—consisting of cymbals, horns, and drums—does not have a discernible melody. It is conducted in accordance with Tibetan notation, so it is not the directionless cacophony so often claimed by outsiders. It reminds me of a night at a Tom Waits concert.

Other Mongolian instruments include the *yatga* (ятга), which is a zither-like instrument similar to the Chinese *zheng* and the Japanese *koto*; the *limbö* (лимбэ), or the six-holed flute; and the *yoochin* (ёочин), or dulcimer.[14]

Returning to our peregrinations, the next main building to the south is the Bayangol Hotel, a 1960s construction that captures the appearance and atmosphere of the hospitality-service sector on the far side of the Iron Curtain in the bad old days. It

14. For Mongolian music, see Atwood at 393–95.

Mural from a by-gone era at the Children's Centre. Photo by Lukas Nikol.

is a 'modernist' building with a touch of Ginzburg's national character in the roof over the auditorium. Some guide books describe it as 'reliable' or 'dependable'. 'Predictable' is my preferred adjective. Keep an eye out for the Birthday Man.[15]

Taking the next turn to the east on Genden Street, we see the green Children's Centre built in the 'individual construction' style of the 1970s. It was here where protesters in 1990 first assembled before marching on Sükhbaatar Square. To the south is the Children's Park, another legacy of the socialist era, with its amusement rides and an ever-shrinking acreage as developers encroach upon its borders.

Across from the Children's Centre is the Exhibition Hall, a 1960s construction that was another adaptation of the ger as a national form. The hall has been surrounded by more recent 'brutalist' construction work. The area is a short hop away from Millie's, one of the favourite restaurants of both the foreign and Mongolian community. See if they offer their magnificent Cuban lunch specials when you visit.

Further down is the Temple of the Choijin Lama or Choijin Lamin Süm (Чойжин Ламын Сүм), a special purpose Buddhist shrine completed in 1908. Its Chinese name *qiaoyi jinmiao* (乔伊进庙) can be translated as the Temple for the Entry of the Lofty Ones, an apt name as we shall see. The building is a beautiful mixed Sino-Mongolian temple with typically Mongolian square cupolas and a Chinese north–south axis and layout.[16] It is now a museum and no longer a site for worship.

The Temple of the Choijin Lama served a special purpose. As noted previously, Vajrayana Buddhists believe personified spiritual forces interact with mortal beings

15. See explanation on pp. 162–63 of Chapter 9, below.
16. See Teleki at 265–69 for a scholarly discussion.

to bless those who propitiate them and harm those who show disrespect. These dharmapalas had been persuaded to take on the role of protectors of Buddhism thanks to the intercession of high lamas such as Padmasambhava or the Third Dalai Lama, who tamed them through force, wisdom, or compassion.

The protectors have two forms: a wrathful appearance to strike terror into the hearts of those who wish to harm the dharma and a peaceful one to help guide and protect the faithful. After their conversion to Buddhism, some of the spirits are said to communicate with the clergy by taking possession of a high lama who then acts as an

Yampai in front of Temple of the Choijin Lama. Photo by author.

Hall of the Maharajas of the Four Directions, Temple of the Choijin Lama. Photo by author.

oracle for the spirit. While possessed by the dharmapala, the oracle speaks in a stylistic language that has to be interpreted by a lama who deciphers the unintelligible noises uttered by the oracle. The lama selected as an oracle has to be periodically replaced by another because of the debilitating effect of the possessions. When a wrathful protector takes over, the oracle may go into a seizure and leap about, flailing his arms and acting aggressively.

The dharmapala Nechung is still an official adviser to the Dalai Lama's court, a post that he has held since the seventeenth century. As an indigenous spirit in Tibet, Nechung originally fought against the construction of the Samye Monastery in the eighth century until his conversion by Padmasambhava. Slightly suggestive of civil service graduated rankings, the next-in-line, Zemer (Зэмэр), took over the role of dharmapala for Samye Monastery when Nechung got his promotion and moved to Lhasa. Nechung continues to play a significant role for the Dalai Lama, who sought Nechung's opinion before deciding to flee Tibet in 1959.

The Eighth Patriarch and his high lamas sought to tap into this resource by having their own oracle in Urga. The chief abbot of Urga, the Venerable Baldanchoimbol, determined that Luvsankhaidav, a younger brother of the Eighth Patriarch, could act as the oracle because of his frequent fainting spells—these were taken as a sign of possession by a spirit. In order to formalize the oracle institution, an older lama, Luvsanpeljee from the Wangain Aimag, composed a text for rituals to invite the dharmapalas to take possession of the oracle. He also was appointed as the translator to make sense of the oracle's utterings.

The Temple of the Choijin Lama was first set up in a ger near the Yellow Palace and then in a wooden temple that burned down in 1903. Construction work for the new temple began in 1904. The project employed hundreds of Chinese carpenters and stonemasons as well as Mongolian bronze-smiths and artists.

At the time of its creation, the institution of an Urga oracle might not have necessarily improved the reputation of the sangha in the eyes of some because Luvsankhaidav had been Luvsanpeljee's catamite.[17] He also pursued pastimes that breached his monastic vows, like shooting anklebones, a game modelled on archery and thus symbolic of the tools of war. In addition to being a wastrel, he also took as his consort a Mongolian woman named Surenkhorloo, a hot number who was known for living a dissipated life with Chinese merchants. She foresaw the advantages of the match; after Luvsankhaidav died in 1918 she returned to her family home with twenty carts filled with loot as her share of gifts from the Choijin Lama.

Despite the oracle's poor 'optics' for monastic discipline, Abbot Baldanchoimbol invited three Tibetan spirits to be the protective deities of the temple. Two were Nechung or Naichün (Найчун) and Zemer (Зэмэр); the third was Dorje Shugden or

17. Some Vajrayana Buddhists believed that non-penetrative sex was an acceptable exception to monastic vows. See Goldstein, Siebenschuh, and Tsering at 26–31 for a discussion of sexual conduct among some of Lhasa's monks in pre-socialist Tibet.

Dorjshüg (Доржшуг), another deity from the Fifth Dalai Lama's reign and an object of controversy among Vajrayana believers today, as we shall see.[18]

During the oracle's possession, the spirits were said to communicate through Luvsankhaidav by a buzzing sound emanating from the oracle's armpit (seriously). The buzzing noise then had to be deciphered by Luvsanpeljee. Most possessions were calm but when Shugden came on the scene, the session became frantic with the oracle 'hopping and leaping about, bobbing up and down and foaming at the mouth', a little like a stranded Air China passenger whose flight to UB has been cancelled once again.[19]

The temple is also said to have been associated with Jamsran. According to an urban legend, the MPR preserved the Temple of the Choijin Lama because of this connection to the red-faced protector. In 1990 student demonstrators demanded a revival of Jamsran's cult at the temple at one point.

With this as background, we begin our visit to the temple at its south end. Here there is grey brick yampai with a depiction of the Eight Immortals (*ba xian* 八仙) on the south wall. The Eight Immortals are legendary figures that entered East Asian literary canons and art work during the Yuan dynasty. They are found in paintings, temple architecture, doorway banners, wall hangings, and what-not from Saigon to Ulaanbaatar and from Gansu province to the islands of Japan. As sages, they scorned conventional society and the folly that accompanies moralizing and pomposity. They bring to mind Ken Kesey's Merry Pranksters playing practical jokes on the self-righteous, helping needy mortals, and getting stone drunk at banquets that transcend time and space. Each immortal's appearance, background, and character are meant to convey a deeper mystical meaning in addition to a satisfying riposte against social convention. Whenever a helpless and socially inappropriate fit of giggles comes over you, rest assured that the Eight Immortals are somewhere nearby.

Fittingly, a khangarid also stares back at the Holy Mountain from the south side of the yampai with two snow lions crouching in reverence at its feet. On the wall's north side, a four-fingered dragon cavorts in the clouds next to bas reliefs of the White Old Man and a deer as symbols of longevity and Tara as a source of compassion.

Going to the vestibule of the complex, we pass through the Temple of the Maharajas, or Makhranzin Sum (Махранзын Сүм), hosting the Maharajas of the Four Directions. The lintels over the passageways are decorated with famous Chinese landscapes, such as Peking's Summer Palace, and scenes from Xuanzang's journey to the western lands.

We come next to the Temple for Awakening Benevolence (or Xingren Si 兴仁寺), which is sometimes just called the main temple, or *gol süm* (гол сүм) in Mongolian. Recently, the temple has been rearranged to simulate a prayer hall by placing four rows of *javans*, or low-standing monks' seats, perpendicular to the main altar. In the centre of the hall is a bronze of the Shakyamuni Buddha. To its right-hand side is a gilded

18. Other sources indicate that there were three other protective deities of the Choijin Lama Temple, namely, Vajrapani, Hayagriva and Perenleijalva.

19. Jambal at 10.

statue of the Choijin Lama perched on his former throne and reportedly containing his ashes. On the Shakyamuni Buddha's left-hand side is the gilded mummified corpse of Abbot Baldanchoimbol. Flanking the approach to the main altar are two noteworthy Tsam masks of deities that were state protectors. One is the red coral mask of Jamsran and across from it is Mahalaka.

In the hall's south-west corner are four Tsam masks: the Khangarid, the White Old Man, Zaluu, who is the spirit of Bayanzurh Mountain, and the Dark Old Man, who was a shaman buried in the Songino Kharkhan Mountain. Tsam masks of Khashin Khan (or the Kangxi Emperor) and his eight sons are in the south-east corner.[20] The north side of the temple has bronzes of Baldan Lkham, Maitreya, Ayush, and Dorj Shugden. A rich assortment of thangkas depicts varying levels of the universe for beasts, men, and gods. Model replicas of heavenly palaces for the deities are on hand as well.

The Temple of Awakening Benevolence is connected to the Chapel of the Protector, or Gonkhon (Гонхон), where there is another throne for the Choijin Lama centred against the north wall as the hall's focal point. Rituals for the spiritual possessions of the Choijin Lama took place there. Along the walls (and also in the portico leading to the main temple) are drawings of human sacrifices and severed body parts illustrating the wrathful power of dharmapalas. On the left side of the throne are bronzes of Tsongkhapa and Padmasambhava. On the right side, Yamantaka is in an ecstatic embrace with his consort. Along the western wall are bronzes of Nechung and Vajrapani while Dorj Shugden and a wrathful version of Ayush are along the eastern wall. In the south-east corner, the King of Shambhala in papier mâché tramples another enemy of the dharma in his eventual triumph over evil.

Outside to the west of the Main Temple is the Temple of the Shakyamuni Buddha, or Zuugiin Süm (Зуугийн Сум). Within it are multiples statues of the Buddhas of the past, present, and future, and the Shakyamuni Buddha's arhats. Protectors Baldan Lkham and Nechung stand guard, flanking the approach to the main altar.

Behind the main temple is the Temple of the Tutelary Deity, or Yadamiin Süm (Ядамын Сум), an exclusive site for the oracle to contemplate a meditational deity, or *yadam*, and engage in Tantric sexual rituals with his consort. Bronze and wooden sculptures of main deities that were once worshipped by the oracle lama are kept here, including bronzes of Vajrasattva, Kalachakra, and Demchengevi, all in ecstatic embrace and cast by Zanabazar.

Continuing around to the east side of the temple complex, the Temple of the First Patriarch, or Öndör Gegeeniin Süm (Өндөр Гэгээнийн Сум), is an octagonal temple constructed in 1907 to the memory of Zanabazar. The artwork inside this building includes a self-portrait bronze by the man himself along with a small bronze stupa reportedly brought back by Zanabazar from Tibet. The bronzes of the Standing Maitreya, Ratnamsambhava, and Vajradeva were also made by Zanabazar.[21]

---

20. Other legends hold that Khasin Khan was a Kashmiri king or the monk Huashang. See Berger and Bartholomew at 156.

21. See Teleki at 165–72; Jambal; Atwood at 105 for further information.

The guides for the Choijin Lama Temple have not been well-versed in its history. Few have been able to answer detailed questions or act at all interested. This is not new. In the 1960s René MacColl, a British journalist with a dry wit but a severe lack of empathy wrote his recollection of a heavily guided trip to Mongolia. His book relentlessly roasted the official guide for the tour group, a gentleman named Lotchin, who, perhaps at the instruction of some higher-up, treated his guests at every turn with deep suspicion and hostility. It does sound like the group did not consist of the most sympathetic collection of visitors from the capitalist world, which might have fuelled concerns about their real purpose. MacColl lampooned Lotchin's talent at pointing out the obvious ('Over here you can see a stone lion') but was in especially fine form in relating Lotchin's description of the paintings of castrated and flayed body parts at the Temple of the Choijin Lama:

> I think that probably my favourite Lotchin remark was at the Temple which has above its main doorway a horrific frieze, showing men who have been castrated and their eyes gouged out, hanging head downwards covered in blood and with frightful expressions of agony on their faces. Said Lotchin: 'Dese bad things. Men most uncomfortable.'[22]

While the temple is a museum rather than a place of active worship, its role as a repository for Buddhist relics was set aside in 2013 to become briefly part of an ongoing controversy in the Tibetan religious community. This is the Shugden schism concerning Dorjshüg, one of the dharmapalas of the temple and a wrathful protective spirit favoured by some Gelukpa adherents.

This dispute arose because of a clash between the Fifth Dalai Lama and an influential lama, the Drakpa Gelsten. The Drakpa was born into a prestigious family with unfulfilled expectations that their scion was to be recognized as the Fifth Dalai Lama. With the selection of another child as the Dalai Lama, the Drakpa's family started a feud which led to personal animosities between the two lamas as they grew older.

Sectarianism was a main bone of contention between the two monks. The Fifth Dalai Lama advocated a non-sectarian relationship with the Red Hat branches of Vajrayana Buddhism while the Drakpa maintained that only the Gelukpa represented the true and pure dharma. All other branches of Buddhism should be rooted out. Depending upon the sources (and their biases), the Drakpa was assassinated by the Dalai Lama's supporters, or he succumbed to an illness after consorting with non-Buddhist 'wild' spirits while trying to learn their dark arts.

After the Drakpa's death the Lhasa valley suffered droughts, plagues, and other calamities attributed to the vengefulness of the Drakpa. Monasteries attempted to 'oust' the Drakpa's spirit through a series of exorcisms, but these all failed—the Drakpa's spirit eluded each attempt at a crucial moment in the rituals. In the end, there may have been a compromise where the Fifth Dalai Lama, or his proxy, agreed to placate the

22. MacColl at 61.

Drakpa's spirit to relieve the suffering of people in the Lhasa Valley. The Drakpa's spirit came to be worshipped as Dorje Shugden.

Subsequent dalai lamas were not as powerful as the Great Fifth, and many 'died suddenly' before coming of age. During this time of unsettled leadership, some Gelukpa monasteries vigorously endorsed the worship of Shugden with his supporters claiming that he readily fulfilled the wishes of his supplicants for wealth and power. As Shugden worship spread in the Vajrayana world, sectarian conflicts broke out with other orders. In the early twentieth century the Thirteenth Dalai Lama came to the conclusion that Tibetan Buddhism needed to embrace a non-sectarianism in support of all branches of the faith. He saw the Shugden sect as being unnecessarily confrontational at a time when Tibet's sovereignty was threatened by China, Russia, and Britain.

The junior tutor of the Fourteenth Dalai Lama was believed to be a partial emanation of the Drakpa, and he trained the young lama in the rituals for Shugden propitiation. However, in 1975 the Dalai Lama after a long debate decided that Shugden worship fuelled sectarianism. He announced that he would no longer initiate Shugden worshippers into the Kalachakra. He acknowledged the other branches of Tibetan Buddhism condemned by the Shugden worshippers as legitimate expressions of the dharma. This spawned an acrimonious dispute between senior lamas at the Dalai Lama's court in Dharamsala and the followers of Shugden, who condemned the Dalai Lama as a traitor to the faith.

In 1996 an important theoretician for the Dalai Lama and his two novice monks were stabbed to death in their quarters not far from the Dalai Lama's residence. The crime remains unsolved but a journalist believes that, on the basis of information from the Indian police, the perpetrators were likely to have been Shugden devotees who fled to China after the murders. This is heatedly denied by Shugden believers.[23]

The Shugden sect has branched out, setting up meditation centres in the West and recruiting Western, Chinese, and Tibetan adherents. In 1997 they launched a media campaign to discredit the Dalai Lama for suppressing religious freedom, comparing him to Hitler and a 'wolf in lama's robes'. The Shugden followers used rhetoric that is similar to the Chinese Communist Party in their attacks on His Holiness, leading some to suspect that the Shugden faction is working closely with China.

In the 1990s the Mongolian Buddhist monasteries were called on to take a position about the dispute. They were not able to reach a unanimous view at first but ten years ago, the Gelukpa monasteries in Ulaanbaatar discontinued Shugden's ceremonies while the lamas of one temple outside of the capital elected to continue its worship of this controversial spirit.

In 2013 the Trijang Rinpoche, a 30-year-old monk believed to be an emanation of the Dalai Lama's junior tutor, arrived in Ulaanbaatar to conduct a Shugden ritual at the Temple of the Choijin Lama. Perhaps the ceremony was staged here because Dorje Shugden is still seen as a protective deity of the temple. This event appears to be another

23. See Bultrini and Dreyfus.

chapter in the geopolitical clash between China and the Dalai Lama. Certainly, there was more to the visit by the Trijang Rinpoche than meets the eye.

Next to the Choijin Lama temple is the Wedding Palace, completed in 1976 as an 'individual construction' as per Soviet architectural trends of the time. The Wedding Palace is an impressive reinterpretation of Mongolian architecture and motifs, but its visual impact is weakened by the surrounding urban sprawl. Whenever the Mongolian lunar almanac identifies an auspicious date for weddings, the marriage registration authorities are deluged with reservations.

Mongolian couples in UB are usually married in a secular ceremony at the Wedding Palace followed by a Western reception. Some families have revived the *ber guih* (бэр гуйх) ceremony, which had fallen out of practice among urbanites during the socialist era. This is a ritual where the male relatives of the groom ask the father of the bride-to-be for permission for the wedding. Neither bride nor groom is in attendance as the participants conduct the ritual on the pretence that the event is unplanned.

The groom's family consults a monk in order to set an astrologically sound time and date for the ceremony on the basis of the natal horoscopes of the couple. The monk also reviews the natal horoscopes of all participants in the ber guih to make sure that there are no unfavourable astrological portents. At least three male relatives of the groom are part of the delegation that visits the bride's immediate family for this strictly private and intimate ceremony.

The preparations for the ceremony fall mainly on the groom's family. They need to purchase suitably prestigious presents as a dowry for the bride's family. For the traditionally-inclined, the colour of each gift should correspond to the birth year of its recipient. When the groom's family arrives at the bride's home, they offer salted milk tea as if they had not expected the visit.

The two fathers exchange snuff bottles with ground tobacco and engage in polite conversation until the bride's father asks for the reason for the visit. Using ornately formal language, the father of the groom asks for the other's consent to the wedding and presents white khadags and a silver cup filled with arul or milk. The bride's father is supposed not to rush into granting his permission but once it is done, the families adjourn for a meal that has been prepared in advance. The ceremony is a reminder that a marriage is not solely an individual choice but also a union of families or clans. Once the newlywed couple sets up their own home, the groom will bring a burning ember from the hearth of his family to light the one in their home.[24]

The main hall of the Wedding Palace has an ornate stained-glass mosaic of a family hearth, or *golomt* (голомт), which symbolizes the Fire Deity, one of the oldest Mongolian spirits. The worship of fire as a holy spirit is an ancient belief that dates back to the middle of the first millennium CE, if not much earlier. Ancient Mongolians perceived the Fire Deity to be a woman, like the Greek goddess Hestia, and called her

24. I am grateful to Nominchimeg Odsuren for this information.

the Mother Fire Deity, or Galaikhan Eke (Галайхан Эх). She has a red face and wears many strips of red silk while casting a yellowish glow like butter.

Given its maternal associations, fire in a hearth is still regarded as a sacred being. It is poor form to put rubbish or water in a hearth or move across a ger by stepping over the hearth. Passing a knife through a flame is also a sign of disrespect to the deity. To kick a hearth is a mortal insult because this implies that the person wishes to destroy the lineage of the entire family.

An important household ceremony occurs before the last day of the twelfth month of the lunar calendar. On that day, the family appears before the hearth dressed in new clothes and offers a sheep's breastbone wrapped in silk and coiled with sheep fat. The bone is waved three times clockwise over the hearth before being placed into the fire, followed by offerings of liquor, jujubes, butter, silk strips, and grain. The family concludes the ritual with the recitation of a prayer, requesting the deity's assistance in the year ahead.[25]

Continuing east we leave Genden Street and turn to the north on Olympic Street where there is an easily overlooked two-storey wooden house. Its existence is an interesting case study on how you can go from the head of government to non-person within a decade and then be rehabilitated in the afterlife (for whatever that is worth). This is the Memorial Museum for Victims of Political Repression in the former home of Peljidiin Genden, a member of the MPRP and the prime minister from 1932 to 1936.

Genden was an early member of the MPRP. Although he was a devotee of Marxism and Leninism, he nevertheless argued in favour of a synthesis of communism and the dharma at first, arguing that Lenin and the Buddha were the two greatest revolutionaries who ever graced humanity, an assertion that might have left both gentlemen scratching their heads in wonder at the comparison. He jumped on the band wagon in support of the disastrous collectivization programme for herders in 1929, a policy that plunged Mongolia into its brief but vicious civil war. Genden survived the purge against the 'Leftist Deviation' and was later selected by Stalin to implement a brief period for the relaxation of state controls.

Genden appears to have risen to power too quickly. He was said to have abused the benefits of office, roaring about town in his official car while raging drunk. He resisted Stalin's instructions repeatedly to crush the monasteries and align himself with every bit of Soviet policy. His luck ran out in 1935. With colossally poor judgement, Genden drank himself into oblivion at a reception in the Mongolian embassy in Moscow, going so far as publicly condemning Comrade Stalin and snatching the Great Man's pipe from his mouth and breaking it. (I can picture Genden sitting on the edge of his bed, hung-over and increasingly terror-stricken, as he pieces together his antics from the previous night's party.) Surprisingly, Stalin did not immediately cashier Genden but allowed him to continue in power until 1936 when he was 'invited' to receive medical

25. Heissig (1980) at 69–76.

treatment in Crimea. He later disappeared into Lubyanka and joined the 'class of '37' of politically inspired collateral damage.[26] He remained a non-person until his rehabilitation in 1956, but his memory was still kept at arm's length as someone best not mentioned until the 1990s.

In 1930 the MPR government built this house for Genden's use. It was designed by Swiss and German specialists working at a brick factory in Ulan Bator. Genden, his wife, and children lived on the first floor while his wife's brothers and sisters, along with a Buryat translator and his Russian wife, lived on the second floor. They were attended to by a Chinese chef named Andre who spoke the pidgin Russian that was formerly the lingua franca in Kiakhta.[27] It must have been a colourful household.

Genden's daughter set up the museum to honour the memory of the 21,000 people who died in the Great Purge. The exhibits are mostly labelled in Mongolian only, but the display of documents from the purges and the macabre collection of skulls with bullet holes tell the story wordlessly.

The building shows the drawback of early modern Russian houses in terms of their dark and claustrophobic atmosphere, a sensation that is not lessened by the gruesomeness of the exhibits. I prefer the snug warmth and conviviality of a ger, with the glow of a hearth and the sighing of the wind across the grasslands.

Memorial Museum for Victims of Political Repression. Photo by Lukas Nikol.

26. Baabar at 346–48.
27. Genden at 132.

8

Between the Monastic Settlements

We start our tour on the corner of Sükhbaatar Street and Jigjidjav Street at the Museum of the History of Mongolia, which was originally opened as the Museum of the Revolution in 1961. As you may gather, the theme of the museum was changed in 1990 when the government unveiled the political repression memorial as part of its reassessment of its political culture.

The museum gives the visitor an impressive overview of Mongolian history. The exhibits track the development of the country from Neolithic days through the Hunnu Empire, the Türkic era, the Chinggisid Empire, the Second Conversion, and to modern times. The oldest artefacts are the usual assortment of stone tools and crumbling bronzes common to such museums in Asia. The exhibit on the Second Conversion selectively presents information that does not shine a light on the clergy's political role or the factionalism among nobles that eventually led the Khalkha elites to an alliance with the Qing dynasty. For me, the exhibits become increasingly interesting as they present items from the nineteenth and twentieth centuries that show the changes in society arising from new technology and global contacts. As you leave the museum, its final exhibits celebrate the 1990 revolution and present a syrupy picture of the 'better days ahead' for all Mongolians as a sampling of the current free-market brainwashing.

Across the street are the neoclassical ZUU residential apartment buildings completed in 1965 with bay windows as a symbol of the luxury of the times. While these buildings were preferential housing allotments then, they look as if they have fallen on hard times with unappealing assortment of restaurants, bars, and shops tacked on at ground level.

Going further to the west, the General Intelligence Agency maintains a low profile on the north side of the street. It was originally the Home Defence Agency, the headquarters of the so-called men in green hats who abducted those suspected of treason for extended discussions in its isolation chambers. It enjoyed a spike in business during the Great Purge but later only the occasional independent thinkers were subjected to its charms. The building was designed in accordance with constructivism and is not too remarkable to the eye. On the south side of the street, a branch of Golomt Bank and its brown pastiche obscure the original structure of the original MongolBank (before it moved further down the street).

To the south of the intersection of Baiga Toiruu and Juulchin Street, there is a 1960s Soviet modernist confection with a beehive assortment of cellular motifs. This once housed the People's Cinema, or Ard Kino Teatr. A 1970 photograph shows the cinema with a sign announcing the screening of revolutionary Soviet films and a poster proudly proclaiming 100 Years of Lenin. After the implosion of Mongolian communism, the People's Cinema became a branch of Anod Bank (until its directors drove the institution into insolvency and fled the country) and now houses branches of Xac Bank and Western Union for receipt of remittances from overseas labourers. Surrounding the former cinema is a series of petit bourgeois shops that have revolving door identities that change from restaurants, to bars, to money-changers, to stores selling cheap imported consumer products and to other tack-on business fronts. To think that you used to come here to see the black and white classics of Sergei Eisenstein.

Going back to Jigjidjav Street and continuing to the west, we come to Builder's Square, the site of the former Khüree Market of Old Urga. The market came into existence around the middle of the nineteenth century as the place for lamas to purchase goods not otherwise made available to them by their aimags. At first, it was a temporary marketplace. Chinese traders used to load goods on poles balanced across their shoulders and made their way from the trading posts in Maimachin to put up lean-tos here, returning to the Chinese enclave at the end of each day. They were joined by other stalls operated principally by Mongolian women.[1]

The former People's Cinema, an example of modernist architecture. Photo by Lukas Nikol.

1. Michie at 153.

Eventually, the more successful Chinese merchants built stores as points of sale and warehouses despite the patriarchs' prohibition against fraternization between lamas and the merchants. The Chinese shops grew in number and were soon joined by stores opened by Russian merchants from Siberia.

The rise of the Khüree Market eventually culminated in administrative litigation of staggering proportions among Mongolian lamas, Manchu ambans, and Chinese merchants. The gravamen of the dispute was whether the stores impinged upon the annual circumambulation of the Maitreya Buddha, a tainting of the sacred by profane commerce that provoked resentment among the clergy. Petitions were filed with the Office of the Administration of Barbarians in Peking, which, in turn, ordered the Manchu authorities to dismantle the unlawfully built Chinese shops. (The functionaries down south shrewdly ignored taking any measures against Russian shops for fear of diplomatic protests about breaches of the 'free trade' treaty between the tsarist government and the Qing dynasty). A token effort was made to tear down some stores.

After a pause the Chinese merchants started up their encroachments once again, spurring another round of complaints lodged with Peking. This time, the Office of the Administration of Barbarians instructed the Manchu amban to investigate the situation and come back with recommendations. The Manchu amban took no action, which provoked the Mongolian lamas to file another round of complaints, with Peking issuing the same instructions to the Manchu amban to investigate the situation.

The litigation went on for almost thirty-two years. When the amban was finally compelled to make a decision, he declared that any rezoning of the market would cause heavy losses to the Chinese merchants and give rise to a claim for indemnification by the Russians under the trade treaty. He recommended that the route of the parade ought to be altered to fit the current configuration of Urga's streets, and there the matter rested, no doubt to no one's satisfaction except the lawyers (assuming they were paid).

With little surprise, this triangular administrative agony appears to have been a cover for some behind-the-scenes subterfuge. It turns out that the Fifth Patriarch had secretly appointed a Chinatown merchant as his agent for sales of goods to the lamas. The agent was allowed to set up a store, thereby eroding the reluctance of other Chinese merchants to flout the rules. I imagine that this arrangement provided for a superb revenue stream for the Patriarch's treasury.

At the beginning of the twentieth century the Khüree market was a bustling site. 'Peking shops' were set up as Urga branches of major retail companies and enjoyed a reputation for being well-kept and properly staffed. Typically, an ornate gateway of a Peking shop welcomed potential customers into the store's courtyard and its main hall where Chinese and foreign products were on display for a Mongolian clientele, such as silks, cotton and woollen clothes, kitchenware, musical instruments, accessories for monks such as red robes, caps and carrying bags, lanterns, wall hangings, and devotional items. The signboards for the Peking shops were artistically designed to be falsely reassuring, with legends such as *The Peking Shop of Batu, Selling Silken Cloth and Woven Damsk and Every Sort of Choice of Wares, The Proprietors Are Well Known for Their Honesty and Easy Dealing.*[2]

Stores set up by traders from Shanxi were the main competition for the Peking shops. The Shanxi stores were of lower quality, retailing inferior goods at lower prices in unkempt and dirty shops. The Russian merchants also mounted a lacklustre showing in terms of presence and initiative. Only a handful of Russian companies had opened stores on the market square purveying Russian goods, primarily in exchange for tea from China.[3]

At the market square Chinese craftsmen also offered services as carpenters, metal smiths, candlemakers, tailors, curriers, and shoemakers. Retired Chinese soldiers sought to earn a few copper coins each day by setting up street-side stalls for the sale of roasted mutton, *khuushuur*, and other savoury pastries.

The Khüree Market retained a lawless atmosphere similar to Wild West towns of the same era. One Russian traveller noted that arguments in the market square would easily escalate into violent, sometimes fatal confrontations without any intervention by the local authorities. If a fight resulted in a death, the body was left in the square until relatives or lamas from the same aimag came to claim the remains. ('Hey Bayar, I saw your uncle in the market today.' 'How's he doing?' 'He's dead; you'd better go collect him.') Unmourned and unnoticed death came to the beggars and the homeless who died while scratching out an existence here.[4]

In March 1911 three drunken lamas got into a brawl with a Chinese in a store that unleashed a sequence of events that would have fit perfectly in one of Laurel and Hardy's short comedies. Chinese soldiers were summoned to arrest the lamas, which provoked a crowd to gather outside the store and loot it. Then the soldiers battled the crowd until Amban Sando showed up to read the riot act. The crowd responded by pelting the amban with stones as he beat a hurried retreat from the scene.

Taking things to a new level, Sando ordered arrests and interrogations of suspects in this mini-drama. In retaliation, the Patriarch undercut the amban's authority and ordered the closing of the Khüree Market. The amban responded by ordering merchants to re-establish a market outside his office near what is today the Lion Bridge. This was meant to be the only authorized marketplace in the city. The Patriarch ordered Mongolians to boycott the amban's market and reopen the Khüree Market to sell their own produce without Chinese middlemen. Sando reported the events to the Peking authorities, who had more pressing problems on their hands as the Qing dynasty was in the final months before its collapse. A tense truce prevailed in Urga until October when Chinese revolted against Manchu rule in China proper and the

2. Pozdneyev at 66.
3. Just as the British set up tea plantations in India and Sri Lanka to break their dependency on Chinese-grown tea, the Russians eventually did the same by setting up tea plantations in Georgia, thereby changing the nature of the tea trade from import to export. These days, Georgian tea sits on the shelves of most UB convenience stores.
4. Pozdneyev at 74–75.

amban, seeing the writing on the wall, fled to the Russian consulate and then to China through Siberia.

Moving into the autonomous period, the Khüree Market swelled in size as commerce continued to grow. A silent film from the time shows Mongolian women wearing popular fan-like headwear and selling root vegetables as Mongolian laymen ride by on horses and carts. As a visiting British diplomat noted in an official report, it was a fun and lively place:

> In the market place, I spent a few mornings haggling with the bright matrons who kept most of the stalls for silver head-dresses, pipes, snuff-bottles, hats, leather boots, sashes, Buddhistic pictures and miscellaneous curios of no great value. Near the stalls, half-a-dozen camels were awaiting purchasers; flocks of sheep were tightly folded close by a bevy of eager women selling hats; a score of ponies were bunched up behind a tangle of carts, on which Mongol butchers were rapidly dissecting carcases of mutton; here a Chinese itinerant blacksmith, there a carpenter or tinker; and everywhere the good-humoured motely throng of Mongols from all parts, sprinkled with Russian Buriats and a few Tibetans.[5]

The market square dealt in services as well as goods. Since the monks were free to roam about in the afternoon lull once their morning prayers were concluded, Chinese entrepreneurs soon hit on the idea of opening small restaurants and drink shops to attract their custom. The next step in the tertiary sector was predictable.

It was probably inevitable that prostitution became a growth industry in a monastic settlement of 10,000 to 30,000 lamas who were leading celibate but boring lives. Since Mongolians had no illusions about the urge to procreate from tending their herds, they were not subject to the same repressed feelings about sexuality as Europeans. In addition, Mongolians were not obsessed about the purity of an imperial seraglio, or by extension, the chastity of the female. Like most ordinary people, Mongolians considered the Chinese institution of court eunuchs to be staggeringly incomprehensible. Because of a less theoretical view of morality, prostitutes did not suffer from social stigma (though as they aged, they went through the ritual of a sham marriage to an imaginary husband, conducted by a lama—this allowed them to wear the formal clothing of a married woman and thus acquire respect and status associated with advancing years).

Off-duty monks solicited the services of the women in the square and then went off to shabby little love motels managed by a lower class of Chinese merchants, who were another source for ready clientele as they were prohibited from bringing their wives and concubines to Mongolia. Unsurprisingly, venereal disease was rife and remained a serious medical problem well into the socialist era.[6]

5. Campbell at 96.
6. Prostitution disappeared with the advances made by progressive Soviet policies for women's rights in the 1930s, only to reappear once Mongolia embraced free-market philosophies in the 1990s.

The charms of Mongolian women did not go unnoticed by the occasional Western traveller to Urga:

> The married [women] wear long robes with shoulders elevated, much like the fashions of women in the reign of Queen Elizabeth. The head ornaments of Mongolian silver work, richly studded with turquoises, which the women wear, are so arranged as to stick the hair out on either side of the head like wings, and this forms an admirable framework for their faces, which are often very pretty. The women's features are almost European.[7]

The Khüree Market reached its cosmopolitan apogee in 1920, as vividly described by a Polish refugee from the civil war in the Soviet Union:

> To the lively coloured groups of men buying, selling and shouting their wares, the bright streamers of Chinese cloth, the strings of pearls, the earring and bracelets gave an air of endless festivity while on another side buyers were feeling of live sheep to see whether they were fat or not, the butcher was cutting great pieces of mutton from the hanging carcasses and everywhere these sons of the plains were joking and jesting. The Mongolian women in their huge coiffures and heavy silver caps like saucers on their heads were admiring the variegated silk ribbons and long chains of coral beads; an imposing Mongol attentively examined a small herd of splendid horses and bargained with the Mongol zahachine or owner of the horses; a skinny, quick, black Tibetan who had come to Urga to pray to the Living Buddha or, maybe, with a secret message from the other 'God' in Lhasa, squatted and bargained for an image of the Lotus Buddha carved in agate; in another corner a big crowd of Mongols and Buriats had collected and surrounded a Chinese merchant selling finely painted snuff-bottles of glass, crystal, porcelain, amethyst, jade, agate and nephrite . . . and everywhere Buriats in their long red coats and small red caps embroidered with gold helped the Tartars in black overcoats and black velvet caps on the back of their heads to weave the pattern of this Oriental human tapestry.[8]

The market drew many Buddhist clerics of various ranks and talents:

> Lamas formed the common background for it all, as they wandered about in their yellow and red robes, with capes picturesquely thrown over their shoulders and caps of many forms, some like yellow mushrooms, others like the Phrygian bonnets or old Greek helmets in red. They mingled with the crowd, chatting serenely and counting their rosaries, telling fortunes for those who would hear but chiefly searching out the rich Mongols whom they could cure or exploit by fortune telling, predictions or other mysteries of a city of 60,000 Lamas. Simultaneously religious and political espionage was being carried out. Just at this time, many Mongols were arriving from Inner Mongolia and they were continuously surrounded by an invisible but numerous network of watching Lamas.[9]

7. Perry-Ayscough at 111.
8. Ossendowski at 192.
9. Ibid. at 192–93.

Flags, carrying an array of meanings, festooned the square:

> Over the buildings floated the Russian, Chinese and Mongolian national flags with a single one of the Stars and Stripes above a small shop in the market; while over the nearby tents and yurtas streamed the ribbons, the squares, the circles and triangles of the princes and private persons afflicted or dying from smallpox and leprosy. All were mingled and mixed in one bright mass strongly lighted by the sun.[10]

By the end of the 1920s the market was gone, replaced by state-owned enterprises. In another twenty years the square had become the Central Bus Station for long-distance travel. The Khüree Market never recovered its bustle and liveliness.

The Builders' Square is the site of several buildings from the Qing dynasty and the early years of the MPR. On the south-east corner of the square is the Zanabazar Museum of Fine Art in a two-storey stone building constructed in 1905 as a store for a Russian merchant. It later served a tour of duty as the State Department Store (before Chinese workers built its seven-storey replacement on Peace Avenue in 1961). Now it hosts a superb collection of Buddhist bronzes cast by Zanabazar and stunningly detailed thangkas.

The museum is also celebrated for its collection of local paintings. Perhaps its most famous work is *One Day in the Life of Mongolia*, painted by Marzan Sharav in 1910. *One Day* is composed in the so-called *zurag* (зураг) style of native themes. It portrays an autumn day with Mongolians going about their chores or enjoying themselves.

Marzan Sharav learned his craft by painting Buddha images for high-ranking lamas, eventually rising to the rank of a court artist for the Eighth Patriarch and his wife. He was active through the autonomous period into revolutionary times, later turning his creative muse to painting a portrait of Lenin as a protective deity of the New Mongolia. He spent his leisure time with Tibetans with whom he shared a taste for rough-cut snuff tobacco and gambling. He was said to forgo washing his hands and face, supposedly as an act of devotion. 'There is no need to consecrate the pure Buddha images painted by Marzan Sharav without washing his hands and face for a few days,' presumably because his unhygienic state indicated that he was in a state of grace. A temperamental artist, Marzan Sharav accepted commissions from those he liked while spurning those whom he did not.[11]

Another famous zurag painting in the museum is *The Old Fiddler* by U. Yadamsuren. This was painted in the late 1950s at a time when the authorities were not frowning at folkloric themes. It depicts a magnificent old bearded gentleman wearing a traditional robe and playing a morin huur.

Two doors directly to the north of the Zanabazar Museum is a one-storey building that once housed the Central Pharmacy, Mongolia's first dispenser of Western medicines and a competitor to the clergy's medical datsans and their traditional remedies. Across the street on the south side of the road is the former People's Motion Picture

10. Ibid. at 193.

11. Jambal at 14–15.

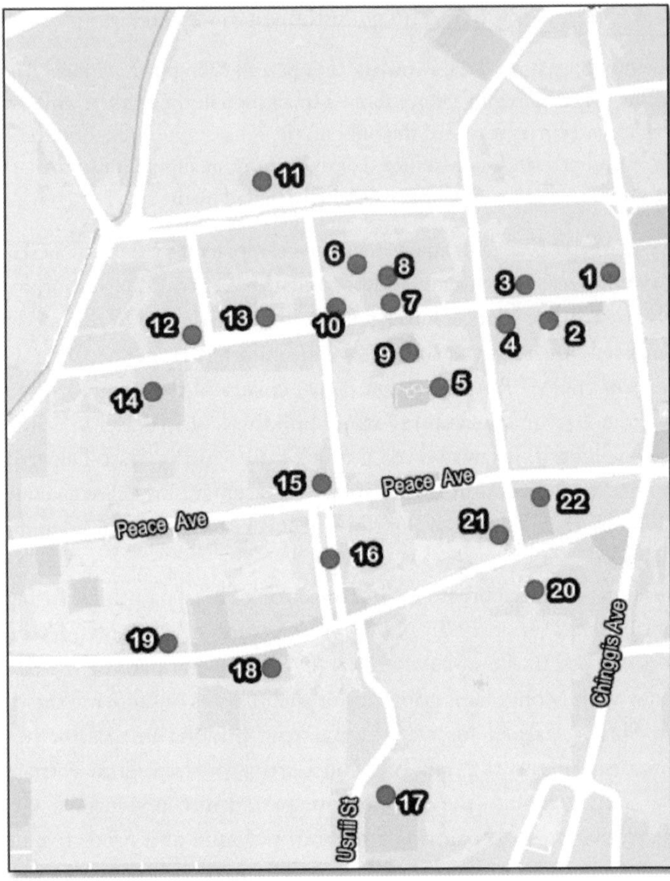

Sites to the west of Sükhbaatar Square. Map by Aubrey Ding-Shan Yang.

Key

1. Museum of History of Mongolia
2. Zuu Residential Apartment Buildings
3. General Intelligence Agency
4. MongolBank
5. Site of former Ard Cinema
6. Builder's Square
7. Zanabazar Museum of Fine Arts
8. Site of former Central Pharmacy
9. Site of former People's Motion Picture Theatre
10. Tuul Restaurant
11. Site of former Lenin Museum
12. Site of former "Yellow Store"
13. Site of former Tibetan colony
14. Site of former Buryat colony
15. State Department Store
16. Beatles Square
17. Asashoryu Private Circus
18. Mercury Market
19. Second Maternity Hospital
20. Prince Khandadorj Palace
21. No. 1 High School
22. Presidential Mansion

Theatre, which opened in 1935 for both film screenings and art exhibitions. Today, it is a house of worship for the Church of the Latter Day Saints. On the south-west corner of the square, the Tuul Restaurant has been in its three-storey building since 1948. Its entranceway is the one with the portico and four thick columns.

Coming to Baruun Road to the west, we can take a right turn and walk past a Burger King to the former Lenin Museum on Sambuu Street. Since the Museum of Natural History has been condemned as structurally unsound, the Lenin Museum is now slated for renovation as the home for the new Central Dinosaur Museum of Mongolia. For the time being, the museum is a superb example of a Soviet 'individual construction' project from the 1970s. The four bas reliefs on the building depict Lenin's early life, his meeting with Sükhbaatar and images celebrating feminism and the peace movement.

Back in the day, the Lenin Museum was a common place of pilgrimage for everyone, from primary school children to work units to veteran groups. Visitors had to remove their shoes upon entering (though I do not know if this was in reverence for ole Vladdy or a reaction to the still thankless task of mopping up muddy boot tracks in the winter time).

The fossilized remains of dinosaurs were known in mainland Asia for centuries, being mistaken for 'dragon bones' and ground into traditional medicines and other 'pick-me-up' restoratives. In 1918 the archaeologist and adventurer Roy Chapman Andrews led an expedition into Mongolia initially to search for human and mammal remains such as those of the 'Peking man' from northern China and the giant mastodons in Siberia. His expedition came across the first widely publicized discovery of dinosaur eggs—the manner of their birth had been unknown. This 'find' led to

'When Vladdy met Damdin', a bas-relief on the former Lenin Museum. Photo by author.

four more expeditions into the Gobi Desert, backed by the New York Museum of Natural History, J. P. Morgan and a coterie of other bankers, as well as the US embassy in Peking.

Andrews created a name for himself as a collector of animal specimens for the New York museum, though he might have covertly engaged in intelligence gathering for the US government given his passion for exploration in the far-flung destinations beyond the comfortable reach of most consuls. In the age that saw the regrettable birth of mass advertising, Andrews wrote extensively about his adventures in the 'uncivilized' corners of the world, with the condescension typical of white male elites towards other peoples. He is sometimes cited as the inspiration for the Indiana Jones character.

On his fourth trip to Mongolia, Andrews encountered suspicion about the real purpose for his scientific investigations. Why would anyone really go through the hardship of digging up old bones in the desert? What gain is there to be had from these things? He was subjected to the standard bureaucratic torture applied to the hyperactive foreigner: he had to wait an excruciatingly long time while the state considered his application for the expedition. He was also forced to hire Mongolian 'specialists' who were, in fact, government spies contributing embarrassingly little to the daily work of the team. At one point, perhaps 'trying it on for size', the Mongolian government demanded that the New York Museum of Natural History take on the cost for two Mongolians to study at Harvard, a request that Andrews politely declined as being beyond the scope of his authority. At the end of this rigmarole, the expeditions were undertaken with the full knowledge and approval of the Mongolian government in accordance with the written terms of a contract that Andrews signed on behalf of the Natural History Museum.

Andrews' expeditions made for great press in the United States. His discovery of dinosaur eggs set off a frenzy for all things dinosaur. Upon his return to the United States, he auctioned off one of the dinosaur eggs to the highest bidder to defray the costs of the expedition. In later years he wrote that he regretted that decision more than any other in his career since this gave rise to the Mongolian assertion that he had made millions from the trade in dinosaur eggs. (The egg was sold under the auction hammer to Colgate College in New York for only US$5,000 incidentally.) Both Soviets and Mongolians relentlessly harped on Andrews's so-called theft. A Russian short story writer went so far as to portray him as a member of a cabal of Japanese militarists, Wall Street bankers, and US imperialists, (an outrageous calumny as there is no evidence that Andrews worked with the Japanese). He was, and remains, an easy target for those who bleat about how foreigners hurt Mongolia.

Nonetheless, there is something about dinosaur eggs that make wealthy white Americans lose their minds. In 1963 the Soviet press reported an incident where an American was deported from Mongolia for having tried to shoplift a dinosaur egg from the natural history museum. Then again, unbelievably, in 1967 a spoiled brat on a tour with his well-heeled American family tried to make off with another dinosaur egg as a lark. These juvenile pranks were not well received by their Mongolians hosts.[12] I wish the Mongolian curators had seized the moment to give the Americans a lecture about the rule of law.

After the collapse of the MPR there was a round of thefts of national treasures, man-made and fossilized. For instance, a journalist was approached by a government official to purchase a dinosaur egg. A noted scholar of Mongolian history observed that an official at another museum could not explain the disappearance of art treasures—evidently, the work of an inside job.[13]

In 2013 the government celebrated the return of a Baatarasaurus dinosaur skeleton, which the US customs authorities had tracked down because of its illegal importation from the United Kingdom to Florida. The culprit was a Russian businessman and enthusiast for old bones. The return of the fossils was given a considerable amount of airplay and heralded as an important achievement, even though it was an easy victory. Getting the US authorities to enforce their own laws, when it is in their interest to show effective enforcement, and then hanging around the airport for the delivery of the bones, is not the sort of thing that requires vast reserves of statesman-like diplomacy or legal finesse. Since 150 cartons of bones were shipped into the Soviet Union in the 1950s and other priceless Mongolian artworks are exhibited internationally, it would be a more worthy success were someone to rise to the challenge and retrieve these from Russia along with other pieces held in the museums of the politically powerful.

As you can tell by my tone, I am not a dinosaur enthusiast. I prefer living cultures and people over fossilized bones. For those who are into long-deceased reptiles, Mongolia is a first-rate destination. There had been a political tug of war recently over the ownership of the former Lenin Museum. Once Vladdy had been disposed of as a national totem of world revolution and clean boots, the museum turned into, ironically, the Chadmana Business Centre. The government declared that it owned the building while the MPP, still nurturing its role as the vanguard of the masses, said it ought to inherit ownership of the site. At the end of it all (and possibly with some undisclosed back-room dealing), the dispute ended in a victory for the government and Barney the Dinosaur.

Turning left into Tömörchnii Street and heading south, we pass the 'Yellow Store', a pharmacy on the corner at the intersection with Urt Tsagaan Road. This one-storey building was originally the Women's Cooperative Retail Store, one of the outlets managed by Montsenkop, the Mongolian Central Cooperative. Montsenkop was the national cooperative established by the government to replace the foreign traders who enjoyed a near monopoly in the export-import market in the 1920s. The store's enrolment of women reflected Soviet support for gender equality. Today, it is a sadly neglected pharmacy which is threatened with demolition.

---

12. Henry Shapiro, 'Pranksters Overseas May End Up in Jail', *Independent Star News*, Pasadena, California, 8 July 1967. The sticky-finger quality of wealthy young Americans even caused a storm in a teacup at Colgate, when the egg sold by Andrews was stolen. 'Dinosaur Egg Stolen', *The Sydney Morning Herald*, 27 March 1957.
13. Becker at 52–53, Rossabi at 185.

'Yellow Store', site of former Mongolian Women's Cooperative. Photo by author.

Turning to the east at the intersection for the Yellow Store, we come to the vicinity of the former Tibetan 'colony' of Urga. Hundreds of learned Tibetan lamas accompanied the third to eighth patriarchs as teachers, translators, and specialists in conducting Kalachakra rituals. The size of the Tibetan colony was given a boost in 1904 when the Thirteenth Dalai Lama sought refuge in Urga from the British occupation of Lhasa.[14] Accompanying His Holiness were large teams of Tibetan lamas who were sheltered in fifty to sixty gers. No women or children came with this exodus because of the Thirteenth Dalai Lama's insistence on strict monastic discipline. Thirty Tibetan lamas eventually settled in Urga and attended daily services at a wooden building that became the Tibetan tsogchin dugan.

Mongolians donated generously to the Dalai Lama as the chief-ranking (and presumably most efficacious) lama in the Vajrayana hierarchy. Because of this windfall, the Dalai Lama set up a treasury and appointed an agent to manage these assets. The Tibetan colony grew next to the Dalai Lama's treasury and, because it was outside the two main monastic settlements, the Tibetan lamas in Urga were permitted to engage in commerce. They achieved pre-eminence in the sale of devotional artwork imported from Tibet, with a sideline in Chinese manufactured goods, until the closing of the country in the 1920s.

The Dalai Lama's agent was the de facto ambassador for the Tibetan government in Mongolia. The political relationship between the two territories grew close in the ensuing decade, culminating in 1915 with a treaty whereby each theocracy recognized the sovereignty of the other.

14. See Chapter 9 for a discussion about the circumstances of the Dalai Lama's flight to Urga in 1904.

An important adviser to the Dalai Lama was the Lonchen Shatra, a high lama at the Lhasa court and one of the three ministers who governed Tibet in the Dalai Lama's absence. He was Lhasa's main negotiator for the Shimla Agreement that sought to formalize Tibetan sovereignty with China and Britain. The Lonchen Shatra stationed a trade agent in Urga who proved to be a fairly astute merchant acquiring considerable wealth. However, during the civil unrest from 1919 to 1921, the agent lost everything, a financial setback that completely unhinged him. As George Roerich recalled,

> I used to see him often in the streets . . . attired in a fine silk coat with a large fur cap on his head, roaming about the bazars. When addressed, he repeated only one sentence, 'Give me my money back.' Curiously enough, he remembers the names of all the persons who had harmed him.[15]

Foreign financiers, beware.

The Tibetan colony faded from the city as the government began to enforce its atheistic policies in 1929. Visitors noted that Mongolians had a universal dislike for Tibetans despite cultural and religious similarities between the two peoples. It is another example of the universal anthropological law that everybody hates the neighbours.

This same vicinity was an informal black market for foreign currency exchange in the aftermath of the Soviet pull-out and thus became the site of several scams. At that time, the area was a plaza without through traffic. The North Korean embassy had gotten itself in trouble here in the 1990s for exchanging counterfeit small-face Benjamin Franklin 100-dollar notes. At another time, Nigerian con artists fooled the money changers by offering to sell bundles of 100-dollar notes. The story was that the United States Mint had marked the bills for destruction by covering them in black ink. The con artists offered to sell the bundles of disfigured bills at a discounted rate, along with a solvent that would remove the ink. Gullible money changers later found to their chagrin that the inked-over currency was simply newsprint. Perhaps the wandering spirit of the Lonchen Shatra's trade agent felt some satisfaction at long last.

The Buryat quarter was next to the Tibetan colony. As subjects of the tsarist empire, Buryats had been exposed to Russian and Western culture and adopted Russian-style names along with Orthodox Christianity. During the autonomous period, Buryat migrants in Urga were numerically insignificant but nonetheless influential purveyors of modernization as sociopolitical workers, teachers, publishers, governmental administrators, craftsmen, and skilled workers such as automobile mechanics, carpenters, and the like. Their influence greatly outstripped their numbers.

Many Khalkha Mongolians distrusted Buryats, who were perceived as having 'somehow betrayed the historical legacy of the Mongol tribes by submitting to the influence of a foreign power'.[16] This was an earlier form of the unthinking nativist reactions to cosmopolitanism that derailed Mongolia's economic development in 2012.

15. G. Roerich at 145.
16. Cheney at 23.

Going on to Peace Avenue, we come to the State Department Store, which was built in 1961 as a miniature modernist version of Moscow's GUM. From that time, the State Department Store has been the main outlet for foreign visitors to purchase souvenirs and other bric-a-brac. Quality has eroded along with marketing ethics, though. These days, the State Department Store fobs off fake jade antiques 'aged' with a generous application of acid and fur hats that come undone in the summer season. Caveat emptor.

The apartment buildings around the State Department Store are elegant neoclassical complexes from the 1960s. However, the original straight-line elegance of the buildings has been lost amid sprouting shopfronts and pizza restaurants, like a formal garden having gone badly to seed.

The 'Beatles Square' is so named, informally, on account of the initiative of a private citizen who raised funds by subscription for a bas-relief of the Fab Four on the street leading to the State Circus. The monument apparently aims to identify Sir Paul as the creative genius of the group since he stands separately from his three bandmates.

The music of the four lads from Liverpool was first aired in Ulan Bator in 1964, thanks to the British diplomat Reginald Hibbert. During a diplomatic soirée, Hibbert broke open a couple of Beatle albums for his Iron Curtain colleagues, who reacted with decided coldness. Certainly no one in attendance that evening would have wagered that a monument to the mop tops would someday grace the streets of the Mongolian capital.

Except perhaps for a member of the Hungarian embassy. In Hibbert's letters to his wife, he asked her to purchase a copy of Ferdinand Lessing's classic, *Mongolian–English Dictionary* (a fantastic resource in traditional Mongolian script for certain historical terms) as a gift for a Hungarian professor of Mongolian and Tibetan, who happened to be a fan of the Beatles.[17] This is a hugely appealing image. I envisage the Hungarian scholar at work in his room at the Ulaanbaatar Hotel, getting gently toasted on a fine duty-free Tokai, translating a satirical poem by Danzanravjaa while listening to *A Hard Day's Night* on loan from the kindly representative of Her Majesty's Government.

Across Seoul Street to the south, you will espy the former State Circus, an institution that was started with Soviet guidance in 1941.[18] This stadium was completed in 1971 and, as black-and-white photographs reveal, the vista from the State Department Store to the circus once had a neat and orderly appearance. Alas, in the relentless pursuit of almighty togrog, urban sprawl has crept up to the stadium and defaced the symmetrical appearance of the area. Now the State Circus is called the Asashoryu Private Circus (with unintended irony) after a Mongolian sumo wrestler.

17. Hibbert at 48–49.

18. Other foreigners had attempted to launch amateur circus performances in Urga much earlier. The missionary James Gilmour reported that in 1870 a French circus had visited Urga on its way from Kiakhta to Shanghai, but the nobles refused to allow any sales of tickets to commoners. The thought of circus wagons crossing the Gobi makes for a powerfully surreal image, not too far removed from the overland importation of huge wind turbines several years ago.

'Back in the MPR'. Photo by Lukas Nikol.

In its day, the circus was a source of uncomplicated good, clean entertainment.

> The circus was sometimes in town, notable for the repellent turns of its contortionists, plus less sinuous camels, foxes, wolves, badgers, horses and a performing yak. A blazing row broke out at one performance between two Mongols in the 'Royal' box, where my family was also situated, alas broken up by the authorities. One part of the safety net broke during the trapeze act. No damage was done, but a large clamp fell within inches of a spectator. A pole thrown by an artist was missed by the attendant and landed in the audience. Finally, the safety net got completely out of hand and enveloped a quarter of the spectators. The Mongols enjoyed all this immensely and would have been disappointed had things gone smoothly. Most of them were doubled up with laughter.[19]

Nearby is a Georgian restaurant called Caucasia, a fine place to take a break in our rambles, if needed.

19. Colvin at 145.

We are in a part of Urga that once was called Meat City. Butchers set up their stalls here since the Buddhist monasteries were far enough away to avoid giving offence to the lamas (who nevertheless consumed meat as part of their daily fare). A tiny group of Russian Jews handled the preparation of meat for the expatriate community and for importation to Russia during the early twentieth century. The name 'Meat City' is ironically unrelated to the Marco Polo strip joint that coincidentally opened near here in the free-market age.

Off to the west of the circus is the Mercury Market, a place that purveys both imported and Mongolian foodstuffs. It is a place where a spirit of curiosity and goodwill makes for a pleasant investment of time. The market is an ideal place to explore truly Mongolian delicacies. I imagine that the good-natured ladies who run the food stalls have the same jovial sense of humour as their forebears in Khüree Market.

'White foods' or dairy products are the staples for herders during the summer season (as opposed to 'red foods' or meats consumed in winter). You will find in one corner of the market a fascinating selection of new tastes from unusual milk products. *Tarag* (тарag) is a sour milk, not unlike Bulgarian yogurt but very liquid. *Beslüg* (бяслаг) is a Mongolian cheese that is quite mild when compared to its more robust European counterparts. *Ezgi* (ээзгий) and *arul* (ааруул) are twisty worm-shaped curds that vary in texture from very hard to nougat-like and with a flavour that ranges from overpoweringly strong to slightly sweet. Their odd shape comes from putting curds through a meat grinder. *Tsötsgii* (цөцгий) is a delicacy made from cream mixed with cane sugar and fried millet. *Öröm* (өрөм) is solid cream cut into rectangular strips—a summertime treat.

Airag (айраг) is the summertime tipple made from fermented mare's milk (which has even been approved for consumption by the Church of Latter Day Saints, earning it the sobriquet the 'Mormon milkshake'). Like any lightly fermented home brew, it does not keep for long. When distilled, it becomes *shimiin* (шимийн) at 10–12 per cent alcohol. Double-distilled, it clocks in at 30 per cent and is called *arz* (арз).

'Mongolian blueberry jam' is on offer here. This makes a nice breakfast companion with slightly sour Russian dark breads. East European sausages and salamis and pickled vegetables from Poland are available for those with a taste for Slavic cuisine. Off to the side is a small enclosure selling ingredients and spices for Chinese cooking. It is operated by umpteenth generation Mongolian-born Chinese who are a little tight-lipped about their heritage.

Elsewhere, you will come across a curious collection of sweet liquors and distilled beverages from former Comecon countries. Experimenting with them is a bit like Russian roulette—it is not an investigation that should be undertaken by the faint-hearted or on a Sunday night.

My favourite memory of the Mercury Market is from the produce section. While I have a liking for fiery South East Asian cuisine, Mongolians do not share my enthusiasm and consider highly spiced foods as inedible torture. Once I spied a stall where the jolly matron offered, among other greens and to my unbridled joy, Thai *prik ki nu* chilli peppers. As I handed her a thumping bundle of peppers to be weighed, her expression went from shock to grave disapproval as if I had just asked Mom to weigh out a kilo or two of heroin.

Retracing our steps to Seoul Street, we come to the Second Maternity Hospital, now hidden behind a fast-food outlet for deep fried poultry parts, marring the well-laid-out appearance of the hospital. Urbanites generally no longer follow the old birth rituals of their ancestors, but most couples still do not purchase items for their baby until after its birth because of the fear that harmful spirits might carry off the child during the pregnancy. Occasionally, an old custom is still practised—a dried bear's paw is supposed to be a sure precaution for a smooth birth if the mother rubs it over her abdomen. Another old ritual is the infant's naming ceremony, which is attended by many relatives. The child is first washed in a chilled broth made from a certain sheep bone. Next the parents and relatives write down suggested names on slips of paper and then mix them in a bowl of rice or wheat. The father chooses one slip and then whispers the selected name to the child's ear.[20]

The site of the Second Maternity Hospital once housed two Nyingma monasteries, the Jagarmolomiin Khural (Жагармоломийн Хурал) and the Tantongjalbiin Khural (Тантонжалвийн Хурал). While Urga was primarily a Gelukpa settlement, the Nyingma monks were permitted to set up temples and practise their rites outside the boundaries of the Eastern and Western monastic settlements. Nyingma adherents had a reputation as 'mad lamas' who did not follow conventional behaviour but exalted in the unorthodox practices of Padmasambhava. Unlike the Gelukpa in Mongolia, the Nyingma recruited nuns and allowed their lamas to marry.

These two temples followed the teachings of Jagarmolom, a Mongolian lama born in the second half of the nineteenth century. After a twenty-year sojourn in Tibet and India, Jagarmolom returned to Urga and set up the first monastery for the Tantric practice of 'cutting through ego', or *zod* (зод).

Zod comes from the teachings of a twelfth-century Tibetan nun named Machik Labdrön.[21] In this form of meditation, a practitioner visually projects his or her spiritual self into the form of a deity that stands apart from the practitioner's body. From this vantage point, the practitioner visualizes the deity slowly carving off parts of his or her body and feeding the gore to horrible gnome-like ghouls who ravenously consume each morsel.

This form of meditation comes as a startling surprise for those who usually associate religion with Christmas carols like 'God Rest Ye Merry Gentlemen' or a basket of chocolate eggs delivered by the Easter Bunny. The exercise is to teach the practitioner that there is no substance to the self or one's sense of emotion. By projecting the self into the deity, the practitioner attempts to achieve the more enlightened perspective of the bodhisattva. By carving up the body, the practitioner is trained to overcome attachment to material matters such as one's own body and to expand perception beyond the

20. I am grateful to Nominchimeg Odsuren for this information.
21. In Mongolian her name is Majiglawdonmaa (Мажиглавдонмаа).

mundane. Feeding the ghouls is meant to reinforce the notion of compassion beyond any judgemental evaluation of the beneficiary of compassion. In all, the practice aims to shatter conventional thinking, leading to a new-found insight into our perceptions of the self and the world.

Machik Labdrön did not confine herself to the secluded world of monasteries but embraced the tradition of a wandering nun who taught unconventional methods for the liberation of the mind. She came to enjoy such considerable fame in the Himalayas and beyond that several revered Indian Buddhist gurus trekked to Tibet to investigate her knowledge and skills. Impressed with her insights, they recognized her practices as fully consonant with Mahayana principles. Her teachings were brought back to India, which is the only instance when a lineage of Vajrayana Buddhism was transmitted from Tibet to India rather than vice versa. It was later absorbed and promoted by the Kagyüpa branch of Vajrayana and ultimately endorsed by the Fifth Dalai Lama.

Moving back towards the city centre, we come across Khandadorj Palace on the south side of Seoul Street, surrounded by a concrete pavement and dreary Brezhnev apartment complexes. Some bright spark hit upon the idea of converting this historic site into a restaurant, alarmingly perhaps as a first step to declare its commercial potential void as an excuse for redevelopment. It is Ulaanbaatar's sole example of early twentieth-century secular Mongolian palace architecture. It was completed in 1913 as the residence for Prince Khandadorj, a leader in the restoration of Mongolian independence.

The prince was an implacable foe of the Manchus. He had battled against the Qing court granting mining concessions to foreign invested enterprises, and generally supported the recalcitrant Eighth Patriarch in resisting Peking's efforts at control. In 1905 the prince welcomed the Thirteenth Dalai Lama during his flight to Urga, assigning his

Former residence of Prince Khandadorj, now taking reservations. Photo by author.

son to accompany His Holiness to Peking in 1906 and hoping for an alliance between Mongolia and Tibet. In retaliation, the Manchu court trumped up a capital charge of lèse majesté against the son, who disappeared into one of the prisons that once bordered on Tiananmen Square. Desperate to locate the boy, the prince hurriedly went to Peking. While attending an imperial court dinner, he was served a large portion of roasted meat wrapped in a cloth towel as one entrée in a multi-course banquet. As the prince unravelled the towel, his wayward son's head rolled out. The story is likely to be an urban legend; nonetheless, it sheds light into the depth of the antipathy that Mongolians feel for the Manchus.

In 1911 the prince secretly travelled with two colleagues to Saint Petersburg to seek Russian support for an independent Mongolia. The three conspirators showed up in Saint Petersburg unannounced, unknown, and confused about how to contact the tsarist authorities to plead their case. They sent a letter for help to the Finnish scholar of Mongolian language and history Gustaf Ramstedt, whom they had met during his earlier visits to Mongolia. Ramstedt duly came to Saint Petersburg to lend a hand.

Professor Ramstedt comes across in his writings as having a sense of balance and good humour. Tracking down the three secret Mongolian envoys in a hotel on Nevskii Prospect, the good professor found his friends under unfriendly interrogation by the police—they had no common language with the gendarmes. Ramstedt explained that the Mongolians were diplomatic dignitaries despite the absence of any credentials or prior warning of such a visit. The cops withdrew and then, as Ramstedt recalled many decades later, the four settled down to a convivial gathering as if in a ger:

> [The prince] sent the Buryat interpreter out to get mutton and to arrange for having it prepared in the hotel kitchen, after which a kettle was brought in and placed in the middle of the room. There we sat, political intriguers, all four of us in Mongolian fashion on the floor around the pot in that fine St. Petersburg hotel.[22]

Thanks to Ramstedt's good offices, the prince and his two colleagues met the Russian Minister of War, who unfortunately gave scant encouragement and offered the Mongolian envoys an arrangement similar to the one between Russia and the emir of Bukhara, a place unknown to the Mongolians. After the meeting, Ramstedt had to explain to the disappointed envoys where Bukhara was and that the former vizier was essentially a Russian captive and not the leader of an independent state.

When Ramstedt returned to Mongolia in 1912, he learned that the prince had been appointed the foreign minister of the Bogd Khan's government.

> I visited the Minister of Foreign Affairs in his official quarters and saw there on his table the same copy of a . . . pocket atlas, which I had given him myself and where I had written beside every country the name of the country in Mongolian. It is possible that [Prince Khandadorj's] geographical knowledge and this very atlas were the chief

22. Ramstedt at 216.

reasons for his being named Minister of Foreign Affairs in the first government of New Mongolia.[23]

Ramstedt recalled with fondness Prince Khandadorj's approachability and sincerity. He was awarded the St Anne's Medal by the tsarist government (or a faction therein) for fostering closer ties between newly autonomous Mongolia and the Russian empire. Undoubtedly, he saw Russia as the less pernicious of the two neighbours, a view possibly reinforced by the supposed murder of his son.

As we continue along to the east on Seoul Street, we pass by No. 1 High School, which opened its doors in 1940, becoming the premiere secondary school in the capital. A friend recalls how, perhaps as a precursor to the 1990 protests, Mongolian mothers gathered in this vicinity in the 1980s to protest the treatment meted out to their sons after their induction into the army. This might have been a foreshadowing of the discontent that was to flare up forcefully against Batmonkh's government several years later.

We next come to the Presidential Mansion, which was originally constructed as a 'Winter Palace' for Choibalsan in 1947. Choibalsan instructed the architects that he wanted his palace to have a European exterior and a Mongolian interior. He did not have the use of it for long, however. The old boy dropped off the twig on Tsagaan Sar eve in 1952 while receiving medical treatment in Moscow, thus fuelling speculation that Uncle Joe might have been doing some spring cleaning. Afterwards, the Presidential Mansion turned into the Museum of Choibalsan and Sükhbaatar, preserving Little Joe's office as he left it along with special exhibits of Sükhbaatar's photographs and weapons. These days, it is less illustriously rented to diplomatic missions for their national holiday celebrations and other such box-ticking social events.

Along the outside walls of the Winter Palace, you will see decorations of the national standard in the shape of a trident and a single-bladed spear. These symbols are part of the *süld* (сүлд), or standards for war and peace, used by Chinggis Khan. The süld initially took the form of a spear planted into the ground with nine horsetails tied below the blade. White horsehair tails capped by a trident symbolized the state in peacetime while a black horsehair tail under a single-bladed spear was used as the state standard in wartime. The two sülds were regarded as the material foundations or depositories of the protective spirit of the nation and thus objects of reverence. Over time, this protective spirit became associated with the soul of Chinggis Khan as the founder of the nation. The white süld of Chinggis Khan was lost about five hundred years ago while the black standard of warfare survived in Shankh Monastery until its disappearance during the Great Purge. New versions were remade in the late 1940s with the white standard in Government House and the black one in the Ministry of Defence.

23. Ibid. at 213–14.

Süld on gate to Presidential Mansion. Photo by author.

Süld presented at the outset of the Naadam ceremony. Photo by Janice Law.

9

Western Monastic Settlement (Baruun Khüree)

Gandantegchenlin Monastery (Гандантэгчинлэн Хийд) is the centre of what was once the Western Monastic District, or Baruun Khüree (Баруун Хүрээ). Known locally as Gandan (Гандан), it takes its name from the Ganden Namgyel Ling, the famous Gelukpa monastery founded outside Lhasa in 1409 by Tsongkhapa. Like its namesake in Tibet, it was established as a centre for scholar-monks to study tsanid philosophy and the other disciplines of the Vajrayana curriculum.

In 1809 the Fourth Patriarch moved one of the aimag colleges from the Eastern Monastic Settlement to a place more conducive to quietude for the intensive hours of study needed for a monk to be well-versed in the esoteric elements of Buddhist scholarship. The Fourth Patriarch selected the summit of Dalkh Hill, or Dalkhiin Denj (Далхын Дэнж), in accordance with the monastic rule that a college ought to be no closer to a village or a market than the reach of human voice. This was meant as a demonstration of the monks' renunciation of worldly concerns.[1] In 1838 the Fifth Patriarch ordered the construction of a permanent stone structure, a tsogchin dugan, or assembly hall for the monks. By 1841 two more colleges were also set up on Dalkh Hill along with a palace for the Fifth Patriarch. When the fifth and sixth patriarchs sequentially died of smallpox in the palace, the lamas and their geomancers concluded that the hill was an inauspicious site. The official palace was moved to the Eastern Monastic Settlement, where it remained until the Great Purge. Meanwhile, Dalkh Hill gradually grew into a 'university town' with the addition of more colleges and monastic residences. In the monastery's heyday, a wooden palisade enclosed the stone temples while other shrines, residences for high lamas, and supporting administrative aimags were established outside the palisade in the standard inverted U-shape of a khüree.[2]

The Gandan lamas followed the Gelukpa disciplinary rules more strictly than other monasteries in Urga. Large, formidable protector-monks were posted at Gandan's gates to deny entry to women, laymen, and especially merchants seeking to pitch their wares when the monks ought to have been memorizing sutras. An exception was made for pilgrim-visitors on the festival on the fifteenth day of the first summer month for the historical Buddha's birth, enlightenment, and *parinirvana*.

1. Pozdneyev (1978) at 49.
2. Teleki at130 et. seq.

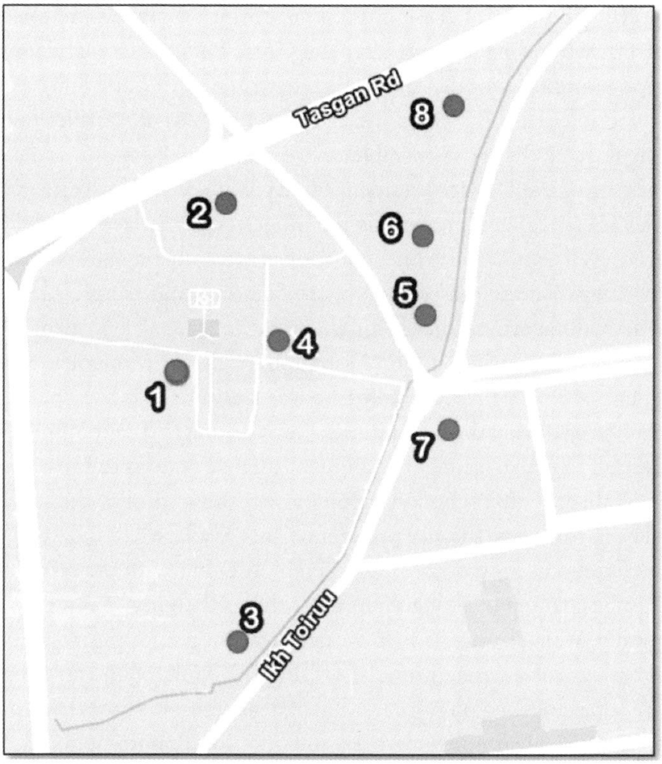

Vicinity of Gandan Monastery. Map by Aubrey Ding-Shan Yang.

Key

1. Gandan Monastery
2. College of the Medicinal Buddha
3. Centre of Shaman and Eternal Heavenly Sophistication
4. Soothsayers and religious stores
5. Geser Temple
6. Zurkhai Datsan
7. Pethub Stangey Choskhor Monastery
8. Tasgan Hill

Compared to Urga's other monastic buildings, Gandan may have had considerably less impact on the eye until 1913 when the theocratic government built the monumental Temple of Avalokitesvara, or Migjid Janraisig Süm (Мигжид Жанрайсиг Сүм), which dominated the city's skyline and became an iconic symbol of Mongolian independence.

To the north and west of the monastic complex stood a walled barrier with twenty-eight stupas. This was the Assembly of White Stupas, or Tsagaan Suvraglin Khural (Цагаан Суваргын Хурал). The most haunting one was a huge Jarankhasar (Жаранхасар) stupa built in the same shape as the stupa at Boudhanath near Kathmandu. The stupa was well-known for the pair of mesmerizing eyes below its crown, a reminder to one and all that no act escapes karmic justice.

Alas, nothing remains of these impressive sentinels as they were torn down and recycled for other building projects after the Great Purge, a fate which was likewise inflicted upon Gandan's wooden datsans at that time. The stone temples within the inner courtyard may have remained intact because they were sturdier buildings that could be redeployed as barracks or stables.

We must thank the US vice president Henry Wallace for inadvertently saving the stone temples at Gandan and preserving the monastery as a place of worship. In 1944 President Roosevelt sent Wallace on a goodwill trip to Siberia, China, and Mongolia, essentially to keep Wallace out of the United States during the presidential primary season. While making arrangements for the trip, the State Department passed along Wallace's request to attend a Buddhist ceremony while in Mongolia. Wallace was a lifelong student of Asian mysticism, but he was unaware that the dharma had been nearly exterminated during the Great Purge. Not wanting to disappoint the Americans or expose himself to embarrassment, Stalin sent off instructions to Little Joe to snap to and provide Wallace with a functioning monastery. A handful of the surviving lamas were hauled back to receive the vice president. Once Wallace left, the MPR authorities retained this Potemkin monastery and its ceremonies but with the restriction that all prayers had to be chanted in Mongolian rather than Tibetan.

Incidentally, Wallace was the first Western tourist 'guinea pig' to be put through the standard paces for a foreign official visiting the Mongolian capital. Aside from watching the lamas tootling on horns and banging drums, his hosts took him to a ger, dressed him up in a del complete with a pointy hat for a photo op, brought him to a culture night featuring some throat singing and morin huur music, and took him out to Terelj National Park for a quick squint at Turtle Rock.[3] Lattimore accompanied Wallace on the trip as translator and cultural adviser. However, by the time of they landed at the military airport in Ulan Bator, Lattimore was fed up with Wallace's notorious lack of focus and his legendary obsession for callisthenics and exercise. (Chiang Kai-shek's representatives knew that Wallace was a fitness nut whom they could distract from raising uncomfortable topics by suggesting a volleyball match, which was never refused.)

By the 1960s the government relaxed its anticlerical policies and permitted the monks to resume Kalachakra initiations at Gandan. This was followed by the founding of the Buddhist University of Mongolia in 1971. In 1979 the Dalai Lama came for an official visit to Gandan, an event blessed by the Soviets who were keen to use this novel way to stick a finger in the eye of the Chinese Communists.

After the implosion of the socialist government, Gandan had a bleak, exhausted appearance, surrounded by barren fields and haunted by the Birthday Man. As all long-term residents know, the Birthday Man is a professional beggar who accosts Westerners near the Bayangol Hotel, loudly proclaiming that that it is his birthday and demanding

3. I am grateful to Jonathan Addleton for his observation on the persistence of this diplomatic protocol for Western visitors.

a cash handout. Twenty years ago he used to hang around the temples at Gandan, where he would hand out an English language note saying that his ger had burned down and that he needed money for a new one. The Birthday Man later transplanted this ploy to the parking lot at Chinggis Khan Airport until the security guards turfed him out. The old boy is a tourist attraction unique to Ulaanbaatar.

Despite the occasional harassment of a beggar or two, Gandan was soon a site for vignettes of revived Buddhist and filial piety, as seen by a British volunteer teacher:

> I once saw a young man in a *deel* staggering like a drunk as he circled one of the temples, a frail and crumpled relative clinging round his neck like a barnacle to a rock. The young man was panting, the crippled older man chanting aloud from the Sutras.[4]

By the end of the decade Gandan had begun to recover its old vitality with the construction of new sites for worship and the induction of young monks. Today, hundreds of worshippers visit the monastery each day to offer juniper incense, spin the prayer wheels, and ask the lamas for a jasaa for spiritual assistance with the trials of modern life.

The main gate of Gandan faces south, like nearly all Buddhist monasteries. The gate is a Chinese monumental structure with a three-bay entrance. The central entrance was reserved for use by the patriarch while lesser officials and lamas used the other two gates. On the exterior of the gate are paintings of the Eight Treasures of Vajrayana Buddhism.

The oldest section of the monastery is the enclosed part to the right once you enter the grounds. The main gate of this section is adorned with the Sanskrit mantra *om mani padme hum*, an invocation of the bodhisattva Avalokitesvara, cast in six colours symbolizing the constituent elements of the universe. The mantra is sometimes rendered into English as 'the jewel is in the lotus' but the Fourteenth Dalai Lama offers this free-verse translation: 'In dependence on the practice of a path which is an indivisible union of method and wisdom, you can transform your impure body, speech, and mind into the pure exalted body, speech, and mind of a Buddha.'[5] The six syllables correspond to the six colours and also allude to the six levels of existence among mortals, deities, and demons. Stone lions flank each side of the entrance; their mouths are stained with butter rubbed on as offerings from pilgrims. The gate's walkway is also flanked by a set of eight huge wooden prayer wheels similar to those once found everywhere in the Eastern Monastic Settlement.

The Main Assembly Hall, or Tsogchin Dugan (Цогчин Дуган), is the yellow ger-temple in the north-east corner of the courtyard. It was built in 1838 and therefore is the oldest structure within the monastic complex. Its formal name, Gandantegchelin,

4. Waugh at 9.
5. From a lecture given by His Holiness the Fourteenth Dalai Lama at the Kalmyk Mongolian Buddhist Center, New Jersey.

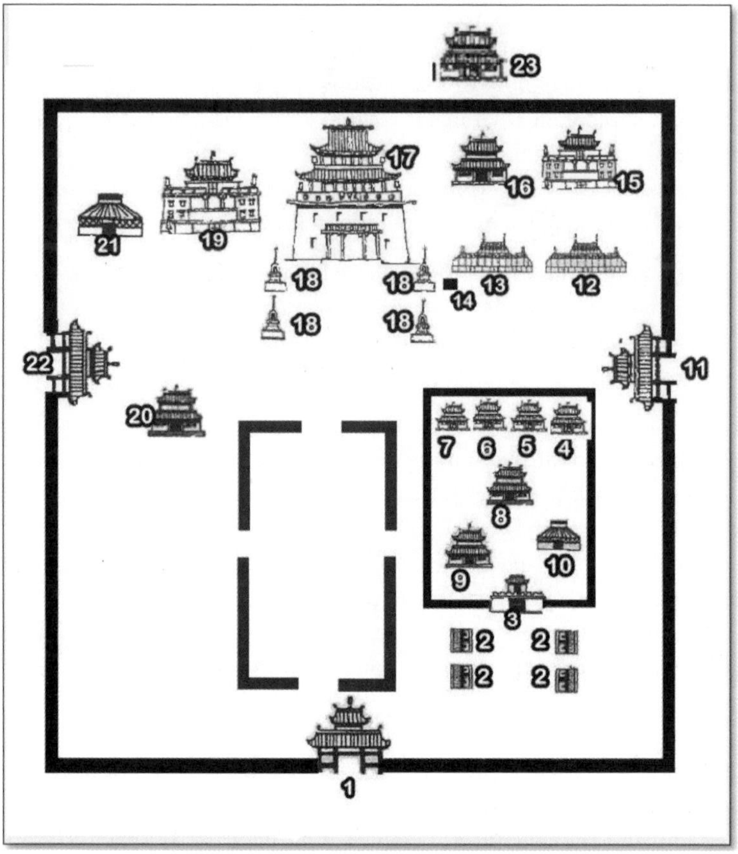

Gandan Monastery. Map by Aubrey Ding-Shan Yang from Gandan's entrance ticket.

Key

1. South Gate (and ticket booth)
2. Prayer Wheels
3. Entrance to Temple Complex
4. Main Assembly Hall, formally Gandantegchenling Monastery
5. Temple of Vajradhara
6. Temple of the Shakyamuni Buddha
7. Shrine to Tsongkhapa and Funerary Stupas
8. Palace of Blissful Emptiness
9. Library (former temple for the Eight Patriarch's Relics)
10. Official reception ger
11. East Gate (to fortune tellers and Geser Temple)
12. College of Expanding Auspiciousness
13. College of Rejoicing
14. Bagana
15. College of Teaching Holder's Happy Heart
16. College of the Kalachakra
17. Temple of Avalokitesvara
18. Stupas
19. Mongolian Institute for Buddhist Art
20. Zanabazar Buddhist University of Mongolia
21. College of Tantric Studies
22. West Gate
23. College of Medicine

Entrance to Gandan Monastery. Photo by Janice Law.

Early morning at Gandan Monastery. Photo by author.

has been co-opted by the entire temple complex. Each morning, monks assemble in this hall for the formal chanting of prayers.[6]

Inside the Main Assembly Hall, a Shakyamuni Buddha statute sits behind the central glass case at the opposite end from the entrance. It was commissioned in 1956 as part of the celebration of the 2,500th anniversary of the Buddha's birth, an event

6. The historical details about Gandan Monastery in this and subsequent paragraphs are based on the work of Teleki; see ibid., among others.

widely celebrated in Buddhist nations and used as political whitewash in Communist ones with Buddhist communities. The shelves on the left-hand wall hold the 108 volumes of the Kanjur. These are woodblock prints made with gold ink on black paper, a sign of reverence and a way for the commissioning patron to accrue more merit than simply ordering a copy printed with black ink on white paper. In the glass case on the right-hand side of the main altar, there is a bronze statue of Zanabazar, cast in the 1680s by the First Patriarch himself at the request of his mother. Surrounding it are statues of the other seven patriarchs. Along the walls are rows of Ayush Buddhas donated by the faithful as offerings for the well-being and extended life of a relative.

To the west of the Main Assembly Hall is the Vajradhara Temple, or Ochirdariin Süm (Очирдарийн Сүм). Built in 1840–1841, the temple originally served as the residence for the Fifth Patriarch. It was converted into a sepulchre in 1842 for the stupa containing his remains. The stupa was destroyed in 1938.

Vajradhara is an exoteric form of the Adi Buddha, the primordial force and substance from which flow all emanations of the universe. 'From the perfect void (*maha-sunyata*), the mystic syllable "aum" became manifest, from which at his own will the Adi-Buddha was produced.'[7] The Gelukpa worship Vajradhara as the supreme power and creator of all things to whom all lesser local deities swear allegiance when they are converted to the dharma.[8] He is usually depicted wearing a bodhisattva's crown and an Indian monk's robes and holding a bronze *dorj*, or thunderbolt. A bronze sculpture of Vajradhara cast by Zanabazar in 1683 sits on the main red-and-gold lacquered altar along the northern wall. Vajradhara is the protective deity of the complex.

In front of the Vajradhara Temple is an incense burner manufactured by a foundry in Peking near the Gate of Excellent Scholarship (or Chongwenmen 崇文门). This is a fitting coincidence. This Peking district has an ancient connection with Mongolia, for in the thirteenth century a Mongolian noble name Prince Hata set up his household near the gate. Later residents colloquially renamed it Hata Gate in his memory. The name and address of the foundry inscribed in Chinese on the incense burner call to mind the unbelievable effort needed for a band of teamsters to lug this heavy piece of iron all the way from Peking by camel caravan.

To the west is the Temple of the Shakyamuni Buddha, or Zuugiin Süm (Зуугийн Сүм). It was built in 1869 to house the stupa for the relics of the Seventh Patriarch (destroyed in 1938) and now displays bronzes of the historical Buddha and his main disciples. Sor offerings and three tiers of bronzes are set out along the north wall while small-scale models of Mount Meru are on the right side of the hall. It is here each morning where the lamas read *gürem*, or prayers for the dead. Relatives gather here while the lamas conduct their prayers for a relative's peaceful passage through the bardo to their next existence.

In the sepulchre to the west of the temple are monuments consisting of a plaster statue of Tsongkhapa, rows of prayer wheels, and a stupa containing portions of the

7. Getty at 2.
8. Ibid. at 3.

relics of the fifth, seventh, and eighth patriarchs. These remains were rescued by lamas at extraordinary personal risk from smouldering trash heaps during the Great Purge.

The two-storey Palace of Blissful Emptiness, or Didanpovran (Диданповран), was completed in 1840 as the winter palace for the Fifth Patriarch. It is used these days for the lamas' morning prayers before they gather in the Main Assembly Hall or the Vajradhara Temple. Astrological projections and prayers for the deceased are also conducted here from 9:00 a.m. to 5:00 p.m.

In the early 1900s the Didanpovran became a nerve centre of geopolitical intrigue in Urga. At that time, Britain and Russia were locked in a century-long struggle for hegemonic supremacy in Central Asia, a contest that had spread into Tibetan politics. The Thirteenth Dalai Lama sought to distance his country from British imperial ambitions by refusing any overture from the colonial government in India to open commerce and establish diplomatic ties. British paranoia reached a climax when Lord Curzon, the viceroy of British India, received intelligence reports about Agvan Dorzhiev, a Russian Buryat lama and supposed agent for the Tsar, acting as an adviser on foreign affairs at the Dalai Lama's court. Agvan Dorzhiev had been a courier for diplomatic correspondence between Saint Petersburg and the Dalai Lama, who was seeking to balance the threat posed to his government by China and Britain. Lord Curzon succumbed to exaggerated fears that Tibet was already controlled by shadowy Russian agents. Despite reluctance in London, Curzon launched a 'pre-emptive strike' into Tibet with Colonel Francis Younghusband at the head of an expeditionary force to compel the Dalai Lama's government to sign a trade agreement. As the British invasion approached Lhasa, His Holiness slipped out of Tibet and fled to Urga, where he took refuge from 1904 to 1906. He attempted to elicit Tsar Nicholas's support for Tibet, but these hopes were dashed because Russia was fully occupied with the growing military confrontation with Japan. Nevertheless, the Tsar made a grand showing of sending valuable gifts to the Dalai Lama and dispatching his ambassador in Peking to Urga for discussions. In 1906 the Dalai Lama left Urga for Inner Mongolia, and from there he went to Peking.

The atmosphere of geopolitical intrigue was compounded when a Japanese spy, Teramoto Enga, arrived in Urga to pay a visit to His Holiness. Teramoto had mastered the skill of impersonating a lama and made an unsuccessful attempt to infiltrate Tibet earlier. He so impressed the Dalai Lama that he was invited to return to Lhasa as an unofficial military adviser. In later years, Teramoto trained Tibetan soldiers in modern military techniques, but his efforts at bringing the Tibetan army into the modern age were not overly successful.[9]

The Dalai Lama and the Eighth Patriarch also did not get along. His Holiness was underwhelmed by the moral laxity in Urga's monasteries while the Eighth Patriarch was peeved by the faithful diverting too many donations to the visiting Tibetan. Urga's learned monks also gave the Dalai Lama a warm welcome because he was an erudite

9. Berry at 250; Kimura at 104.

teacher and an accomplished debater of Vajrayana philosophy, talents which the syphilitic and alcoholic Eighth Patriarch could not hope to match.

Other pettiness plagued a relationship that had been strained historically. The seventeenth-century Zungharian rebel Galdan used an alleged breach of protocol by Zanabazar to stir up conflict when, during a meeting of high lamas, the throne of the Dalai Lama's representative was placed 'disrespectfully' in a lower position than the throne for Zanabazar. This chestnut of a quarrel erupted once again over the positioning of thrones during the Thirteenth Dalai Lama's stay along with other acrimonious arguments between the courtiers of the two high lamas over protocol and decorum.[10]

Next to the Didanpovran, the library was originally constructed in 1925 to house the stupa for the remains of the Eighth Patriarch. These days, the library's archives hold an extensive collection of philosophical, historical, literary, and scientific treatises in Mongolian, Tibetan, and Sanskrit including a rare Derge version of the Kanjur as well as assorted works by Tsongkhapa, the dalai lamas, the panchen lamas, and renowned Mongolian philosophers such as Agvanbaldan and Bragriin Gegeen. Some of the manuscripts in the library's collection have jewel-studded covers with texts written in gold or silver ink made from pulverized precious jewels. It was in the library where Professor Damdinsuren first discovered sections of the *Moon Cuckoo* in the late 1950s.[11]

Roy Chapman Andrews happened to be in Urga in 1925 during the Bogd Khan's funerary ceremonies and caught a glimpse of the internment. Since non-Buddhists were forbidden to attend the event, a Mongolian friend helped smuggle Andrews and another foreigner into the proceedings, dressing them in robes, darkening their complexion with walnut dye, and telling the lamas in attendance that the two odd-looking mourners were deaf-mutes from Alashan in China proper. The ruse worked. Andrews and his colleague were brought into the temple where 'at the far end of the room facing the entrance sat my old friend the Hutukhtu [the Eighth Patriarch] on a golden throne. He looked natural enough to speak except that he was half his normal size and completely gilded in gold leaf. His features were perfect.'[12]

Near the library there is a two-storey tower called *burayin shat* (бүрээн шат) or the 'trumpet platform' for summoning the clergy to prayers. Two monks ascend the tower each day to take turns blowing a continuous note on a conch-shell trumpet before morning prayers. This is also a request to the spirit of the Buddhas and protective deities to join the ceremonies. The ger to the south-east of the courtyard serves as a reception area for distinguished visitors.

In the newer buildings on the eastern side of the inner courtyard, the faithful submit their requests for a *jasaa* (жасаа), or the reading of a prayer. Ground juniper leaves are also given out here as offerings for incense burners. The smell of juniper incense is highly evocative of Vajrayana Buddhism, and it is a scent that perfumes holy

10. Goldstein at 46.
11. Teleki at 137; Heissig (1967) at 220 et seq.
12. Andrews (1935) at 114.

sights all the way from the Mongolian Plateau to the Himalayas. It is another one of UB's timeless sensations, like glimpsing the khangarid on the municipal flag.

Directly to the north of Gandan's walled inner courtyard is the location where many of the monastic colleges had been set up in the nineteenth century and where now we can see the revival of tsanid learning in post-Communist Mongolia. Directly behind the Main Assembly Hall is the College to Spread Auspiciousness, or Dashchoimbel Datsan (Дашчоймбэл Дацан). The Dashchoimbel Datsan was established under the Second Patriarch as the first Mongolian monastic school for tsanid studies in 1756 and moved by the Fifth Patriarch to Dalkh Hill in 1837. The datsan was revived in 1989 with help of the Nineteenth Bakula Rinpoche, a Ladkhaki lama and the Indian ambassador to Mongolia at that time. The Fourteenth Dalai Lama officially consecrated the revived college during a Kalachakra initiation in 1995. The datsan's curriculum is now the same as in pre-Communist times with philosophical examinations held for granting higher degrees. In the mornings young monks chant their prayers under the watchful eye of the disciplinary master. He goes on patrol with a heavy staff with blue khadags whenever the students become distracted. Sometimes in the afternoon, you can see student monks honing their debating skills here.

To the west is the College of Rejoicing, or Güngaachoilin Datsan (Гунгаачойлин Дацан). The Fourth Patriarch established this datsan in 1809 as the second centre for tsanid Buddhist philosophical studies in Mongolia. It follows the philosophical teachings of the sixteenth-century Tibetan scholar Wanchin Sonomdagva of Drepung Monastery, which is one of the three great Gelukpa monasteries in Lhasa. Its traditional course of studies was revived in 1990 in a classroom in the Buddhist university. The new datsan was rebuilt on its original site in 2001.

Two datsans. Photo by Janice Law.

To the south-west of the college, there is a pillar that might be one of the bagana of the original 1809 datsan. People still recount the legend about how an enemy of the dharma tried to desecrate the bagana in the twentieth century. Depending upon the teller of the story, the villain varies from Manchu amban Sando to one of Little Xu's gamin soldiers, or sometimes a 'green hat' from the Ministry of Internal Security. (One hundred years from now people will say it was Robert Friedland.) Whoever it was, the villain attempted to saw down the pillar, but at each attempt to draw the blade, the pole bled or let out a deafening scream, which frightened off the attackers.

The lamas attached to the datsan explain that this event actually occurred in 1937. Baldan Lkham, the protectress of the datsan, was the spirit who struck back against the desecration. In truth, it seems that the cadres probably just forgot to complete the job, having been ordered to take care of some other task. Or this might be the exoteric explanation of an esoteric incident.

The bagana is best viewed as a 'connector' between the earth and sky, very much like trees venerated with blue khadags. People circumambulate the pillar clockwise (or in the 'sun direction') as with prayer wheels and peregrinations around Vajrayana temples. The supplicants also insert coins or matches into the pole and tie khadags as offerings to Baldan Lkham. If you wish to join in this ritual, place your right hand on the bagana as you circle it. Your hand will pick up a scent of juniper, mutton fat, coal, and pinewood, all of which powerfully convey the essence of the steppes and the spirituality of Central Asia. This sight is one of my favourites in all Ulaanbaatar in that it testifies to a living connection with Urga and centuries-old traditions.

The College of the Teaching Holder's Happy Heart, or Idagachoinzenling Datsan (Идгаачойзинлин Дацан), was established by the Eighth Patriarch in 1910 for the

Bagana near the College of Rejoicing, or Güngaachoilin Datsan. Photo by author.

study of philosophical treatises composed by the monk-scholars of Sera Monastery in Lhasa. It is now housed in the cement building with a golden roof completed in 2004.

To the south-east corner of the Temple of Avalokitesvara is the College of the Aeon of Great Bliss, or Dechengalpa Datsan (Дэчэнгалба Дацан). The datsan had been set up as a Kalachakra monastic school in the Eastern Monastic Settlement in 1806 by the 'Terrible Fourth'. It was re-established here in 1992, with its new building completed in 1994 for an initiation of Kalachakra teachings during a visit by the Dalai Lama. Today, the lamas here follow the same practices as the re-established Namgyal Monastery in New Delhi and revive traditional ceremonies of old Urga, such as the Great Düinkhor festival, the Kalachakra sand mandala, and the annual procession to the source of the Tuul River in Gachuurt. When the Fourteenth Dalai Lama comes to Ulaanbaatar for a Kalachakra initiation, he sits on the throne on the northern wall, which was also used by the Ninth Patriarch after he moved to Ulaanbaatar in 2011.

The main site in the Gandan complex is, of course, the Temple of Avalokitesvara, which was built after Mongolia's declaration of independence. Foreign Minister Prince Khandadorj led the effort to raise funds for its construction as an offering to Avalokitesvara for the restoration of the Eighth Patriarch's eyesight. As the bodhisattva of compassion, Avalokitesvara is associated with sight because he sees the suffering of all sentient beings and thus was the appropriate deity to beseech for help in overcoming the Patriarch's blindness. The temple initially housed a 25-metre bronze statue of the bodhisattva cast by Chinese coppersmiths in Doloon Nor and gilded by Mongolian and Chinese craftsman in Urga. On 13 June 1913 the temple was consecrated and ten thousand statues of Ayush cast by craftsmen in Urga and Warsaw were installed around the main statue.[13] The ganjirs placed on the roof were filled with copies of the Prajnaparamita Sutra and along the entranceway builders erected stupas marking the eight events in the Shakyamuni Buddha's life.

In his last days in Urga during the spring of 1921 the 'Mad Baron' came to this temple seeking a fortune-teller's prediction for his fate. The soothsayer said that he would meet his doom in one hundred thirty days.[14] He was captured by the Bolsheviks in August and shot on 15 September 1921, roughly one hundred thirty days later. The Eighth Patriarch ordered prayers to be said for his soul.

Roy Chapman Andrews also visited the temple and left us a record of his impressions, although distastefully tainted with his bias:

> I was fortunate in being present one day when the temple was opened to women and the faithful in the city. Somewhat doubtful as to my reception, I followed the crowd as it filed through an outer pavilion between a double row of kneeling lamas in high-peaked hats and robes of flaming yellow. I carried my hat in my hand and tried

13. This odd connection might be explained because, at that time, Poland had not yet recovered its sovereignty from tsarist Russia. Someone in the Russian consulate might have made the recommendation to commission a noted Warsaw bronze smith.

14. Ossendowski at 217.

Temple of Avalokitesvara. Photo by Janice Law.

> to wear a becoming expression of humility and reverence. It was evidently successful, for I passed unhindered into the Presence . . . Silent with awe, the people . . . prostrated themselves before the gigantic figure standing on the golden lotus blossom, its head lost in the shadows of the temple roof . . . From niches in the walls, hundreds of tiny Buddhas gazed impassively on the worshipping Mongols.
>
> The scene was intoxicating in its barbaric splendour. The women in their fantastic headdresses and brilliant gowns; the blazing yellow robes of the kneeling lamas; the chorus of prayers which rose and fell in meaningless half-wild chant broken by the clash of cymbals and the boom of drums—all this set the blood leaping in my veins. There was a strange dizziness in my head, and I had an almost overpowering desire to fall on my knees with the Mongols and join in the chorus of adoration. The subtle smell of burning incense, the brilliant colours, and the barbaric music were an intoxicating drink which flamed the sense but dulled the brain. It was then that I came nearest to understanding the religious fanaticism of the East. Even with a background of twentieth century civilization I felt its sensuous power. What wonder that it has such a hold on simple, uneducated people, fed on superstition from earliest childhood and the religious traditions of seven hundred years.[15]

In 1938 the Mongolian Communists sent the temple's bronzes to the Soviet Union where they were reportedly melted down for the manufacture of ammunition. Elsewhere it is written that the bronzes were still in storage in Leningrad in 1958.[16]

In the 1950s the MPR authorities offered 10,000 togrogs to any work unit willing to take on the task of pulling down the temple, but there were no takers, perhaps

15. Andrews 1921 at 72–73.
16. Becker at 74.

because of the bad karmic effect that would result from such sacrilege. Or no one wanted to go through the bother of filling out a Soviet version of those damn World Bank bidding documents. In the 1990s plans were launched to reconstruct the bronze statue, which was completed and consecrated in 1996.

The temple is a combination of Tibetan and Chinese styles, with the white tapering walls replicating the appearance of a sanctuary common to Tibetan temples and the gabled two-tiered roof commonly seen in China. There are eight windows on the southern facade symbolizing the Eight Treasures. The roof is topped with the usual Vajrayana decorations.

The Avalokitesvara statue, standing at 26.5 metres, wears the crown of a bodhisattva prince. It has four arms holding a mirror, a silken scarf, a vessel filled with sacred water, and a pair of bronze balls symbolizing the ability to perceive suffering. Its elongated ears refer to the bodhisattva's ability to hear the cries of all sentient beings while its third eye symbolizes insight into reality unclouded by desire. At the base of the statue, there are photographs of the Fourteenth Dalai Lama and the Ninth Patriarch along with bronzes of Avalokitesvara and Dorje Drolo, a wrathful form of Padmasambhava. Around the inner perimeter of the temple are bronze prayer wheels and along the walls are countless Ayush Buddhas donated to the temple. The pillars are decorated with images of water, earth, and clouds to represent the three realms of earthly existence. Stupas are to be found to the south-west of the temple and along its north perimeter.

On the west side of the Gandan complex is a fenced area with residences for the lamas as well as the Mongolian Institute for Buddhist Art with its three-storey building for lectures and conferences. The Mongolian Institute for Buddhist Art provides undergraduate- and graduate-level courses for laymen and lamas on traditional Buddhist arts, such as thangkas, sculptures, appliqué, stupas, and other objects of veneration.

The Zanabazar Buddhist University of Mongolia is in the yellow two-storey administration building directly to the south-west of the Janraisig Temple. Established in 1970, the university offers a four-year degree programme with a faculty of internal sciences for majors in Buddhist philosophy and chanting, and a faculty of common knowledge for Sanskrit, English, Tibetan traditional medicine, and astrology. Its graduates include students from Mongolia, Tuva, Buryatia, and Kalmykia.

The College of Esoteric Knowledge, or Jüd Datsan (Жүд Дацан), established in 1739 by the Second Patriarch in the Eastern Monastic Settlement, was reconsecrated in 1998 within a humble ger as a site for higher-level tantric rituals. The monastic authorities later moved it into the present red brick building, which, in keeping with its role as a centre for esoteric studies, is usually not open. However, graduates of the three datsans on the east side of the monastery complex may continue their studies of esoteric rituals and philosophy here. At the time of writing, the datsan was under renovation.

Outside the north wall of Gandan is the College of the Medicinal Buddha, or Manla Datsan (Манла Дацан), which serves as the medical school attached to the

Bronze statue of Avalokitesvara. Photo by Janice Law.

monastery. To get there, you will have to walk along the outer wall of the monastery. After 1990 the Manla Datsan was re-established in the Geser Temple, relocating to its current temple in 2001. Mandal Zuu, or the Medicine Buddha, usually depicted in blue, is the main deity of the datsan. Supplicants come to seek prayers for health or for a good rebirth of a deceased relative or friend. It also trains students in traditional medicine and astrology. I found the lamas here to be an outgoing bunch, and their college is appealing in its ramshackle elegance.

Zanabazar Street is the main avenue leading up to the monastery's grounds. It hosts many newly established datsans, temples, and Buddhist paraphernalia shops, some with grand names that suggest a connection with the city's illustrious monastic heritage. For the most part, they are not affiliated with Gandan Monastery, however. These datsans have been set up as the UB equivalent of store-front churches in urban America and seek to earn alms for prayers and astrological projections.

The Centre of Shaman and Eternal Heavenly Sophistication is a departure from the layout of Buddhist temples. It is in the large ger on the south-east side of Zanabazar Street with the peacetime and war standards of Chinggis Khan flying overhead. Zorigbaatar Banzar and his wife set up the centre to promote worship of Chinggis Khan and shamanistic beliefs in post-Communist Mongolia. The couple receives numerous supplicants each day, seeking redress from financial, romantic, or other crises.[17] The centre's interior is a meaningful lesson in the visual difference between shamanism and Buddhism. Its decorations are arranged helter-skelter without the symmetry that is characteristic of a Buddhist temple. Beneath the gonkhon of the ger, a stuffed vulture appears to rise up. Horsehair sülds are prominently displayed between the baganas, which are decorated with fox and wolf pelts. Two stuffed tigers stare out from beneath the toono, and along the perimeter of the ger are a jumble of shaman's robes and mirrors, arrows and quivers, conch shells, butter lamps, swords, spears, and multiple Chinggis portraits. You will easily recognize Mr Zorigbaatar as he is the fabulously robed gentleman with a long beard and a hairdo reminiscent of that worn by Khitan warriors in the eleventh century. The overall effect of the centre is not unlike a mystical version of a Salvation Army thrift shop managed by a benevolent Hell's Angel. (I mean this as a compliment.) The centre amply illustrates an observation once made by the author and poet Bill Porter that Taoism is just a housebroken version of shamanism.

I prefer to leave Gandan Monastery by its east gate because the appearance of the surrounding neighbourhood has been mostly unchanged over the past hundred years, judging by the 1913 Jügder map. The alleyways lead you past khashaas enclosing felt tents and wooden houses. Several log houses with red wooden lintels over the gateway invoke the same scene as witnessed by travellers in the nineteenth century. The shops immediately by the gate are those engaged in applied tsanid sciences, such as fortune telling and astrology, as well as in the business of selling Buddhist articles, some of recent manufacture and others old to the eye.

Many Asian traditions have been sacrificed in the march to modernity, whether it is architectural heritage, folk art and crafts, or cuisine. However, fortune telling is a field that remains authentic and resistant to change, regardless of greater social upheavals in the twentieth century. In this corner of Ulaanbaatar, the past blends with the present as it openly and seamlessly began to do once again in the early 1990s, as observed by the journalist Tiziano Terzani:

> I saw an old Mongolian telling a soldier's fortune. On a red cloth with a geometric pattern he dropped a handful of white pebbles. He divided them into pairs and groups of threes and fours, moved them about and gathered them up again while

17. Levin.

> murmuring formulae that sounded like poems. An old system: one reads the future in the way the stones fall . . . with the advantage that stones can be found everywhere on the plain, and the squares and circles can be drawn on the ground. In front of one of the new department stores I saw another old man calling out to the passers-by, offering to read their future by burning some *ars*, the scented Mongolian herb which is dried and ground to a fine powder.[18]

In another instance, a lama revived a prognostication ritual by drawing patterns on incense ash in a box:

> [The lama's] method was to ask first for my year of birth and then for a number under 109. With a silver chopstick he drew some complicated signs in the ashes, cancelled them and drew some more. He traced a picture of my life that was there one moment and vanished the next, as with a simple movement of the box, he restored the ashes to a perfectly smooth surface . . . I liked his truths because they were more ephemeral than horoscopes written on paper . . . At the end he traced a perfect circle in the ashes, inscribed some signs in it, and went to consult a sheaf of handwritten papers. The original basis of his system lay in the 108 volumes of the Ganjur, the sacred book of the Mongols.[19]

At the bottom of the hill is the King Geser Temple, or Geser Khaan Süm (Гэсэр Хаан Сүм), the pink building with green tiled roofs at the intersection of the Outer Ring Road and Sambuu Street. A Chinese merchant built the temple in 1919 as an offering to a legendary Mongolian deity who had been fused in popular imagination with the Chinese 'God of War'.

King Geser is a pre-Buddhist Mongolian and Tibetan folk hero hailing from eastern Tibet. Some philologists see a connection between Geser and the imperial title Caesar, pointing for support to a poem by the Tibetan mystic Milarapa about a Geser of Phrom, possibly meaning Caesar of Rome. In the legend, King Geser is destined to re-establish order and morality in a world that lost its spiritual bearings. For centuries, travelling bards spread his legend from the Himalayas to the steppes and on to the forests of Buryatia.

However, he was not always regarded favourably by the Buddhist clergy. Gelukpa lamas viewed the legend disdainfully as a story about a crass superhero rather than a true protective deity or a mystical lama well-versed in the wisdom of the tsanid treatises, but with time his popularity grew even among conservative Yellow Hat lamas. This was justified on the basis of a legend holding that King Geser appeared to a dalai lama in a vision to explain how to free the material world from disorder.

In the seventeenth century the Manchus adopted Geser as the spiritual patron of martial prowess, merging him with Guan Gong Di (关公帝), the so-called Chinese God of War. Lord Guan was a historical military commander during the late Han dynasty. His exploits were absorbed into the Chinese novel *The Romance of the Three*

18. Terzani at 287.
19. Ibid. at 302.

Temple of King Geser of Ling, also known as Guan Yu. Photo by author.

Kingdoms as one of its main protagonists. Subsequent generations of Chinese worshipped him as a powerful spirit capable of granting their wishes. His appearance was that of a consummate warrior, wearing armour with a flowing beard and a red face that symbolized his aggressive military abilities, not unlike the red-faced wooden statues of the Abatai Khan in the Eastern Monastic Settlement.

The conflation of King Geser and Lord Guan was well suited to the mixed congregation of lay Mongolians and Chinese who worshipped here. A second courtyard was added for the syncretic worship of Tara and Guan Yin as goddesses of compassion.[20]

The temple survived the Great Purge because it had been previously allocated as a dormitory for state artists. Later, the temple was put to various uses as a 'cultural revival' office of the government, a library for Gandan Monastery, a Buddhist medical college, and a Buddhist secondary school for young lamas between the ages 12 and 16. In 2002 the Lotus Yoga College, or Badam Yoga Datsan (Бадам Ёга Дацан), first established by Second Patriarch in 1745, reopened here along with institutions for the study of traditional medicine and astrology.

On the east side of the building someone has painted the Tibetan mantra *om mani padme hum*. The pillars for the main entrance are decorated with clay depictions of multicoloured clouds and four-fingered dragons. In the main hall of the first courtyard, there are bronzes of Padmasambhava along with Green and White Taras on the altar. In the second courtyard are gers for astrological and other rituals as well as a consulting room for the patients of the Buddhist physicians. The temple's windows are decorated with Siberian frames, which, for me, are a pleasant image of the cultural accommodation that is so characteristic of Mongolians.

20. For more on King Geser, see Atwood at 197–98; David-Neel and Yongden; and Penick.

Siberian window frames on the second hall of the Temple of King Geser. Photo by author.

Behind the Geser Temple is the Zurkhai Datsan, a newly constructed astrological monastic college, set in an octagonal building at the foot of Tasgan Hill.

The Tibetan style Pethub Stangey Choskhor Monastery, or Bakula Rinbüüchiin Betüv Khiid (Бакула Ринбүчийн Бэтүб Хийд) is across from the temple on Sambuu Street. It was built in the 1990s with support of the Nineteenth Kushok Bakula Rinpoche, a key figure for the revival of Vajrayana Buddhism in Mongolia and an interesting illustration of the ongoing role of religion in geopolitics.

The Bakula Rinpoche was a Ladkhaki Gelukpa lama who was recognized by the Thirteenth Dalai Lama as an emanation of one of the disciples of the Shakyamuni Buddha. He became an important personage on the Indian political stage. His public role began when he was the minister of state in his native province of Indian-administered Jammu and Kashmir. Later, he became a member of the Indian Parliament and worked in the government's Commission on Minorities. In the 1970s he played a significant role in arranging for the Dalai Lama's pastoral visit to the Soviet Union's Buddhist community in Buryatia.

The Bakula Rinpoche sought to visit Mongolia in the late 1980s but the MPR authorities rejected his visa application, presumably because he was a Buddhist cleric. In late 1989 he was able to circumvent this obstruction when the government of India appointed him as its ambassador to the MPR in a move curiously mixing diplomatic and religious functions. The Bakula Rinpoche's tenacity to come to Ulan Bator might have been fuelled by a Gelukpa prediction that the year 1989 would witness the end of a harmful and destructive sixty-year cycle for the dharma. Once in post, the Rinpoche was sought out by student demonstrators, though he remained politically neutral. The following year witnessed the political reform that seemed to fulfil the prophecy. His efforts at proselytization assured that the revival of Mongolian Buddhism proceeded with strong ties to the exiled Tibetan community in India. He retired in 2000, passing away in New Delhi four years later.

We can draw our visit to the Western Monastic Settlement to a close by going to Tasgan Hill, which is the setting for the only *ovoo* (овоо) within downtown Ulaanbaatar.

An ovoo is a circular cairn of stones that forms the material foundation for the home of a spirit living in a mountain, by a crossroad, or in some other auspicious location. Passers-by seek the spirit's blessings by circumambulating the ovoo three times and adding a stone at each turn. When stones are added to the ovoo, the spirit supposedly blesses the supplicants and, if they are travelling, the spirit will summon a wind horse to hurry them to a successful completion of their journey.

Ovoos are an ancient custom in Central Asia. Records from the twelfth century indicate that these collections of stones were already atop mountain passes and other places as border or caravan markers. After the Second Conversion, ovoos entered into the world of Buddhist rituals and were built at sites of Buddhist miracles or historic events for the sangha.

Traditionally the appropriate celebrants of ovoo rituals were lamas or community elders rather than shamans. Ovoo worship was a ritual meant to exalt the spirits of nature while shamans were supernatural fixers, enquiring into the cause of a dispute and negotiating a solution. Women were excluded from the ceremonies since the underlying spirits were thought to be narrow-minded men resentful of the intrusion of women into their man-caves.[21]

An eighteenth-century lama from Inner Mongolia, the Third Mergen Lama, brought ovoo worship into the mainstream of the Gelukpa faith and wrote several treatises on the correct way to build one. In the treatises, the reincarnate lama recommended that ovoos should be built around a symbolic 'wishing tree' consisting of several types of tree trunks lashed together. The 'father of the trees', the juniper, is placed at the top of an ovoo under construction. This is followed by the reed as the 'mother'. Lower down the choice of timber changes to the tamarisk as the son, to be followed by the rooted birch as the uncle and the willow as the daughter.[22]

In addition to three stones, a passer-by might offer kumis, arkhi, milk, butter or a blue khadag to an ovoo. The UB clergy has launched a campaign against environmental spoilage at ovoos where people thoughtlessly leave empty bottles of vodka or beer, cigarettes, and piles of non-biodegradable nylon khadags. (I once recall seeing a brassiere on top of an ovoo.) In the countryside, some supplicants hang spare car parts on an ovoo as a prayer against breakdowns or accidents during a trip. ('Why are you late for work?' 'My car broke down.' 'Didn't you have any spare parts?' 'Well, uh . . .'). The abbot of Gandan Monastery has issued encyclical letters discouraging people from leaving such environmentally harmful articles at ovoo sites.

---

21. Wallace at 231.
22. Bawden (1994) at 121.

Prior to philosophical examinations for their monastic qualifications, Urga monks gathered at the ovoo on Tasgan Hill for a ritual specific to the occasion.[23] Another source suggests that the Thirteenth Dalai Lama and the Eighth Patriarch had an extended 'off-the-record' conversation here. In the free-market era, some geniuses hit upon the bright idea of putting a roadway through Tasgan Hill on its northern end, to facilitate the flow of traffic, and thereby offended the spirit within.

Tasgan Hill allows a fine view into the ger districts to the north and west as well as a vista to observe the gradual expansion of the gers along the surrounding mountains, as more herders are forced to seek sedentary lives in Ulaanbaatar.

Ovoo on Tasgan Hill. Photo by author.

23. Wallace at 239.

10

'Consulate Hill' and Environs

Consulate Hill, or Konsuliin Denj (Консулын Дэнж) is the archaic name for the part of UB where the Russian community first set down roots on a ridge in the 1860s. We will point out a few notable places on our way there.

Along the north side of Embassy Street, the Japanese Embassy is a reminder of the relationship between Japan and Mongolia in modern times. By the beginning of the twentieth century, Tokyo had extended its influence into north-east Asia after defeating China in the Sino-Japanese War of 1894. Within ten years, Japan took control of Korea and used it as a springboard for incursions into Manchuria. Under a secret concordat between Tokyo and Saint Petersburg, the two powers agreed to separate their respective spheres of influence along a north–south axis that ran through Peking. Everything to the east was Japan's 'territory' while all points to the west, including most of Mongolia, were deemed within Russia's sphere of influence.

This modus vivendi did not last long. With the collapse of the Qing dynasty, Japan accelerated its commercial and military intrusions into Manchuria by building the South Manchurian Railway while allying with the Peking gamin government. The plan was greased by loans and other gifts to Chinese warlords and local elites.

By 1915 Japan had extended its footprint into Mongolia, as companies such as Mitsui set up representative offices in Urga. The city also became a destination for Japanese migrants working as prostitutes, physicians, pharmacists, barbers, and restaurateurs as well as in other jobs that were conducive as cover for intelligence agents. These migrants stayed put in Urga even during Ungern-Sternberg's occupation of the city because Japan had looked hopefully to him as a potential ally; later, the Japanese community fled upon the arrival of the Red Army. By 1927 a physician named Kojima was the only Japanese who remained behind in Urga. He was married to a Russian woman and operated a successful clinic for venereal disease.[1]

In the early 1930s Japan sought to influence Inner Mongolian politics by supporting the Gelukpa sect and covertly dispatching Japanese agents posing as lamas. The militarists hoped to lure the Panchen Lama, who was then in exile in northern China, to throw in his lot with the Greater East Asian Co-Prosperity Sphere. They also

1. Ma at 129.

courted Inner Mongolian aristocrats by offering the usual inducements of money and titles. The Japanese hoped to launch a revival of Buddhism as a political force and then eventually merge it under the Nichiren Buddhist church, which was an imperialist and nationalistic version of Mahayana Buddhism that dominated Japan after the Meiji Restoration.

Both the Soviet Union and the MPR correctly saw the growing influence of Japan as a threat. With support from the Soviet secret police, the MPR government seized upon the Japanese expansion as a pretext for purging politicians and lamas who had fallen afoul of its rule.

At this time, Mongolia really did have a third neighbour but, unlike the rhetorical make-believe of twenty-first-century politicians, this third neighbour was the Japanese puppet state Manchukuo established in 1932 with the last Qing emperor as its sovereign. There was an ill-defined boundary between the MPR and Manchukuo, which gave the excuse for an undeclared war in the late spring of 1939 when Japan's army chieftains successfully petitioned Tokyo for an attack on the Soviet Union. Its troops infiltrated the eastern border of Mongolia but were eventually beaten back by joint Mongolian and Soviet forces. The severe loss of face for the Japanese army led the militarist cabal in Tokyo to throw its support to the Imperial Navy and its 'strike south' policy in China and South East Asia.

There is a book that captures the intrigue of this era. *Japanese Agent in Tibet* records the experiences of Kimura Hisao, a Japanese agent who not only succeeded in passing himself off as an Inner Mongolian monk but travelled incognito to Lhasa at the end of the war to gather intelligence on local conditions there. This riveting read illustrates Japan's intricate plans to infiltrate the Central Asian region with agents trained to pass themselves off as locals.

After the war, Mongolian-Japanese relations remained in hibernation until Prime Minister Eisaku Satō relaunched Japanese activism in East Asia. After the normalization of diplomatic relations between the two countries, John Colvin recalled the arrival of the first Japanese diplomats:

> The Japanese, after negotiation over war damage, re-established diplomatic relations half-way through our tour. Their first chargé d'affaires, never wholly sober, was a Mongol speaker. At one of Ulan Bator's frightful receptions, he addressed a Mongol Minister:
>
> 'You have an Inner Mongol accent,' said the latter . . .
>
> 'Yes, I was based there in 1943.'
>
> 'In what capacity?'
>
> 'A monk at the Yellow Faith Lamasery, cover for espionage on behalf of the Japanese forces against your country. I was caught just across the frontier by an Outer Mongol military patrol. The soldiers did not kill or seize me because, knowing your customs, I instantly removed the saddle from my horse and lifted it in the gesture of surrender.'
>
> 'And then?' harshly enquired the Minister.

> 'The patrol let me go, thinking that I would die in the desert. They took the horse, naturally. But they did not know that, behind a sand dune, I had another horse.'
>
> 'What!' said the Minister. 'We've been looking for you for 30 years.'[2]

Japan's foreign policy towards Mongolia lapsed into quietude until the 1990s when it decided to exert its soft power in post-Communist Mongolia through Monbusho scholarships. It has been an extremely successful policy in light of the quality of the Mongolian alumni who completed their studies in Japan.

Further down Embassy Street and closer to the Selbe River is a sad relic of old Urga. It is a Siberian log cabin or izba with typically ornate window frames and a light-blue gingerbread fretwork. This quaint little building was not conveniently located when the Ulaanbaatar municipal geniuses elected to expand its pedestrian-unfriendly urban design. Half of it was torn down, leaving it looking lopsided and forlorn.

Moving to the north, the blue neoclassical University of Finance and Economics sits on the north side of Peace Avenue. Nearby, the Ministry of Agriculture is the grey building with Greek columns, stone lions, and gilded statues of a woman herder and a male farmer in Grecian heroic poses on each side of its entrance. These days, the intersection in front of the Ministry supports a less heroic trade in the world's oldest profession.

Peace Avenue crosses the Selbe River at the Lion Bridge. The stone lions which give the bridge its name are from the King Geser/Guan Yu Temple in Chinatown. The Selbe River has been at alarmingly low levels for decades on account of its diversion for the municipal water supply. The area to the south of the bridge on the east bank was the vicinity of the official residence of Amban Sando, who was chased out of Mongolia in 1911 after hiding in the Russian consulate. No structures of that era remain. One can imagine this area being a beehive of activity during the showdown between Amban Sando and the Eighth Patriarch.

At the intersection of Tokyo Street and Peace Avenue, the Ulaanbaatar City Museum is a wooden single-storey building constructed in classic Siberian style by the Russian Buryat merchant Tsogt Garmaevich Badamjan in 1919. The building was the site of the meeting of the Central Committee of the MPP in July 1921 and later became the embassy of the little known Tuvan Republic.[3]

In the museum there is a wonderful 1970s painting of Ulan Bator, with its power stations, opera houses, Peace Bridge, and all other incidentals of progress, executed in Mongolian *zurag* style. Several years ago, the museum still exhibited mementos of the Cold War, such as makeshift landmines given by the Vietnamese Communists as a souvenir of their ongoing war with the United States. As observed by the sniffy MacColl, weapons of selective destruction once figured prominently in the museum:

---

2. Colvin at 163.
3. For a story about Tannu Tuva and the physicist Richard Feynman's fascination with the country-that-hardly-existed, see Leighton. *Genghis Blues* is an enjoyable documentary about bluesman Paul Pena participating in a throat-singing competition in the Tuvan capital Kyzyl.

> It is a strange little retreat, oddly engaging in a pathetic way, with its scratch collection of lop-sided pictures and crude drawings, ill-executed portraits of heroes, large scale models of the Ulan Bator of the future, propaganda and general bric-a-brac, including a machine gun which was said to be the gift of North Vietnam, and which was identified by one of our party as of the same type used by Communist forces in Laos.[4]

(How could a tourist identify military hardware from Laos? Maybe old Lotchin had reasons to be suspicious of MacColl and Company.)

Across the street is the light blue Terra Europe Restaurant and a collection of bakeries, convenience stores, and what-not in the former Office of Radio, Communications, and Post. This building was the 'last mile' for telegraph lines that came up around the east flank of Bogd Uul from Kalgan and then went onward to Siberia. The telegraph poles were installed and operated by a Danish company and soon became a handy guide for trade caravans. Old photographs show these to be in the same curious shape as fixed-line electricity poles in use today—two wooden poles are joined by brackets at the top to form an A-frame, which is secured to concrete foundations as a protection against water damage. (Water-logged poles explode with a booming crack in winter as the ice expands outward in the log.) The final approach of these telegraph poles to the Office of Communications gave an eerie and surreal touch to Urga's monastic cityscape in the late nineteenth century.

Continuing towards the east on the north side of Peace Avenue, the British Embassy is a 1930s building initially assigned to Cuba after Castro took power. It later changed hands when the United Kingdom recognized the MPR. Among the expatriate community, the British Embassy is famous for its Steppe Inn, a pub set up in one of its outer buildings and open to members on Friday evenings, with last orders at 9:30 p.m. The Steppe Inn has gone from being one of the few places for Anglophone nightlife in the socialist era to now another bar competing for custom, having lost its former uniqueness.

While Britain enjoys the prestige of being the first Western country to have diplomatic ties with Mongolia, the British Foreign Office did not know what to expect when they met their Mongolian counterparts in the 1960s. To their surprise, they found a people with a sense of humour, irony, and perspective with whom communication came easily. 'We found out that they were just like us,' or so was the recorded reaction of a British diplomat in the Foreign Office archives, echoing the pleased impressions of the Bishop of Norwich sixty years earlier.

Ambassador Colvin and his wife offered Owen Lattimore a warm welcome during his visits to the country in the 1970s. The British couple appreciated the depth of Lattimore's knowledge of local culture and custom. In his memoirs, Colvin referred to Professor Lattimore as 'the most electric of writers, teacher, friend and the greatest

4. MacColl at 63.

traveller in Central Asia of this century'.[5] Colvin also recorded Lattimore's dry sense of humour:

> One day, while he was having tea with us, we heard him referred to on Peking radio as 'an international spy'.
>
> 'Owen, do international spies get a lot of money?' my wife enquired.
>
> 'Well, they ought to get *more*, oughtn't they?'[6]

Continuing to the east, we pass American Hill, which is the escarpment that rises behind the Kempinski Hotel. Its name recalls a long-vanished trading house run by the 'Williams', an American-born Chinese family who understood the commercial wisdom of playing down their ethnicity.[7] They eventually branched out into a makeshift cinema which might have offered an assortment of popular films by Charlie Chaplin and Douglas Fairbanks, Sr. Most Mongolians learned of Western romance, specifically kisses, from American cinema for the first time. At the time audiences convulsed in laughter at this outlandish gesture of affection.

Further to the north and next to the Sansar Tunnel is the first high-rise residential complex built in Ulaanbaatar in the late 1960s. Sansar means 'space' and refers to the Soviet Union's early successes in space travel. This was the trendy part of Ulan Bator in the years of the Soviet space programme and the national pride felt for cosmonaut Jügderdemidiin Gürragchaa's trip into space in 1981. Nearby is the Opanos Ukrainian restaurant, a superb choice for well-prepared Slavic cuisine.

At the north-east corner of Ikh Toiruu, there is a modern interpretation of the Vajrayana image of the Four Friends or Tumbashi (Тумбаши). This statue is based on the *jataka* story of a prior animal incarnation of the Buddha. The story tells of an elephant, a rabbit, a monkey, and a partridge coming together to harvest fruit from a tree. Each animal speaks about the time it first saw the tree, thus determining seniority and the correct way to arrange themselves to gather the fruit. The jataka story aims to remind the sangha of the priority that should be afforded to older monks and the value of cooperation.

To the south-west of the intersection at the Kempinski Hotel are the burned-out ruins of a building, which look like a Dairy Queen that has seen better days. Some say that this derelict building is haunted because it is located on the site of a Qing dynasty prison, the 'Massive White', or Bat Tsagaan (Бат Цагаан). Old photographs show that the prison was a rectangular-shaped wooden building painted white and enclosed by a palisade. This was where the Qing government imposed punishments of medieval harshness on convicts. Morbid tourists made a beeline to the prison to gawk at its assortment of boxes, or *mulen* (мулэн) measuring one by one and a half metres with a small hole cut into the side. Into these were crammed prisoners for sentences ranging from five years to decades. These living coffins paralysed the legs and arms

5. Colvin at 166.
6. Ibid. at 167.
7. Baabar at 303; Addleton at 4–5.

'Haunted house' on site of former Urga prison. Photo by author.

of their inmates, who were often driven to madness. The Soviets were aghast at this punishment. Once they helped to install the MPR, prison reform was one of the first items on their agenda.

The memory of the prison was invoked in a popular song from the 1960s:

On top of Battsagaan,
If you look at right side,
The colonial school that I was in when I was young,
Grandstanding on where it was.[8]

From here, we enter Consulate Hill with its remnants of the 150 years of Russian influence in Mongolia.

The Russian settlement in Urga came into existence because of the trade in tea, which was conveniently sourced for the Russian market at this staging post. In fact, tea drinking was not an indigenous custom in Mongolia. Tea brewed in the Tibetan way became popular in Mongolia at the time of the Second Conversion when the custom arrived from Tibet along with Buddhist rituals, one of which was the tea-offering ceremony to the lamas. In contrast to Chinese custom of plain tea, Mongolians learned from Tibetans to add milk and salt. The latter as a necessity in their landlocked homelands. *Suutei tsai* (сүүтэй цай) is an acquired taste but a soothing beverage that is evocative of Mongolia. Herders served it in the silver-lined wooden bowls that doubled as dinner bowls, not the handleless porcelain cups found elsewhere in East Asia. Suutei tsai is also taken with butter or used as a soup stock for a mutton-and-barley stew,

8. Thanks to Turuu Bat-Erdene for this translation.

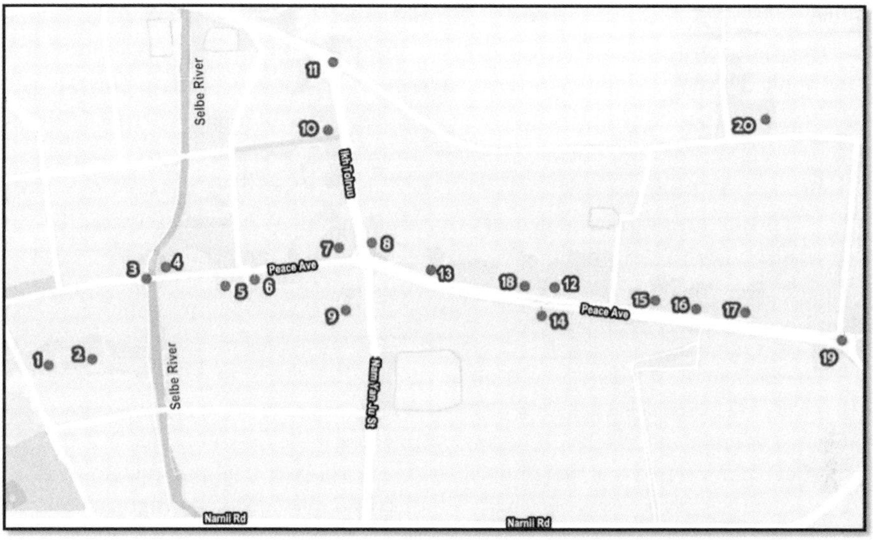

Sites to the east of Sükhbaatar Square. Map by Aubrey Ding-Shan Yang.

Key

1. Japanese Embassy
2. Sawed-off Siberian cabin
3. Ministry of Agriculture
4. Lion Bridge
5. Ulaanbaatar City Museum
6. Europa Restaurant
7. British Embassy
8. American Hill
9. Site of former Qing prison
10. Sansar Tunnel and Residential Complex
11. Tumbashi
12. Buildings of tsarist Russian consulate
13. Microdistricts Nos. 12 and 15
14. Russian Orthodox church
15. Nicholas Roerich Museum
16. MongolKino
17. Former Mongolor building
18. Marshall Zhukov Museum
19. Monument to Mongolian Ard Squadron
20. Russian cemetery

a departure that shocks the expectations of more conventional tea drinkers but is quite tasty.

Later on, Ulan Bator's urbanites exchanged their silver-lined wooden bowls for crystal glasses in steel frames and flavoured their tea with lemon or sugar in the Russian fashion. Chinese tea disappeared from the markets once the MPR government established exclusive trade links with the USSR. It was replaced by Georgian tea, which still enjoys popularity as seen on the shelves of convenience stores.

Imperial expansion and trade were the motivations for Saint Petersburg to set up a permanent diplomatic presence in Mongolia. Under the 1860 treaty between the Qing court and the Tsar's representative, Count Nikolay Pavlovich Ignatieff, an influential player in the Great Game rivalry (and a sinister character in the Flashman novels by George MacDonald Fraser), Russia acquired the right to set up a consulate in Urga. Construction work began the next year and by 1863 the first Western building was added to the city's landscape. It was a two-storey rectangle with a green iron roof that was the source of its nickname, the 'Green House'. The iron roof was an innovation later applied to the rebuilt Maitreya Temple in the Eastern Monastic Settlement. Gradually, other buildings grew up around the consulate building—a barracks for the Cossacks, stables for their horses, storehouses, and, later, a Russian Orthodox chapel.

In addition to diplomatic functions, the Russian Consulate played a secondary role as a hostel for nineteenth-century European travellers trekking between Peking and Irkutsk. The Russian diplomats were delightful and sympathetic hosts, keen to discuss international and local affairs as a way to relieve the boredom of their isolation. Their hospitality was legendary.

> On reaching the house of a merchant on whom I had a letter of credit, and where I had anticipated being able to find lodging, I learned, to my disappointment, that there was no room to spare for the moment, but that the Russian consul had sent word that I was to stay at the Consulate . . . I received a very kind and truly Russian welcome from the Consul, M. Feodroff. The fact of my being a total stranger, unprovided even with a letter of introduction to him, appeared to make no difference. He had heard I was coming, so took it for granted that I, like other travellers, would stay at the Consulate.[9]

A contingent of Cossacks, and their wives, supported the Consulate and formed the initial nucleus of the Russian colony. According to one British traveller, the wives of the Cossacks seemed to have the marital monopoly on common sense. When Harry de Windt and his travelling companions arrived at the gate of the Russian consulate after an arduous crossing of the Gobi Desert, the thickheaded Cossack on duty refused to be helpful, let alone show any of the fabled Russian hospitality, and tried to turn them away. The Cossack's sturdy Siberian wife came to the rescue. She browbeat her lumpen spouse into submission and arranged for a warm welcome for the exhausted travellers by giving them rooms and refreshments. De Windt recorded his satisfaction at hearing her hector her lout of a husband all afternoon as he and his fellow travellers recovered from their journey in comfortably plush guest rooms, languidly smoking cigarettes, and drinking well-prepared Russian tea from fine crystal glasses.[10]

This seed of a community soon attracted Russians peasants coming as homesteaders. The settlers and Mongolians enjoyed friendly and non-threatening ties that were totally absent of the tensions with the Chinese, who set up insular communities, 'creating a patch of "the Chinese way of life" that excluded everyone else'. Instead of roosting in a self-contained closed community, the Siberian Russians preferred to strike out on their own, settling in forests with open meadows where they could farm, hunt, raise livestock, and keep honey bees. Russians also consumed dairy products, kept cows as well as oxen, and lived a life that was not too alien to their Mongolian neighbours in

9. Price at 273–74.
10. Windt at 165–66.

contrast to the threat posed to the Mongolian way of life by Chinese moneylenders and merchants.[11]

Naturally, some misunderstandings did arise between the early Russians and Mongolians but they were not fatal to the cultivation of friendly ties. The lamas once lodged a protest when it turned out that the flagpole at the Russian consulate was higher than the ganjirs on Urga's Buddhist temples. Another complaint was that the Russians had set up a cemetery for their citizens, thereby polluting the earth and insulting the spirits below.[12] These clashes blew over, unlike the prolonged friction between Mongolians and Chinese.

The Russian merchants set up warehouses as trade depots initially but then expanded into the domestic retail market for manufactured goods. They were fewer than the large Chinese enterprises and generally the first Russians were not energetic entrepreneurs, selling imperfect goods at excessive markups. A British traveller recorded one Russian as saying that since he earned only a 20 per cent margin on his wares, he regarded his business in Urga as a patriotic exercise to support Russian industry rather than a truly commercial one. Others mentioned profit margins of no less than 50 per cent but ignored any suggestion of expanding or improving their businesses.[13] In 1910 a Moscow manufacturers' trade delegation arrived in Urga, and its members were generally underwhelmed by their confrères. They found their countrymen to be disorganized, quarrelsome, and indifferent to any innovation in business.[14]

While Russian trade prospects were limited, the tsarist Russia authorities acknowledged the need to tend to the spiritual well-being of their citizens in Urga, but, as in China, they refrained from widespread proselytization. The first Orthodox liturgy was celebrated in the consulate in 1864. When more Cossacks were assigned to protect the consulate during an outbreak of civil unrest in North China in the 1870s, the minister procured funds to build a chapel within the consulate grounds. Priests from the Orthodox Russian ecclesiastical mission in Peking periodically came to Urga to hold services. Later the Russian Orthodox Church transferred the congregation to the diocese of the Irkutsk and Baikal Clerical Missions. In 1892 the missions approved the permanent stationing of a clergyman in Urga.

The Russian congregation came to be a pivotal presence for the growing expatriate community, especially during Christian festivals, as described in this vignette:

> The time spent in Urga passed very pleasantly, for, in addition to the daily rambles in and about the capital, there was a social side to life in this unique place that could not be neglected. Easter came and was celebrated by the Russian community in the orthodox way. There were calls to be made upon the officials and the commercial community, and an almost unbroken round of dinners at various houses during the

11. Lattimore (1962) at 69.
12. Rupen 1957 at 163–64.
13. Perry-Ayscough at 104–5.
14. Endicott at xlv et seq.

> 14 days the festival was celebrated. Never shall I forget the scene outside the little Church in the Consulate compound on Easter morning when, after the services, the congregation came out with the joyful greeting on their lips '*Christos Voskres!*' and embraced their friends.[15]

There were undeniable hardships associated with life in the Russian colony. Climate, disease, and isolation compounded the challenges of daily life. Travel to Urga was not an ordeal to be lightly taken. For those making their way south from Siberia, there was a choice of two Russian carriages, the tarantass or the telega (aside from the dreaded Peking cart). These were springless four-wheeled wagons tethered to three horses. The beasts were typically whipped at by Mongolians drivers at breakneck speeds to cover the distance between Verkhneudinsk and Urga in as short of a time as possible, usually three days.

Boredom was another hardship for those with little interest in local culture. In his memoirs Ramstedt told of a Russian pharmacist sent to Urga by his Saint Petersburg headquarters to manage a branch of their drug stores. Having no clear image of life in Mongolia, the poor fellow became inconsolable upon realizing the limited opportunities for cultural pursuits. He tried to drown his sorrows in gramophone records of Chaliapin's arias shipped to him from Irkutsk but, to his chagrin, his fellow settlers did not share his tastes in classical music. So he drowned his sorrows in more conventional ways with drink, gossip, and social cliques.[16]

By the early twentieth century the Russian community had grown such that it was feasible for Russians to set up businesses for services to other Russians rather than retailing goods to local purchasers. Russian bakers, doctors, dentists, butchers, printers, engineers, and teachers were members of the Consulate Hill community. This pool of expatriates trained Mongolians in new technologies or brought in skilled Buryat Mongolians from the Transbaikal region. This, in turn, accelerated popular awareness about the changes occurring beyond Mongolia's borders.

As Russia went through social upheaval and world war broke out in Europe, the Russian community was divided in its views about how to respond to the troubles in their homeland. Some adjuncts working in Russian-sponsored schools and printing presses advocated Marxist solutions to Russia's problems while more conservative tsarist officials assured the theocratic government of Saint Petersburg's ability to handle both domestic unrest and the war with the Kaiser. Just as in our times, Mongolians watched and listened carefully to the debates among the foreigners in their midst.

With the fall of the Romanovs, the Russian community was left to its own devices. They formed a self-governing executive council to organize their own affairs, though its members fell into fractious political factions. Along with other nationals in Urga in early 1921, the Russians were paralysed with terror by the arrival of the 'Mad Baron', who soon lived up to his reputation by committing idiotically brutal acts at the

15. Kent at 57–58.

16. Ramstedt at 192 et seq.

slightest demented whim. His men hunted down Urga's Jewish residents in a competition to find the cruellest way to murder them—one young Jewish baker's assistant was burned to death in an oven. In another instance, a Mongolian nurse working for a Jewish family vainly sought to save the infant in her charge by rushing to the Orthodox chapel and having the child baptized, only to be slaughtered by the Cossacks. Ungern-Sternberg had so traumatized the population that any subsequent liberator would have been welcomed, irrespective of ideology or great power affiliation.[17]

The first 'Red' Russians arrived in Urga in the summer of 1921. They consisted of Comintern agents, spies, and soldiers, but later more rank-and-file types arrived as Mongolia settled into its system of socialist reform. The Soviets did not establish a formal embassy in Ulan Bator but instead worked through a plenipotentiary representative on account of Soviet sensitivity to China (which had not renounced its claims to Mongolia but nonetheless turned to Moscow for political remedies for its own domestic troubles). The need for the Soviets to keep a low profile ended with the Mongolian plebiscite endorsing the country's independence in 1945. The Soviet embassy moved to downtown Ulan Bator, though the old Consulate Hill area continued to be a main base for Soviet personnel and Soviet-Mongolian joint ventures, like Mongoltrans, the state enterprise responsible for hauling freight between the two countries. By the 1950s Ulan Bator's Russian community consisted of people who had set down roots in Mongolia by choice, though there were some involuntary residents like Vladimir Molotov, who was exiled to Mongolia as the Soviet ambassador as a punishment when de-Stalinization went forward in earnest.

Many commentators have reheated Reagan's clichés about the evil empire, but I do not subscribe to the Washington Consensus that the word *Russian* has always and wholly been a synonym for 'sinister'.[18] While Communist political horrors are known to all, the Soviets made altruistic contributions to life in Mongolia, at least before the bureaucratic stagnation coming from Brezhnev's policies for 'developed socialism'. I recall a Mongolian friend commenting about a site visit to the countryside with a group of grey-suited Western investors. Separate tables and chairs were set up for a luncheon for the esteemed guests while most Mongolians picnicked separately on a blanket on the ground. One elderly Mongolian sat down and sighed, 'This would not happen if our Soviet brothers were here'.

Be that as it may, Russian-Mongolian friendship plummeted as the Soviet Union declined and Mongolians felt themselves freer to express resentment against the perceived or actual attitude of Russian superiority put on by Brezhnev bureaucrats. When Russians left Ulaanbaatar in a mass exodus in 1992, film footage shows crowds of Russians milling about at the Ulaanbaatar Railway Station, waiting for the train home and lamenting acts of violence committed against them in their homes or at work.

17. See Teleki at 186–87.

18. While it is beyond the scope of this book, my rationale for this viewpoint can be glimpsed in Kuralt at 226–40.

Among some Mongolians today there is nostalgia for the Old Soviets and distrust of New Russians (among the other new breeds of foreign interlopers). I wonder if this is because of the pioneering 'can-do' spirit of the Soviet Siberians who arrived in the early years in contrast to the Western Russian nouveau riche class. However, others still feel bitterness about the phenomenon of 'Russian privilege' that prevailed in Residential Microdistricts Nos. 12 and 15. These were exclusive compounds built in the 1960s for Russian expatriates and military personnel—the equivalent of today's gated communities for the well-off. Special 'Soviets-only' stores provided for imported luxuries to lessen the hardship of life in Mongolia. Hegemonic attitudes always poison the well of solidarity among allies.

Since Mongolia went with the free-market crowd, this part of Ulaanbaatar underwent a rapid transformation into a sacrifice zone, marred by brutalist construction projects and chaotic development. Some Russian sites have managed to survive, though.

In Microdistricts Nos. 12 and 15 the Soviet-built expatriate apartments are still owned by Russians, who are mostly absentee landlords. The neighbourhood has grown some anomalies, such as an ersatz Kremlin that houses a karaoke parlour, a restaurant, and a pawnshop for automobiles. The constructivist-style Centre of Geophysics has been joined by an anomalous neighbour, the Tibetan-style Yellow Hat Tarvalin Monastery (Тарвалин Хийд), with a statue of the White Old Man on its approach rather than a bushy Karl Marx. Farther to the north is the Mongolian Military Museum in another constructivist building, with exhibits on the application of force from the Chinggisid Empire to the alliance between Moscow and UB in 1921 and on to the Second World War. The museum is surrounded by Khanburger outlets and auto-repair shops operated by Vietnamese expatriates.

UB's own Kremlin. Photo by author.

Centre of Geophysics, constructivist-style building. Photo by author.

Going back to Peace Avenue and up along the ridge of Consulate Hill, the Marshall Zhukov Museum is located in the house where the Soviet general stayed during the summer of 1939. The museum commemorates the memory of a man who is often likened to Saint George in the Russian pantheon of national saviours. In May 1939 Stalin dispatched General Zhukov to lead the joint Soviet-Mongolian armed forces against the Japanese at Khalkha Gol (or Nomohan in Japanese) on the eastern border. Zhukov applied his 'deep penetration' strategy, which he devised to fight an enemy on a massively wide-front on steppes and plains, with phenomenal success. (Battle debris still litters the fields in Khalkha Gol.) The 'deep penetration' strategy aimed to disrupt supply lines and proved to be effective when deployed against the Nazi army on the Western Front.[19] On the outside walls of the museum there are mosaics of Zhukov and, fittingly, Saint George slaying the dragon, and nearby is a bust of the marshal.

Farther east, the remnants of the tsarist consulate are well hidden, having been converted to other less vaunted uses. The former Russian Orthodox chapel from the nineteenth century survives in the form of a yellow building with a red roof and a portico with columns, now hosting something called a Zolboo store. Next to it is an overlooked and partially hidden grey brick building that was the original consulate. It now houses a Korean hotel and restaurant.

The remains of the chapel on the former Consulate's grounds always bring to mind Father Feodor Parnakowyz. He was appointed as the twentieth century's last Orthodox priest in Urga in 1914. The good father sought to build ties among his congregation and the Jewish, Chinese, and Buddhist communities. He carried out frequent pastoral visits to the countryside and set up a library and the first commercial college

19. See Colvin (1999).

Former Russian Orthodox chapel. Photo by author.

Former tsarist Russian consulate. Photo by author.

in Mongolia. When Urga was occupied by Ungern-Sternberg, Father Parnakowyz bravely remonstrated with the baron against his atrocities. The baron's Cossacks tortured Father Parnakowyz for days before he died an agonizing death.

The landmark of the neighbourhood is once again the Russian Orthodox church, which was rebuilt in 2007. It is a delightful building looked after by kindly Russian and Mongolian lay caretakers. When you enter the church, you are surrounded by beautiful gilded Byzantine paintings of the Last Supper, Saint John the Baptist, the Archangels,

Russian Orthodox chapel. Photo by author.

the Ascension of Christ, and Biblical quotes in Slavonic script. An image of Christ looks down from the dome of the cathedral. The airiness and lightness of the cathedral are extraordinarily invigorating and peaceful. It is fitting to spend a moment here reflecting on Father Parnakowyz and perhaps lighting a candle for him.

In a back street on the north side of Peace Avenue is an izba that has been converted into the Roerich Museum.[20] In 1927 this building was the Ulan Bator residence of the famous Russian artist, theosophist, and possible Soviet agent, Nicholas Roerich.

Born in Saint Petersburg in 1874, Roerich first came to fame for his brilliant effervescent paintings of Russian legends and historical landscapes. He was outside Russia at the time of the October Revolution and its aftermath and therefore escaped its mayhem. Being outside the fray, he was able to maintain cordial ties with the Soviets even after travelling to the West in search of fortune and further fame. In London he advocated his own theosophical theory for a merger of Eastern and Western mysticism and lectured about a mystical Shambhala homeland somewhere in Central Asia. In the 1920s he secured the financial support from wealthy New Yorkers for a Central Asian expedition with his wife and son George, ostensibly to seek out this El Dorado. When

20. Otgontsetseg.

Roerich was passing through India, the British intelligence authorities concluded that he was a Soviet agent and refused him entry into Tibet. Undeterred, he launched the expedition from north-western India into Xinjiang and then on to Siberia, Mongolia, and parts of Tibet, marching across the steppes behind the stars and stripes and a victory banner of the Maitreya bodhisattva. Interestingly the Soviet authorities did not interfere with his expedition and allowed him to travel through Siberia to Mongolia.

The expedition stayed in Ulan Bator for seven months. Mongolians were impressed with Roerich and his theories about the compatibility of the Bolshevik revolution and the new age of Maitreya. He donated a painting, *The Red Protector*, to the MPR. Its theme combined the Shambhala legend and the inevitability of a workers' revolution. (It can still be seen at the Zanabazar Museum.) His visit coincided with efforts by a small faction of Soviet agents seeking to expand Soviet influence into Tibet by sending Agvan Dorzhiev to Lhasa.

Upon his return to the United States, Roerich used his charm and artistic talents to befriend the high and mighty. He fashioned a 'world peace mission' that was endorsed by the administration of Franklin Roosevelt, primarily because of the enthusiastic support of then-secretary of agriculture Henry Wallace.

With Wallace's help, Roerich launched another official expedition to Central Asia ostensibly to look for drought-resistant grasses as a part of a New Deal programme to support Dust Bowl farmers. Roerich arrived in Yokohama and then went on to Manchuria, pressing upon the Japanese his role as the leader of an official US expedition. In his diary he wrote about how he sought to locate 'Kansas', his code word for a Shambhala-like kingdom to be found somewhere in Central Asia.

However, his well-stocked inventory of arms and ammunition alarmed the Japanese and seriously annoyed the two US agricultural specialists who had been assigned to the expedition. (Taking it on faith that the purpose of the trip was to gather grass seedlings, they were anxious to get to work.) At length, the Japanese authorities expelled them all from Manchukuo. Roerich later settled in India, dodging a massive US tax bill and passing away in 1951.[21]

Wallace lived to regret his relationship with Roerich. In the 1940 US presidential race, several Republican operatives had gotten hold of copies of the personal correspondence between Wallace and Roerich and hoped to derail FDR's campaign by publicizing them. In these letters, Wallace called himself Roerich's 'disciple' and used the honorific name Galahad, given to him by Roerich. (Roerich gave mystic nicknames to all his financial supporters, probably in lieu of official receipts.) Fighting fire with fire, the Roosevelt election machine threatened to reveal Wilke's extramarital affairs and thus crushed the move to discredit Wallace. In 1944 Roosevelt dropped Wallace from the presidential ticket, choosing instead Harry Truman, a failed haberdasher from Missouri, to be his running mate.

21. Errico and Walker.

We are left with an unclear image of Roerich. His paintings are movingly beautiful visions of a spiritual dream spanning Russian mythology and Tibetan legends. When Indira Gandhi asked Yuri Gaugin what the earth looked like from space, he said it was just like a Roerich painting. His followers in Russia continue to laud him as an important spokesperson for universal peace.

On the other hand, he disillusioned many of the patrons who fell under his spell. Wallace wrote bitterly of Roerich as a con man, and other financial supporters drifted away with time. These days, occult conspiracy theorists take his legend to extremes by posting YouTube lectures where they pitch Roerich as a satanic figure in league with the forces of darkness and the Federal Reserve Bank. It is not clear whether he was in fact a Soviet spy or simply an artist who knew how to appeal to the Russian fascination with Central Asian mysticism. A positive interpretation of his legacy is on display at the museum.[22]

In addition to displaying several paintings by Roerich and various memorabilia, the museum is also a tribute to the scholarship of Shagdaryn Bira, an eminent scholar and student of Roerich's son, George, a well-regarded Tibetologist in his own right. Bira's lifelong work continues on in the fine tradition pioneered by Rinchen, Damdinsuren, and others at the Mongolian Academy of Sciences.

This area of Consulate Hill also stirs long-forgotten memories of the Protestant efforts at proselytization in Mongolia. In the late nineteenth century, a Swedish missionary named Ola Naestegard spent time in Urga seeking to convert the inhabitants and preaching in the streets and markets of a city where many of the monastic community had spent years studying Vajrayana argumentation and logic. Poor Naestegard found that his own skills at conversion floundered on the shoals of a tough audience.

> For instance, once he was explaining . . . that men are saved and go to heaven solely by believing in Christ, when one of his listeners inquired in a loud voice, 'but what has happened then to all those who died before you came here? Are they all lost?' Naestegard answered without thinking, 'Yes, certainly.' Another Mongol, also a priest, then cried, 'But this is too cruel a god. After all, it wasn't their fault that you came here so late.' The next time Naestegard was on his guard and conceded that those who had heard nothing about Christ could be saved if they led a pious and honest life and were generous to the poor. This concession then inspired a priest, who had listened to Naesteagard's sermonising, to say aloud, 'But why did you come here then, since thus we don't need you and your religion here with us?'[23]

Naestegard eventually set aside street preaching in favour of distributing Mongolian language versions of the Bible that were often used by Mongolians as padding for worn-out footwear.

---

22. A severely unsympathetic portrait of Roerich is painted in Errico and Walker. Both Roerich and his son left accounts of their 1927–1928 journeys in Central Asia. Znamenski writes about the convergence of Soviet geopolitics and the Shambhala prophecy.
23. Kemp at 435, citing Ramstedt at 41–42.

In 1919 the Swedish Mongol Mission sent Gerda Ollen to establish a small medical clinic on Consulate Hill. Despite initial reluctance among Mongolians to seek treatment from the 'foreign medical man' who happened to be a woman, she soon found herself swamped with forty to fifty patients each day waiting for medical treatment. The patients had usually sought the advice of lamas for Tibetan medical cures beforehand without success. Others from the Swedish Mongol Mission joined Ollen and later looked to buy a small farm as a base. In 1924 the Swedes were forced to leave the capital with the rising leftist politics of the 1920s. After the implosion of the communist state, the missionary society attempted to reclaim the rights to the log cabin that once housed the clinic but were ignored by the new government.[24] The log cabin must be hidden somewhere in the backstreets near the Roerich Museum.

On the north side of Peace Avenue, the University of Cinematic Art, or Kino Üildver, is a fine example of constructivist architecture. Initially built as the Military Culture Palace, black-and-white photos from the 1930s show it decked out with posters of Lenin in mid-speech, Sükhbaatar, Stalin, Choibalsan, Molotov, and other Communist luminaries. From 1961 to 1998 it housed MongolKino, the Mongolian motion picture production unit, and the Higher School of Motion Picture Arts. This is an appropriate place for a digression on Mongolian cinema, a subject unknown outside the country.

The MongolKino Studio was founded in 1935 with the active support of Soviet directors. Its first film was a Mongolian-Soviet joint production called *The Mongolian Boy*, or *Mongoliin Khüü* (Монголын Хүү), co-directed by Ilya Trauberg and Demberel Baldan. Trauberg was an assistant director to Sergei Eisenstein for the classic silent Soviet film *October*. His co-director, Demberel Baldan, went on to direct the first solely Mongolian production, a black-and-white short feature called *Norjmaagin's Destiny*, or *Norjmaagiin Zam* (Норжмаагийн Зам) in 1938.

Mongolian cinema absorbed the techniques of classic Soviet film-making with themes based on historic revolutionary heroes, such as *Tsogt Taij* (Цогт Тайжи) filmed in 1945 with a screenplay written by Rinchen. *Tsogt Taij* is an unsung classic of black-and-white cinema and should enjoy wider fame because of its accuracy in portraying the customs of seventeenth-century Mongolia.

Mongolian cinema was not just politically themed depictions of proletarian struggle, however. In the 1950s films moved into the genre of musical comedy. Based on a folk tale, the first colour film, *Altan Örgöö* (Алтан Өргөө), appeared in 1961 along with a soundtrack recorded by the German Democratic Republic Symphony. Selections from the soundtrack became standard in the Mongolian orchestral repertoire and the film itself had many special effects that were advanced for its time. Another famous film was 1970's *The Clear Tamir*, or *Tungalag Tamir* (Тунгалаг Тамир), by Ravjaagiin Dorjpalam, based on a novel set during the 1921 revolution by Chadraabalyn Lodoidamba.

24. Kemp at 437–40.

While the withdrawal of Soviet economic assistance in the 1990s brought a halt to Mongolian film production, it has recovered in recent years. *A Pearl in the Forest* deals with the Great Purge, and *The Weeping Camel* became a huge arthouse hit in the Western world. *My Beautiful Jingjiimaa*, directed by Ochir Mashbat in 2008, is a story of injustice inflicted upon two people living on the edge of society, a deaf mute man and a woman raped by a local official, and their eventual vindication.

In contrast, Western pop culture has produced B-grade dreck whenever it turns its limited attention to Mongolia. By this, I do not refer to things such as Nobel Laureate Bob Dylan's innocuous reference to Chinggis Khan in his bluegrass classic *You Ain't Going Nowhere*. I am alluding to the celluloid counterparts of 'Dschinghis Khan', a cringingly bad West German entry to the 1979 Eurovision song contest.

The list of these B-grade films is nearly endless. Hollywood moguls evidently thought it sensible to cast John Wayne as the lead in a 1950s biopic about Chinggis Khan, *The Conqueror*. This low-grade formula was repeated in 1966 with Omar Sharif saddled with the starring role in yellow-face for *Genghis Khan*. An Italian studio offered the world *Hercules vs. the Mongols* (a slight historical anomaly). The low-budget 1940s film noir *State Department File 649* pitches a pistol-packing Sam Spade–like State Department official into an unintentionally hilarious plot of psychopathic intrigues among vicious Mongolians and Chinese communists in the fight for the good ole US of A.

Schlockmeisters never sleep. *Charlie's Angels: Part II* starts off with an escape from Mongolia by Cameron Diaz and her colleagues outwitting a stock group of Orientals-as-Commie thugs. The former governor of the state of California started his lamentable film career by starring in *Conan the Barbarian*, a low-grade offering that included a Mongolian sidekick imaginatively named Khan. Even though it is a polished product cleverly tied to multimedia marketing ploys to extract more revenue from theatregoers, Disney's *Mulan* recycles stale Chinese stereotypes of Mongolians.

Destination Gobi is a tortured Second World War film that has at least some merit since it is based on an obscure historical event. During the Second World War, the US army posted weathermen in the Gobi Desert to send back radio intelligence on storm fronts as an aide for the saturation bombing of Japan. In the film, circumstances force the GIs to leave their base in Inner Mongolia and make their way to the coast of Japanese-occupied China. Underlying the film is the plot (if you can call it that) about whether the GIs should trust the Chinese or the Mongolians as they make their way across North China. Despite tedious plot twists and stock characters of Oriental inscrutability, Mongolians come out as the heroes in the story, though Hollywood filmed the motion picture on location in Arizona, using Navajos as extras and their hogans as gers. At least the flick is arguably pro-Mongolian in its sentiment.

However, the palm for the eye-clawing nadir has to go to *Mongolian Death Worm*, a recent 'thriller' based on the legend of killer worms in the Mongolian desert. In this masterpiece of bad taste, giant worms lurk beneath a power station (CHP5 backers, take note) and a combination of C-grade white actors and a Stetson-wearing Mongolian sheriff go to battle in a setting oddly reminiscent of Orange County.

There is only a small community of outsiders with sincere sympathy for Mongolia. We often encounter distasteful jocularity from non-Mongolians who utter tedious and tiresome stereotypes without fear of having these comments called out for being ignorant and disrespectful. If you wonder about the root of these prejudices, this dreary dirge of B-grade movies shows us the origins of negative images fobbed off on Mongolia by Western pop culture. The dreck stands in contrast with products of the golden age of Mongolian cinema that were made by MongolKino.[25]

Resuming our tour and moving on farther to the east, a nondescript grey two-storey building marks the former site for the Mongolor company and the Urga branch of a Russian-Chinese joint venture bank. This was a stage for multiple dramas in the early twentieth century concerning foreign investment and mining.

Mongolor is mostly forgotten today, but in the early 1900s it was regarded as a crucial engine for Mongolia's modernization. In 1899 the Peking authorities granted the Yero Valley gold mining concession to Mongolor LLC, or, to give its none-too-snappy full name, the 'Joint Stock Company for the Mining Enterprise in the Tüshetu and Tsetsen Khan Aimags of Mongolia'.[26]

The proposal for the mining concession spurred fierce debate among nobles, lamas, and the Qing authorities. The points of contention sound uncomfortably familiar to the ears of contemporary foreign investors. Some Mongolians argued fiercely against allowing foreign capital into the country for fear of a loss of autonomy; others claimed that the gold mine would offend the spirits. Everyone heatedly complained that all the good jobs would go to foreigners, and so forth. On their end, the Manchu ambans were painfully aware of the need to raise tax revenue for their uneconomical colony while juggling the agendas of competing political factions.

Victor von Grot, a former secretary to Chinese Premier Li Hongzhang and a Russian citizen, pulled the short straw and got the job of being the country manager for the project. He was hired by the Russo-Asiatic Bank, one of the primary financial institutions for tsarist interests in the Far East, to keep an eye on how the loan proceeds were applied to the mining operations.

Grot had unknowingly stepped into a whirlwind of Central Asian politics and intrigue that could sink the efforts of any slippery investment bank spin doctor to gin up a set of reasonable 'risk factors' for a prospectus. The company was hit at the outset by high transportation costs for importing European mining equipment. Given the scarcity of Mongolians with qualifications, Grot had to hire Chinese labour and Russian supervisors, a move that sparked a further dispute over foreign worker quotas. One former employee of Mongolor noted that:

25. For the classic groundbreaking work on American impressions of Asia, see Isaacs.

26. Rupen at 58.

Former Mongolor building. Photo by author.

> There was plenty of gold in the locality. The Mongols looked on interestedly at the work, but did not cooperate in it. Digging great quantities of gold out of the earth did not appeal to the Mongol as a profitable way in which to spend his days.[27]

Amid fears that they were 'losing the Mongols' hearts', Mongolian elites demanded higher royalty rates on the output of the mine. After that attempt floundered on the rebuttal that 'a contract is a contract', the authorities eventually circled back and shut down the mine in 1908 until the company conceded to higher royalty rates.[28] Mongolor went into bankruptcy, and Grot left Mongolia for San Francisco 'without a penny to his name . . . as a common labourer'.[29] 'The many years of local protests and renewed negotiation had drained the investor's finance.'[30]

The anxiety about the spirits of nature proved to be a movable feast in those days. Some Mongolians argued that mining enraged the spirits in the ground; however, these objections were overruled by the clerical authorities when it became clear that Urga could not supply its heating needs by burning argol indefinitely. In 1915 the objections were set aside and coal mining began in nearby Nalaikh.

Urga did get a permanent brick building out of the Mongolor fiasco. The two-storey building also housed a Sino-Russian bank branch until its collapse upon the default by Mongolian nobles on their loan repayments in 1911. Later attempts to start up a bank in Mongolia during the autonomous period needed to overcome the reluctance of other Russian banks fearing the same fate.[31]

27. Larson at 245–46.
28. High at 11.
29. Romanov at 510; High at 11.
30. High at 11.
31. Perry-Ayscough at 124.

Russian cemetery. Photo by Lukas Nikol.

In 1921 the Chinese warlord army made its last stand against Ungern-Sternberg in the Mongolor building. Once his Cossacks had driven out the gamin troops, the baron installed himself in the building. His touring car used roar out of the courtyard, scattering passers-by and speeding its way to hangings and executions. His victims were sometimes strung up on meathooks installed in the courtyard.[32] Later in the 1930s the building became a military hospital. These days, it is rented out as commercial space for a pharmacy.

The Ministry of Defence is the neoclassical building on the north side of Peace Avenue. It has a pastiche front similar to the facelift given to Government House. It is not open to the public unless you take a photograph within 150 metres of its perimeter, which means any spot closer than the sidewalk. If you do this, several officers with aerodynamic caps and scrambled egg on their lapels will snap to and demand that you delete the photographs. When this happened to me, I asked the fellow to show me the basis of his authority to do so. Into the ministry we went as the officer went through the drill of showing me the recently enacted regulations. No petition to common sense, or reference to the multitude of existing photographs of the building on the Internet, made any difference. Soon, we were joined by a younger man in an unstylish grey track suit and the haughty attitude that young bucks usually reserve for matters requiring diplomat finesse. He stormed into our discussion, proclaiming that he was in military intelligence—a contraction in terms, but I elected not to push it. I could see that the spy was haranguing my newly made friend, who could not escape the idiocy of having to follow regulations. I deleted the photos, the officer became my best friend, and the

32. See Ossendowski and Alioshin.

MI poser was off both our backs. I was then escorted from the ministry, to the salutes of every passing soldier and beaming smiles. I returned their salutes.

At the end of Peace Avenue is the Monument to the Mongolian Ard Air Squadron, depicting three aircraft rising vertically from a metal exhaust stream. This is a memorial to the air squadron funded by donations from Mongolia during the war with Nazi Germany. Its silvery exhaust stream makes me think of the jet streams of flights passing overhead to or from Europe and the conceit of many people on those flights who dismiss Mongolia as a 'flyover' country.

Let's close our visit to Consulate Hill by paying our respects to the Russian Cemetery, a lonely, dusty site well to the north of Peace Avenue. The graveyard began in the late nineteenth century though nearly all the tombstones are of much later dates. Perhaps the oldest ones have crumbled away. The Russian embassy sends out teams to repair the graveyard from time to time.

A nineteenth-century visitor recorded his reflections at this melancholy site:

> We passed the European cemetery on the way back, eight or ten roughly made graves, mere mounds of earth, with huge stones heaped on them to keep away the dogs. The crevices between were riddled with holes where rats had tried to get at the dead. Only one grave boasted the smallest attempt at adornment, a white wooden cross with black letters, bearing the name and age of a young Russian girl who had died in Ourga a few weeks back. I could not help wondering if the poor child ever realized, during lifetime, that this lonely, neglected spot would ever be her last resting place.[33]

33. Windt at 169.

11

'Chinatown' (Maimachin)

Ulaanbaatar's 'Chinatown' is a ghost town—a long-vanished community that once was the main centre of the commercial life of the capital.[1]

In ancient times, the name of this quarter was the Red Hill, or Ulaan Dov (Улаан Дов). As the settlement expanded with the arrival of more and more Chinese merchants, its official name was changed to the Village of Abundant Peace, or Elbeg Amgalan Gatsaa (Элбэг Амгалан Гацаа) from which the district takes its current name, Amgalan.

By 1807 the settlement had a population of 4,000 Chinese. With the loosening of Qing restrictions on Chinese migration, Maimachin gradually grew the standard hallmarks of nineteenth-century sedentary Chinese society—courtyard-style houses and stores with tiled roofs, temples dedicated to Chinese deities, hostels set up as caravanserai, theatres, restaurants, taverns, and brothels, as well as guild halls for Chinese merchants to set standards and regulate their business activities.

By the end of the nineteenth century a square-shaped wooden palisade enclosed Chinatown, with a gate at each of the cardinal directions. More houses and shops spilled outside the settlement walls—this is where most of the Mongolian residents of Chinatown lived. To the immediate north of the settlement were plots of land under cultivation for vegetables otherwise not available on the steppes. Unlike the two monastic settlements, there was an attempt to construct a typical urban Chinese chequerboard street grid by building three main avenues running from east to west, with Customs Street, or Gaalin Gudamj (Гаалийн гудамж), along the southern wall. Manchu and later MPR officials levied duty on goods brought into and from Khalkha Mongolia at this spot. (This was also where travellers in the 1920s encountered delays by the officials of the newly founded MPR.)

Maimachin in the early twentieth century boasted a Confucian temple where Manchu officials and Chinese residents attended the annual ceremonies in reverence of the sage and his philosopher-disciples. While Confucian political philosophy never took root among Mongolians, its ethical principles struck a responsive chord. The *Great Learning*, or *Da Xue* (大学), one of the canonical Four Books of Confucianism,

---

1. For more information on Maimachin, see Teleki at 191; Pozdneyev I (1977) at 77 et seq.; Ma at 125–28; and Rupen (1957).

was translated into Mongolian under the title *Ikh Sürtakhüi Bichig* (Их Суртахуй Бичиг). The social virtue of respect for parents and ancestors had its mirror image in local custom, which certainly must have been reinforced with the Mongolian translation of the *Book of Filial Piety*, or *Xiao Jing* (孝经), into *Achilat Nom* (Ачлалт Ном).

Aside from the Confucian temple, the settlement contained temples dedicated to a wide assortment of the gods of the Chinese pantheon, some of whom were regarded as the alter egos of Mongolian Vajrayana deities, like Lord Guan and his mirror emanation King Geser. Maimachin also had a temple dedicated to the Chinese patron saint of carpentry, Lu Ban, because many Chinese carpenters plied their trade here. Chinese Muslim merchants and caravan men attended to their daily prayers in a mosque while outside the inner settlement wall were Red Hat Buddhist monasteries and hovels for shamans. Travelling Peking opera troupes performed for the Chinese community in the open courtyards of the district's temples or at specially built theatres modelled on those in China.

In contrast to the liveliness of Maimachin, the Chinese cemetery was a forlorn sight, set up at a distance from the north wall of the settlement. The remains of deceased Chinese were placed in above-ground wooden coffins until friends or relatives could arrange for repatriation of the deceased to their hometowns. This temporary above-ground storage conformed to Mongolian sensitivities by not putting the dead into the ground, a practice that was offensive to the supernatural 'owners' of the earth. However, the stench from the graveyard could reach as far as Consulate Hill. For penniless nobodies, the cemetery and its wooden coffins were the 'end of the road' with no chance of repatriation or being honoured in the afterlife by their descendants. In Chinese beliefs, they became aggrieved ghosts, doomed to wander the steppes mourning their fate and casting harm on mortals.

In the spring of 1921 the Mad Baron had a catastrophic effect on the Chinese merchant community. Russian and Mongolian soldiers under his command ruthlessly looted Chinese shops and imposed a psychotic vengeance in fits of madness. In one case, Ungern-Sternberg arrested two Cossacks and a Mongolian for stealing brandy from a Chinese shop and brought the three thieves back to the store, returned the brandy, and ordered his soldiers to hang the offenders from the front gate of the shop. An eyewitness recalled,

> That seemed expeditious and just enough [to Ungern-Sternberg] until the Chinese proprietor came in dire distress to the Baron and pleaded with him: 'General! Baron! General Baron! Please take those men down from my gateway, for no one will enter my shop?'[2]

The panic-stricken Chinese proprietor feared a calamity of supernatural proportions. The ghosts of the hanged men would haunt the threshold and take revenge on those entering or passing by the store. Presumably the bones of these three brandy thieves wound up littering the approaches to Urga.

2. Ossendowski at 200.

After the Mad Baron fled, Maimachin rebounded and resumed its role as the commercial centre of the capital because of the essential role of Chinese trade for the country. Some Mongolian nobles and even revolutionaries saw the advantage to the local economy (and themselves personally) of permitting Chinese merchants to return as commercial agents and financiers. However, by 1927 the political winds had changed and the revolutionaries were squeezing Chinese businesses to leave the country. Soon they were long gone, though some Chinese workers elected to remain in the country and quietly assimilate into Mongolian society. For a brief while in the 1950s, Maimachin's role as a centre for expatriate Chinese was revived when the government provided temporary housing for guest workers from Mao's China, but with the onset of the Sino-Soviet split, the district drifted back into obscurity, occasionally used as a film set but otherwise neglected as the city constructed microdistricts elsewhere under Soviet guidance.

The Monastery of Great Tara, or Dar'ekh Khiid (Дарь Эх Хийд), is the only surviving structure that recalls the days of Maimachin. It was originally built in 1778 under an imperial decree issued by the Qianlong Emperor. In 2001 it was given to a congregation of nuns who hold services there under its new name Dolmalin Khiid (Долмалин Хийд). As the oldest building in Ulaanbaatar, it is an unsung jewel that has been shamefully neglected by the municipal authorities. This neglect is even more inexcusable given laudable efforts by the nuns to preserve the temple while cultivating their knowledge and practice of the dharma.

The entrance to the monastery is at its north-east corner. The main hall of the temple is dedicated to Great Tara, who was synonymous with the bodhisattva Guan Yin to Chinatown's residents. The portico of the doorway to the main hall is supported by sagging *dougong* wooden brackets, richly decorated with images of elephants, *makaras*,

Temple of Great Tara in 'Chinatown'. Photo by Lukas Nikol.

nagas, and the three jewels. Stone lions stand guard at each side of the entrance and an incense burner is directly in front of the main hall. Inside the hall, many Ayush bronze statues cloaked in yellow or blue khadags are set out along the north wall while thangkas of the Green and White Taras hang from the ceiling by the side walls. The nuns congregate here each morning for prayers.

The side halls to the east and west of the courtyard are now used as a meditation hall and a dormitory. Back when the monastery was an active site for worship in Chinatown, the eastern hall was a shrine dedicated to the White Old Man while in the western hall, the monks paid reverence to an image of the Kangxi Emperor, or Khashin Khaan (Хашин Хаан), as a patron of Vajrayana Buddhism. The Chinese agent Ma Ho-t'ien mentions that in the 1920s Peking opera performances were staged in the courtyard where there was preferential seating in temporary two-storey structures for officials and lamas while the hoi polloi were crammed together on the ground.

On the south end of the courtyard, there are two 11-metre granite ceremonial pillars that were erected in 1783 and now are protected as national historical monuments. Each pillar contains one part of a couplet in classical Chinese about the purpose of the Mahayana faith:

> 普渡迷津济群生
> To Save All Crossing the Deluded Stream
> 大发慈悲救万苦
> To Spread Compassion to Relieve a Myriad of Sufferings

'Deluded stream' means the process of samsara and the misperception of an enduring self. A 'myriad of sufferings' refers to the Shakyamuni's first noble truth that life is suffering.

The pillars are decorated with standard Buddhist motifs, such as the Buddhist victory flag celebrating the Shakyamuni Buddha's triumph over suffering and evil, *makara*s, the eight-spoke dharma wheel, various deities, and clouds coiling around the pillar.

Ma penned a description of the Temple of Great Tara at the time of the Chinese New Year celebration in 1927. This was probably the last time that the holiday was celebrated with any verve in Chinatown.

> Farthest to the east stood the imposing structures of a Taoist [*sic*] temple, inside of which was a pair of delicately carved stone flagstaffs thirty or forty feet high. They had been erected at a cost of more than eight thousand ounces of silver. As a festival was in progress, the inside of the temple was specially decorated. A straw hut had been set up and then transformed into a mountain of ice, with an image of the seated Shakyamuni below, Buddhist images insides, and a cave behind a waterfall on top, all made of ice. Another ice mountain in the rear was topped by the figure of Hsuan-tsang collecting scriptures.[3] There were also several lanterns of ice, cleverly arranged so that large

3. Hsuan Tsang (Xuanzang 玄奘) was a seventh-century Buddhist monk who travelled overland from China to India to collect Buddhist philosophical texts and other literature for the Buddhist community in China.

> candles could be lit inside in the evening. Within the central hall were a few Chinese sitting on the ground at their prayers.[4]

On the north-west corner of the nunnery stands a 200-year-old poplar tree (*Populus diversifolia*), which looks like one of J. K. Rowling's 'whomping willows'. Its twisted trunk and clawing branches are adorned with blue khadags placed there by the residents of the district. As an indigenous desert species, the poplar easily absorbs water and becomes alkaline, making its wood bitter to the taste. The bitterness symbolizes how the spirit within the poplar blesses those who adore it by absorbing their pain.

With a touch of empathetic imagination, you might be able to hear the sotto voce echoes of the feverish prayers by people who lived in Maimachin as they tried to decipher every rumour about the Chinese revolution or the Mad Baron's Cossacks. I prefer a visit to the temple when the harsh cold of winter and the December sunlight from a deep-blue sky lend themselves to imagining the ghosts of the long-deceased residents of this forgotten part of the city. The Monastery of the Great Tara and the wizened poplar tree are the only surviving witnesses to Maimachin's tumultuous past.[5]

Oldest resident in Chinatown. Photo by Lukas Nikol.

4. Ma at 127.
5. At the time when I moved to Ulaanbaatar, I learned that two Manchu-era warehouses somehow managed to survive in Maimachin. These were two-storey buildings with roofs constructed at a 45-degree angle, abruptly descending straight to the ground at the apex. The municipal government made a lamentably ignorant decision to proceed with a residential apartment complex to the north of the temple and tear down the last two examples of Chinese warehouse architecture in Maimachin.

12

To the South

The Ulaanbaatar Rail Station is one of the two main points of entry for visitors to Mongolia. It is a curious mixture of Soviet-style waiting rooms, high ceilings, polished marble walls, and crystal chandeliers with newly-added rickety and tarnished metal benches of Chinese manufacture, mom-and-pop convenience stores purveying junk food, and tacky souvenir stands selling Chinggis Khan memorabilia and little toy gers. The tannoy reverberates with the echoed announcements of arriving and departing trains, an effect that preserves a slight impression of the bad old days at Checkpoint Charlie and other Cold War crossing points. The rail station also proves the foresight of Nikolai Spathary, a seventeenth-century Greek-Russian diplomat in the service of the Romanovs.

Ulaanbaatar Railway Station. Photo by Lukas Nikol.

In 1676 Peter the Great appointed Spathary to be his ambassador for a 150-man mission to Peking for the purpose of establishing diplomatic relations and demarcating the boundary between Russia and China. Spathary managed to secure an audience with the Kangxi Emperor and even obtained an invitation to an imperial banquet at the Forbidden City, but otherwise, his mission did not succeed in its objectives. However, he did bring back the first dependable logistical intelligence on the eastern lands bordering on Peter's expanding empire.

In his report Spathary observed that there were three main routes for travelling to Peking. One route passed through Xinjiang, but it was impassable at that time because of the Manchu-Zungharian conflict. The second route—the one that Spathary took—was the long and arduous journey to a remote border crossing in Manchuria where the city called Manzhouli (or Manchu Village) now exists. Both routes were dismissed by Spathary as impractical. He recommended future Russian envoys to travel to Peking through the Tuul River Valley. In 1706 this became the official trade route between the two empires, an agreement that was formally ratified in the Treaty of Kiakhta of 1726 between Catherine the Great and the Yongzheng Emperor.

The overland trade route reconnected Mongolia to the outside world for the first time since the collapse of the global Chinggisid Empire three centuries earlier. Mongolian teamsters and wagoners were the backbone of a transportation network that was completed in stages between Siberia and Inner Mongolia. The lives of the caravan men created a vibrant subculture that lasted well into the first part of the twentieth century but was inevitably doomed. In the 1860s Knox could sense the end coming for the caravan men and their way of life:

> The Mongols engaged in the caravan service pass a large part of their lives on the road, and are as merry as larks over their employment. They seem quite analogous to the teamsters and miscellaneous 'plainsmen,' who used to play an important part on our overland route, and are destined to disappear when the Pacific Railway is completed.[1]

By the late nineteenth century foreign investment firms and other fantasists had begun to pitch plans to connect the Trans-Siberian Railway and the new rail artery in north China but they received no encouragement from financial syndicates. Cost and the remoteness of the region cooled enthusiasm for building a railway when more immediate returns were to be had by constructing railways to connect the bustling markets in the coastal provinces of China proper. In the 1910s the Peking warlord government briefly revived interest in the project and considered appealing for Japanese financing for a rail link between Mongolia and China. The 1921 revolution put an end to these plans and any further discussions of a rail line built from the south.

One decade later, the Soviets contemplated the need for a spur line running into Mongolia as a defensive manoeuvre against Japanese encroachment into Siberia. As an initial test project, they built Mongolia's first railway running between Ulan Bator and the Nalaikh mines—a narrow gauge track covering 22 miles for hauling coal for the

1. Knox at 169.

city's power plant. After the Great Purge and the Second World War, a cross-border rail line was opened between Ulan Bator and Verkhneudinsk (now Ulan-Ude) on 7 November 1949 along the original 338 miles of the Mongolian caravan route. Once the Chinese Communists took power, the Soviet Union pushed on with an extension of the line to Jining, the first major city on the Chinese side of the border. The Trans-Mongolian Railway was inaugurated with great socialist fanfare on 1 January 1956. Black-and-white photographs of the ceremony show a diesel engine emblazoned with Stalin's portrait, carrying the flags of the three socialist fraternal allies as an optimistic portent for a new world. 'Three centuries of use have proven the logic and efficiency of this route for connecting the two great empires of Russia and China, and the completion in 1955 of a railroad along the same route confirms Spathary's foresight.'[2]

The railway brought about more extensive change to Mongolia than any other event in its modern history. It permanently connected the country to the distant ports of the Atlantic and Pacific oceans. It also brought into existence a new class of Mongolians skilled in modern technical trades, such as machinists, track engineers, locomotive and car masters, truck brigadiers, telegraph specialists, locksmiths, electricians, and many others. Only thirty years before a few Western writers had predicted the demise of Mongolians as a dying race incapable of material progress. The Trans-Mongolian Railway was a strong rebuttal to the social Darwinists and an alarming shock for Cold War warriors in the West.[3]

The optimism of this achievement did not last long. At first in the interests of socialist unity, China adopted the larger Russian gauge for the 210-mile Erlian–Jining domestic rail spur, which expedited shipments across the border. However, the integration of the Chinese and Soviet rail networks depended upon geopolitics and preservation of trust between the two communist giants. This ended in short order.

In 1962 within days of reaching agreement with Zhou Enlai over boundary disputes, Prime Minister Tsedenbal took an abruptly anti-fraternal step and deeply offended Peking by condemning China's interpretation of socialism in a show of loyalty to Moscow. China retaliated against Mongolia by tearing up its Russian gauge spur line and insulated its transportation network from the threat of Soviet invasion by rail. The question of the railway gauge continues to be a heated domestic issue for Mongolia, which now fears Chinese social and economic infiltration. These days, the rail trip across the Chinese border entails a four-hour delay at the Zamyn-Ude–Erlian border crossing to change the train's bogies (a ritual that works to slow down commerce and inflate Mongolian commodity prices).

During the tense years of the Sino-Soviet split, the railway crossing between Mongolia and China took on all the melodrama of a John le Carré novel:

> In the moonlight, one can just pick out the border post, and almost immediately the train halts and Mongolian soldiers in jackboots approach with dogs. The nice thing

2. Rupen (1957) at 160–61.
3. Rupen at 274.

> about Mongolia is that it really looks the way you think it should look. It resembles a set for a 1930s movie about Mongolia, if there ever was such a thing. And the customs and immigration men who board the train at Zamyn-Ude look like extras prone to over-acting.[4]

A venerable China hand told me about his experience crossing the Sino-Mongolian border late one night in 1979. During an interrogation by Mongolian immigration officials, he admitted he did not have a standard yellow WHO vaccination card, a mandatory requirement for transiting passengers in those days. With no common language between them, the Mongolian officials took him off the train and led him into the pitch-black night and up a spiral staircase in an unlit building. He was suddenly brought into a blindingly lit clinic staffed by a buxom nurse suckling an infant. A battery of Mongolian was fired off with only one decipherable word: cocktail. At first my friend was puzzled by the prospect of a nightcap but then the nurse filled a massive stainless steel and glass hypodermic needle with various pharmaceutical concoctions and gestured to my friend to take off his T-shirt. As he raised the shirt over his head and without a word of forewarning, the nurse stabbed the needle with its 'cocktail' of vaccinations into his back. He did not succumb to any mutated vaccines that night and was able to get a brief glimpse of Ulan Bator the next morning. He confirms that the city still had the same attractive appearance described by Lattimore in 1962.[5]

The Ulan Bator Rail Station itself was also a place for other less-than-welcoming conduct by Mongolian officialdom. A 1986 British travel guide to the Trans-Siberian Railway warned of customs officials spitefully troubleshooting acts of espionage. One guard coaxed a Western tourist with a zoom-lens camera to the other side of the train where, out of the sight of the other tourists, the guard unscrewed the zoom lens and scratched it with a pair of nail clippers right in front of the apoplectic tourist.[6] In another instance, the author Paul Theroux recorded how, as the Chinese train pulled out from the station and into the desert south of Ulaanbaatar, Mongolians threw stones at the rail car's windows, an experience encountered by other travellers in the days of frosty relations with China.[7]

These days, soft-sleeper train travel to and from Ulaanbaatar is dependable and puts far less wear-and-tear on the body and soul than flying. If you pack a well-provisioned hamper with a few bottles of wine, a good book, and an MP3 player with headphones, a soft-sleeper berth is the most civilised way to travel to or from UB.

The neighbourhood directly to the north of the station was the main railway workers residential district in the 1950s. Its pastel-yellow three-storey buildings have now fallen into an unsightly tangle of shops, bars, and karaoke parlours, looking more like a sacrifice zone in urban America than the homes for people working in an

4. Pringle.
5. His Excellency Clifford Borg-Marks, ambassador of the Republic of Malta to Mongolia, personal conversation, May 2011.
6. Strauss at 68.
7. Theroux at 63.

essential sector of the national economy. The neighbourhood is still dotted with a few neoclassical buildings allocated for use by state enterprises like Ulaanbaatar Railways. The district could be the site of a handsome restoration project, but sadly these grand old buildings will probably be torn down and replaced by modern monstrosities in the fate typically reserved for Asian cities.

There is an interesting addition to the neighbourhood, however. On Magsarjav Street just to the east of Jarg Street, the Puntsoglin Monastery (Пунцоглин Хийд) was founded in 1990 by the Railway Association of Mongolian Believers for the revival of a branch of Red Hat Buddhism. The monastery follows the lineage of the Tibetan lama Thang Tong Gyalpo, or, in Mongolian, Tonton (Тонтон), a contemporary of Tsongkhapa and the founder of a branch of the Kagyüpa. The present building is a modern Tibetan-style construction. The monks hold daily prayers to Padmasambhava and a special ceremony on the tenth day of the first month of autumn for the deities revered by their lineage.

Thang Tong Gyalpo was a legendary Tibetan polymath. His fame rested partially on his mechanical-engineering skills; he constructed iron-chain bridges throughout the Himalayas, some of which are still in use. Perhaps it was because of his engineering skills that the railway workers decided to found a temple in his honour. To fund his building projects, Thang Tong Gyalpo became a music impresario and a composer, creating an influential form of Tibetan opera called Ache Lha-mo that incorporates legendary stories about the past lives of the historical Buddha. Using his considerable medical talents, he also founded the famed Chapo Ri Medical College in Lhasa. He wrote highly regarded medical treatises as well as countless religious texts that expressed his 'mad monk' philosophies and compassionate regard for all sentient beings.

In the late nineteenth century the Mongolian lama Jagarmolom brought Thang Tong Gyalpo's teachings to Mongolia and founded two Red Hat temples on the site of what became the Second Maternity Hospital. The lamas of the newly constructed Puntsoglin Monastery aim to revive this tradition.[8] On the *arsh*-scented second floor of this sturdy building, lamas attend daily prayer sessions while others recite jasaas for the faithful. A Shakyamuni Buddha bronze holds pride of place on the main altar while thangkas of Padmasambhava and the bearded Thang Tong, among others from the Vajrayana pantheon, are enclosed in a glass cupboard.

Near the intersection of Peace Avenue and P. Jasray Avenue, directly to the north of the Railway Station, stands the Islamic Centre of Ulaanbaatar, a mosque constructed with Saudi funding for the Sunni Muslim community and the Kazakh residents of the capital. The Kazakhs were about 4 per cent of the population of Mongolia in 2010, or just over 100,000 people. They are a Türkic-speaking people who practise Sunni Islam flavoured with pre-Islamic steppe traditions and customs, such as reverence for the sky, their ancestors, and the hearth. In the mid-nineteenth century Kazakh nomads settled

8. Mongolian Temple Project website; for Tonton, see Gyatso.

in what is now Bayan Ölgii province in the far west of the country and in the early twentieth century were joined by other Kazakhs fleeing civil unrest in Xinjiang.

The Kazakhs have become a staple image in the Mongolia tourism industry because of their eagle-hunting tradition, which undeniably cuts a cool image. Less well-known is the Kazakh tradition of an oral epic literature, shamanism, and legendary stories about an enchanted world populated by goblins, giants, and other supernatural beings. The Kazakhs of Mongolia have faced some discrimination as outsiders despite being loyal citizens of the Mongolian state, but those Kazakhs who elected to immigrate to an independent Kazakhstan found an even less warm welcome there. The Nalaikh district in Ulaanbaatar is the site of the largest Kazakh community in the capital. Should the invitation arise, it would be memorable to participate in the feasting of one of their holiday festivals, though be forewarned: they are prodigious vodka drinkers.

The Islamic Centre has been the focus of on-again, off-again construction work over the years depending upon the flow of funding from wealthy Gulf States. When completed, the centre will have a Middle Eastern appearance.

Returning to the Railway Station and going towards the east on Narnii Road, we pass a wall that has become an open-air gallery for Ulaanbaatar's graffiti artists, who certainly demonstrate no inconsiderable amount of talent. Further along, the Railway Museum shows off its collection of historically important locomotives on the lot abutting on Narnii Road. In addition to the tiny black steam-powered engine that served on the Nalaikh–Ulan Bator line, there is a 1950s diesel engine proudly bearing a portrait of Comrade Stalin. Behind the museum is the UB railway depot, which gives you a chance to see where old Soviet engines and carriages go to die in a cyber-steampunk setting.

We next visit the southern suburbs by crossing Peace Bridge, which is one of the last tangible examples of cooperation between China and the Soviet bloc in Mongolia before the withdrawal of Chinese workers in the 1960s. Even before the clash between the two powers, Mao had provoked considerable anxiety among Mongolians when in 1952 he offered to send 300,000 Chinese as 'helpers', a transparent attempt to reclaim what Chiang Kai-shek had abandoned only seven years earlier. Mao also relentlessly lobbied Khrushchev throughout the late 1950s for the return of Mongolia to China. These machinations would not have been lost on the Mongolian politburo as the love affair between Moscow and Peking cooled off.

On the south side of Peace Bridge, the Museum of the Bogd Khan is the official name for the two historical buildings at the place where the airport road comes into UB proper. One of these buildings is the Green Palace, or Nogoom Laviran (Ногоон Лавран,) and the other the Winter Palace. These were constructed as additional palaces and a personal chapel for the Eighth Patriarch.

After one of the Patriarch's palaces in the Eastern Monastic Settlement burned down in 1893, the Urga government retained Chinese artisans to build the Green Palace in the style of a late Qing-era Buddhist temple graced with Mongolian touches, such as the square cupolas constructed over the main gate and central halls. In 1904 the

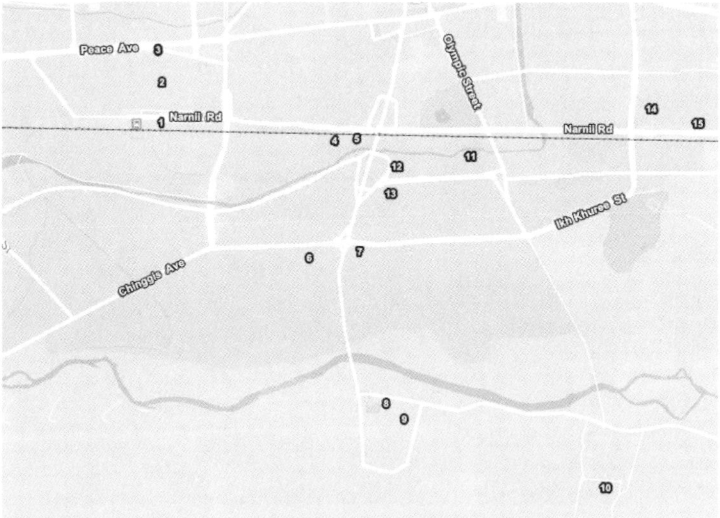

Sites on the south side of Ulaanbaatar. Map by Aubrey Ding-Shan Yang.

Key

1. Ulaanbaatar Rail Station
2. Puntsoglin Monastery
3. Islamic Centre of Ulaanbaatar
4. Railway Museum
5. Peace Bridge
6. Museum of Bogd Khan
7. Brown Palace
8. International Buddha Park
9. Zaisan Memorial
10. Ikh Tengri
11. Mahatma Gandhi statue
12. Monument to Mongolian Independence Referendum
13. National Sports Stadium
14. Narantuul Market
15. Cathedral of Saints Peter and Paul

Eighth Patriarch ordered the additional construction of a modern Western building based on a photograph of a palace in a portfolio collection sent by Tsar Nicholas II as a gift. The secular design of the building caused some disquiet among Manchu administrators, who probably sensed that the Patriarch was angling to make a statement about independence, or at least a pitch for support from Saint Petersburg. The controversy blew over once the Patriarch agreed to place a ganjir on the roof of the palace, thereby reaffirming his status as a clerical and not temporal authority.

The most ornate structure in the Green Palace is the Gate of Settled Peace, or Amgalan Enkhiin Khaalga (Амгалан Энхийн Хаалга), which is a name derived from the Chinese Andingmen (安定门). Built in 1915, the gate is a classic Chinese three-tiered triumphal arch with interlocking *dougong* brackets, which use no nails whatsoever. (Nails were considered to be an uncouth form of construction.) Along with the Temple of Avalokitesvara at the Ganden Monastery, the Gate of Settled Peace is one of the two main monuments built to commemorate Mongolian independence.

Steam locomotive at the Railway Museum. Photo by author.

I suspect that the Gate of Settled Peace was an irresistibly mischievous idea dreamed up by the Mongolian theocratic elites to tweak the nose of gamin warlords and politicians in Peking. When returning from a campaign in Central Asia during the Ming and Qing dynasties, Chinese armies re-entered Peking by marching under a gate on the north side of the city's wall. This gate, called the Gate of Settled Peace, was meant to symbolize Chinese invincibility and assure the citizenry of Peking that the imperial troops had successfully sorted out any threat from troublemakers to the north. The name of the gate implied that China had imposed a settled peace on those nomads with a penchant to be forever chasing 'water and grass'. Given how often Peking had been sacked by invaders from the north, the name was ahistorical, not unlike the false pageantry surrounding the proclamation 'Mission Accomplished'.

Revelling in his newly acquired imperial title, the Bogd Khan, or perhaps a sycophantic official in the theocratic government, thought up a way to pay back Han chauvinism in its own coin. This splendidly ornate gate appropriated the same name as the gate in Peking. The designers positioned the Gate of Settled Peace for their Mongolian sovereign to face south towards China, implying that Mongolians had taught the southern rice-growing troublemakers a lesson by driving them from the steppes.

As in the case with vanity projects, there were unintended consequences. The construction of the gate had incited the ire of the Russian consulate because the theocratic government has misappropriated the proceeds of a Russian gold rouble loan meant for infrastructure projects and the training of the Mongolian army, and not for what was perceived as a frivolous and self-indulgent expression of nationalism. Within a decade both the tsarist and theocratic governments had been swept away, leaving us this fine example of Sino-Mongolian architecture.

The Green Palace is positioned symmetrically along a north–south axis that served as the Holy Walkway for the Bogd Khan. At the southernmost point is a grey brick *yampai* sporting dragons with, cheekily enough, five fingers (a motif once reserved for exclusive use by the Chinese emperors and perhaps another example of the Bogd Khan cocking a snoot at China). Next is the triple gate, or *yamba yosloliin khaalga* (ямба ёслолын хаалга), a feature of Asian royal architecture dating back to the second millennium BCE. At each side of the triple gate is a flagpole, or *tugnii mod* (тугны мод) or *chii-gaa* (чий гаа), a standard feature of both imperial and religious architecture in Asia. During the autonomous period, the pole on one side flew the yellow flag of Gelukpa Buddhism as a symbol of the state religion while on the other pole was the blue flag of the state, which was an emulation of blue khadags and a reference to Möngke Tenger.

The door guardians on the Gate of Settled Peace are legendary protectors borrowed from a Chinese custom dating at least to the early years of Tang China. The founding emperor of the Tang dynasty complained about ghosts that came to haunt him each evening. Concerned about the emperor's well-being, two of his generals stood guard outside the emperor's bedroom. The ghostly visitations ceased, but since the emperor did not want to do without the protection of his generals, he had their images painted on his bedroom doors. This legend soon yielded door guardians on temple doors and outer courtyard entranceways.

The main entrance to the Green Palace leads us into an antechamber built in 1903 for the Maharajas of the Four Directions. The first courtyard comports with Qing temple architecture in having a bell tower, or *jin honk* (жин хонх) and a drum tower, or *jin khengereg* (жин хэнгэрэг), on each side of the Holy Walkway. The main hall directly

The Green Palace, Museum of Bogd Khan. Photo by Janice Law.

Winter Palace's bay window where the Bogd Khan distributed his gifts. Photo by author.

in front of us is the Temple of the Disciples, or Naidan Süm (Найдан Сүм). This was where the Bogd Khan held annual summer ceremonies in honour of the eighteen disciples of the Shakyamuni Buddha. It now houses bronzes of deities granting long life and well-being—Ayush, White Tara, and Vijaya or Tselkhanamsüm (Цэлханамсүм). The Bogd Khan's servants lived in the shrine rooms on the east and west sides of the courtyard; today they contain thangkas in appliqué or painted with natural minerals. On display are exceptionally well-executed depictions of Avalokitesvara, the Amitabha Buddha, and the legendary twelve deeds of the Shakyamuni Buddha, among others.

Going into the next courtyard, the Green Palace is the main hall of the second courtyard. As the principal temple of the complex, it was dedicated for use by the Bogd Khan. His throne, with its twenty-one cushions, is on display—the higher a monk's status, the more cushions allocated to him—along with a bronze of the palace's main protective deity, Vajradhara. The exquisite twenty-one bronzes of Tara cast by Zanabazar in 1706 are also on display here.

According to legend, Zanabazar modelled the Tara statuettes on a young woman known simply as the Princess, a renowned beauty who became his consort. Despite the intimacy of their relationship, she was reputed to have cultivated the advanced spiritual powers ordinarily possessed by daginas. When several aimag khans visited Zanabazar to express their concerns about his unchaste behaviour, they were reduced to silence when the Princess came out from a workshop holding a molten lump of bronze, which she then moulded by hand into a bronze Buddha.

In the early twentieth century, the Bogd Khan and several high lamas gathered at the main temple for the Summer Oath-Taking, or *Yar Khailen* (Яр Хайлэн), a forty-five-day meditational retreat during the Buddhist Lenten period. The custom goes back to the Buddha having his disciples remain indoors during the monsoon season so that they would not accidentally hurt insects that were stirring and coming out of the ground.

The hall on the west side served as lodgings for princes and other nobles visiting the Bogd Khan; it later became his treasury. Inside are nineteenth- and twentieth-century thangkas with portraits of the Fourth Panchen Lama (who was the seventeenth-century tutor of the only Mongolian-born Dalai Lama), the Maitreya Buddha, Tsongkhapa, Yama, and Ganesh, the elephant-headed Hindu god, or, in Mongolian, Ganapati (Ганапати). The building on the east side was divided into lodgings for visiting religious leaders and the Bogd Khan's library.

The Western-style two-storey Winter Palace stands separately at the south-east corner of the museum's grounds. It contains exhibits that made up only a small fraction of the personal possessions of the Patriarch, such as his robes, hats, jewels, a throne, a golden overcoat worn by Zanabazar, and a collection of glassy-eyed stuffed and mounted animals from his zoo, looking decidedly worse for the wear. The yellow carriage that took the Patriarch to his coronation in 1911 is on the first floor but without any description of its historic use. On the second floor is a royal ger made from snow leopard skins. The Winter Palace has eight rooms on each floor, complete with a telephone, an electric bell, and a generator for the Patriarch to summon his servants, who must have rued the day that technology came to Mongolia.

The Winter Palace's large bay window overlooking the street always reminds me of Frans Larson, the Swedish missionary who came to Mongolia in the 1890s but later wore many other hats—such as a dealer in horses and furs, a retail merchant, a guide for visiting Westerners, and a consultant to the Patriarch's government—until the political revolution forced him to leave Khalkha Mongolia in the late 1920s. Fluent in Mongolian, Larson became a friend of the Bogd Khan, who awarded him the title of duke, or *gün* (гүн), because of which he was known among the foreign community as the 'Duke of Mongolia'. (In truth, he was only a duke in Mongolia; many people had been granted the title gün.) He was later recast during the revolutionary era as an agent of Wall Street trying to enslave Mongolia, a proposition that would have left capitalist financiers doubled over with laughter—they had no interest in seeking economic hegemony in fringe border areas far from the highly populated urban centres of Asia.[9] The silent Soviet film *Storm from the East* carries this fiction to absurd levels, depicting *British* imperial soldiers occupying Khalkha Mongolia to protect the business dealings of a ruthless cigar-chomping fur merchant (as if high-end ladies fashions were a core industry for imperialism). The character is supposedly based on Larson. (This is a cracking good film despite the goofy storyline.)

Larson recorded that the Bogd Khan was a compulsive consumer of Western luxury goods and curios, perhaps because of the relentless boredom of monastic life. Since the Manchus had forbidden him to leave the country, he brightened his days by ordering a tremendous volume of goods from Sears and Roebuck–style catalogues sent

9. Lattimore tried to explain this to his Mongolian colleagues when he visited Ulan Bator in 1962. See Lattimore (1962) at 115–16.

by mail-order supply companies in Europe, North America, and Asia. Once he had the chance to examine these consumer gadgets, he lost interest and periodically announced a distribution of gifts to all comers. On the chosen day, the Bogd Khan appeared at the bay window and tossed out all manner of goods that he no longer cared to keep.

> You can imagine my surprise when a window in the upper story of the palace was flung open and a jolly man, dressed in a gown of glittering gold, appeared and flung out a lady's corset . . . A shower of watches followed—good watches of Swiss manufacture. There was a terrific scramble for these . . . After the watches came clocks, all of foreign makes, dainty things, such as ladies admire; but he heaved out one tall grandfather clock, which fell with a thud and was broken to pieces. Lamps followed clocks . . . He disappeared from the window. The mob called him back. They cheered when he returned with his arms filled with Western ladies' dresses. These he threw out one at a time . . . Hats which must have been designed to match each costume were tossed out as if they were so many cakes. Both men and women put these on over their own headgear. The Living Buddha even tried one—a concoction of straw and ostrich feathers—and thrust his head through the window for the admiration of the crowd before he threw it down. Shoes came next . . . These were followed by a shower of face powder punctuated with fluffy puffs. There were even a pair of skates, a toy windmill, a Noah's ark, and a small sailboat. He ended the afternoon's sport by scattering hundreds of horns and whistles and some Christmas tree tinsel . . . All that afternoon and evening they [the people] rollicked through the streets on horseback, blowing whistles and horns like children on circus day in Sweden.[10]

The Bogd Khan delighted in all sorts of indulgence. The Qing court sent him an elephant as an imperial gift and a sign of his religious authority. When the poor beast died from exposure in 1913, the Bogd Khan's officials diverted funds from the national treasury to purchase a replacement. (A photo of the severely traumatized pachyderm is on display in the museum—look at its desperate expression.) A Russian consultant to the theocratic government was given the thankless task of purchasing an elephant from the Saint Petersburg Zoo and accompanying it to Urga. They must have had to travel by freight train to the rail station in Verkhneudinsk, from where the beast had to be led by foot to the capital. A far-sighted mahout had trained the animal to bow down at a signal from its handler. The elephant did so when presented to the Bogd Khan, causing a minor sensation in town as people exclaimed that it recognized the sovereign's holy status.[11]

Despite Larson's fond memories of the Bogd Khan as a jolly figure, other observers left reports that contradict this impression. The Bogd Khan bestowed benefits upon his obvious constituency, the clergy, while increasing the tax burdens of everyone else and cutting the dole previously handed out to the aristocracy. Herders were left to fend for themselves against the increasing exactions by nobles. The Bogd Khan's

10. Larson at 113–15.

11. Rupen (1964) at 98.

own extraordinary taste for luxury goods was never abated. Unfortunately, like other Mongolian elites throughout history, he delighted in secret scheming and factional politics.

There is an even darker side to him, one of cruelty and murder. He banished one of his former lovers, a lama, to exile and then later arranged to have him buried alive. Another lama who offended him was beaten, castrated, and finally killed. (The coroner's report went so far as to conclude that the cause of death was suicide by self-mutilation.) While in his cups, yet a third lama made the mistake of disparagingly talking about the Bogd Khan's Tibetan birth. As a punishment, he was slowly beaten to death.[12]

People do love gossip, and truth has never been a barrier to a good story. The veracity of these disturbing stories may be contested, especially since some foreign visitors, including those who mastered the language, had such fond memories of the Bogd Khan. I have no doubt that, as a representative of his times, he could have been a discomfiting mixture of kindness and cruelty.

The area around the Green Palace along the Tuul River was the part of Urga where the well-to-do preferred to set up their homes. Mongolian and Manchu nobles built their 'townhouses', or *khoroo* (хороо) here. These were courtyard houses that were often left vacant and in ill-repair until official business brought their owners to Urga. A few of the Bogd Khan's neighbours in this district maintained residences as an inherited privilege of great wealth. For example, the descendants of Zanabazar's wet nurse (and surrogate mother) were granted hereditary estates and lived in this neighbourhood during the days of the Bogd Khan.

Despite the grandeur of the Green and Winter Palaces, the Bogd Khan preferred to while away his private hours at another residence known as the Summer Palace, which was also colloquially called the Brown Palace, or Khaistai Laviran (Хайстай Лавран). The Brown Palace had originally been the residence of Abbot Baldanchoimbol, the tutor of the seventh and eighth patriarchs. (We saw his gilded mummy at the Temple of the Choijin Lama.) Upon the abbot's death in the late nineteenth century the palace became part of the estate of the Patriarch where he went for rest and seclusion. From its main gate there were magnificent views of the river; herds of grazing horses and sheep were kept in the abundant grasslands surrounding the palace. The Bogd Khan's 'adopted' children—actually his sexual partners—also lived here.[13]

Only three buildings survive. They are to be found to the south of the Management Academy, or Udirdlgaiin Akademi (Удирдлагын Академи) and to the east of the road that leads to the Bogd Khan Museum. The first is a renovated two-storey white building with blue coloured window frames. Around the corner is a one-storey white building decorated with Siberian gingerbread fretwork under its eaves. This is now the Child Welfare Department of the Metropolitan Police Department (ironically enough, given that pederasty was one of the Bogd Khan's pastimes). To the south of this is another Urga-era building, a one-storey rectangular house with a brown-coloured

12. Jambal at 26–27, 31–32, and 53.
13. Teleki at 160; Jambal at 23–26.

Crumbling building in the former Brown Palace complex. Photo by author.

Zaisan Soviet-Mongolian Memorial. Photo by Janice Law.

exterior. It appears to be under renovation. These three buildings were constructed in secular Russian style.

The vicinity of the Brown Palace is still the preferential location for the homes of Ulaanbaatar's elite. Housing prices here are among the most expensive in the city, though little had gone into crafting an urban appearance that appeals to the eye.

Further to the south we come to the International Buddha Park with its 18-metre statue of the Shakyamuni Buddha, a gift from the Buddhist community in Korea. The Zaisan Memorial to the Soviet Union stands atop the hill behind it. The memorial depicts a victorious Soviet soldier and features a panorama of scenes of Soviet-Mongolian cooperation. The mural rolls out images of the 1921 revolution, the battle of Khalkha Gol, the victory over fascism, and the Soviet-Mongolian space programme. Nearby is a tank that used to greet visitors on the airport road into Ulaanbaatar. It had been paid for with contributions raised by Mongolians for the Soviet war effort and took part in the final assault on Berlin in May 1945. In the first decade of the twenty-first century, the Ulaanbaatar city fathers decided that a tank on the main access road into the city was sending a mixed signal to visitors and decided to move it to Zaisan Hill.

Off further to the east is Ikh Tenger (*Их Тэнгэр*), a government villa and ceremonial complex located in the northern foothills of the Bogd Uul. It was built as the personal dasha of Choibalsan and later became a governmental conference centre. Visits to Ikh Tenger are usually arranged by invitations to investment conferences and state events that offer a surfeit of predictably uncontroversial platitudes by businessmen and an unduly generous dose of meaningless canned speech by officials. Waiters dressed in national costume offer mutton dumplings and shots of vodka while a few string musicians saw away at traditional melodies.

Ikh Tenger's conferences lose their lustre the longer one lives in Ulaanbaatar, but nothing can match the disaster occasioned by the 1966 Great Flood that paralysed the Tuul River Valley at the onset of Naadam, as witnessed by Hibbert. This tragic farce foreshadowed the decline of the MPR's competency over the next quarter century.

The rain began to fall torrentially on 9 July, turning the annual memorial services at the tomb of Sükhbaatar and Choibalsan into soggy confusion. Even though the rain had worsened by 11 July, the leadership insisted on sticking to the schedule of parades and political rallies. With no protective clothing, thousands of people were drenched in a downpour that brought one-third of Ulan Bator's annual rainfall at one shot. 'Even the hardened [Soviet bloc] residents began to murmur that it would have been cancelled in Prague or Bucharest or Warsaw.' The event was 'carried through to the bitter end according to the programme, down to the last [tannoyed] word of the Defence Minister's inaudible speech and the last detail of imitation of the way these things are done in Moscow.' The opening of the Naadam games was delayed in the downpour because Tsedenbal was an hour late for the event. By then, the stadium grounds were almost under water while 'the wrestlers splashed at every fall'.

As the waters of the Tuul River flooded into thousands of homes, the municipal power station, and the industrial zone, the government soldiered on with an official national day reception at Ikh Tenger amid the dangerous conditions. 'We had to endure a full round of speeches by the delegations followed by a somewhat incoherent and long improvisation by Tsedenbal'—talk about the persistence of tradition! Some officials and diplomats became raucously drunk in the side rooms. 'This and the pelting rain and rushing water and the start of the scheduled fireworks display created a more demented atmosphere than is usual on diplomatic occasions,' which is quite a statement. The bridge across the Tuul River washed away later that night.

The next afternoon, the diplomatic corps was hurried back for the finals of the wrestling competition despite the relentless rain. The Tuul River soon broke its banks and flooded the area around the stadium, inundating the residential districts where children were swept away while their parents attended the mandatory Naadam sport events. 'No one had been warned and no one was ready . . . Families and individuals struggled to safety as best they could.'

The flood devastated a large part of the capital. Soviet troops helped stiffen rescue efforts and flew in helicopters for the stranded, bringing them to Sükhbaatar Square, which was turned into a makeshift camp of shivering homeless refugees.[14]

The flood waters came nowhere near the Bogd Khan's Museum, which was left high and dry during the catastrophe. It spurred many comments that the Bogd Khan certainly knew his business when it came to casting an effective spell.

Farther to the east of Ikh Tenger, there is a newly created park for practising shamans with a dozen three- or four-legged towers covered with khadags and wind horse flags. At the top of each shrine is an identifying logo for the specific sect that erected the tower. The shamans enter into a trance inside the shelter in order to leave the earthly realm for a visit to the spirits in the sky.

Let us retrace our steps and continue our tour on the north bank of the Tuul River, turning into Mahatma Gandhi Street where a statue of Mahatmaji graces the east end of the boulevard. On this road, we can also see a white obelisk; this marks the central polling headquarters for the referendum of 20 October 1945 on Mongolian independence.

During the Yalta Conference in February 1945, Stalin pushed Churchill and Roosevelt to agree that 'Outer Mongolia' should be allowed to determine its future despite its murky status under international law. Churchill was indifferent and Roosevelt sympathetic. On a personal level, Roosevelt had a romantic fascination for the history of nomadic peoples in Central Asia. He also understood that it was foolhardy to oppose the accomplished fact of more than twenty-three years of Mongolian independence from China. By consenting to Stalin's proposal, Roosevelt had set events into motion so that the Chinese Nationalists had no choice but to accept the de facto situation and permit a face-saving referendum on Mongolian sovereignty. It

14. Hibbert's account of the 1966 flood is at 206–9.

Shaman's park. Photo by author.

is remarkable that Chiang Kai-shek did not resist more forcefully but then he held Roosevelt in high regard as the only true anti-imperialist among the leaders of the Allies.[15]

The referendum took the form of an open ballot with voters affixing signatures or thumbprints next to their names in official registry records. Choibalsan insisted upon the completion of the election nationwide by 8:00 p.m., a considerable logistical challenge for a huge county without a modern communications network. I suspect that he wanted to send Moscow a sycophantically worded telegram timed to be received just as the 'boss' was finishing his lunch. The vote was 483,281 to 0.[16]

To the south is the National Sports Stadium, which is the site for the opening of the annual Naadam festival and the hosting of its wrestling contests. The stadium is a Russian construction project completed with Chinese labour in 1958.

The Naadam celebration is the modern equivalent of a thirteenth-century Mongolian summer festival, featuring wrestling, archery, and horse-racing contests. The traditional summer festival also included annual ovoo worship ceremonies and rituals for the formal aspersion of the season's new kumis and other dairy products as offerings to the spirits. (This latter ritual later morphed into the more informal custom of dipping a finger into a drink and flicking drops into the air three times.)

After the Second Conversion, this summer festival also incorporated the *danshig* (даншиг) ceremony for the patriarchs. Danshig rituals are held in remembrance of the occasion when the disciples of the 80-year-old Shakyamuni Buddha pleaded with him to extend his earthly existence. In 1697 the Khalkha monastic community inaugurated a triennial danshig festival for Zanabazar, which began a tradition whereby

15. See R. Newman.
16. Atwood at 438.

the laity donated lavish gifts to the patriarchs in an act of fealty. These contributions accounted for the stupendous wealth of the estates of the patriarchs (and a drain on capital accumulation for productive investments). During the autonomous period the Urga danshig ceremonies were expanded to include participation by all Mongolians, not just the Khalkha.

In 1922 Sükhbaatar moved the date for the summer festival's sporting contests to 11 July of the Western calendar in celebration of the first anniversary of the Mongolian revolution. He kicked off the festival himself by riding out to the sporting field 'at full gallop, leaning from the saddle to pick up silver dollars from the ground—a show to delight the cavalryman in every Mongol heart'.[17] In subsequent years, the festival became the national holiday with its opening ceremonies taking the form of Soviet-style military parades passing in front of the tomb of Sükhbaatar and Choibalsan and watched by the leadership of the MPR. These days, an honour guard in traditional military attire opens the ceremony by marching the white horsehair süld from Government House. The jolly atmosphere outside the stadium on the opening day is reminiscent of the festive air of the international quidditch tournaments in the Harry Potter novels.

The Naadam festival continues the thirteenth-century tradition of the 'three manly sports', which are featured in contests for different classes of participants. Mongolian wrestling takes centre stage at the opening ceremonies. This is a highly stylized sport played by beefy opponents wearing skimpy costumes that belie the fierceness of the competition. (During his state visit to Mongolia, US vice president Joseph Biden was jokingly paired with a Mongolian wrestler for a match, though he was warned beforehand that his opponent could snap his clavicle like a wishbone.) A contestant wins the bout when he forces the other wrestler's trunk, knee, or elbow to touch the ground. Upon entering the stadium, the wrestlers conduct a ceremonial dance imitating the flight of a khangarid. Before each individual match, the wrestler turns his traditional Mongolian conical hat over to a herald who extols the wrestler's virtues. As the contest begins, each wrestler tries to grab hold of his opponent's shirt sleeve or jacket, which then turns into a head-to-shoulder hold. The match can last for as long as forty minutes as one contestant tries to wear down the other or push his opponent off his balance by a sudden shifting of weight. At the end of the match, the losing wrestler passes under the winner's arm while the winner executes the khangarid victory dance. The winner then takes a handful of crumbled hard cheese and tosses it as an offering to the local gods in a distant reflection of the aspersion rites of the thirteenth century.[18]

The archery contests take place in other sites around UB. The bow and arrow have been closely tied to Mongolian culture and history for centuries—for instance, the earliest example of written Mongolian script is a stone carving made in 1226 recording an arrow shot 575 metres by a nephew of Chinggis Khan. For the Naadam festivals, the contestants shoot at a *sur* (сур), which is a target made of leather rolled into a

17. Lattimore (1962) at 105.

18. Atwood at 588–89; Lattimore (1962) at 20–22.

Opening ceremony for the Naadam festival. Photo by Janice Law.

Mural of victorious wrestler. Photo by Lukas Nikol.

cylindrical shape. As the contestants enter the competition ground, they give out a cry of *uukhai* (уухай) while making a clockwise circular motion ('in the sun direction') with their arms towards the sky as a petition for good fortune. The arrows are shot in a trajectory rather than a straight line at the target, which is about 100 metres away. The umpires and the contestant cry out *uukhai* when the arrow hits the mark. A victorious archer is called a *mergen* (мэргэн), a title which refers both to a sharpshooter and someone with profound wisdom. In 1960 women contestants were permitted to compete against other women archers.

Lamas were precluded from archery contests because of monastic rules against using weapons. To circumvent this, they invented a modified version of archery which is played by flicking pieces of ivory or horn at a target made from sheeps' ankle bones. This too has become absorbed into Naadam festivals, though initially high lamas prohibited monks from ankle-bone contests as a form of archery in disguise. While this might be a 'less manly' sport than the others, it is nonetheless a major event during the festival.[19]

On the grasslands outside Ulaanbaatar, the Naadam horse-racing contests take place over a course that runs 30 kilometres in a straight line. For steppe dwellers, a horse's endurance is more highly prized than its ability to sprint for a short distance as in Western horse racing. The races are separated into categories based on the age of the horses. The jockeys are children, boys or girls aged between 6 and 10 with 1,300 to 1,600 horses participating in the contests. The first five horses to cross the finish line in a race win titles. A judge gives the five jockeys handfuls of crumbling cheese and then anoints the horse's head with kumis. He then shares a cup of kumis with the jockeys and the horse owners.[20]

Spectators gather in blue and white maikhans at the finish line to watch the results, though some prefer to bounce along over the countryside in SUVs next to the contestants, swerving in and out of dust storms and narrowly missing other vehicles in an adventure where excitement outdistances common sense.

Because of this equestrian tradition, Urga became a market for the sale of horseflesh to foreign agents of the elites who raced Mongolian ponies on the tracks that sprung up in the treaty ports along the China coast in the nineteenth century. As observed by one traveller:

> At certain times of the year, Mongolia was overrun with agents from Shanghai and Tientsin racing men on the look-out for promising young 'griffins' (a young untrained horse which shows signs of speed) and comparatively big sums of money are paid for them. Apart from racing purposes, the Mongolian ponies make capital hacks when trimmed up a bit and knocked into shape. I could hardly believe that the smart, well-fed, carefully groomed animals I saw in Peking, Tientsin and Shanghai were originally rough, unkempt brutes of the desert, so great was the transformation.[21]

19. Atwood at 20–21; Lattimore (1962) at 22–23.
20. Atwood at 221–22; Lattimore (1962) at 16–20.
21. Price at 293; see also Coates at 193–99.

Horse-racing at the Naadam festival. Photo by Janice Law.

The 1921 revolution cut off Mongolia as a source of horses for China coast equestrian racing. In its aftermath, rumours made their way to Shanghai about Khalkha Mongolian compradors being shot as enemies of the state, something that was unlikely to upset the 'horsey set' in those cities too much.

Going back to Narnii Road and heading east, we come to Narantuul Market, a place where you can sample a slice of real life in UB that has echoes of the old Khüree Market. The market sells a wide array of household articles for daily life as well as some interesting curios, both of ancient and modern vintage. In the north-east corner, merchants offer traditional orange-coloured Mongolian wardrobes, cast-iron coal stoves, herding equipment, shaman utensils like mirrors and drums, and Buddhist paraphernalia. The market is the best place to buy a pair of decorated Mongolian leather boots with upturned toes or a traditional robe, or *del*. (It is not a good idea to buy a *del* 'off-the-rack'. If you fancy owning one, you should be properly measured by a tailor and have one made specifically for your build at the market.) Bargaining is the order of the day, as is being on guard against pickpockets.

Continuing farther east along Narnii Road, the Cathedral of Saints Peter and Paul is the location for the Apostolic Prefecture of Ulaanbaatar. The Roman Catholic Church has a time-honoured pedigree in Mongolia stretching back to the thirteenth century, though these ties were subject to extended gaps as a result of geopolitical shifts in world affairs. William of Rubruck was an observant thirteenth-century writer and diplomat who recorded Mongolian customs, which he described with a detached objectivity for the times. Arriving in Kharakhorum in 1254, he had uncomplainingly walked from the Black Sea in the depth of winter, passing by trees exploding in the frost and other unimaginable deprivations. At Kharakhorum, he gave Roman Catholic sacraments to a small European community who had been seized as slaves during

Shaman's wares for sale at Narantuul Market. Photo by author.

Mongolian raids in Europe. He presented diplomatic credentials from King Louis IX of France to the khans and tried to elicit their interest in Christianity. He noted that the khans sponsored theological debates among Christians (Roman and Nestorian), Muslims, Buddhists, Taoists, and Hindus for both education and entertainment but invariably concluded that their own beliefs were as sound as the others offered by missionaries. In the words of Möngke Khan, they came to regard religions as different fingers on the hand of God and thus did not choose to slaughter those guilty of 'doctrinal errors'.[22] It was an attitude of tolerance that was still centuries away in Europe.

In the same century, Father John of Montecorvino was another Roman Catholic missionary who achieved (late) posthumous renown on account of his travels in the Mongolian empire. In 1291 he arrived in Peking, where he received permission from Kublai Khan's court to build churches and later introduced Western choral music. Father John periodically sent reports back to the Vatican along with pleas for more support but was miffed never to receive a reply, let alone a set of clear instructions, from 'headquarters.' He spent the remainder of his life in Peking.[23]

With the collapse of the Yuan dynasty, the Roman Catholic Church had no further contact with Mongolia until the seventeenth century when Jesuit scholars arrived in Peking, impressing the Manchu emperors with Western science, erudite knowledge, and extraordinary language skills. The Jesuits acted as linguistic and cultural intermediaries for the negotiations among Russians, Manchus, Mongolians, and Chinese that led to the Treaty of Nerchinsk in 1689, delineating the border between China and

22. See, generally, Rubruk; Cameron at 90 et seq.; Kemp at 186 et seq.; Weatherford (2016).

23. Kemp at 207 et seq., Cameron at 90 et seq.

Russia.[24] Because of the Jesuits' participation in the negotiations, the sole authoritative and binding version of the treaty was drafted in Latin, an interesting footnote to this landmark meeting of cultures.

The Jesuit influence in the Qing Empire was soon to wane, however, because of Manchu suspicions about their motives and quarrels between Catholic orders regarding Jesuit interpretations of Chinese customs. When the Jesuits ran afoul of the Vatican in 1773, the Pope charged the Lazarists with responsibility for Catholic affairs in China as well as the Jesuit congregations in Peking, which came under increasingly restrictive controls by the Qing government. In 1834 the Lazarists moved the centre of their operations to a small settlement about 30 kilometres to the north-east of Kalgan. Around that time, the French Lazarists Évariste Régis Huc and Joseph Gabet were sent to Khar Us, an even more remote Catholic settlement where they learned Mongolian and Manchu. The two Frenchmen are deservedly famous for their entertaining record of travel in Mongolia, Amdo, and Lhasa. They might have even visited the Tuul River Valley in the 1840s, though their account lacks a detailed description, suggesting that they only reported hearsay.[25]

In 1866 the Lazarists handed over their responsibilities to another order, the Scheut Missions—CICM (Congregatio Immaculati Cordis Mariae). Father Antoine Mostaert, another French Lazarist, set up a mission to the south-west of the Inner Mongolian city of Hohhot in 1906 where he acquired a profound knowledge of Ordos Mongolian customs and culture. A Mongolian named Munkhjargal was ordained the first Mongolian Roman Catholic priest.

Roman Catholic ties with Mongolia entered another hiatus after the communist revolution. Pope Pius XI approved an apostolic vicariate for Urga in 1922 and entrusted its administration to the CICM, but its members were denied entry into the country by the newly installed Communist authorities. This is where the matter was left until 1990 when the government reached out to the Holy See to establish diplomatic ties. The Apostolic Vicariate for Central Mongolia, a mission that had existed only in paper from the 1920s, came alive again with the arrival in July 1992 of Bishop Wenceslas Padilla. In August 2016 Bishop Padilla ordained Joseph Enkh as the first Mongolian priest since the Vatican's fledgling attempts to establish a congregation in the 1920s.[26]

The design of the Cathedral of Saints Peter and Paul is based on the shape of a ger, but it reminds me of the round cathedrals built in the Eastern Mediterranean by the successors of Constantine, which is an apt symbol for the combination of East and West, even if the similarity is unintended.

---

24. See Cameron, Lee, and Sebes for the Jesuit role as cultural and diplomatic advisers.
25. See Huc and Gabet for their account of their Central Asian travels.
26. For a discussion of Christian missions in the Mongolian world, see Kemp at 329 et seq.

13

Farther Afield

To the north-west of the city on a windswept hill is the cemetery known as Level 70, or Dalan Davkhar (Далан Давхар). Public cemeteries are a comparatively recent custom in Mongolia. As noted by a nineteenth-century British traveller,

> When a Mongol dies, the body is wrapped up in an old coat and is taken a short distance outside the city on to the hills, where it is placed on the ground, with only a 'prayer flag' over it to protect it, and is then abandoned, not to the mercy of the elements, but to the hundreds of dogs who have already scented their feast and are waiting patiently by. No sooner are the mourners out of sight than the dreadful repast commences, and in an incredibly short time nothing remains of the lifeless body. As there is no cemetery or particular spot for depositing the dead, one not infrequently comes across a stray bone or a skull which has escaped those hungry canine sextons, and these poor vestiges of frail humanity certainly add to the desolate surroundings of the desert city.[1]

The elites had different arrangements for meeting eternity. High lamas were immured in stupas while nobles were buried in a *bunkhan* (бунхан), a small brick pyramid in which the bodies of the deceased were positioned sitting upright

Burial practices for ordinary people were based upon the practicalities of life on the steppes. Nomads did not have shovels and pickaxes among their household tools since these were as useful as a diving bell to life on the steppes. The long winters saw the ground frozen as hard as iron, and an inordinate amount of scarce fuel would be needed for a cremation even in less inclement weather. While Westerners saw this method of the disposal of loved ones as callous, Mongolians thought Westerners were excessively morbid and incomprehensibly attached to lifeless remains. What use is there of a broken vessel once the spirit is gone?[2]

As part of Tsedenbal's modernization campaign, Ulan Bator established a municipal cemetery in 1955. At Level 70 there are hundreds of graves dating from the 1950s. The tombstones are in Cyrillic or traditional script, with the latter coming into fashion from the 1990s. A few tombstones are in Arabic script, presumably for

1. Price at 289.
2. Lattimore (1941) at 185.

Kazakh Mongolians, and others are in Chinese for people who moved to Mongolia from Hebei or Shanxi provinces (as indicated in the epitaphs).

In remembering the deceased, the modern custom is to place a candle in a small boxed altar on the grave and leave an offering of three cups of vodka and some wheat or rice. Prayers are recited in Tibetan to the extent that the mourners know them. Occasionally you will see a red-robed lama performing a ceremony at the edges of the cemetery.

A plusher necropolis is featured in the north-east suburbs in the Altan Ögil National Cemetery, where in the centre of the burial grounds a mausoleum, once defined as the final and funniest folly of the very rich, houses the remains of Sükhbaatar and Choibalsan.[3] It is surrounded by the tombs of other Mongolian luminaries, sometimes decorated with sculpted busts of the deceased and totemic symbols from the Soviet era. The statues do not stand up very well to the winter temperatures and soon become cracked and broken, which makes for an interesting contrast to feudal-era *balbal*s that have remained intact on the windswept steppes for centuries.

The historian Baabar has recently spoken out about the failure of Soviet-trained politicians to conduct themselves as statesmen for the sake of Mongolia's future. He recommends that the best thing for this generation is to die off as rapidly as possible, mirroring a sentiment felt by millennials around the globe towards the 'baby boomer' generation. Since the grounds of the national cemetery are spacious enough to pot quite a few, let's hope they get a move on soon.

* * *

Altan Ögil National Cemetery. Photo by author.

3. Bierce at 304.

Starting from the mid-seventeenth century, many monasteries filled the landscape of the outlying districts of Urga though only a few have managed to make it to the twenty-first century.

On the north side of Ulaanbaatar in the Chingeltei Mountain Valley, the remnants of the Monastery of the Spreading and Flourishing of the Teaching, or Dambadarjaalin Khiid (Дамбадаржаалин Хийд), are located near the confluence of the Western and Eastern Selbe rivers.[4] The monastery is not often mentioned in nineteenth- and twentieth-century travellers' memoirs because it was outside the main caravan route between Urga and Siberia. In 1761, the Qianlong Emperor ordered its construction for the stupa holding the relics of the Second Patriarch. In the nineteenth century the remains of the third and fifth patriarchs were also entombed here.

A mid-nineteenth-century visitor, Alexander Michie, noted that the monastery had a Tibetan appearance:

> The buildings are of vast extent, almost as plain as if they were barracks; but the ornamentation there about them is quiet and in good taste. They differ considerably from the Chinese style of architecture and are no doubt Thibetan. An inscription in the Thibetan language has been placed on the slope above the monasteries. The characters are formed by means of white stones, and the size of them is to render them legible at the distance of a mile.[5]

Later, the monastic authorities added Mongolian gers and Chinese-style temples to the grounds as the clerical population expanded, reaching 1,500 monks at its height during the autonomous period. At this time, the main assembly hall and its related temples were enclosed by a wall outside of which aimags were arranged in the customary inverted U-shape of a khüree.

Only eleven buildings survived the Great Purge. In 1939 these were turned into a hospital for wounded Japanese POWs under the care of a Japanese physician. (I wonder if this was Dr Kojima, the venereal disease specialist in Ulan Bator during the 1920s, being recycled by the Choibalsan regime while he was waiting for his exit visa to leave Mongolia.) After the monastery's provisional use as a hospital, the authorities built a white neoclassical health resort on the foundations of the assembly hall in 1940 and later converted it for use as a tuberculosis hospital. The abandoned hospital fell into ruin by the first decade of the twenty-first century.

These days, the temple grounds are still enclosed by a faded red brick and plaster wall. The south, east, and west gates have crumbling Vajrayana decorations, such as the endless knot, stone lions, and *makara*s. As you enter the grounds through the east or west gate, you will see the drum and bell towers and two pavilions hosting imperial stelae recording a Mongolian version of the Qianlong Emperor's decree for the establishment of the monastery. A modern grey three-storey tsogchin dugan has been constructed on the site where the tuberculosis hospital once stood.

4. See Teleki at 200 et seq.
5. Michie at 154.

Faded outer wall, Monastery of the Spreading and Flourishing of the Teaching. Photo by author.

Behind the tsogchin dugan, the newly-revived Palace of Coolness, or Serüün Laviran (Сэрүүн Лавран), contains a statue of Lokecvara, or Longhsir Janraiseg (Лонгхсир Жанрайсэг), who is regarded as an emanation of Avalokitesvara by Vajrayana Buddhists and a form of Shiva by Hindus. Two decaying chapels also stand on the eastern and western flanks of the courtyard of the Lokecvara temple. The square-faced stupa in honour of the Shakyamuni Buddha was erected in the courtyard in 2003.

The monks have tried to restore the three Tibetan mantras mentioned by Michie on the hill behind the monastery. The mantras are spelled with white stones but are in a state of significant disrepair. The top line appears to be a hybrid version of the Manjusri mantra, which is chanted as *om ah ra pa za na di*. The second line appears to be a full version of the Avalokitesvara mantra, *om ma nin pa de ma/ah hm hri*, but it has deteriorated. The third line may contain a separate mantra but it is unclear because it also contains elements that form parts of the compound letters from the Avalokitesvara mantra on the line above.[6]

The impressive Jarankhasar stupa with its brooding eyes at the north-west corner of the monastery is modelled on the Great Stupa of Boudhanath, which has been a major site for pilgrimages between India and Kathmandu since the sixth century.

According to Buddhist legend, a social outcaste built the Great Stupa of Boudhanath Stupa as a votive offering to the dharma. She was a poor woman who had given birth to four sons by four low-caste fathers. Somehow she scraped together enough savings from her Kathmandu market stall to construct a stupa on the site believed to be the burial place of an earlier incarnation of the Shakyamuni Buddha.

6. I am grateful to Scott Palmer for this information.

Pavilions for imperial edicts. Photo by author.

Jarankhasar Stupa. Photo by author.

Seeking a royal grant, she submitted a petition to the Newari king to be given a parcel of land at the site 'no larger than an 'oxhide'. Once her petition was approved, she measured the boundaries for her stupa by cutting an oxhide into a lengthy strip of rope and stretching it to enclose much more space at the site than was intended by the king, who good-naturedly agreed to keep his word. Her four sons took charge of the construction work. As a karmic reward, the sons were reincarnated as great promoters of Tibetan Buddhism. One became Padmasambhava in his next life while another was reborn as King Trisong Detsen, one of the great early Tibetan Buddhist monarchs. The other two sons became Shantarashita, a famous Buddhist scholar of Sanskrit and the pious prime minister of King Trisong Detsen, Bhami Thri Zher.[7] All four reincarnates played important roles for the introduction of monasticism in Tibet.

Like its progenitor in Nepal, the main stupa in the monastery is built in the style of the 'Mind of All Buddhas', which is distinguished by the two eyes of the Buddha painted under the crown. The straight line descending from the two eyes means 'one', referring to the unity of all material and spiritual phenomena.

Further to the north of the monastery is the former site of the cemetery for Japanese prisoners of war. In pre-revolutionary times, this area had been reserved as a charnel ground for the remains of monks. After the establishment of diplomatic ties with the MPR, the Japanese government arranged for the repatriation of the soldiers' remains in 1966, and the site was converted into a memorial in 1995. The monument includes a granite stone altar with a map of Mongolia and an arrow pointing to a circular opening in a graceful arch, indicating the direction home for any wandering Japanese spirits.

The former site of the Monastery of Theory and Practice, or Shaddüvlin Khiid (Шадувлин Хийд), is located further to the north. It was initially established by the Fourth Patriarch in a temple that housed a bronze of Tsongkhapa. The monastery later grew into a retreat for religious rituals and meditation and was favoured by the Eighth Patriarch, who sought refuge here from the hundreds of supplicants seeking his blessings each day. The discipline masters of the Monastery were known for enforcing monastic discipline strictly as set out in the Tanjur canon. For instance, no beggars were permitted near the grounds since they were a distraction from meditation, and monks had to follow monastic protocol strictly, such as wearing the correct clerical wardrobe corresponding to their rank at all times. Perhaps such attention to detail was a requirement for espionage work.

During the autonomous period, the Bogd Khan set up an espionage training centre, or *nuuts tagnuulin gazar* (нууц тагнуулын газар), at the monastery for qualified monks to learn the dark arts of deception and intelligence gathering. The recruits studied foreign languages and customs before embarking on clandestine missions to China, Japan, Russia, and Germany. One of the last lamas trained in these skills was the Dilov Khutugtu Jamsranjav, an emanation in a lineage of high lamas that includes the Tibetan Buddhist poet Milarepa. In 1932 the communist authorities brought the Khutugtu to trial at the Green Domed Theatre on the charges of being a Japanese spy. He was acquitted but, sensing which way the wind was blowing, the Khutugtu escaped to Inner Mongolia and later went to the United States, thanks to a helping hand from his old friend Lattimore. He became the spiritual leader of the New Jersey Kalmyk refugee community, which had migrated to the United States in the early 1950s.

It is fitting that an institution connected to espionage has left us almost no traces of the monastery where it was established. Summer houses have crept in along the

7. Berry at 57–59.

Memorial to Japanese Prisoners of War. Photo by author.

Showing the way home. Photo by author.

valley and up the sides of the mountains. The only tangible legacy of the monastery is a recently built shrine, two ovoos, and a tree adorned with blue khadags.[8]

On the left side of the road to the Dar'ekh and Dambadarjaa suburbs, a hot spring is in a fenced area with a wooden pavilion and a small bridge. This is the 'Place with Holy Water', or Rashaant (Рашаант), whose waters have been revered as a sacred medicinal cure-all since the early 1700s.[9] Throughout the day, families come to the spring to fill yellow water jugs and bring the medicinal water back to their homes. The

8. Ibid. at 212 et seq.
9. Ibid. at 220.

Temple of the King of the Naga Spirits, or Lowon Jalbiin Süm (Лован Жалбын Сүм), was next to the hot springs. The temple was another victim of the Great Purge.

In pre-revolutionary years Mongolians believed that powerful nagas, or serpent-spirits, lived in rivers and springs. They were conceived of as having the form of humans with their lower bodies shaped like the tail of a snake. Nagas were said to be devotees of the Shakyamuni Buddha, assisting him in his quest to spread the dharma. South East Asian statues of the historical Buddha often have a multi-headed naga acting as a protector arching over his meditating body from behind.

Mongolians believed that nagas aggressively protected their watery domains and struck down those who were foolish enough to waste water, but they might grant a supplicant's wishes when approached reverentially. It was risky to call on the nagas blithely, however, especially at the wrong time in the year. Nagas often travelled long distances from their watery homes to hibernate during the last winter month of the lunar calendar. They were said to react with wrathful outrage if someone disturbed them while they were asleep or recently returned from hibernation, a little like a cranky Air China passenger with jet-lag after a long and unexplained delay. When angered, a naga could strike at a human by inflicting an illness or a painful death.[10] Mythical interpretations aside, the nagas were a symbolic reminder of the imperative for a desert-dwelling people to respect and preserve sources of water.

Rashaant, or Holy Spring. Photo by author.

10. Wallace at 230–31. See also Beer at 70–73.

Former site of the Monastery of Theory and Practice. Photo by author.

* * *

Several other sights can be visited on day trips from Ulaanbaatar. Heading first to the east, we come across a relentlessly promoted tourist location. This is the gargantuan Chinggis Khan Statue Complex, which looks like it is built from recycled beer cans. It is a freakish place that is not to the taste of many discerning Mongolians, who have dismissed it as a monument to the vainglory and hubris of the nouveau riche classes.

The Terelj River Valley and its national park host many trendy ger encampments and weekend homes for urbanites escaping UB's summer heat. As the valley widens to the east, the landscape is noteworthy for its freestanding rock formations, Turtle Rock being the most celebrated. Its name tells you all you need to know.

The Terelj Hotel, located within the Terelj National Park, was formerly the State Guest House where party officials and other elites took their holidays in the MPR days. Bronze statues of Lenin and a milkmaid were placed out front to remind visitors of the ideological tunes of the time. One night here Bill Douglas was corralled into singing a song for his hosts in the pre-karaoke era. He sang Yale University's Whiffenpoof Song, a college anthem warbled by American elites, government officials, and spies throughout Asia during the Cold War.[11]

A year later, René MacColl's delegation visited the State Guest House. With his customary dry nastiness, he wrote dismissively of the place:

> The rest house was one of the best spoken of in the country, the resort of party officials, top government men, the elite in general, and it was said that pull was necessary to get into it. The place itself looked exactly like any other 'rest house' you will find

11. Douglas at 301.

Turtle Rock. Photo by Lukas Nikol.

> in the Communist empire, all the way from the Baltic to the China Sea: red plush curtains, standard glassware, piped music, cement already starting to crumble, and that frightful air of silence and sadness.[12]

These days, the State Guest House has been transformed into a luxury hotel that probably could pass muster with the old curmudgeon. The statue of the Mongolian milkmaid still stands in front, with a hand shielding her eyes from the sunshine while she scans the horizon for something, perhaps solvent guests. The statue of Lenin has been hustled out of sight to the back of the hotel.

Nearby, the Aryaval Meditation and Initiation Centre (Арьяабал Бурханы Номлол Бутээлийн Төв) is a recent construction testifying to the revival of the dharma in Mongolia. It is located at the northern head of the valley in Terelj National Park. The centre is in a white Tibetan style temple reached by walking across an iron chain bridge (calling to mind Thang Tong Gyalpo) and climbing a stairway with 108 steps. The shape of the temple is supposed to resemble an elephant's head, with the long staircase as its trunk. The prayer hall is beautifully decorated with bronzes, thangkas, and various representations of Buddhas and bodhisattvas. Portraits of grand lamas and the Shakyamuni Buddha's arhats are painted in a style reminiscent of Sino-Tibetan artwork. On the outside beams of the temple are depictions of various levels of existence, starting with the tortures awaiting those reborn in Buddhist 'hells', continuing on to the mortal world of faithful practitioners, and finally to the celestial deities above.

12. MacColl at 170.

Peonies, Mongolian landscapes, and mystical symbols of the Kalachakra abound. Rock paintings on the surrounding mountains look down on the temple.

* * *

Approximately 45 kilometres to the east of Ulaanbaatar, in the Nalaikh district, the eighth-century tomb of Prince Tonyukuk is a forlorn site that serves as a reminder that ancient peoples once traversed the steppes as easily as the Phoenicians sailed the Mediterranean Sea. For instance, several centuries after Prince Tonyukuk, a renowned Taoist monk named Qiu Chuji (丘处机) *walked* from western Shandong province through Khalkha Mongolia to Afghanistan, and *then back again*, at the invitation of Chinggis Khan for a personal tutorial on philosophy.[13]

Prince Tonyukuk was a respected Türkic statesman when China was recovering from four hundred years of disunity. In 617 a Sino-Türkic family founded the Tang dynasty in the former Chinese capital Chang'an, extending the reach of Chinese influence through the Gansu corridor and across the Gobi Desert into Central Asia. The Tang Empire was China's most cosmopolitan dynasty and its people eagerly absorbed new customs and cultures from the surrounding regions. Türkic, Korean, Persian, and Sogdian were among the many languages spoken in the corridors of power in the capital.

The Türkic rulers, on the other hand, recognized the threat of cultural assimilation. While he was not a khan, Tonyukuk was a capable minister and a military leader with perceptive insights into Asian geopolitics. He speaks from the stones about the historic clash between 'the steppe and the sown', the perpetual conflict that characterized the relationship between sedentary and nomadic Asia since antiquity. As a staunch but reasoned opponent of Sinicization, Tonyukuk advised his followers to reject Buddhism and Taoism as unsuited to the culture of the people of the grasslands. He warned that the Türks numbered only one-hundredth of the population of China. To set up urban settlements would give the Chinese an advantage in warfare. Nomadic life promised a chance of long-term survival for the Türks while sedentary life meant extinction at the hands of their eternal enemies.[14]

The two stelae here are written in the Orkhon runic script, of which we have seen samples at the Monument of the Great Seal behind Government House. The word *runic* is a misnomer; the alphabet of the Türkic people only bore a superficial similarity to the writings of northern Europeans of the same age. Tonyukuk describes how he was born a subject of the Chinese but joined the Türkic revolt against the Tang Empire in 681. He fought in many campaigns against Chinese, Kirghiz, and other hostile neighbours and assisted with the annexation of territory in the Yenisei Region, the Khitan lands, and what is now Xinjiang. Tonyukuk died around 734.

13. See Li Chih-Ch'ang.
14. Sinor at 312 and 315.

Prince Tonyukuk's windswept pillars. Photo by author.

Runic script on one of Tonyukuk's pillars. Photo by author.

The Finnish Mongolist Gustaf Ramstedt visited the tomb in 1898 to take rubbings of the two pillars:

> Mongol passers-by, both caravans and individuals, who watched our labour were greatly astonished and apparently understood nothing of what we were up to nor of the significance of the stones. Tonyukuk's fame had died a thousand years ago. It seemed peculiar to read the bombastic, self-conscious words on the stones, when the natives of the country who were present had no idea of the earlier history of their country. Round about spread only verdant grass fields, and over us shone the blue sky and the birds sang their summery songs.[15]

* * *

Around 90 miles to the south of Ulaanbaatar is Mother Rock, or Eej Khad (Ээж Хад), a natural rock formation and a site of pilgrimage and prayer. It is a granite outcropping resembling a maternal figure that is thought to be the female counterpart to the male spirit of Avdar Bayan Mountain, or Avdar Bayan Uul (Авдар Баян Уул). *Avdar Baya* means 'rich chest', an allusion to the traditional wooden chests that herders use to store precious belongings, which in this instance means Mother Rock. Local people believe that the rock had been a site of worship for hundreds of years. Others say that historical records show that it became associated with the feminine power of nature only after an earthquake in 1970.[16]

On the approach to Mother Rock, you pass by a triumphal arch announcing your imminent arrival to the presence of 'your own mother'. Mother Rock is located within a circular shrine that replicates the shape of a ger. The rock is about one and a half

Mother Rock and her devotees. Photo by author.

15. Ramstedt at 196.
16. Gohen; Robinson at 204.

metres tall with two arm-like protrusions and a round-shaped bulge resembling a head. It wears a golden woven hat and matching robe with its sizeable 'waist' wrapped in blue khadags and a train of jewellery on its 'back', looking like braided hair. Men form a queue to the left of the rock while women stand to the right (as in a ger). The supplicants separately lean their heads on the rock's 'shoulders' one at a time to make their silent petition to the spirit. People place gifts of candy, Mongolian cakes, and *arul* in a silver bowl on an altar table. Wheat and tea leaves are placed on a side table next to an altar of burning butter lamps. Afterwards, supplicants circle the outside of the shrine in the 'sun direction', splashing vodka or milk into the air. An ovoo stands on the hill near the shrine. You are supposed to keep your request to the spirit as a secret, but if it is granted you are to return to give thanks, just as any dutiful offspring ought to.

The Mother Rock shrine has produced its own set of administrators who supervise parking, collect tickets, and maintain the grounds. Clustered outside the shrine are a few simple, family-run restaurants, serving khuushuur, khorkhog, and salted milk tea, which nicely enhance the Mongolian flavour of a visit here.

About two kilometres from Mother Rock is a small shrine formed by a granite boulder in the shape of a silver ingot. This is Yembuu Rock, which promises material wealth to its petitioners. The custom is to place one's wallet against the boulder while circumambulating it, a manoeuvre that is supposed to help the increase the value of your portfolio (or at least put a few more togrogs in your wallet). Signs have been posted warning people off chipping pieces of the stone as a souvenir or wealth charm. Nearby are other rocks that are supposed to guarantee fertility.

* * *

The ruins of the Monastery of Manjusri, or Manjushri Khiid (Манзушри Хийд), are on the south side of Bogd Uul. The monastery was built in honour of the bodhisattva in 1733 and administered directly by the Second Patriarch. By the late nineteenth century, it had grown to be one of the largest monasteries in Mongolia with a strong reputation for monastic discipline and scholarship. It certainly competed with the monastic settlements in Urga in terms of the number of monastic residents and religious significance. The monastery was razed by Choibalsan during the Great Purge and its abbot, Tserendorj, and eighteen other high lamas, were executed outside Ulan Bator after a year-long show trial in the Green Domed Theatre.[17]

The thick brick and adobe walls of the former assembly hall stand in ruins and the grounds are littered with stone relics, such as a marble tablet with the Chinese word for the 'Buddha', *fo* (佛),[18] and a two-ton bronze cauldron cast in 1726. (The cauldron could cook up to ten sheep or two cows at one time for the clerical community.) A two-storey museum and shrine has been built, with a small display of sorrowful black-and-white photographs recalling the monastery during its days of splendour. In one

17. See Kaplonski (2014).
18. In Mongolian, this is Zuu (Зуу).

Ruins of Monastery of Manjusri. Photo by author.

Memorial Hall, Monastery of Manjusri. Photo by author.

corner, the portrait of Abbot Tserendorj recalls his philosophical acumen and leadership of the monastery. A few Tsam masks are on display along with a bronze for the supplications of the faithful. The museum is sadly underfunded.

The foothills leading to the museum are dotted with the ruined foundation stones of the aimags and datsans that once stood here. Behind the museum are several cave shrines that have been reconstructed with painted carvings of Buddhas and bodhisattvas on their rock walls. The cave shrines call to mind the ritual of lamas, seeking refuge in caves to practise deep meditation without worldly distractions, sometimes going so far as to immure themselves in a cave for an extended round of meditation lasting from three months to three years.[19]

The ruins exude a strongly mournful feeling as if the grounds are still seeped with grief from the smashed icons, the burned thangkas, and the brutality meted out to the lamas and their disciples. It is a moving experience to visit the ruins in the depth of winter when the wind sighs through the snow-clad fir and pine trees.

* * *

Circling back into the city, we pass by the Chinggis Khan International Airport where, to the north side of the airport entrance, you will see the old terminal building. It recalls the time when air travel to Ulaanbaatar was a unique adventure made more colourful by MIAT stewardesses handing out pint bottles of blue-labelled Mongolian vodka in business class. Deplaning passengers jammed the tiny arrivals hall and jostled each other in the search for embarkation cards. Once these were in hand, the scramble began for linguistic help because the embarkation cards were printed only in Mongolian and Russian. For plane-spotting enthusiasts, vintage biplanes and Soviet helicopters slowly decay on the side of the runway.

Air travel to the capital has an older pedigree in Mongolia than train travel, surprisingly. Regular air service began between Ulan Bator and Verkhneudinsk in 1926. A Russian company drafted a group of pilots who, in the words of the English language website for Baikal International Airport, *had to* fly on the Buryat-Mongolian run. The maiden flight covered the distance of 500 kilometres between the two cities in an astonishingly short four and a half hours.

The airport is destined for domestic service upon the completion of the new international airport. The new airport road will give visitors an impressive taste of the steppes while travelling into UB (at least for a little while before the inevitable urban creep).

Some wags say that MIAT actually stands for 'Maybe I Arrive Today'. There is some truth to this as flights from Peking are frequently delayed for hours during the spring and autumn season as continental weather patterns shift. While this is annoying, it is a small matter compared to the trials of taking Air China, whose pilots are unfamiliar with weather conditions at Chinggis Khan International Airport and often

19. For a sensationalist early-twentieth-century account of immured lamas, see Waddell at 238–41.

abort landings only after they have flown all the way from Peking and circled over UB several times. Once my two-hour flight turned into a fifty-two-hour ordeal as Air China made five passes over the UB airport before returning to Peking and locking all passengers into a shabby hotel reeking of cigarette smoke.

Nevertheless, things are not as bad as they once were during the days of the Leftist Deviation. In 1931 a Sino-German airline began a multi-stop 'direct' flight between Berlin and Shanghai. In one instance, weather forced the pilots to make an emergency landing in Ulan Bator. The authorities promptly arrested the German pilots and sentenced them to five years in prison for espionage. When there was no word about their fate, the Germans sent a relief plane to find the pilots. It was shot down. Eventually, the German government appealed to the good offices of the Soviet Union to secure the release of the pilots.[20]

So, if your flight is delayed and information not forthcoming, cheer up. Things could be worse.

* * *

The Aglag Buteeliin Monastery (Аглаг Бүтээлийн Хийд) is another excellent destination to observe the revival of Mongolian Buddhism. Located 100 kilometres to the north-west of UB, it is a classic Vajrayana forest monastic retreat. Behind the main prayer hall is an impressively broad collection of Buddhist sculptures, such as a womb-like cave said to symbolize rebirth, stupas of the twelve deeds of the Buddha, the White Old Man, a pair of dragon claws, heavenly footprints, the Tathagata Buddhas, and bodhisattvas. A visit there is the equivalent of a Buddhist sermon in stone and makes for a splendid excursion.

20. Friters at 270–71.

14

The Holy Mountain (Bogd Uul)

Since the Holy Mountain provided shelter for each of the three cities of Urga, Ulan Bator, and UB, it is a fitting place to bring our perambulations in the Mongolian capital to a close. The mountain stands like a silent and stable older brother to the feckless city and its ceaseless changes in priorities, appearance, and values.

The Holy Mountain has been a site sacred to Mongolians since the time of Chinggis Khan. Chinese officials, European Jesuits, Russian envoys, and Western explorers have left us their impressions of the Bogd Uul as the most impressive of the four mountains surrounding the Tuul River Valley. Its majestic appearance gave rise to the belief that a protective spirit lived in Bogd Uul as well as in its three smaller neighbours: Bayanzurh to the east, Chingeltei to the north, and Songino Hairhan to the west.[1]

In their reverence for the mountain, Mongolians forbade hunting, tree cutting, and any disruption of the earth on the Bogd Uul, all of which were capital offensives in the days of the patriarchs. No bloodshed was even permitted within its sight for fear of offending the spirit. For this reason, executions took place in a hidden hollow to the west of Urga. Travellers noted that deer and antelopes in the mountain sanctuary were tame and forests of birch, pine, and larch grew thickly.

In the late eighteenth century the Mongolian amban Yondendorj petitioned the Qing court to grant titles to the two peaks of the Holy Mountain. The name of the mountain was changed from Khaan Uul to the more honorific Bogd Uul while its two peaks were granted the titles of 'duke' and named after the two main aimags—Tsetee Gün (Цэцээ Гүн) and Tüshee Gün (Түшээ Гүн).[2] Yondendorj also spelled out the Tibetan phrase *Om As Kun* in white stones on the eastern and western slopes of the mountain as an offering for the purity of the Tuul River water used by the patriarchs.[3]

Because of these honorific titles, the Bogd Uul was entitled to receive a stipend, paid in silver ingots twice annually, as well as an annual tribute of the 'nine whites', which consisted of nine white camels, nine white horses, nine white sheep, nine white

1. The Qing court also bestowed the title of the White Shell Protector, or Dünjigarav (Дүнжигарав), to the Bogd Uul. The title refers to the conch shell, one of the eight auspicious symbols and a token of the sovereignty of the dharma.
2. Teleki at 270 et seq.; Jambal at 17.
3. Jambal at 17, Wallace at 224.

cows, nine white goats, and a white dog, all paid for by the patriarch's treasury. The number and colour of the annual tribute was based on nine as an auspicious number for good fortune and white as a symbol of purity and power since the time of Chinggis Khan. These animals were allocated to the herds of livestock maintained for the mountain spirit just like the herds kept for the benefit of the monasteries and the nobility.[4]

Every year, the Mongolian and Manchu ambans in Urga had to trundle over to the mountain to honour the spirit of the Bogd Uul and present the semi-annual stipend. In this ritual, they were joined by five representatives from the aimags and the patriarch as well as high lamas, Mongolian nobles, and other dignitaries. The silver ingots were pitched into a crevice next to a temple atop the mountain.

In addition to its supernatural power to grant wishes, protect supplicants, and inflict harm, people believed that the mountain was a wilful being with peevish expectations for the benefits and entitlements accruing to the elite. However, an amban could punish the spirit of the mountain for its maliciousness. In the eighteenth century, a severe snow storm impeded a Manchu amban's entourage as it laboured to the top of the mountain. The amban fulfilled his duty and completed the ritual despite the storm, the cold, and icy trails, but then he also lashed back, 'I am worshipping you because it is my duty, not because I want to. What do you think you are up to?' As a punishment, the amban ordered twenty lashes to be given to the mountain and had put its ovoo in wooden fetters.[5] It did not take long for some ambans to wake up to the pointlessness of the tribute and to figure out ways to embezzle the silver and confiscate the herds. I wonder if this was the motivation in petitioning the Qing court to grant titles to the mountain in the first instance.

Coming to the twentieth century, Baron Ungern-Sternberg violated the centuries-old precedent of the Bogd Uul being a peaceful preserve free from bloodshed and disruption. In February 1921 his soldiers crossed the mountain from the Manjusri Monastery on its southern side and rescued the Bogd Khan from house arrest. It was the first and last time of a breach of the mountain's sacred status until the encroachment by illicit construction projects from UB upon its northern foothills in recent years.

In the aftermath of the Great Purge the MPR authorities replaced the Tibetan mantra written in white stones with the Soyombo and the Mongolian words for 'Long Live the MPRP' (МАНДТУГАЙ МАХН). During the 1990 revolution protesters tapped into Mongolia's fine satirical tradition by removing the last letter from the acronym so that it read 'Long Live Meat', a superb taunt to the Communist government's failure to fulfil basic needs.[6] In the 1990s the phrase was changed so that every year it reads 'Long Live the [umpteenth] Anniversary of the Revolution'. Reflecting the spirit of the age, the government set out a white stone portrait of Chinggis Khan on another peak. This iconic image becomes less easy to see as Ulaanbaatar's urban blight

4. Wallace, ibid.
5. Jambal at 16.
6. Becker at 44.

Bogd Uul foothill overlooking Ulaanbaatar. Photo by Janice Law.

continues apace. In 1995 the government officially reinstated ceremonial worship of the Holy Mountain. Ministers, officials, and lamas attend the annual ritual at the foot of the mountain and do not bother with clambering up to the peak.

Facing the city, the Soyombo (Соёмбо) is the important Tantric symbol designed by Zanabazar. It is supposed to represent the Mongolian word for the Sanskrit *Svayambhu*, meaning 'self-creating', an ancient metaphysical term referring to the mystical origins of all forms of being. In Vajrayana Buddhism, Svayambhu is also an allusion to the Kalachakra philosophy generally and a specific reference to the Adi-Buddha.

The top of the Soyombo has the same features found on stupas throughout Mongolia and Tibet—a sun, a crescent moon, and a three-pointed flame. Below this is a circular image perhaps borrowed from Taoist philosophy but more likely to have been derived from the Tibetan Buddhist symbol of two golden fish. On each side is a vertical pillar with downward-facing triangles and a short bar. In its pre-revolutionary format, a lotus flower was the foundation for the Soyombo image. Collectively, the symbol stood for the union of feminine wisdom and masculine skill producing the flame of enlightenment.[7]

The theocratic government adopted the Soyombo as a symbol of Mongolian independence in 1912. During the communist era, a star representing the party was placed on the apex of the symbol (only to be discarded after the 1990 revolution). In 1945 Choilbalsan became alarmed about the potential embarrassment from the continued use of a feudal superstition as a national emblem. To remedy the problem, Choibalsan ordered Rinchen to help him out and come up with a politically correct reinterpretation. (Can't you just picture the sage at his desk, opening the letter with

7. Atwood at 518–19.

these instructions, and then leaning back in his chair and sighing?) Rinchen borrowed liberally from Marxist theory to concoct an anachronistic explanation of the image. The downward-pointing triangles were said to represent the destruction of class enemies while the horizontal bars were the people's struggle for justice. The two fish were recast as unblinking vigilance against the enemies of the state and so on. Rinchen's interpretation is the one most commonly known by Mongolians today as most people are not aware of the symbol's religious origins.[8]

A Newari mystical symbol was Zanabazar's inspiration for the design of the Soyombo. This is the Ratna, or the 'All Powerful Ten', an interlocking set of symbols, combining the initial seven syllables from the Kalachakra mantra written in the Lantsa script and a depiction of the sun, the moon, and fire, all symbolizing enlightenment. The Ratna was often set out in plaques over the gateways to lamas' khasaas in Urga and can be seen in temples of today's UB.[9]

Turning back to the mountain itself, Tsetee Gün has reassumed its status as a sacred summit of the mountain. During the Great Purge, the 'men in green hats' destroyed the wooden temples and pavilions on the peak. These days, there is a stone altar, a rusting incense burner, and ovoos bundled up with wind horse flags and blue khadags. Tsetse Gün can be reached from Manjusri Monastery on a two-hour hike, but it is best to go with a guide who truly knows the way. People have been known to get lost.

8. Ibid. at 519.
9. Beer at 123.

Afterword

The ghosts of a city are never more evident than when you take a late night stroll along its deserted streets or its empty spaces. It is said that long-deceased urban spirits are drawn to places where they have an unhampered view of the scenes that meant so much to them in life.

When I lived in Ulaanbaatar, I sometimes found the occasion to wander through the grounds of the Temple of Avalokitesvara in the evenings, seeking a glimpse of a scene from UB's elusive past, if only for a moment or two. I remember one night sitting on a bench near the temple, contemplating the moon over the city and allowing myself the luxury of letting my thoughts drift as the evening wore on. While lost in this reverie, I heard a far-off horn. At first, the long and mournful sound made me think of a lama blowing into a conch shell to summon the clergy to prayers. This impression soon faded as I became aware that it was only a horn on a train rumbling past the south of the city. Then another vision passed across my mind's eye. It was the grand ceremony in 1956 for the opening of the Trans-Mongolian Railway and the long-forgotten promise of a Mongolia without want. This flickering impression dissolved as I realized that, in fact, I had just heard a train hauling timber illicitly harvested in Siberia or coal destined to pollute the lungs of UB's citizens.

With another blast of the locomotive's horn, all three images returned, swirled together, and then disappeared, leaving me to sense the sound of chuckling from the spirit who performed this ethereal legerdemain for a fellow eccentric who had come out that night to pay him a visit.

Glossary

Key:

(M)	Mongolian	(T)	Tibetan
(Ma)	Manchu	(S)	Sanskrit
(C)	Chinese	(R)	Russian

Abatai Khan (1554–1588): Khalkha prince in Tüshetu Khan Aimag, promoted the Second Conversion north of the Gobi Desert after meeting the Third Dalai Lama.

Adi-Buddha (S): formless primordial Buddha who was present before all existence and from whom all existence arises.

Agvaankhaidav: nineteenth-century monk, devotee of Maitreya, and author of a widely used Tsam handbook.

Agvan Dorzhiev (1854–1938): Buryat monk-scholar, consultant to the Thirteenth Dalai Lama, agent for Tsarist interests in Tibet with ties to the Soviets after 1917.

Agvanbaldan (1797–1864): a Mongolian Buddhist philosopher, tsorji of Urga from 1836 to 1847, author of a three-volume history of Indian Buddhism.

aimag (M): (1) province, (2) territorial subdivision of Khalkha Mongolia ruled by a hereditary khan, (3) a monastic residence for monks from the same region or in the same trade.

Akshobya (S): the Imperturbable, one of the five Tathagata Buddhas, associated with compassion, the direction east, and the colour blue-black.

altan gadas (M): see golden nail.

Altan Khan (1508–1582): Mongolian prince who initiated the Second Conversion in Greater Mongolia after meeting the Third Dalai Lama.

amban (Ma): high-commissioner of non-Han territories in the Qing Empire.

amgalan (M): peace, name of district in south-east Ulaanbaatar.

Amgalan Enkhiin Khalgaa (M): Gate of Settled Peace, triumphal arch built at the southern end of the Bogd Khan Museum to commemorate Mongolia's independence.

Amitabha (S): the Infinite Light, one of the five Tathagata Buddhas, associated with longevity, the direction west, and the colour red, his statue is a frequent offering in Ulaanbaatar temples.

Amoghassiddhi (S): the Unfailing Success, one of the five Tathagata Buddhas, associated with triumph over envy, the direction north, and the colour green, symbol of Mongolia.

Andrews, Roy Chapman (1884–1960): American explorer, adventurer and possible spy, 'discoverer' of dinosaur-bone fossils in the Gobi Desert, supposed basis for the character Indiana Jones.

ard (M): ordinary people.

argol (M): dried sheep dung, commonly used for fuel on the steppes.

arsh (M): juniper, commonly ground into powder and used as incense.

asar (M): rectangular gatehouses for temples and on archways.

Atisha: eleventh-century Bengali missionary and reformer of Tibetan Buddhism, founded precursor of Gelukpa branch of Vajrayana Buddhism.

autonomous period: the period between Mongolia's declaration of independence from the Qing Empire and the forced cancellation of Mongolian sovereignty by the Peking warlord government, 1911–1920.

Avalokitesvara (S): bodhisattva of compassion, one of the most important deities in the Buddhist pantheon throughout East Asia, depicted in female and male forms.

Ayush (M): see Amitabha.

bagana (M): supporting column for a temple or assembly hall.

balbal (M): anthropomorphic stone statues made by ancient Türkic people and placed near royal tombs.

Baldan Lkham (M): see Sri Devi.

balin (M): an anthropomorphic dough offering to a deity for a community's atonement of sins.

Bakula Rinpoche (1917–2003): incarnate lama, Ladkhaki statesman, Indian ambassador to Mongolia, and supporter of the revival of Vajrayana Buddhism in post-Communist Mongolia.

bandi (M): novice monk.

baruun (M): western or 'right-hand side' as perceived by a monarch on a throne facing towards the south.

Jambyn Batmonkh (1926–1997): last communist leader of Mongolia, voluntarily ended one-party government.

Battle of Nomohan: battle between Imperial Japanese Army and joint Soviet-Mongolian troops on the border between Mongolia and Manchukuo during the summer of 1939.

Bayanzürkh Uul: mountain located to the east of Ulaanbaatar, literally 'wealthy heart mountain'.

Bazarsad (M): see Vajrasattva.

Begtse (M): see Jamsran.

bodhisattva (S): a sentient being who has achieved enlightenment but elects to remain in the world until the liberation of all sentient beings, embodiment of the union of wisdom and compassion.

Bogd Khan (M): (1) title of the Manchu emperors of the Qing Empire, (2) title of the Eighth Patriarch upon assumption of sovereign powers in 1911.

Bogd Uul (M): the 'Holy Mountain', the main mountain in the Tuul River Valley located to the south of Ulaanbaatar.

boipar (M): metal incense burner.

bö (M): male shaman.

Bon (T): pre-Buddhist shamanistic religion in Tibet, now regarded as one of the five branches of Vajrayana Buddhism.

Bragriin Gegeen (1781–1848): Mongolian monk-philosopher, studied in Tibet and Urga, wrote famous work titled *Pandelamsan*.

Bu-Ton Rinche Drup (1290–1364): Tibetan lama, Sakyapa master, historian, and chief editor for the translation and compilation of the Kanjur and the Tanjur.

S. Buyannemekh (?–1937): early twentieth-century Mongolian poet and satirical writer.

bunkhan (M): pyramid-shaped brick tomb for nobles.

burayin shat (M): 'trumpet platform', raised platform for monks to summon lamas to prayers by blowing into conch shells.

burkhan (M): (1) god, (2) Buddha, (3) statue of a Buddhist deity.

Buryat: Mongolian ethnic group living in northern Mongolia and Siberia, early transmitters of Russian culture.

buuz (M): Mongolian steamed dumplings.

chimeglel luu (M): see zhiwen.

Chingeltei Uul (M): mountain to the north of Ulaanbaatar.

Khorloogin Choibalsan (1895–1952): Mongolia's paramount dictator from 1939 to 1952, commonly regarded as Joseph Stalin's 'enforcer' in Mongolia.

choijin (M): see sakhius.

Choijin Lama: the title for a Mongolian lama who acted as the vehicle for possessions by dharmapalas, see Luvsankhaidav.

Choijoo: see Yama.

Citipati (T): lesser Buddhist deities in the form of two dancing skeletons.

constructivism: Soviet architectural theory popular in the 1920s, emphasized utilitarian function over form.

dagina (T): female wisdom deities.

Dalai Lama (M): title of the leading monk of Vajrayana Buddhism.

Damdin (M): see Hayagriva.

Tsendiin Damdinsuren (1908–1986): Mongolian scholar and author, sought to preserve pre-revolutionary folk culture, discoverer of the lost Moon Cuckoo libretto.

Jamsrangiin Damdinsürüng (1874–1920): Mongolian general who fought against Chinese warlord armies, died in captivity.

danshig (M): Buddhist ceremony where supplicants make offerings to an incarnate lama requesting that he prolongs his life.

Danzanravjaa (1803–1856): an unorthodox incarnate lama and Mongolia's greatest premodern poet and playwright.

Dar' Enkh (M): see Tara.

Dark Old Man: honorary title given to a shaman buried in Songgino Mountain to the west of Ulaanbaatar, the spirit of the Songgino Mountain.

datsan (M): monastic college for Buddhist learning.

dayanchi (M): Buddhist contemplation or meditation, sometimes involving withdrawal from society.

del (M): Mongolian robe.

dharmapala (S): a 'protector of the dharma', often depicted as a wrathful deity, pre-Buddhist local spirit converted to Buddhism.

Dilov Khutugtu Jamsranjav (1884–1965): incarnation of the Dilov Khutugtu, a lama accused of being a Japanese spy, later fled to Inner Mongolia and then the United States.

dogshid (M): a dharmapala in wrathful form.

Dolma (M): see Tara.

Doloon Nor (M): site of the meeting between the Khalkha elite and the Kangxi Emperor in 1691, city formerly renowned for its Buddhist art work.

Dongogdulam (M): name of consort of the Eighth Patriarch at time of Mongolia's declaration of independence.

dorj (T): thunderbolt, symbol of Vajrayana Buddhism, often depicted as a sceptre.

Dorjshüg (1618–1655): a wrathful protective deity, supposed incarnation of a highly placed Tibetan lama and rival of Fifth Dalai Lama, see Shugden Controversy.

Douglas, William O. (1898–1980): American Supreme Court Justice, visitor to Mongolia in 1963, noted civil libertarian.

dougong (C): wooden brackets placed on top of a column to absorb evenly the weight of tiled roofs.

dharma (S): Buddhist teachings.

Drepung (T): famous monastery near Lhasa, one of the 'three seats' of Gelukpa Buddhism.

Duan Qirui (1865–1936): premier and acting president of Chinese warlord government in Peking, sent Xu Shucheng to Urga to reclaim Mongolia for the Republic of China.

Düinkhor (M): see Kalachakra.

Dürteddagwa (M): see Citipati.

Eastern Monastic Settlement: centre of Urga surrounding the Yellow Palace of the patriarchs.

Eight Sages: a group of legendary, anti-establishment Taoist spirits, common East Asian decorative motif.

Erdene Zuu (M): see Monastery of the One Hundred Treasures.

Erlig Khan (M): see Yama.

Eternal Sky: formless, yet male, primordial spiritual force of heaven.

Etügen Ükh (M): see Mother Earth.

Galdan Boshogtu Khan (1644–1697): leader of Zungharian war against Khalkha Mongols and the Qing Empire.

gamin: (M from C): 'revolutionary', derogatory term for early twentieth-century Republic of China.

Gandan Monastery: main site of Buddhist datsans in Urga, primary Gelukpa monastery in Ulaanbaatar.

Ganden Monastery: famous monastery near Lhasa, one of the 'three seats' of Gelukpa Buddhism.

Ganesha (S): elephant-headed Hindu god of fortune, absorbed into Buddhist pantheon.

ganjir (M): gilded vase-shaped container of sutras placed on the main beam of temple roofs.

gazriin ezen (M): 'owners of the earth', local spirits living in significant geographical sites

gelen (M): fully ordained monk having taken 253 monastic vows.

Gelukpa (T): the 'system of virtue', one of the five main branches of Vajrayana Buddhism, founded by Tsongkhapa, emphasizes monastic discipline and scholarship.

Peljidiin Genden (1895–1937): prime minister of Mongolia from 1932 to 1937, executed in Moscow for failing to implement instructions from Moscow and quarrelling with Stalin.

genen (M): Buddhist layman.

ger (M): traditional circular Mongolian felt tent.

Geser (M): legendary king from Mongolian and Tibetan epic folk stories.

gesgüi (M): disciplinary master at a monastery.

getsül (M): novice monk having taken ten monastic vows.

gol süm (M): main hall of a temple or monastery.

golden nail: the North Star, the 'peg' that holds the sky in place.

Gombo: see Mahalaka.

Gombodorj: son of the Abatai Khan, father of Zanabazar.

Great Purge: the destruction of the sangha in Mongolia between 1937 and 1940.

Guan Yin (C): see Avalokitesvara.

Guan Yu (C): historical Chinese general from the Three Kingdoms Period who was deified after death, revered as the god of war and protector of the Qing dynasty, associated with King Geser in popular belief.

gün (M from C): noble title, often translated as 'duke'.

gürem (M): prayer by monks for a good reincarnation for a deceased.

Hayagriva (S): horse-headed dharmapala, popular with herders.

Holy Mountain: literal translation of the name of the mountain directly south of Ulaanbaatar, symbol of the city.

individual construction: Soviet architectural theory popular in the 1970s, emphasized monumental special-purpose buildings, such as memorials.

izba (R): log cabin.

Jagarmolom: nineteenth-century Mongolian lama, founded first zod monastery in Mongolia.

jaltsan (M): gilded decoration on temple roofs in the shape of victory banners.

Jamsran (M): red-faced pre-Buddhist Mongolian deity absorbed as a dharmapala, frequently regarded as the main protective deity of Mongolia, also known as Begtse.

Tsyeben Jamstrano (1880–1942): Buryat scholar, collector of Mongolian folklore, publisher of the journal 'Shine Toli', translator of European literature.

Janraiseg (M): see Avalokitesvara.

Jarankhasar (M): stupa based on the Great Boudhanath Stupa in the Kathmandu Valley.

jasaa (M): readings by monks requested by individuals for health, happiness, or prosperity.

javdan (M): low bench for monks in temples.

Jonom (T): a branch of Vajrayana Buddhism, supressed in seventeenth-century Tibet but continuing in a remote community in China's Qinghai province, the Ninth Patriarch was declared its leader by the Dalai Lama.

Jebzundamba Khutugtu (M): title of the third highest ranking lama in Khalkha Mongolia after the Dalai Lama and the Panchen Lama.

Jüd (M): esoteric Vajrayana teachings.

Jügder: Mongolian artist attached to the court of the Bogd Khan, famous for a detailed map of Urga painted in 1913.

Kadampa (T): reformist branch of Vajrayana Buddhism founded by Atisha.

Kagyüpa (T): one of the five main branches of Vajrayana Buddhism, emphasizes meditation and ritual more than scholasticism, lineage of Milarepa.

Kalachakra (S): (1) Vajrayana teaching called the 'Wheel of Time', emphasizes the primacy of wisdom and ritual and esoteric and exoteric knowledge, (2) treatise by the same name, (3) a deity representing a visual depiction of the Kalachakra in an ecstatic embrace with his consort.

Kalgan (M): former name for a major trading city in Inner Mongolia on the south side of the Gobi Desert, now known as Zhangjiakou.

Kalmyk: name of Mongolian ethnic group living near the mouth of the Volga River.

Kangxi Emperor (1654–1722): emperor of the Qing Empire, consolidated the alliance between Khalkha Mongolia and the Manchu throne.

Kanjur (T): a 108 volume Vajrayana canonical compilation of sayings attributed to the Shakyamuni Buddha.

karma (S): Buddhist belief that all acts, omissions, and thoughts inelastically yield spiritual and material consequences.

khadag (M): ceremonial scarf, commonly blue-coloured in Mongolia, offered as a show of respect or reverence.

khailen (M): oath-taking, annual forty-five-day summer retreat for monks.

khajid (M): see dagina.

Khalkha (M): the main ethnic region in Mongolia, originally referred to the three northern aimags that aligned themselves with the Qing dynasty in 1691.

Prince Khandadorj: (1870–1915): anti-Manchu noble who led a secret diplomatic mission to Saint Petersburg at the end of the Qing dynasty. First Mongolian foreign minister.

Khangarid (M): Garuda, spirit of the Holy Mountain, later a symbol for Ulaanbaatar.

khasaa (M): yard enclosed by wooden palisade.

Khashin Khan (M): figure based on the Kangxi Emperor in the Tsam ceremony, protector and supporter of Gelukpa, also seen sometimes as a Ladkhaki or Chinese monk character in a tsam ceremony.

khiid (M): monastery.

khoshun (M): a subdivision of an aimag, sometimes called a banner.

khüree (M): monastic complex arranged in the shape of an inverted *U* with a high lama's residence located at its centre.

khutugtu (M): title for Buddhist incarnate lamas.

khuushuur: (M) fried mutton-meat pie.

Kiakhta (M): 'having spear grass', Russian trading town on the Khalkha Mongolian border, staging post for overland trade with Qing China.

kirtimukha (S): 'face of glory', legendary monster and servant of Lord Shiva, door knocker in the shape of a jawless monster protecting homes, common decorative motif throughout Asia.

lama (T): a highly learned Buddhist monk.

King Langdarma (?–842): Tibetan king who launched a purge against Buddhism in Tibet, later compared to Vladimir Lenin by Mongolian lamas.

Larson, Frans August (1870–1957): Swedish missionary and Mongolian expert, sometime adviser to the Bogd Khan.

Lattimore, Owen (1900–1989): pioneer American Mongolist, author of celebrated works on Central Asia.

Leftist Deviation: extremist programmes pursued by the MPRP and its Youth Revolutionary League from 1930 to 1932.

Ligdan Khan (1588–1634): last emperor-descendant of the Yuan dynasty.

Logshir Janraisig (M): see Lokecvara.

Lokecvara (S): the 'protector of the World', an emanation of Avalokitesvara.

lu (M): see naga.

Luvsankhaidav (1872–1918): younger brother of the Eighth Patriarch, state oracle, the sole Choijin Lama in Urga's history.

Luvsanpeljee: early twentieth-century monk and translator of the Choijin Lama's utterances during the lama's possessions.

Machik Labdrön (1055–1149): a Tibetan Tantric practitioner who developed the zod form of meditation.

Sandagdorjiin Magsarjav (1877–1927): Mongolian general who fought victoriously against White Russian and Chinese warlord armies during the autonomous period.

Maharajas: see Maharanz.

Maharanz (M): the guardian-deities of the four cardinal directions, protectors of Mount Meru, frequently depicted in statues in the antechamber of Buddhist temples.

Mahalaka (S): one of the ten wrathful protectors, the 'Great Black One', a significant protective deity of Mongolia in pre-revolutionary times.

Maidar (M): see Maitreya.

maikhan (M): rectangular cloth tent, typically used for summer gatherings.

Maimachin (M): 'Buy-Sell City', the Chinese traders' settlement to the south-east of Urga.

Maitreya (S): the Future Buddha, the last of the Buddhas whose coming will mark the end of time.

makara (S): a sea-dragon decoration on temple roofs.

mandala: symbolic representation of a Buddhist deity's palace, an offering of a mandala symbolizes an offering of the universe, object of concentration for meditation exercises.

Manjusri (S): the bodhisattva of wisdom.

Manla (M): Supreme Healer, Bhaishayaguru, the medicine Buddha.

mergen (M): skilled archer.

Mergen Gegeen (M): an incarnate lama and head of the Mergen Monastery in Inner Mongolia, the third incarnation of the Mergen Gegeen promoted Mongolian translations of Tibetan canonical works.

Meru (S): legendary mountain at the centre of the Buddhist universe.

Milarepa (circa 1052–circa 1135): Tibet's most famous poet and hermit, adherent of Kagyüpa branch.

modernism: Soviet architectural style popular in the 1960s, emphasized restrained geometric shapes.

Monastery of the One Hundred Treasures: first Gelukpa monastery in Khalkha Mongolia, founded in 1586.

Möngke Tenger (M): see Eternal Sky.

Mongolor: abbreviated name of Urga's first ill-fated foreign-invested mining company.

Mönke Khan: Grand Khan of the Mongolian empire, grandson of Chinggis Khan, reigned from 1251 to 1259.

morin huur (M): horse-head fiddle.

Mother Earth: main feminine earth spirit, counterpart to Eternal Sky.

Naadam (M): summer festival, once held as a danshig, with three types of sports contests.

naga (S): half-human and half-serpent water spirit

Naichün (M): state oracle of the Dalai Lama's court.

naidan (M): arhats, first eighteen disciples of the Shakyamuni Buddha.

Nalaikh (M): district to the south-east of Ulaanbaatar, site of coal mine put into operation in 1915 and a terminus for the first rail line to Ulan Bator, site of UB's largest Kazakh community.

natsagdorj: double thunderbolt in the form of a cross.

Dasdorjiin Natsagdorj (1906–1937): modern Mongolian author, playwright, and poet.

neoclassicism: Soviet architectural style popular in the 1930s because of its modest use of steel, influenced by classical Greek architectural design.

Ninety-Nine Tengers: lesser heavenly deities under Eternal Sky.

nuuts tagnuulin gazar (M): an early twentieth-century espionage training centre for lamas in a monastery to the north of Urga.

Nyingma (T): the 'ancient teachings', an early form of Buddhism in Tibet, one of the five major branches of Vajrayana Buddhism.

Ochirdara (M): see Vajradhara.

Ochirvaan (M): see Vajrapani.

Oirat (M): seventeenth-century alliance of western Mongolians, fought against the Manchus and Khalkha elites.

om mani padme hum (S): 'the jewel is in the lotus', a popular mantra in Vajrayana Buddhism.

ongon (M): a figurine used as the material foundation for an ancestral spirit.

Ordos: part of Inner Mongolia located within the bend in the Yellow River.

örgöö (M): residence of an important personage, root for the name 'Urga'.

ovoo (M): a cairn built on a mountaintop or at a crossroad as a material foundation for local spirits.

Padmasambhava: eighth-century Indian guru, founder of Nyingma teachings, overpowered hostile local spirits in order to establish first Tibetan monastery.

Panchen Lama (T): title of the second most important lama in Vajrayana Buddhism.

parinirvana (S): enlightenment, state of bliss achieved beyond karmic consequences.

Qianlong Emperor (1711–1799): emperor of the Qing Empire, restricted the autonomy of Mongolian nobles and decreed candidates for the Third Patriarch and his successors must be found in Tibet.

Qing Empire: a multi-ethnic empire ruled by Manchus, consisting of China, Manchuria, Mongolia, Xinjiang, and Tibet.

Rashaant (M): 'place with hot springs, holy water'.

Ratna (S): the 'jewel' or the 'All Powerful Ten', symbol of the Kalachakra, basis for the Soyombo, a Buddhist symbol combining images of enlightenment, i.e., the sun, moon and fire, and the first seven syllables of the Kalachakra treatise.

Ratna Sambhava (S): the Jewel Born, one of the five Tathagata Buddhas, associated with triumph over pride, the direction south, and the colour yellow.

rationalism: Soviet architectural theory popular in the 1920s, emphasized elaborate geometric shapes.

Red Hat Sect: imprecise name for Vajrayana Buddhist branches other than the Gelukpa, name taken from the colour of the headwear of the branch's lamas.

Rinpoche (T): jewel, gem, a title for incarnate lamas.

Byambyn Rinchen (1905–1979): multitalented Mongolian scholar, writer, and intellectual maverick.

Roerich, Nicholas (1874–1974): Russian artist, writer, mystic, and possible Soviet spy.

Sain Noyon Khan Aimag: one of the four aimags that made up Khalkha Mongolia.

sakhius (M): protective deity.

Sakyapa (T): one of the five main branches of Vajrayana Buddhism, came into existence in the twelfth century.

Jamsrangiin Sambuu (1895–1972): Mongolian politician and statesmen, known for his layman's expertise in animal husbandry.

samsara (S): reincarnation, emanation of constituent parts of the soul into a new being.

Khuulichi Sandag: early nineteenth-century Mongolian poet known for his satirical writings.

sangha (S): Buddhist monastic community.

Second Conversion: the conversion of Mongolians to Vajrayana Buddhism beginning in the 1580s.

Sera Monastery: famous monastery in Lhasa, one of the 'three seats' of Gelukpa Buddhism.

Seven Old Men: the seven gods of fate, represented by the stars of the Great Bear constellation.

shabi (M): clerical serfs working in estates owned by the patriarchs.

Shakyamuni Buddha: 'the Awakened One', the historical Buddha, Siddhartha Gautama, born in the sixth century BCE.

shaman: mystic healer, soothsayer, intermediary with the spirit world.

Shambhala (S): legendary kingdom that will arise when the Maitreya Buddha reigns over the world.

Marzan Sharav (1869–1939): Mongolian religious painter, credited with founding zurag style of painting.

Shine Toli (M): 'New Mirror', name of Mongolian language journal that introduced modern topics to the Mongolian reading public.

shireetü: a lama presiding over divine services.

Shugden Controversy: a current dispute between the Dalai Lama and the followers of Dorjshüg with geopolitical overtones.

Songino Uul (M): mountain to the west of Ulaanbaatar, home of the Dark Old Man, literally 'Onion Mountain'.

King Songtsen Gampo (605–649): founder of the first Tibetan empire and credited with the introduction of Buddhism to Tibet.

sor (M): triangular sacrificial cake, presented as a Buddhist offering.

Soyombo (M): first letter of the script invented by Zanabazar as Mongolian word for the Svayambhu, Mongolia national emblem.

Sri Devi (S): one of the ten wrathful protectors and the only female member of the dharmapalas.

stupa (S): a structure originating in India symbolizing events in the Shakyamuni's life, also used as a reliquary for the remains of a high lama.

suburgan (M): see stupa.

Damdiny Sükhbaatar (1893–1923): Mongolian revolutionary leader, credited as the founder of the Mongolian People's Republic.

süld (M): a standard or banner that acts as the host for a spirit.

süm (M): shrine temple.

Svayambhu (S): 'self-originating', reference to Adi-Buddha

Tanjur (T): 225 volumes of canonical treatises and other commentary on Buddhism.

Tanton: see Thang Tong Gyalpa.

Tara (S): female bodhisattva, often depicted in white or green, loosely based on the Chinese and Nepalese wives of Tibetan King Songtsen Gampo.

Taranatha (1575–1634): last leader of the Jonam branch of Vajrayana Buddhism in Tibet, believed to have been reincarnated as the First Patriarch.

tarantass (R): Russian horse-drawn carriage, frequent means of conveyance between Siberia and Urga.

Tathagata (S): the 'victors' or the 'thus gone ones', enlightened beings who have entered parinirvana, often represented by five spiritual Buddhas, symbols of constituent elements of existence.

telega (R): Russian carriage.

tenger (M): deities associated with forces of nature.

Terrible Fourth: nickname for the Fourth Patriarch because of his emphasis on discipline.

Thang Tong Gyalpa (1361–1485): Tibetan lama polymath skilled at composing religious operas as well as civil engineering, philosophy, and medicine.

thangka (T): Vajrayana Buddhist painting meant to serve as a sermon in images.

Tonyukuk: eighth-century Türkic prince who advocated against assimilation into China.

toono (M): wooden ring at the top of a ger that is connected to the circular wooden lattice framework of the ger's circular wall.

Tsagaan Ögön (M): see White Old Man.

Tsagaan Sar (M): 'white month', the festival at the start of the first month of the Mongolian lunar calendar, most important holiday in the Mongolian calendar.

Tsam (M): a slow-paced Vajrayana Buddhist dance ceremony performed by lamas wearing masks of bodhisattvas and dharmapalas.

tsanid (M): Buddhist metaphysics and scholarly learning.

Yumjaagin Tsedenbal (1916–1991): Mongolian prime minister from 1953 to 1984, ruled during era of gradual stagnation, dedicated follower of the USSR.

Tsetsee Gün (M): the highest peak of the Holy Mountain.

Tsetsen Khan Aimag: one of the four aimags that made up Khalkha Mongolia.

tsogchin dugan (M): main assembly hall in a Buddhist monastery.

Tsogt Taij (1580–1636): Khalkha prince opposed to Manchu alliance and influence.

tsorji (M): chief administrative officer of a monastery.

Tsongkhapa (1357–1419): the 'Man of the Onion Valley', the monk who founded the Gelukpa branch.

tsuivan (M): fried mutton noodles.

Tuul River: river flowing to the south of Ulaanbaatar.

Tüshee Gün (M): second peak of the Holy Mountain.

Tüshetu Khan Aimag: one of the four aimags that made up Khalkha Mongolia.

ubashi (M): a Buddhist layman who has taken five monastic vows.

udgan (M): female shaman.

Ulaanbaatar: romanized transliteration of the name for the capital of Mongolia, used in this book to refer to the city since 1990.

Ulan Bator: romanized transliteration of the name for the capital of Mongolia, used in this book to refer to the city from 1924 to 1990.

umzad (M): chanting master.

uni (M): one of the two supporting beams for a ger.

Urga: name given by Westerners to the monastic capital of Khalkha Mongolia, used in this book to refer to the city until 1924.

Wallace, Henry (1888–1965): American vice president, acolyte of Nicholas Roerich, highest ranking Western diplomatic visitor during the Communist period.

wenshou (C): zoomorphic decorations on the eaves of a temple roof.

Western Monastic Settlement: formal name for the section of Urga with the Gandan Monastery at its centre.

White Old Man: pre-Buddhist local deity absorbed into the Buddhist pantheon.

White Shell Protector: title granted by Qing court to khangarid or the protective deity of the Holy Mountain.

Vairocana (S): the Illuminator, one of the five Tathagata Buddhas, associated with emptiness, the centre, and the colour white.

vajra (S): thunderbolt, also diamond, a sceptre used in Buddhist ceremonies, symbol of Vajrayana Buddhism.

Vajradhara (S): the exoteric primordial Buddha equivalent to the Adi-Buddha, Buddhist patron saint of Mongolia.

Vajrapani (S): bodhisattva, protector of the Shakyamuni Buddha, exoteric primordial Buddha equivalent to the Adi-Buddha, emanation of Chinggis Khan.

Vajrasattva (S): bodhisattva associated with purification process.

Vajrayana Buddhism: branch of Mahayana Buddhism that developed in Tibet and spread to Mongolia, currently believed to consist of five orders: Bon, Gelukpa, Kagyüpa, Nyingma, and Sakyapa

Xu Shucheng (1880–1925): Chinese warlord general who forced the revocation of Mongolian independence in 1920.

yadam (M): tutelary deity selected by a monk as a model for meditation and spiritual cultivation.

Yama (S): Lord of Death, bullheaded wrathful deity.

Yamantaka (S): destroyer of the Lord of Death, bullheaded wrathful deity who defeated Yama.

yampai (M): protective wall against harmful spirits in front of a main gate.

Yellow Hat Sect: informal name for the Gelukpa branch of Vajrayana Buddhism, name taken from the colour of the headware worn by Tsongkhapa.

Zanabazar (1635–1723): Mongolian polymath, First Patriarch of the Gelukpa lineage in Khalkha Mongolia.

Zasagtu Khan Aimag: one of the four aimags that made up Khalkha Mongolia.

zeebad (M): see kirtimukha.

Zemer (T): protective deity of Samye Monastery in Tibet.

zhiwen (C): sea dragon decoration placed on the ends of a temple's main roof beam.

Zhukov, Georgy Konstantinovich (1896–1974): Soviet general who defeated the Japanese Imperial Army at the Battle of Nomohan.

zod (M): a meditation technique used in the Nyingma and Kagyüpa sects where the practitioner envisages cutting away the body as an offering, later endorsed by the Fifth Dalai Lama.

Sanjaasurengiin Zorig (1962–1998), charismatic leader of the 1990 revolution, murdered on the eve of being nominated as prime minister.

zurag (M): 'traditional' Mongolian folk painting, a popular style beginning in the early twentieth century.

Zuu (M): the Shakyamuni Buddha.

züün (M): eastern or 'left-hand side' as perceived by a monarch on a throne facing south.

Bibliography

Addleton, Jonathan S., *Mongolia and the United States: A Diplomatic History*, Hong Kong University Press, Hong Kong, 2013.

Akim, Hatagin Gotov, *Just One Genghis Khan on Earth: The Sitting Pretty of Blue Mongols*, Munkhiin Useg, Ulaanbaatar, 2014.

Alioshin, Dmitri, *Asian Odyssey*, Henry Holt and Company, New York, 1940.

Allen, Thomas B., 'Time Catches Up with Mongolia', *National Geographic Magazine*, February 1985, 242–69.

Alley, Rewi, *Journey to Outer Mongolia: A Diary with Poems*, Caxton Press, Christchurch, New Zealand, 1957.

Allsen, Thomas T., *Culture and Conquest in Mongolian Eurasia*, Cambridge University Press, Cambridge, 2004.

Altangerel, Z., and Ch. Khatanbaatar, *A Brief History of Khamar Monastery*, Space Entertainment, Ulaanbaatar, 2009.

Altannavch, D., *Bogd Khan Palace Museum: A Brief Guide*, Interpress Publishing, Ulaanbaatar, 2001.

Amarsana, C., and S. Mainbayar, *Concise Historical Album of the Mongolian Democratic Union*, Ulaanbaatar, 2009.

Amglan, M., *The Cultural Monuments of Western Mongolia*, Monsudar, Ulaanbaatar, 2008.

Amitai-Preiss, Reuven, and David O. Morgan, eds., *The Mongol Empire and Its Legacy*, Brill, Leiden, Boston, and Cologne, n.d. [1999].

Anderson, Richard, *Russia: Modern Architectures in History*, University of Chicago Press, Chicago, 2015.

Andrews, Roy Chapman, *Across Mongolian Plains: A Naturalist's Account of China's "Great Northwest"*, Blue Ribbon Books, New York, 1921.

Andrews, Roy Chapman, *Ends of the Earth*, Garden City Publishing Company, Garden City, New York, 1929.

Andrews, Roy Chapman, *The New Conquest of Central Asia*, American Museum of Natural History, New York, 1932.

Andrews, Roy Chapman, *On the Trail of Ancient Man: A Narrative of the Field Work of the Central Asiatic Expeditions*, Garden City Publishing Company, Garden City, New York, 1926.

Andrews, Roy Chapman, *This Business of Exploring*, G. P. Putnam Sons, New York, 1935.

Appignanesi, Richard, and Oscar Zarate, *Lenin for Beginners*, Icon Books, Cambridge, 1994.

Arlington, L. C., and William Lewisohn, *In Search of Old Peking*, Oxford University Press, Hong Kong, 1991.

Atkinson, Thomas Witlam, *Oriental and Western Siberia: A Narrative of Seven Years' Explorations and Adventures in Siberia, Mongolia, the Kirghis Steppes, Chinese Tartary, and Part of Central Asia*, Asian Educational Services, Delhi, 2000.

Atwood, Christopher P., *Encyclopedia of Mongolia and the Mongol Empire*, Facts on File, New York, 2004.

Avery, Martha, *The Tea Road: China and Russia Meet across the Steppe*, China Intercontinental Press, Beijing, 2003.

Baabar, *History of Mongolia: From World Power to Soviet Satellite*, White Horse Press, Cambridge, 1999.

Baasansuren, Khandsuren, *Erden Zuu: The Jewel of Enlightenment*, Ulaanbaatar, 2011.

Bamana, Gaby, *On the Tea Road: A Journey into Mongolian Life and Culture*, Admon, Ulaanbaatar, 2008.

Barfield, Thomas, J., *The Perilous Frontier: Nomadic Empires and China 221 BC to AD 1757*, Blackwell Publishers, Cambridge, Massachusetts, 1992.

Barzini, Luigi, *Peking to Paris: A Journey across Two Continents in 1907*, Library Press, New York, 1973.

Batsaikahn, Ookhnoi, *Bogdo Jebtsundama Khutuktu, the Last King of Mongolia*, Admon, Ulaanbaatar, 2009.

Batsaikahn, Ookhnoi, *Mongolia: Becoming a Nation-State (1911–1952)*, Bit Press, Ulaanbaatar, 2013.

Bawden, Charles R., *Confronting the Supernatural: Mongolian Traditional Ways and Means—Collected Papers*, Harrassowitz Verlag, Wiesbaden, 1994.

Bawden, Charles. R., tr., *The Jebtsundamba Khutukhtus of Urga*, Otto Harrassowitz, Wiesbaden, 1961.

Bawden, C. R., *The Modern History of Mongolia*, Kegan Paul International, London and New York, 1989.

Bawden, C. R., *Mongolian Traditional Literature: An Anthology*, Kegan Paul, London, 2003.

Bawden, Charles R., *Mongolian–English Dictionary*, Kegan Paul International, London and New York, 1997.

Bawden, C. R., *Shamans, Lamas and Evangelicals: The English Missionaries in Siberia*, Routledge and Kegan Paul, London, 1985.

Bawden, C. R., tr., *Tales of an Old Lama*, Buddhica Britannica Press, London, 1997.

Bayasgalan, Bayanbat, *Ulaanbaatar Then and Now: Amazing Images of Ulaanbaatar's History*, Monsound and Vision Foundation, Ulaanbaatar, 2013.

Becker, Jasper, *Mongolia: Travels in the Untamed Land*, Tauris Parke Paperbacks, New York, 2008.

Beer, Robert, *The Encyclopedia of Tibetan Symbols and Motifs*, Shambhala Publications, Boston, 1999.

Bell, Charles, *The Religion of Tibet*, Oxford University Press, Oxford, 1931.

Bell, John, *A Journey from St. Petersburg to Peking 1719–1722*, edited by J. L. Stevenson, Edinburgh University Press, Edinburgh, 1965.

Berger, Patricia, and Terese Tse Bartholomew, eds., *Mongolia: The Legacy of Chinggis Khan*, Asian Art Museum of San Francisco, San Francisco, 1995.

Berry, Scott, *A Stranger in Tibet: The Adventures of a Wandering Zen Monk*, Kodansha International, Tokyo and New York, 1989.

Berzin, Alexander, 'Exploitation of the Shambhala Legend for Control of Mongolia', *The Alexander Berzin Buddhist Archives*, April 2003 at http://www.berzinarchives.com/web/en/archives/advanced/kalachakra/shambhala/exploitation_shambala_legend_mongolia.html.

Bierce, Ambrose, *The Collected Writings of Ambrose Bierce*, Citadel Press, New York, 1996.

Billé, Franck, *Sinophobia: Anxiety, Violence and the Making of Mongolian Identity*, University of Hawai'i Press, Honolulu, 2015.

Binsteed, G. C., 'Life in a Khalka Steppe Lamasery', *Journal of the Royal Asiatic Society*, October 1914, 869–70.

Bisch, Jorgen, *Mongolia: Unknown Land*, E. P. Dutton & Co., New York, 1963.

Blunden, Jane, *Bradt Guide to Mongolia*, Bradt Travel Guides, London, 2004.

Bodio, Stephen J., *Eagle Dreams: Searching for Legends in Wild Mongolia*, Lyons Press, Guilford, Connecticut, 2003.

Boyle, J.A., ed., *The Cambridge History of Iran Volume 5: The Saljuq and Mongol Periods*, Cambridge University Press, Cambridge, 1968.

Bredon, Juliet, *Peking: A Historical and Intimate Description of Its Major Sights*, Kelly & Walsh, Shanghai, 1922.

Brown, William A., and Urungunge Onon, *History of the Mongolian People's Republic*, Harvard University Press, Cambridge, Massachusetts, and London, 1976.

Budge, E. A. Willis, tr., *The Monks of Kublai Khan Emperor of China*, Religious Tract Society, London, 1928.

Buell, Paul D., and Eugene N. Anderson, *A Soup for the Qan: Chinese Dietary Medicine of the Mongol Era as Seen in Hu Sihui's Yinshan Zhengyao*, Brill, Leiden and Boston, 2010.

Bulag, Uradyn E., and Hildegard G. M. Diemberger, eds., *The Mongolia-Tibet Interface: Opening New Research Terrains in Inner Asia*, Brill, Leiden and Boston, 2007.

Bulstrode Gull, Beatrix M., *A Tour in Mongolia*, Methuen & Co., London, 1920.

Bultrini, Raimondo, *The Dalai Lama and the King Demon: Tracking a Triple Murder through the Mists of Time*, translated by Maria Simmons, Tibet House US, New York, 2013.

Buyagndelger, Manduhai, *Tragic Spirits: Shamanism, Memory, Gender in Contemporary Mongolia*, University of Chicago Press, Chicago and London, 2013.

Cable, Mildred, and Francesca French, *Through Jade Gate and Central Asia: An Account of Journeys in Kansu, Turkestan and the Gobi Desert*, Hodder and Stoughton, London, 1937.

Cameron, Nigel, *Barbarians and Mandarins: Thirteen Centuries of Western Travellers in China*, Oxford University Press, Hong Kong, 1989.

Cammann, Schuyler, *The Land of Camel Tents and the Temples of Inner Mongolia*, Isha Press, New Delhi, 2013.

Campbell, C. W., *Travels in Mongolia, 1902: A Journey by C. W. Campbell, The British Consul in China*, Stationery Office, London, 2000.

Campi, Alicia, *The Impact of China and Russia on United States–Mongolian Political Relations in the Twentieth Century*, Edwin Melle Press, Lewiston, New York, Queenston, Canada, and Lampeter, United Kingdom, 2009.

Carruthers, Douglas, *Unknown Mongolia: A Record of Travel and Exploration in North West Mongolia and Dzungaria*, Hutchison & Co, London, 1914.

Chandra, Lokesh, *Buddhism across the Grasslands of Chinggis Khan*, Aditya Prakashan, New Delhi, 2013.

Chapman, F. Spencer, *Lhasa: The Holy City*, Bodhi Leaves Corporation, Delhi, 1992.

Ch'en, Kenneth K. S., *Buddhism: The Light of Asia*, Barron's Educational Series, Woodbury, New York, 1968.

Cheney, George A., *The Pre-revolutionary Culture of Outer Mongolia*, Mongolia Society, Bloomington, 1968.

Clubb, O. Edmund, *China and Russia: The "Great Game"*, Columbia University Press, New York, 1971.

Coates, Austin, *China Races*, Oxford University Press, Hong Kong, 1994.

Colins, Perry McDonough, *Overland Exploration in Siberia, Northern Asia and the Great Amoor River Country, with Incidental Notices of Manchooria, Mongolia, Kamchatka and Japan*, Appleton, New York, 1864.

Colvin, John, *Nomohan*, Quartet Books, London, 1999.

Colvin, John, *Twice Around the World: Some Memoirs of Diplomatic Life in North Vietnam and Outer Mongolia*, Leo Cooper, London, 1991.

Conze, Edward, *Buddhism: Its Essence and Development*, Harper & Brothers, New York, 1959.

Cramer, Marc, *Imperial Mongolian Cooking*, Hippocrene Books, New York, 2003.

Croner, Don, *Guide to Locales Connected with the Life of Zanabazar, First Bogd Gegeen of Mongolia*, BookSurge, 2006.

Croner, Don, *Travels in Northern Mongolia*, Polar Star Publishing, Anchorage, Alaska, 2004.

Danzanravjaa, *A Song Arising from Contemplation: Selected Poems*, translated by Simon Wickham-Smith, Mongolian Academy of Culture and Poetry, Ulaanbaatar, 2013.

Dashdondov, Ts., *Mongolian Traditions at a Glance*, Khokh Sudar, Ulaanbaatar, 2007.

Dashpurev, D., *Reign of Political Terror and Repression in Mongolia 1920–1990*, Institute of International Studies [Ulaanbaatar], 2014.

David-Neel, Alexandra, and Lama Yongden, *The Superhuman Life of Gesar of Ling*, Shambhala, Boston and London, 1987.

Davis, Matthew, *When Things Get Dark: A Mongolian Winter's Tale*, St Martin's Press, New York, 2010.

Dawson, Christopher, ed., *The Mongol Mission: Narratives and Letters of the Franciscan Missionaries in Mongolia and China in the Thirteenth and Fourteenth Centuries*, Sheed and Ward, New York, 1955.

DeFrancis, John, *In the Footsteps of Genghis Khan*, University of Hawai'i Press, Honolulu, 1993.

Delaplace, Gregory, 'Chinese Ghosts in Mongolia', *Inner Asia*, Vol. 12, 127–41, 2010.

Delgerjargal, A., *Your Friendly Guide in Ulaanbaatar*, Irmuun Agency, Ulaanbaatar, 2008.

Desjacques, Alain, *Melodies de flûte d'un berger Mongol*, Ulaanbaatar, 2004.

Di Cosmo, Nicola, *Ancient China and Its Enemies: The Rise of Nomadic Power in East Asian History*, Cambridge University Press, Cambridge, 2002.

The Diluv Khutagt, *Political Memoirs and Autobiography of a Buddhist Reincarnation*, translated by Owen Lattimore and Fujiko Isono, reprinted by Polar Star Books, Ulaanbaatar, 2009.

Dorje, Hungkar, ed., *Tangkas in Golog: The Tangka Album of Lung-ngon Monastery*, Quangmin Books, Ho Chi Minh City, n.d. [2001].

Douglas, William O., 'Journey to Outer Mongolia', *National Geographic Magazine*, March 1962, 289–345.

Dreyfus, Georges, 'The Shuk-dun Affair: History and Nature of a Quarrel', *Journal of International Association of Buddhist Studies*, Vol. 21, No. 2, 1998, 227–310.

Eberhard, Wolfram, *A Dictionary of Chinese Symbols: Hidden Symbols in Chinese Thought and Life*, SMC Publishing, Taipei 1994.

Elverskog, Johan, *Our Great Qing: The Mongols, Buddhism and the State in Late Imperial China*, University of Hawai'i Press, Honolulu, 2006.

Elverskog, Johan, 'Tibetocentrism, Religious Conversion and the Study of Mongolian Buddhism', *The Mongolia-Tibet Interface: Opening New Research Terrains in Inner Asia*, Urdadyn E. Bulag and Hildegard G. M. Diemberger, eds., Brill, Leiden and Boston, 1977.

Elvin, Harold, *The Incredible Mile: Siberia – Mongolia – Uzbekistan*, Heinemann, London, 1970.

Endicott, Elizabeth, tr., *Pages from the Past: The 1910 Moscow Trade Exhibition to Mongolia*, Eastbridge, Norwalk, Connecticut, 2007.

Ermakov, Dmirtry, Bө *and* Bön*: Ancient Shamanic Traditions of Siberia and Tibet in Their Relation to the Teachings of a Central Asia Buddha*, Vajra Publications, Kathmandu, 2008.

Errico, Charles J., and J. Samuel Walker, 'The New Deal and the Guru', *American Heritage*, Vol. 40, No. 2, 1989, 92–99.

Even, Marie-Dominique, 'Spirituality Versus Ritual? On Modern Tibetan Buddhism in Post-Communist Mongolia', https//:halshi.ariches-ouvertes.fr/halshs-00274087, 17 April 2009.

Fairbank, John K., ed., *The Cambridge History of China Volume 10: Late Ch'ing 1800–1911*, Part 1, Cambridge University Press, London, 1978.

Fairbank, John K., Edwin O. Reischauer, and Albert M. Craig, *East Asia: Tradition and Transformation*, Houghton Mifflin Company, Boston, 1973.

Forsyth, James, *A History of the Peoples of Siberia: Russia's North Asian Colony 1581–1990*, Cambridge University Press, London, 1994.

Franck, Harry A., *Wanderings in Northern China*, Century Co., New York and London, 1923.

Franke, Herbert, and Denis Twitchett, eds., *The Cambridge History of China Volume 6: Alien Regimes and Border States, 907–1368*, Cambridge University Press, Cambridge, 1994.

Friend, Tad, *Lost in Mongolia: Travels in Hollywood and Other Foreign Lands*, Random House, New York, 2001.

Friters, Gerard, M., *Outer Mongolia and Its International Position*, George Allen & Unwin, London, 1951.

Geleta, Joseph, as related to Ladislaus Forbath, *The New Mongolia*, translated by Lawrence Wolfe, William Heineman, London and Toronto, 1936.

Gerasimovich, Ludmilla K., *History of Mongolia Literature (1921–1964)*, Mongolia Society, Bloomington, Indiana, 1970.

Gernet, Jacques, *Daily Life in China on the Eve of the Mongol Invasion 1250–1276*, translated by H. M. Wright, Macmillan, New York, 1967.

Getty, Alice, *The Gods of Northern Buddhism*, Dover Publications, Mineola, New York, 1988.

Gilmour, James, *Adventures in Mongolia*, Religious Tract Society, London, 1886.

Gilmour, James, *Among the Mongols*, Religious Tract Society, London, 1883.

Gilmour, James, *James Gilmour of Mongolia: His Diaries, Letters and Reports*, Religious Tract Society, London, 1893.

Gilmour, James, *More about Mongols*, Religious Tract Society, London, 1893.

Gohen, Ethan, 'The Story of Eej Khad: Mother Spirit of the Earth and Her Children', Fall 2007, *Independent Study Project (ISP) Collection*. 136, http://digitalcollections.sit.edu/isp_collection/136

Goldstein, Melvyn C., *A History of Modern Tibet Volume I 1913–1951: The Demise of the Lamaist State*, University of California Press, Berkeley, Los Angeles, and London, 1989.

Goldstein, Melvyn C., and Cynthia M. Beall, *The Changing World of Mongolia's Nomads*, Guide Book Company, Hong Kong, 1994.

Goldstein, Melvyn C., William Siebenschhuh, and Tashi Tsering, *The Struggle for Modern Tibet: The Autobiography of Tashi Tsering*, M. E. Sharpe, Armonk, New York, and London, 1997.

Goppal, Sarvepalli, and Sergei Tikhvinsky, eds., *The History of Humanity: The Twentieth Century*, Vol. 7, Routledge, New York, 2008.

Grousset, René, *The Empire of the Steppes: A History of Central Asia*, translated by Naomi Walford, Barnes & Noble Press, New York, 1996.

Gulik, R. H. van, *Hayagriva: Horse Cult in Asia*, Orchid Press, Bangkok, 2005.

Guo, Qinghua, *Visual Dictionary of Chinese Architecture*, Images Publishing, Victoria, Australia, 2002.

Gyatso, Janet, 'Thang-stong rGyalpo, Father of the Tibetan Drama Tradition: The Bodhisattva as Artist', *Zlos-gar*, edited by Jamyang Norbu, Library of Tibetan Works and Archives, New Delhi, 1986.

Hangin, John Gombojab, 'Dashdorjiin Natsadorg (1906–1937)', *The Mongolia Society Bulletin*, Vol. 6, No. 1 (11), Spring 1967, 15–22.

Hart, Guy, *White Month's Return: Mongolia Comes of Age*, Book Guild, Sussex, England, 1993.

Haslund, Henning, *Tents in Mongolia*, Kegan Paul, London, 1934.

Hauts-de-Seine, Conseil général, and Albert-Kahn, Musée et Jardins, *La Mongolie entre deux ères, 1912–1913: Catalogue de l'exposition*, Paris, 2011.

Hedley, John, *On Tramp among the Mongols*, North-China Daily News & Herald, Shanghai, 1908.

Heissig, Walther, *A Lost Civilization: The Mongols Rediscovered*, Thames & Hudson, London, 1966.

Heissig, Walther, *The Religions of Mongolia*, translated by Geoffrey Samuel, Routledge and Kegan Paul, London and Henley, 1980.

Heller, Amy, 'The Great Protector Deities of the Dalai Lamas', *Lhasa in the Seventeenth Century: The Capital of the Dalai Lamas*, edited by Françoise Pommaret, Brill, Leiden and Boston, 2003.

Hibbert, Reginald, and Ann Hibbert, *Letters from Mongolia*, Radcliffe Press, London and New York, 2005.

High, M. M., and J. Schlesinger, 'Rulers and Rascals: The Politics of Gold in Qing Mongolian History', *Central Asian Survey*, 29 (3), 2010, 289–304.

Hogan, Brian, *There's a Sheep in My Bathtub: Birth of a Mongolian Church Planting Movement*, Asteroidea Books, Bayville, California, 2008.

Hopkirk, Peter, *Setting the East Ablaze: Lenin's Dream of an Empire in Asia*, John Murray, London, 1984.

Howard, Christopher R., *Tea of Ulaanbaatar*, Seven Stories Press, New York, 2011.

Howard-Gibbon, and John Edward, *Hsu Shu-Cheng and the Cancellation of Self-government in Outer Mongolia*, MA thesis, University of British Columbia, May 1971.

Howarth, Henry, *History of the Mongols from the 9th Century to the 19th Century: Volumes I to IV*, Longmans, Green, London, 1876.

Huc, Évariste-Régis, and Joseph Gabet, *Travels in Tartary, Thibet and China, 1844–1846*, translated by William Hazlitt, Dover Publications, Mineola, New York, 1987.

Humphrey, Caroline, and Hürelbaatar Ujeed, *A Monastery in Time: The Making of Mongolian Buddhism*, University of Chicago Press, Chicago and London, 2013.

Hyer, Paul, 'Mongolian Politics and Religion in Inner Mongolia: Japan's Plans for the 9th Jebtsundamba "Living Buddhas"', *Mongolian Journal of International Affairs*, No. 17, 2012, 64–74.

Isaacs, Harold R., *Scratches on Our Minds: American Images of China and India*, John Day & Co., New York, 1958.

Jackson, David, and Janice Jackson, *Tibetan Thangka Painting: Methods and Materials*, Snow Lion Publications, Ithaca, 1988.

Jagchid, Sechin, and Paul Hyer, *Mongolia's Culture and Society*, Westview Press, Boulder, Colorado, 1979.

Jerryson, Michael K., *Mongolian Buddhism: The Rise and Fall of the Sangha*, Silk Worm Books, Chiang Mai, 2007.

Jisl, Lumir, *Mongolian Journey*, translated by Till Gottheiner, Batchworth Press, London, 1960.

Jisl, Lumir, *One Hundred Eight Images of Mongolia: The Photographs of Czechoslovak Archaeologist Lumir Jisl 1957–1963*, Admon, Ulaanbaatar, 2014.

Juergensmeyer, Mark, *The New Cold War? Religious Nationalism Confronts the Secular State*, University of California Press, Berkeley, Los Angeles, London, 1993.

Kalsang, Ladrang, *The Guardian Deities of Tibet*, translated by Pema Thinley, Winsome Books India, Delhi, 2010.

Kamata, Takyua et al., *Managing Urban Expansion in Mongolia: Best Practices in Scenario-Based Urban Planning*, World Bank, Washington, DC, 2010.

Kaplan, Robert D., *Imperial Grunts: On the Ground with the American Military from Mongolia to the Philippines to Iraq and Beyond*, Vintage Books, New York, 2006.

Kaplonski, Christopher, *The Lama Question: Violence, Sovereignty and Exception in Early Socialist Mongolia*, University of Hawai'i Press, Honolulu, 2014.

Kaplonski, Christopher, *Truth, History and Politics in Mongolia: The Memory of Heroes*, RoutledgeCurzon, London and New York, 2004.

Kapstein, Matthew T., *Tibetan Buddhism: A Very Short Introduction*, Oxford University Press, Oxford and New York, 2014.

Kemp, Hugh P., *Steppe by Step: Mongolia's Christians: From Ancient Roots to Vibrant Young Church*, Monarch Books, London, 2000.

Kendall, Elizabeth, *A Wayfarer in China: Impressions of a Trip across West China and Mongolia*, Houghton, Mifflin and Company, Boston and New York, 1913.

Kent, A. S., *Old Tartar Trails*, North-China Daily News and Herald, Shanghai, 1919.

Kimura, Hisao, as told to Scott Berry, *Japanese Agent in Tibet*, Serindia Publications, London, 1990.

King, Matthew, 'Modernities, Sense Making, and the Inscription of Mongolian Buddhist Place', *Buddhism in Mongolian History, Culture and Society*, edited by Vesna A. Wallace, 53–69, Oxford University Press, Oxford and New York, 2015.

Kingsley, Peter, *A Story Waiting to Pierce You: Mongolia, Tibet and the Destiny of the Western World*, Golden Sufi Center, Point Reyes, California, 2014.

Knox, Thomas W., 'A Journey to Mongolia', *The Galaxy*, Vol. 6, No. 2, August 1868, 160–72.

Kohn, Michael, *Lama of the Gobi: How Mongolia's Mystic Monk Spread Tibetan Buddhism in the World's Harshest Desert*, Blacksmith Books, Hong Kong, 2010.

Kohn, Michael, *Mongolia*, Lonely Planet Publications, Victoria, Australia, 2014.

Kollmar-Paulenz, Karenia, 'Buddhism in Mongolia after 1990', *Journal of Global Buddhism*, Vol. 4, 2003, 18–24.

Komaroff, Linda, and Stefano Carboni, eds., *The Legacy of Genghis Khan: Courtly Art and Culture in Western Asia, 1256–1353*, Metropolitan Museum of Art, New York and Yale University Press, New Haven and London, 2002.

Kotkin, Stephen, and Bruce A. Elleman, *Mongolia in the Twentieth Century: Landlocked Cosmopolitan*, M. E. Shape, Armonk, New York and London, 1999.

Krueger, John R., *Mongolian Folktales, Stories and Proverbs*, Mongol Society, Bloomington, Indiana, 1967.

Kunsang, Roger, 'The Reawakening of Buddha-Dharma in Mongolia', *Mandala*, January–February 2000, 38–41.

Kuralt, Charles, *A Life on the Road*, G. P. Putnam's and Sons, New York, 1990.

Laird, Thomas, *The Story of Tibet: Conversations with the Dalai Lama*, Atlantic Books, London, 2006.

Lane, George, *Daily Life in the Mongol Empire*, Hackett Publishing Company, Indianapolis and London, 2006.

Lankov, Andrei, *The Real North Korea: Life and Politics in the Failed Utopian State*, Oxford University Press, Oxford and New York, 2013.

Larson, Frans August, *Larson: Duke of Mongolia*, Little, Brown, and Company, Boston, 1930.

Lattimore Owen, *Desert Road to Turkestan*, Kodansha Press, New York, 1995.

Lattimore, Owen, *High Tartary*, Kodansha Press, New York, 1994.

Lattimore, Owen, *Inner Asian Frontiers of China*, Beacon Press, Boston, 1962.

Lattimore, Owen, *Mongol Journeys*, Doubleday, Doran and Co., New York, 1941.

Lattimore, Owen, *The Mongols of Manchuria*, Macmillan, New York, 1935.

Lattimore, Owen, *Nationalism and Revolution in Mongolia*, Oxford University Press, New York, 1955.

Lattimore, Owen, *Nomads and Commissars: Mongolia Revisited*, Oxford University Press, London, 1962.

Lattimore, Owen, *Studies in Frontier History: Collected Papers 1929–58*, Oxford University Press, New York, 1962.

Laube, Lydia, *Slow Boat to Mongolia*, Wakefield Press, Kent Town, Australia, 1997.

Lawless, Jill, *Wild East: Travels in the New Mongolia*, Summersdale Publishing, Chichester, West Sussex, United Kingdom, 2002.

Lee, Robert H. G., *The Manchurian Frontier in Ch'ing History*, Harvard University Press, Cambridge, Massachusetts, 1970.

Le Munyon, Ethan C., 'The Lama's Motor-Car: A Trip across the Gobi by Motor-Car', *National Geographic Magazine*, May 1913, 641–70.

Leighton, Ralph, *Tuva or Bust: Richard Feynman's Last Journey*, London, Penguin Books, 1992.

Lessing, Ferdinand D., ed., *Mongolian–English Dictionary*, University of California Press, Berkeley, 1960.

Lessing, Ferdinand Diedrich, *Ritual and Symbol: Collected Essays on Lamaism and Chinese Symbolism*, Oriental Cultural Service, Taipei, 1976.

Lessing, Ferdinand Diedrich, *Yung-Ho-Kung: An Iconography of the Lamaist Cathedral in Peking*, Elanders Boktryckeri Akteibolao, Stockholm, 1942.

Levin, Dan, 'Shamans' Spirits Crowd Air of Mongolian Capital', *New York Times*, 10 July 2009.

Li Chih-Ch'ang, *The Travels of an Alchemist*, translated by Arthur Waley, Broadway Travellers, London, 1931.

Li Ung Bing, *Outlines of Chinese History*, Cheng Wen Publishing Company, Taipei, 1967.

Liang, Ssu-Ch'eng, *Chinese Architecture: A Pictorial History*, Dover Publications, Mineola, New York, 1984.

Luvsandorj, G., *Decoration of the Mongolian Architecture*, Admon, Ulaanbaatar, 2011.

Ma Ho-T'ien, *Chinese Agent in Mongolia*, translated by John DeFrancis, Johns Hopkins Press, Baltimore, 1949.

Maclean, Fitzroy, *To the Back of Beyond: An Illustrated Companion to Central Asia and Mongolia*, Little, Brown and Company, Boston and Toronto, 1975.

MacColl, René, *The Land of Genghis Khan: A Journey in Outer Mongolia*, Oldbourne, London, 1963.

Madrolle, Claudius, *Northern China—The Valley of the Blue River—Korea*, Hachette & Company, Paris and London, 1912.

Majer, Zsuzsa, and Krisztina Teleki, *History of Zaya Gegeenii Khüree: The Monastery of the Khalkha Zaya Pandita*, Admon, Ulaanbaatar, 2013.

Man, John, *Genghis Khan*, Bantam, New York, 2005.

Man, John, *Kublai Khan: The Mongol King Who Remade China*, Bantam, New York 2007.

Man, John, *Xanadu: Marco Polo's and Europe's Discovery of the East*, Bantam, New York, 2009,

Marshall, A. E., 'French Business Association Mission to Mongolia–October 1990', not published, 1990.

Marshall, Robert, *Storm from the East: From Genghis Khan to Khubilai Khan*, Penguin Books, London, 1993.

May, Timothy Michael, *Culture and Customs of Mongolia*, Greenwood Press, Westport, Connecticut, and London, 2009.

McArthur, Meher, *Reading Buddhist Art: An Illustrated Guide to Buddhist Signs & Symbols*, Thames & Hudson, London, 2004.

Meignan, Victor, *From Paris to Pekin: Over Siberian Snows*, S. Sonnenschein & Co., 1885.

Metternich, Hilary Roe, *Mongolian Folktales*, Avery Press, Boulder, Colorado, 1996.

Micheli, Silvio, *Mongolia: In Search of Marco Polo and Other Adventures*, Hollis & Carter, London, 1964.

Michie, Alexander, *The Siberian Overland Route from Peking to Petersburg through the Steppes of Mongolia and Tartary*, John Murray, London, 1864.

Middleton, Nick, *The Last Disco in Outer Mongolia*, Sinclair-Stevenson, London, 1992.

Montagu, Ivor, *Land of Blue Sky: A Portrait of Modern Mongolia*, Dobson Books, London, 1956.

Moses, Larry William, *The Political Role of Mongol Buddhism*, Asian Studies Research Institute, Bloomington, 1977.

Moses, Larry, and Stephen A. Halkovic Jr., *Introduction to Mongolian History and Culture*, Research Institute for Inner Asian Studies, Bloomington, 1985.

Mostaert, Antoine, CICM, *Manual of Mongolian Astrology and Divination*, Harvard University Press, Cambridge, 1969.

Murphy, George G. S., *Soviet Mongolia: A Study of the Oldest Political Satellite*, University of California Press, Berkeley and Los Angeles, 1966.

Namgyal Monastery, *Kalachakra*, Tibet Domani, Rome, 1996.

Natsadorj, D., *Three Fateful Hills*, State Publishing House, Ulaanbaatar, 1978.

Nebesky-Wojkowitz, René de, *Oracle and Demons of Tibet: The Cult of Iconography of the Tibetan Protective Deities*, Mouton & Co., Netherlands, 1956, reprinted by SMC Publishing, Taipei, 1990.

Newman, John R., 'A Brief History of the Kalachakra', *The Wheel of Time: The Kalachakra in Context*, edited by Beth Simon, Snow Lion Publications, Ithaca, 1991.

Newman, Robert P., *Owen Lattimore and the "Loss" of China*, University of California Press, Berkeley, Los Angeles, and Oxford, 1992.

Ngawang Paldan of Urga, *Shakyamuni Puja: Worshipping the Buddha*, translated by Martin Willson, Wisdom Publications, London, 1988.

Nyamdavaa, O., and Gurdip Singh, eds., *Mongolia and India: Spiritual Neighbours*, Himala Publishers, New Delhi, 2000.

Olschki, Leonardo, *Guillaume Boucher: A French Artist at the Court of the Khans*, Johns Hopkins Press, Baltimore, 1946.

Onon, Urgunge, tr., *Mongolian Heroes of the 20th Century*, AMS Press, New York, 1976.

Onon, Urgunge, *My Mongolian World: From Onon Bridge to Cambridge*, Global Oriental, Kent, UK, 2006.

Orleans, Pierre Joseph d', *History of the Two Tartar Conquerors of China*, Hakluyt Society, London, 1854.

O'Rourke, P. J., *Holidays in Hell*, Grove Press, New York, 2000.

Ossendowski, Ferdinand, *Beasts, Men and Gods*, E. P. Dutton & Company, New York, 1922.

Otgontsetseg, S., 'Roerich Museum Opened', *The Mongol Messenger*, 19 August 2009.

Palmer, James, *The Bloody White Baron: The Extraordinary Story of the Russian Noble Man Who Became the Last Khan of Mongolia*, Basic Books, New York, 2009.

Penick, Douglas J., *The Warrior Song of King Gesar*, Wisdom Publications, Boston, 1996.

Perdue, Peter C., *China Marches West: The Qing Conquest of Central Eurasia*, Harvard University Press, Cambridge, Massachusetts, and London, 2005.

Perry-Ayscough, Henry George Charles, and Robert Bruare Otter-Barry, *With the Russians in Mongolia*, John Lane/Bodley Head, London, 1914.

Petrov, Victor P., *Mongolia: A Profile*, Pall Mall Press, London, 1970.

Piasetsky, Pavel Ivakvolech, *Russian Travellers in Mongolia and China*, translated by J. Gordon-Cummings, Chapman & Hall, London, 1884.

Pokotilov, Dmirtii, *History of the Eastern Mongols During the Ming Dynasty from 1368 to 1634*, translated by Rudolf Lowenthal, West China University Press, Chengdu, China, 1947–1949.

Polmar, Norman, and Thomas B. Allen, *Spy Book: The Encyclopedia of Espionage*, Random House, New York, 1997.

Polo, Marco, *The Travels of Marco Polo: The Complete Yule-Cordier Edition*, Dover Press, Mineola, New York, 1993.

Popov, Vladimir, *Steel and Slag*, Foreign Language Publishing House, Moscow, 1948.

Poppe, Nicholas, *The Heroic Epic of the Khalkha Mongols*, Mongolia Society, Bloomington, 1979.

Poppe, Nicholas, *Reminiscences*, Western Washington University, Bellingham, Washington, 1983.

Poussielgue, Achille, *Voyage en Chine et en Mongolie de M. de Bourboulon, ministre de France, et de Madame de Bourboulon 1860–1861*, Librairie L. Hachette et Cie, Paris, 1866.

Powers, John, *Introduction to Tibetan Buddhism*, Snow Lion Publications, Ithaca, 1995.

Pozdneyev, A. M., *Mongolia and the Mongols Volumes I and II*, edited by John R. Krueger, Mongol Society, Bloomington, Indiana, 1977; reprinted by Curzon Press, Richmond, Surrey, United Kingdom, 1997.

Pozdneyev, A. M., *Religion and Ritual in Society: Lamaist Buddhism in Later 19th Century Mongolia*, edited by John R. Krueger, Mongol Society, Bloomington, 1978.

Prawdin, Michael, *The Mongol Empire: Its Rise and Legacy*, translated by Eden and Cedar Paul, George Allen and Unwin, London, 1940.

Price, Julius M., *From the Arctic Ocean to the Yellow Sea: The Narrative of a Journey, in 1890–91, Across Siberia, Mongolia, the Gobi Desert and North China*, Sampson Low, Marston & Co., London, 1892.

Pringle, James, 'Guest Traveller's Tales', *Far Eastern Economic Review*, 31 August 1989, 33.

Prosek, James, *Fly-Fishing the 41st: Around the World on the 41st Parallel*, HarperCollins, New York, 2003.

Przhevalskii, Nikolai Mikhailovich, *Mongolia, The Tangut Country and the Solitudes of Northern Tibet*, translated by E. Delmer Morgan, S. Low, Marston, Searle and Rivington, London, 1876.

Purev, Otgony, and Gurbadaryn Purvee, *Mongolian Shamanism*, Ulaanbaatar, 2007.

Ramstedt, Gustaf John, *Seven Journeys Eastward 1898–1912 Among the Cheremis, Kalmyks, Mongols and in Turkestan and to Afghanistan*, translated by John R. Krueger, Mongolia Society, Bloomington, Indiana, 1978.

Rees, Helen, *Echoes of History: Naxi Music in Modern China*, Oxford University Press, Oxford, 2000.

Riasanovsky, V. A., *Fundamental Principles of Mongol Law*, Indiana University Publications, Bloomington, 1965.

Riasanovsky, V. A., 'Mongol Law—A Concise Historical Survey', 23 Wash. L. Rev. & St. B. J. (1948), 166–78.

Richardson, Hugh, *Ceremonies of the Lhasa Year*, Serindia Publications, London, 1993.

Roberts, James Hudson, *A Flight for Life and an Inside Look of Mongolia*, Pilgrim Press, Chicago, 1903.

Robinson, Carl, *Mongolia: Nomad Empire of Eternal Blue Sky*, Odyssey Books and Guide, Hong Kong, 2010.

Rockhill, William Woodville, *The Land of the Lamas: Notes of a Journey through China, Mongolia and Tibet*, Century Company, New York, 1891.

Roerich, George N., *Trails to Inmost Asia: Five Years of Exploration with the Roerich Central Asian Expedition*, Bookfaith India, Delhi, 1996.

Roerich, Nicholas, *Altai-Himalaya: A Travel Diary*, Book Faith India, Delhi, 1996.

Ross, E. Dennison, 'The Tonyukuk Inscription: Being a Translation of Professor Vilhelm Thomsen's Final Danish Rendering', *Bulletin of the School of Oriental Studies*, Vol. 6, No. 1, 1930, 37–43.

Rossabi, Morris, *Kubilai Khan: His Life and Times*, University of California Press, Berkeley and Los Angeles, London, 1988.

Rossabi, Morris, *Modern Mongolia: From Khans to Commissars to Capitalists*, University of California Press, Berkeley, Los Angeles, London, 2005.

Rubruck, William van, *The Journey of William of Rubruck to the Eastern Parts of the World 1253–55*, translated by William Woodville Rockhill, Hakluyt Society, Washington, DC, 1900.

Rupen, Robert A., 'The City of Urga in the Manchu Period', *Studia Altaica: Festshrift für Nikolaus Poppe*, Otto Harrassowitz, Wiesbaden, 1957.

Rupen, Robert A., *How Mongolia Is Really Ruled: A Political History of the Mongolian People's Republic 1900–1978*, Hoover Institution Press, Stanford, California, 1979.

Rupen, Robert A., *Mongols of the Twentieth Century*, Indiana University Publications, Bloomington, 1964.

Rupen, Robert A., *The Mongolian People's Republic*, Hoover Institutions on War, Revolution and Peace, Stanford, California, 1966.

Sabloff, Paula L., ed., *Modern Mongolia: Reclaiming Genghis Khan*, University of Pennsylvania Museum of Archaeology and Anthropology, Philadelphia, 2001.

Sambuu, Jamsrangiin, *Herdsman to Statesman: The Autobiography of Jamsrangiin Sambuu of Mongolia*, translated by Mary Rossabi, Rowman & Littlefield, Lanham, Maryland, 2010.

Sanders, Alan J. K., *Historical Dictionary of Mongolia*, Scare Crow Press, Lanham, Maryland and London, 1996.

Sanjdorj, M., *Manchu Chinese Colonial Rule in Northern Mongolia*, translated by Urgunge Onon, C. Hurst & Company, London, 1980.

Sarangerel, *Chosen by the Spirits: Following Your Shamanic Calling*, Destiny Books, Rochester, Vermont, 2001.

Sarközi, Alice, *Political Prophecies in Mongolia in the 17th–20th Centuries*, Otto Harrassowitz, Wiesbaden, 1992.

Schaik, Sam van, *Tibet: A History*, Yale University Press, New Haven and London, 2011.

Sebes, Joseph S. J., *The Jesuits and the Sino-Russian Treaty of Nerchinsk (1689): The Diary of Thomas Pereira, S.J.*, Institutum Historicum Societatis Iesu, Rome, 1961.

Severin, Tim, *In Search of Genghis Khan*, Collier Books, New York, 1991.

Shapiro, Henry, 'Pranksters Overseas May End Up in Jail', *Independent Star News*, Pasadena, California, 8 July 1967.

Sheepshanks, John, Bishop of Norwich, *My Life in Mongolia and Siberia: From the Great Wall of China to the Ural Mountains*, Society for Promoting Christian Knowledge, London, 1903.

Sinor, Denis, 'The Establishment and Dissolution of the Türk Empire', *The Cambridge History of Early Inner Asia*, edited by Denis Sinor, Cambridge University Press, Cambridge, 1990, 285–316.

Smith, Donald E., *Ducks, Yaks and Camels and the Vast Mongolian Sky, Oh My!*, AuthorHouse, Bloomington, 2009.

Snellgrove, David L., and Hugh Richardson, *A Cultural History of Tibet*, Orchid Press, Bangkok, 2003.

Spuler, Bertold, *History of the Mongols Based on Eastern and Western Accounts of the Thirteenth and Fourteenth Centuries*, translated by Helga and Stuart Drummond, Dorset Press, New York, 1988.

Starr, S. Frederick, *Red and Hot: The Fate of Jazz in the Soviet Union 1917–1980*, Oxford University Press, Oxford and New York, 1983.

State Printing Office, *Mongolia through Camera Lens*, State Printing Office, Ulaanbaatar, 1976.

Stewart, Stanley, *In the Empire of Genghis Khan: A Journey among Nomads*, Lyons Press, Guilford, Connecticut, 2002.

Stone, I. F., *The Trial of Socrates*, Little, Brown and Company, Boston and Toronto, 1988.

Storey, Robert, *Mongolia: A Travel Survival Kit*, Lonely Planet Publications, London, 1993.

Strasser, Roland, *The Mongolian Horde*, translated by R. T. G., Jonathan Cape & Harrison Smith, New York, 1930.

Strauss, Robert, *Trans-Siberian Rail Guide*, Bradt Publication, Bucks, United Kingdom, 1987.

Ssu-ma Ch'ien, *Records of the Grand Historian of China*, Vol. 2, translated by Burton Watson, Columbia University Press, New York, and Chinese University Press, Hong Kong, 1993.

Swoboda, Edi, *Mongolia Land of Nomads*, privately published, Hong Kong, 2005.

Sydney Morning Herald, 'Dinosaur Egg Stolen', 27 March 1957.

Teleki, Krisztina, 'Bogdiin Khüree: Monasteries and Temples of the Mongolian Capital (1651–1938)', PhD thesis, 2008.

Teleki, Krisztina, *Introduction to the Study of Urga's Heritage*, Admon Print, Ulaanbaatar, 2015.

Terzani, Tiziano, *A Fortune Teller Told Me: Earthbound Travels in the Far East*, HarperCollins, London, 1997.

Theroux, Paul, *Riding the Iron Rooster: By Train through China*, G. P. Putnam's Sons, New York, 1988.

Timkowskii, George, *Travels of the Russian Mission through Mongolia to China and a Residence in Peking*, translated by H. E. Lloyd, Longman Rees, Orme, Brown and Green, London, 1827.

Tolme, Andre, *I Golfed across Mongolia: How an Improbable Adventure Helped Me Rediscover the Spirit of Golf (and Life)*, Thunder's Mouth Press, New York, 2006.

Tseden-Ish, B., *From the History of the Formation of Mongolian Borders*, Sodpress, Ulaanbaatar, 2003.

Tserendulam, G., *P. Genden: To the Memory of My Father*, Ulaanbaatar, 2000.

Tsultem, N., *Mongolian Architecture*, State Publishing House, Ulan Bator, 1988.

Tsultemin, Uranchimeg, 'The Power and Authority of Maitreya in Mongolia Examined through Mongolian Art', *Buddhism in Mongolian History, Culture and Society*, edited by Vesna A. Wallace, Oxford University Press, Oxford and New York, 2015, 137–59.

Tucci, Giuseppe, *The Religions of Tibet*, New Age Books, New Delhi, 2011.

Tung, Rosemary Jones, *A Portrait of Lost Tibet*, Holt, Rinehart, and Winston, New York, 1980.

Turbat, Tsaangan et al., *Deer Stones of the Jargaltyn Am*, Nomkhur Printing, Ulaanbaatar: n.d. [2011].

United States Department of War, 'Economic Potential for War: Outer Mongolia', Industrial College of the Armed Forces, 7 November 1947.

USSR Academy of Sciences and MPR Academy of Sciences, *A History of the Mongolian People's Republic*, University of Press of the Pacific, Honolulu, 2000.

Visser, Marinus Willem de, *The Dragon in China and Japan*, J. Muller, Amsterdam, 1913.

Waddell, L. Austine, *Lhasa and Its Mysteries*, John Murray, London 1905.

Waddell, L. Austine, *Tibetan Buddhism: With Its Mystic Cults, Symbolism and Mythology, and in Its Relation to Indian Buddhism*, Dover Publications, Mineola, New York, 1972.

Wallace, Vesna A., editor, *Buddhism in Mongolian History, Culture and Society*, Oxford University Press, Oxford and New York, 2015.

Wallace, Vesna A., 'Buddhist Sacred Mountains, Auspicious Landscapes, and Their Agency', *Buddhism in Mongolian History, Culture and Society*, edited by Vesna A. Wallace, 221–40.

Wallace, Vesna A., 'What Do Protective Deities, Mongolian Heroes, and Fast Steeds Have in Common?' *Buddhism in Mongolian History, Culture and Society*, edited by Vesna A. Wallace, 202–20.

Watt, James C. Y., *The World of Khubilai Khan: Chinese Art in the Yuan Dynasty*, Metropolitan Museum of Art, New York, and Yale University Press, New Haven and London, 2010.

Waugh, Louisa, *Hearing Birds Fly: A Nomadic Year in Mongolia*, Abacus, London, 2007.

Weatherford, Jack, *Genghis Khan and the Making of the Modern World*, Crown Publishers, New York, 2004.

Weatherford, Jack, *Genghis Khan and the Quest for God: How the World's Greatest Conqueror Gave Us Religious Freedom*, Viking, New York, 2016.

Weatherford, Jack, *The Secret History of the Mongol Queens: How the Daughters of Genghis Khan Rescued His Empire*, Crown Publishers, New York, 2010.

Wickham-Smith, Simon, 'A Literary History of Buddhism in Mongolia', *Buddhism in Mongolian History, Culture and Society*, edited by Vesna A. Wallace, Oxford University Press, Oxford and New York, 2015,160–78.

Wickham-Smith, Simon, and Tsog Shagdarsuren, *An Anthology of Mongolian Literature*, Academy of Culture and Poetry, Ulaanbaatar, 2008.

Williams, C. A. S., *Outlines of Chinese Symbolism and Art Motives*, Caves Books, Taipei, 1983.

Williamson, Alexander, *Journeys in North China, Manchuria and Eastern Mongolia*, Smith Elder & Co., London, 1870.

Windt, H. de, *From Peking to Calais by Land*, Chapman and Hall, London, 1892.

Wolff, Serge M., 'Mongol Delegations in Western Europe, 1925–1929', *Journal of the Royal Central Asian Society*, Vol. 32, Nos. 3–4, 1945, 289–98.

Zamcarano, C. Z., *The Mongol Chronicles of the Seventeenth Century*, translated by Rudolf Loewenthal and Otto Harrassowitz, Wiesbaden, 1955.

Znamenski, Andrei, *Red Shambhala: Magic, Prophecy and Geopolitics in the Heart of Asia*, Theosophical Publishing House, Wheaton, Illinois, and Chennai, India, 2011.

Index

Abatai Khan, 11, 89, 97, 177
Academy of Sciences, 122, 123, 197
Adi-Buddha, 55, 166, 251
Aglag Buteelin Monastery, 248
Agvaankhaidav, 90
Agvanbaldan, 168
aimag, 10, 13, 14, 91, 92, 97, 140, 142, 234, 247, 250
Akshobya, 55
'All Powerful Ten', 252
Altai Hotel (former), 109
altan gadas, 42
Altan Khan, 10, 11, 57
Altan-Orgil National Cemetery, 108, 233
American Hill, 185
Amitabha, 55, 218
Amoghassiddhi, 55, 56, 94
Ananda, 46
Andrews, Roy Chapman, 147–49, 168, 171
Angkhan Burkhan. *See* Adi-Buddha
archery, 225, 226, 228
architectural styles, 63–79
  'brutalist', 34, 129, 192
  constructivist, 73, 75, 77, 78, 118, 192, 193, 198
  futurism, 73
  individual construction, 79, 128, 136, 147
  modernist, 78
  neoclassicism, 7, 78
  rationalism, 78
  Siberian log cabin, 73
  temple architecture and decorations, 65–73
Ard Cinema, 78
arkhi, xviii, 110, 117, 179
Aryaval Meditation and Initiation Centre, 241
Asokha, 70
Assembly of White Stupas, 161
'A Story of Cars', 118
automobiles, 118–20
autonomous period; 22, 23, 30, 108, 143, 145, 151, 201, 217, 226, 234, 237
  atmosphere in Urga upon proclamation, 22–23
  proclamation ceremony, 96–97
  renunciation, 97–98
Avalokitesvara, 56, 88, 163, 171, 218, 235
Avdar Bayan Mountain, 244
Ayush, 133, 166, 171, 173, 207, 218

Baabar (historian and commentator), 233
Badamjan, Tsogt Garmaevich, 183
bagana, 65, 71, 170, 175
Baga Toiru Street, 78
bagsh, 45, 45n10
Baikal International Airport, 247
Bakula Rinpoche (Nineteenth), 169, 178
balbal, 113, 233
Baldanchoimbol, 131, 133, 221
Baldan Lkham, 57, 84, 133, 170
bandi, 45, 45n10, 60
Barkhor, 92
Baruun Road, 147
Batmonkh, Jambyin, 35, 104, 158
Bat-Ohiruyn Eldev Children's Cinema (former), 78, 110, 120
Bawden, Charles, ix

Bayangol Hotel, 92, 128, 162
Bayanzurh Mountain, 133, 249
'beads' (architectural decoration), 71
'Beatles Square', 76, 152
Becker, Jasper, 35
Bell, John, 15
beverage, Mongolian, xviii, 154
Bierce, Ambrose, xi, 233n3
Bira, Shagdaryn, 197
'Birthday Man', 129, 162–63
'Blue Chronicle', 18
Blue Sky Tower and Hotel, 111
bö, 43, 58
bodhisattva, 42, 50, 53–57, 155
Bodio, Steve, 38
Bogd Khan, 22, 26, 27, 32, 59, 86, 84, 85, 96, 97, 115, 116, 118, 157, 168, 214, 216–21, 224, 250
Bogd Uul. *See* Holy Mountain
Bo'orchu, 108
Boucher, Guillaume, 112
Boudhanath, 161, 235
Bragriin Gegeen, 168
Brezhnev, Leonid, 34, 79, 104, 124, 156, 191
British Embassy, 114, 184
Brown Palace, 221, 223
Budai, 42
Buddha
  meaning of, 48
  Shakyamuni Buddha, 49, 50, 54, 55, 58, 69–72, 84, 89, 96, 132–33, 160, 165–66, 171, 178, 207, 213, 218, 223, 225, 235, 239, 241
  Tathagata Buddhas, 55–56, 84, 90
Builders' Square, 145
bunkhan, 232
Buryat quarter, 151
Bu-ton Rinche Drup, 53
buuz, xvii
Buyannemekh, S., 103, 118
'by-pass capitalism', 26, 30

Café Bear Cub, 78, 120
Cathedral of Saints Peter and Paul, 229, 231
Central Pharmacy (former), 145
Central Square, 85, 86, 95, 97, 107
Central Tower, 104, 109
Centre of Geophysics, 192
Centre of Shaman and Eternal Heaven Sophistication, 175
Chandra, Lokesh, 123
Chiang Kai-shek, 162, 214, 225
Children's Centre, 129
Children's Park, 115, 120, 127, 129
Chimed, B., 124
chimeglel luu. See *zhiwen*
'Chinatown', 4, 16, 20, 141, 183, 204–8
Chinese cemetery, 205
Chingeltei Mountain, 234
Chinggis Khan, xviii, 9, 25, 41, 56, 99, 100, 108–9, 158, 163, 175, 199, 209, 226, 240, 242, 249, 250
Chinggis Khan International Airport, 247
Chinggis Khan Square, 99
Chinggis Khan Statue Complex, 240
Chinggünjav, 16, 16n11
Choibalsan, Khorloogiin, xvi, 23n29, 25, 30–31, 58n36, 59, 89, 102–4, 107–8, 115, 116, 121, 124, 158, 198, 223, 225–26, 233, 234, 245, 251
choijin. See *dharmapala*
Choimbol, S., 109
citipati, 58, 95, 96
College (Buddhist monastic centres of study)
  College of Aeon of Great Bliss, 171
  College of Esoteric Knowledge, 173
  College of Medicinal Buddha, 173–74
  College of Rejoicing, 169
  College of the Teaching Holder's Happy Heart, 170
  College to Spread Auspiciousness, 169
Colvin, John, 34, 182, 183–85
Communal Apartment Building District, 34
Consulate Group, 25
Consulate Hill, 6, 181, 186, 190, 191, 193, 197, 198
Council of Shamans, 44
Customs Street, 205

dagina, 58, 84, 97, 218
Dalai Lama, 11–14, 16, 46, 53, 57, 59, 89, 131, 135, 168, 176, 219

Fifth, 95, 132, 134, 156
Fourteenth, 59, 60, 135, 162, 163, 169, 171, 173, 178
Thirteenth, 135, 150, 156, 167, 168, 178, 180
Da Lama, 23, 46
Dalkh Hill, 160, 169
Dambijantsan, 54
Damdin. *See* Hayagriva
Damdinsuren, 126, 127n12, 168, 197
Damdinsüren, Bilgerinin, 102
Damdinsuren, Prince, 108
danshig, 225–26
Danzan, 120
Danzanravjaa, 18, 125–26, 127n12, 152
Dark Old Man, 41, 133
dartsug, 58
Dashcholin Monastery of Eastern Monastic Settlement, 83–85
datsan, 17, 92, 145, 162, 169–71, 173–75, 177–78, 247. *See also* college for specific datsans
Da Vinci, Leonardo, 14
dayanchi, 47
Dechingalav Temple, 88
deer (as architectural decoration), 48, 69
Deer Park, 48, 69, 73, 96. *See also* Sarnath
del, 229
Demchengevi, 133
Deng Xiaoping, 35
De Windt, Harry, 188
dharmapala, 52, 54, 56, 57, 84, 95, 130, 131, 133, 134
Didanpovran, 167
divination, 42, 58, 61, 68
dogshid, 56
Dolmalin Khiid, 206
Doloon Nuur, 13, 90, 171
Dongogdulam, 84, 97
Dorzhiev, Agvan, 167, 196
Douglas, William O., 116–17, 240
dougong, 67, 206, 215
Drakpa Geltsen, 134–35
Duan Qirui, 24, 98
Eastern Monastic Settlement, 4, 83–98, 107, 160, 163, 171, 173, 177, 188, 214
East Khüree Group, 25
Eight Immortals, 132
Eight Treasures, 70, 163, 173
Eisenstein, Sergei, 140, 198
Elbegdorj (former president), 99
Enkh, Joseph, 231
Enkhbayar, Nambaryn, 108
Enkhem Tonni Aimag, 84
Erdene Zuu Khiid, 11
Erling Khan. *See* Yama
espionage, 56, 122, 144, 182, 212, 237, 248
Eternal Sky, 41, 55, 63
Etügen Ükh, 41
Europa Restaurant, 73
Exhibition Hall, 79, 129

feng shui, 66
Filatova, Anastasia Ivanovna, 124
Fire Deity, 136–37
food, Mongolian, xvi–xviii, 154
Foster, Stephen, 102
'Four Friends', 185
Fraser, George MacDonald, 187
funerary customs, 20, 232–33

Galdan Boshogtu Khan, 12–13, 13n7, 168
Gandanchoinkhorin Aimag, 84
Gandantegchenlin Monastery, 59, 60, 66, 68, 72, 79, 89, 126, 160–75, 177
Ganesh, 219
ganjir, 79, 171, 189, 215
Garden Park, 112, 115
Gate of Excellent Scholarship, 166
Gate of Settled Peace, 215–17
Gautama, Siddhartha, 48, 51
Gavaa, 'Bonehead', 104
gazriin ezen, 41
Gelata, Joseph, 100
gelen, 45, 47
Gelukpa, 52–54, 57, 125, 134, 135, 155, 160, 166, 169, 175, 178, 179, 181, 217
Genden, Peljidiin, 137–38
General Intelligence Agency, 139
General Post Office, 111

ger, 63–65
Geser (King), 176–77, 183, 205
getsül, 45
Gilliam, Terry, 8
Gilmour, James, 152n18
Ginzburg, Moisei, 75, 77, 79, 125, 129
Gobi Desert, viii, ix, 9n2, 12, 15, 48, 112, 148, 152n18, 188, 199, 242, 248
God of Longevity, 42
gokhon, 65
'golden nail', 42
Government House, 32, 99, 101, 107, 108, 112, 115, 116, 158, 202, 226, 242
Grand Khan Irish Pub, 120
Great Purge, 30–31, 59, 61, 78, 83, 102, 111, 123, 138, 149, 158, 160, 162, 167, 177, 199, 234, 239, 245, 250, 252
Great State Seal of Mongolia Monument, 115
Green Domed Theatre, 77, 100, 101, 103, 104, 237, 245
Green House, 188
Green Palace, 97, 214, 215, 217–18, 221
Green Tara, 56
Guan Gong Di, 176
Guan Yin, 177, 206
Gürragchaa, Jügderdemidiin, 104, 185

Haslund, Henning, viii–ix, 29
Hata, Prince, 166
Hayagriva, 58, 96
Herodotus, x
Hessig, Walther, 125
Hibbert, Ann, 127
Hibbert, Reginald, 33, 114, 152
Hisao, Kimura, 182
Hollow of the Stone Man, 113
Holy Mountain, viii, 9, 41, 132, 249–52
'Hong Gil-Dong', 110
'horse-head fiddle'. See *morin huur*
horse-racing, 225, 228
Hunnu-Syanbi runic symbols, 116

Ignatieff, Nikolay Pavlovich, 187
Ikh Daginiin Aimag, 84
Ikh Tenger, 223–24
Independence Palace, 114
Indra's Knot, 71
Injannashi, 18
Inner Mongolia, viii, 10, 12, 13, 30, 31, 121, 144, 167, 179, 181, 182, 199, 210, 231
International Buddha Park, 223
Irkutsk and Baikal Clerical Missions, 189
Islamic Centre of Ulaanbaatar, 213–14

Jagarmolom, 155, 215
Jagarmolomiin Khural, 155
jaltsan, 70
Jambal Namdo Choiji, 59
Jamsran, 26, 42, 57, 71, 84, 89, 96, 116, 117, 132, 133, 237
Jamsranjav, Dilov Khutugtu, 237
Jamstrano, Tseyeben, 22–23, 108
Japan, 21, 24, 30, 31, 111, 112, 113, 167, 181–83, 199
Japanese Embassy, 181
Jarankhasar, 161, 235
Jarg Street, 213
jasaa, 60, 84, 163, 213
javdan, 69
Jebzundamba Khutugtu, 4, 11, 22, 46, 59, 98
Jigjid. *See* Yamantaka
Jigjidjav Street, 78, 139, 140
John of Montecorvino, 230
Johns Hopkins University, 121–22
Jokhang Temple, 67, 90
'Journey into Hell', 125
Jügder, 85
Juulchin Street, 140

Kadampa, 52
Kagyü, 52, 53, 156, 213
Kalachakra, 53, 54, 59, 88, 133, 135, 150, 162, 169, 171, 242, 251, 252
Kalgan, viii, 9n2, 184, 231
Kangxi Emperor, 13, 14, 133, 207, 210
Kanjur, 53, 57, 89, 166, 168
karma, 48, 71, 86
khadag, 58–59, 103, 169, 170, 179, 207, 208, 217, 224, 238, 245, 252

Khalkha, 4, 9, 10, 12–17, 31, 46, 47, 88–89, 91, 139, 157, 204, 219, 225, 226, 229, 242
khamba, 46
Khandadorj, Prince, 156–58, 171
Khandadorj Palace, 156
Khangarid, 9, 41, 115, 132, 133, 169, 226
khanjid. See *dagina*
Kharakhorum, 11, 63, 112, 113, 229
khasaa, 78, 90–92, 108, 252
Khishigt, A., 124
Khön, 52
khoshun, 13
Khrushchev, Nikita, 78, 124, 214, 245
khüree, 4, 14, 17, 19, 234
Khüree Market (former site), 102, 140, 141–45, 154, 229
khushur, xvii, 142
khutugtu, 14, 17, 53
Kiakhta, 9n2, 123, 138, 152
King Geser Temple, 174, 176, 178
King Lear, 127
Kirghiz, 242
kirtimukha, 69
Knox, Thomas, 19, 21, 94, 210
Kojima (early twentieth-century Japanese physician), 181, 234
Kozel, Gerhard, 109
Kublai Khan, 10, 112, 230
kumis, ix, 110, 112, 179, 225, 228

'La Banniere Bleue', 22
lama, 49
Larson, Franz, 219–20
Lattimore, Owen, 31, 33, 40, 46, 114, 118, 120–22, 162, 184–85, 212, 237
Lazarist Order, 231
Leeds University, 122
Lenin, Vladimir, 25–27, 35, 73, 115, 140, 145, 147, 198, 240, 241
Lenin Club (former), 77, 111
Lenin Museum (former), 79, 147, 149
'Level 70', 232
Lhamsuren, 'Horsehead', 124
Library (at Gandan), 168
'Life History of the Moon Cuckoo', 126, 168
Ligdan Khan, 115
Li Hongzhang, 200
Lingkhor, 92
lion, 70, 73, 85, 108, 114, 132, 134, 163, 183, 207, 234
Lion Bridge, 142, 183
lion throne, 72, 89–90
'Living Buddha', 14, 144, 220
Lkhagavasuren, Jamyangiin, 31
Lokecvara, 235
Lonchen Shatra, 151
Lotchin (travel guide for Rene MacColl), 134, 184
Lotus Yoga College, 177
Lu Ban, 205
Luvsankhaidav, 131–32
Luvsanpeljee, 131–32

MacColl, Rene, 33, 134, 183, 184, 240
Machik Labdrön, 155–56
Magsarjav, Sandagdorjiin, 23, 25
Magsarjav Street, 213
Mahabharata, 9
Mahalaka, 57, 84, 133
Maharajas of the Four Directions, 58, 66, 84, 132, 217
Mahatma Gandhi Street, 224
Mahayana Buddhism, 49–50, 60, 63, 156, 182, 207
Maher, Kavel, 108
Ma Ho-T'ien, 27, 207
Maidar. *See* Maitreya
maikhan, 65, 228
Maimachin, 4, 140, 204–8
Maitreya, 27, 55, 56, 84, 90, 94, 96, 133, 141, 196, 219
Maitreya festival in Urga, 94–96
Management Academy, 221
Manchukuo, 31, 182, 196
Manchus, 11–17, 22, 24, 114, 156, 157, 176, 219, 230
Manjusri, 16, 56, 57, 88, 235, 245, 250, 252
Manla, 55, 173, 174
Manthose, 67
Manzhouli, 210
Mao Zedong, 34, 206, 214

Mara, 23
Marshall Zhukov Museum, 193
'Massive White' (early twentieth-century prison), 185
'Massive White' (main assembly hall), 89
McCarthy, Joseph, 121
'Meat City', 154
Méliès, George, 83
Memorial Museum for Victims of Political Repression, 137–38
Mercury Market, 154
Mergen Lama (Third), 179
Merry Pranksters, 132
MIAT, 247
Michie, Alexander, 234–35
microdistricts, 6, 79, 192, 206
Milarepa, 237
Military Museum, 192
mining, 156, 200–201
Ministry of Animal Husbandry and Crops (former), 118
Ministry of Defence, 158, 202
Ministry of Foreign Affairs, 112, 115
'mirrors' (as architectural decoration), 71
Monastery of Great Tara, 206
Monastery of Manjusri, 245
Monastery of Spreading and Flourishing of the Teaching, 234
Monastery of Theory and Practice, 237
Möngke Tenger, 41, 217
MongolBank, 140
Mongolian Cooperative Centre, 29
Mongolian Institute for Buddhist Art, 173
Mongolian National Gallery of Modern Art, 108
Mongolian People's Party (or MPP), 24–26, 99, 114, 115, 118, 140, 183
Mongolian People's Republic (or MPR), 3, 26–31, 34, 35, 77, 78, 85, 98, 00, 100, 105, 111, 116, 118, 128, 132, 137, 138, 145, 149, 162, 172, 178, 182, 184, 186, 187, 196, 203, 223, 226, 232, 240, 250
Mongolian People's Revolutionary Party (or MPRP), 26, 26n35, 27–31, 35, 102, 114, 124, 137, 250
Mongolian Stock Exchange, 110
Mongolian Theatre Museum, 108
MongolKino, 198, 200
Mongolor Stock Company, 200–202
Montagu, Ivor, 32, 110
Montsame News Agency Building (former), 118
Monument to Mongolian Ard Air Squadron, 203
Monument to Mongolian Referendum on Independence, 224–25
morin huur, 127–29, 145
Mostaert, Antoine, 231
Mother Earth, 41
Mother Rock, 244–45
Mount Meru, 58, 67, 166
Munkhjargal, Fr. (early twentieth-century Roman Catholic priest), 231
Muqali, 108
Museum of Bogd Khan, 68, 214
Museum of History of Mongolia, 139
Museum of Natural History, 85, 147–48
musical instruments
  limbö, 128
  morin huur, 127–29
  Tibetan liturgical, 128
  yatga, 129
  yoochin, 128
'My Homeland', 101

Naadam Festival, 86, 104, 223–28
Naestegard, Ola, 197
naga, 56, 58, 67, 207, 239
Nagarjuna, 46
Narantuul Market, 229
Narnii Road, 214, 229
National Academic Theatre of Opera and Ballet, 109
National Pedagogical University, 115
National Sports Stadium, 225
natsagdorj. *See* 'double-vajra'
Natsagdorj, Dasdorijiin, 101–2, 115
Nechung (oracle), 131, 133
Nicholas II, 215
'nine whites', 92, 249
norbu, 58
'Not I', 101–2

Noyin Khutugtu Lama, 125
No. 1 High School, 158
Nyamsuren (poet), 42
Nyingma, 52, 125, 155

Ochirdara. *See* Vajradhara
Office of Telecommunications and Postal Services, 110, 112
Ogedei Khan, 108
'Old Fiddler', 145
Old Man of the South Pole, 42
Ollen, Gerda, 198
Olympic Street, 137
'One Day in the Life of Mongolia', 145
ongon, 41–42, 44, 70
Ordos, 10, 11, 231
Örgöö, 3, 14
Orkhon runic script, 242
O'Rouke, P. J., 34
Otochi. *See* Manla
ovoo, 59, 179–80

Padilla, Wenceslas, 231
Padmasambhava, 51–52, 130, 131, 133, 155, 173, 177, 213, 236
Palace of Blissful Emptiness. *See* Didanpovran
Palace of Coolness, 235
Panchen Lama, 14, 16, 90, 168, 181, 219
parinirvana, 49–50, 55, 160
Parnakowyz, Feodor, 193–95
Patriarch
  Eighth, 18n14, 22, 85, 96, 96, 97, 131, 145, 150, 156, 157, 167, 168, 170, 171, 180, 183, 214, 215, 221, 237
  Fifth, 90, 141, 160, 166, 167, 169, 234
  First, 133, 166
  Ninth, 59, 171, 173
  Second, 14, 16, 84, 88, 169, 173, 177, 234, 245
  Seventh, 18n14, 166
  Sixth, 18n14, 160
  Third, 17, 88
  Tenth, 60
Peace Avenue, 76, 111, 112, 114, 145, 152, 183, 184, 193, 195, 198, 202, 203, 213
Peace Bridge, 75, 76, 183, 214, 215
Peking cart, 93, 190
Peking shops, 141–42
People's Cinema (former), 140
Peter the Great, 210
Pethub Stangey Choskhor Monastery, 178
Phakyepo, 67
Poe, Edgar Allan, 102
Polar Star, xiii, 42
Polo, Marco, 19n19, 112, 154
poplar, 208
Porter, Bill, 175
Pozdneyev, Aleksei, 21, 89
Prajnaparamita Sutra, 50, 54, 83, 171
prayer wheels, 70, 85, 163, 166, 170, 173
Presidential Mansion, 158
Prince's Aimag, 83
'Prince Sando', 101
prostitution, 18, 143
protective deity. See *sakhiu*
Przhevalskii, Nikolai, 93
Public Retail Store No. 8 (former), 116
Puntsoglin Monastery, 66, 213

Qianlong Emperor, 13, 16, 17, 47, 206, 234

Rahu, 69
Railway Museum, 214
Ramstedt, Gustav John, 21, 23, 157–58, 190, 244
Rashaant, 238–39
Ratna, 252
Ratna Sambhava, 55
Red Army, ix, 25, 30, 98, 104, 204
'red food', 154
'Red Hat' Buddhism, 52, 134, 205, 213
'Red Hero', 9, 26
Red Hill, 204
Remington, Frederic, 113
Residential Microdistricts Nos. 12 and 15, 192
Revolutionary Youth League, 29, 124
rhubarb, 15
Rinchen, Byambyn, 122–24, 197, 198, 251–52
Roerich, George, 151

Roerich, Nicholas, 195–97
Roerich Museum, 195, 197, 198
Roman Catholicism, 56, 229–31
Roosevelt, Franklin D., 162, 196, 224–25
Rowling, J. K., 208
Russian Cemetery, 283
Russian Consulate (former), 73, 143, 183, 188–89, 216
Russian Orthodox Chapel (current), 194–95
Russian Orthodox Chapel (former), 73, 188, 191, 193
Russo-Asiatic Bank (former), 200

Sain Noyon Aimag, 10
Saint Nicholas, 42
Saint Petersburg, 21, 111, 157, 167, 181, 187, 190, 195, 215
sakhiu, 68
Sakyapa Buddhism, 4, 52, 53
Sambuu, Jamsranglin, 23, 117
samsara, 48, 70, 207
Samye Monastery, 52, 131
Sandag, 'Khuulich', 19
Sando, Amban, 101, 142, 170, 183
sangha, 46, 49, 97, 131, 179, 185
Sansar Tunnel, 185
Sarnath, 48, 69, 96
Sato, Eisaku, 182
scapulimancy, 43, 58, 61
Scheut Missions—CICM, 231
'scientific socialism', 73
Secondary School No. 40, 34
Second Maternity Hospital, 155, 213
'Second Turning of the Wheel', 50
Second World War, 31, 103, 121, 192, 199, 211
Selbe River, 9, 183
Senggerinchen, Prince, 18n14
Seoul Street, 115, 152, 155, 156, 158
Seven Old Men, 42
'Seventy-Year-Old Woman and the Seven-Year-Old-Boy Scout', 103
shabi, 19
Shabolovka Radio Tower, 75
shamanism, 12, 44, 59, 123, 175, 214
Shambhala, 26, 27, 53, 55, 56, 195, 196
Shanxi stores, 142
Sharav, Marzan, 145
Sheepshanks, John, 21
Shine Toli, 22, 108
shireetü, 46
Shiva, 50, 69, 79, 235
Shugden, 131–35
Shugden Controversy, 134–36
Shukov, Vladimir, 75
Siberia, 6, 9, 25, 27, 30, 43, 57, 73, 88, 121, 141, 143, 147, 162, 177, 178, 183, 184, 188, 190, 192, 196, 210, 221, 234, 253
Siberian window frames, 73
Sonam Gyatso, 10, 11
song
  long song, 128
  short song, 128
  throat singing, 128, 162, 183n3
Songgino Mountain, 41
Songtsen Gampo, 51
sor, 71, 166
Soviet Union, 27, 28, 29, 30, 31, 32, 34, 35, 73, 75, 78, 107, 144, 149, 172, 182, 185, 191, 211
soyombo, xviii, 223, 248, 250–52
Spathary, Nikolai, 209–11
spirit screen. See *yampai*
Sridevi, 57, 84
Ssu Ma-Chien, x
Stalin, Joseph, 22, 25, 29, 30, 31, 32, 38, 58, 59, 78, 116, 122, 123, 124, 137, 162, 198, 211, 214, 224
State Central Library, 120, 122
State Circus, 152
State Department Store, 145, 152
State Drama Theatre, 124, 125, 127
State Guest House (former), 240, 241
State Printing Press (former site), 79, 108, 123
State University of Mongolia, 78, 115, 116, 123
Steppe Inn, 184
'Storm from the East', 219
stupa, 67, 71, 72, 73, 84, 88, 133, 161, 166, 168, 171, 173, 232, 234, 235, 236, 237, 248, 251

suburgan. *See* stupa
Sükhbaatar, Damdiny, 25, 26, 89, 104, 105, 108, 115, 147, 158, 198, 223, 226, 233
Sükhbaatar Square, 78, 99–117, 129, 234
Sükhbaatar Street, 139
süld, 158, 175, 226
'summer oath-taking', 210
Summer Palace. *See* Brown Palace
Summer Palace (Peking), 132
'sun direction', 63, 170, 228, 245
Sun Yat-sen, 24
suutei tsai, 110, 186
svayambhu, 90, 251
Swedish Mongol Mission, 198

Tagore, Rabindrnath, 9
tanjur, 53, 237
Tantonjalbiin Khural, 155
Tara, 14, 56, 58, 84, 132, 177, 218
tarantass, 190
Tasgan Hill, 178–80
tea, 15, 15n10, 186, 187, 188
'Tears of the Reverend Lama', 102
telega, 190
Temple of Avalokitesvara, 66, 161, 171, 215, 253
Temple of Choijin Lama, 129, 130–32, 134, 135, 221
Temple of Disciples, 218
Temple of First Patriarch, 133
Temple of King of Naga Spirits (former), 239
Temple of Maharajas, 132
Temple of Maitreya, 90
Temple of Shakyamuni Buddha, 133, 166
Temple of Three Bodhisattvas, 88, 97
Temple of Tutelary Deity, 133
Terelj River Valley, 240
'Terrible Fourth', 17, 171
Terzani, Tizano, 61, 175
thangka, 63
Thang Tong Gyalpo, 213, 241
Theravada Buddhism, 49
Theroux, Paul, 212
Third Apartment Building District, 34
'Third Turning of the Wheel', 50
Three Jewels, 49, 125, 207
'Three Sorrowful Hills', 102
Tiananmen Square, 35, 86, 157
Tianjin, 15, 118, 121
Tibet, 10, 11, 13, 16, 17, 21, 45, 50, 51, 52, 53, 56, 57, 58, 69, 70, 88, 90, 92, 94, 96, 125, 131, 133, 135, 156, 157, 167, 196
Tibetan colony (former), 150–51
Tomb of Prince Tonyukuk, 242–44
Tömörchnii Street, 149
Tonyukuk, Prince, 242
toono, 63–65, 84, 175
tortoise stelae, 113
Trade Union Council Building (former), 109
Trans-Siberian Railway, 30, 210, 212
Treaty of Kiakhta, 210
Treaty of Nerchinsk, 230
'tree of life', 42, 63
Trijang Rinpoche, 135, 138
Trotsky, Leon, 29
Truman, Harry S., 196
tsam, 86, 94, 95, 96, 133
tsanid, 47, 48, 160, 169, 175, 176
Tschepetinikov, N. M., 115
Tsedenbal, Yujaagin, 31, 34, 35, 100, 103, 104, 114, 124, 211, 223, 224, 232
Tserendorj, Abbot, 245, 247
Tsetee Gün, 249, 252
Tsetsen Khan Aimag, 10, 200
tsogchin dugan, 68, 83, 89, 150, 160, 163, 234, 235
Tsogt Taij, 115, 198
Tsongkhapa, 52, 54, 84, 133, 160, 166, 213, 219, 237
tsorji, 46
tsuivan, xviii
tulku, 53, 59
Tumbashi. *See* 'Four Friends'
Tumen Enkh, 127
Türkic revolt, 242
'Turning of the Wheel', 48
Turtle Rock, 162, 240
Tüshee Gün, 249
Tüshetu Khan Aimag, 10, 11, 99, 200
Tuul River, viii, x, 4, 5, 16, 38, 110, 125, 171, 221, 224, 249

Tuul River Valley, 9, 13, 14, 15, 16, 17, 73, 210, 223, 231, 249

ubashi, 45, 46
udgan, 42, 58
Ulaan Dov, 204
'Ulaanbaatar' (as used in this book), 3
Ulaanbaatar History Museum, 73
Ulaanbaatar Hotel, 103, 110, 114, 115, 124, 152
Ulaanbaatar Railway Station, 191, 209
'Ulan Bator' (as used in this book), 3
Ulan Ude, 211
umzad, 46
Ungern-von Sternberg, Roman, 25, 56, 171, 181, 190, 191, 194, 202, 205, 206, 250
uni, 64
University of Cinematic Art, 198
University of Finance and Economics, 183
'Urga' (as used in this book), 3
Urga Dawn, 28
Urgoo Cinema, 78
Urt Tsagaan Road, 149

Vairocana, 55
Vaisali, 49
vajra, 50
  'double vajra', 71
Vajradeva, 133
Vajradhara, 55, 68, 88, 89, 166, 218
Vajrapani, 56, 84, 132, 133
Vajrasattva, 133
Vajrayana Buddhism, 10, 48, 50–55, 58, 59, 60, 65, 67, 68, 70, 73, 84, 92, 129, 132, 134, 150, 156, 160, 163, 168, 170, 173, 178, 185, 197, 205, 207, 213, 234, 235, 248, 251
Verkhneudinsk, 190, 211, 220, 247
Village of Abundant Peace, 204
von Grot, Victor, 200

Waits, Tom, 128
Wallace, Henry, 121, 162, 196, 197
Waugh, Louise, 40
Wedding Palace, 79, 136
wenshou, 67
Western Palace, 89, 97
Wheel of Time. *See* Kalachakra
'white foods', 154
White Old Man, 42, 58, 84, 96, 132, 192, 207, 248
White Palace, 68
White Shell Protector, 249n1
White Tara, 56, 177, 207, 218
Wickham-Smith, Simon, 61
William of Rubruck, 63, 112, 229
wind horse, 58, 179, 224, 252
Winter Palace, 158, 167, 214, 219, 221
Women's Cooperative Retail Store (former), 149
World Peace Bell, 112
wrestling, 225–26

Xinjiang, 16, 21, 196, 210, 214, 242
Xuanzang, 132, 207n3
Xu Shucheng, 24, 25, 97, 170

yabyum, 54
yadam, 53, 133
Yadamsuren, U., 145
Yama, 56, 57, 84, 96, 219
Yamantaka, 57, 84, 133
yampai, 66, 132, 217
'Yellow Hat' Buddhism, 10, 11, 12, 14, 52, 176, 192
Yellow Palace, 85, 86, 88, 89, 90, 92, 93, 97, 107, 131
'Yellow Store', 149–50
Yembuu Rock, 245
Yondendorj, Amban, 249
Yongzheng Emperor, 14, 210
Yulkhorsung, 67
yurta, 63

Zaisan Memorial, 223
Zanabazar, 11–14, 84, 89, 133, 145, 166, 218, 219, 221, 225, 251, 252
Zanabazar Museum of Fine Arts, 145, 196
Zasagtu Khan Aimag, 10
zeebad, 69–70, 85
Zemer, 131
zhiwen, 69

Zhou Enlai, 211
zod, 155
Zorig, Sanjaasurenglin, 111
Zurkhai Datsan, 178
Zuu Residential Apartment Buildings, 139